QUESTIONING THE SOLUTION:

The Politics of Primary Health Care and Child Survival

with an in–depth critique of
ORAL REHYDRATION THERAPY

David Werner and David Sanders
with Jason Weston, Steve Babb and Bill Rodriguez

Original drawings by Alicia Brelsford

Published by

HEALTHWRIGHTS
Workgroup for People's Health and Rights

QUESTIONING THE SOLUTION:
The Politics of Primary Health Care and Child Survival
with an in–depth critique of
ORAL REHYDRATION THERAPY

By David Werner and David Sanders
with Jason Weston, Steve Babb and Bill Rodriguez
Original drawings by Alicia Brelsford

Library of Congress Catalog Card Number: 96–79528
Werner, David
        Questioning the Solution: The Politics of Primary Health Care and Child Survival, with an In–Depth Critique of Oral Rehydration Therapy / David Werner and David Sanders with Jason Weston, Steve Babb and Bill Rodriguez
        Includes bibliographical references and index.
        ISBN 0–9655585–1–7 (hardcover)
        ISBN 0–9655585–2–5 (paperback)

Published by

HEALTHWRIGHTS

Workgroup for People's Health and Rights

964 Hamilton Avenue
Palo Alto CA 94301

Published in association with:
The International People's Health Council (IPHC),
Third World Network, and
Partners in Health

10 9 8 7 6 5 4 3 2 1

Not until the creation and maintenance of decent conditions of life for all people are recognized and accepted as a common obligation of all people and all countries—not until then shall we, with a certain degree of justification, be able to speak of mankind as civilized.

Albert Einstein, 1945

For Whom This Book Is Written

We wrote this book for:

- **Students, health workers, activists, and everyone concerned about global issues,** including health, development, nutrition, human rights, the environment, and quality of life—especially as these issues relate to children in difficult situations. We have tried to provide enough background so that readers relatively unfamiliar with international health questions can follow our discussion.

- **People working or interested in primary health care** and allied fields, particularly in the Third World.

- **Health and development planners and policy-makers,** especially those working or concerned with child survival and children's quality of life, alternative development strategies, and oral rehydration therapy.

How This Book is Organized

In this book we explore the problems of primary health care and child survival in underprivileged countries and communities. To do this, we must look into some of the most thorny issues of economic and social development. We have chosen diarrheal disease—one of the biggest killers of impoverished children—as a focus for exploring the complex determinants of child health and quality of life.

We begin, in **Part 1,** with a brief historical overview of health services from colonial times until the 1970s. Next we discuss the concept of *Primary Health Care* as formulated in 1978 at Alma Ata. We analyze the forces that have led world institutions to abandon the comprehensive, potentially revolutionary concept of Primary Health Care in favor of the more limited strategy of Selective Primary Health Care and the vertical interventions of Child Survival. Finally, we consider some of the prevailing concepts and policies that need to be challenged. We ask if quick-fix technologies and top-down planning are sufficient to solve health problems related to poverty and unfair social structures.

In **Part 2,** as a case study, we look at one of the most touted interventions of Selective Primary Health Care—oral rehydration therapy (ORT)—which is widely promoted in poor countries to lower the appallingly high death rate from diarrhea. We see how the medical establishment has dragged its heels in accepting breakthroughs, especially those that demystify knowledge and give ordinary people more control over their health care. In this context, we examine different methods of ORT, including those which are dependency creating and those which foster self-reliance. We see how the commercialization of ORT has turned a potentially life-saving technology into yet another way of exploiting the poor. In the last analysis, this *simple, low-cost solution* has been made unduly complex and costly.

Part 3 looks at determinants of the health of populations from an historical and contemporary perspective. We examine factors that have reduced child mortality and improved health in northern industrialized countries, and compare these with events in the South. We trace colonial exploitations of the past to the "new colonialism" of today's globalized economic order. We examine how the international financial institutions have perpetuated underdevelopment by imposing structural adjustment policies on debt-stricken countries. We then discuss the impact of these policies on health and the quality of life of the world's neediest people and explore how the growing power of transnational corporations—and specifically the infant formula, pharmaceutical, and arms industries—influence public policies and endanger child health. Then we look at how a few countries that have taken an alternative path of development have achieved *good health at low cost.* And we see how factors of equity—and inequity—relate to increase in population and AIDS.

On a more positive note, **Part 4** concludes with a few examples of equity seeking, health promoting initiatives. These range from programs focusing on specific urgent health problems (such as diarrhea and undernutrition), to comprehensive efforts which place health care within the context of working toward fairer, healthier social structures. However, given the current socially regressive climate of the so-called *New World Order,* we see that even these equity-oriented initiatives are suffering setbacks. In view of the escalating global obstacles to this process, we close by discussing the international solidarity and grassroots networks that are needed to counter the current regressive trends. We conclude that child survival strategies are not enough. Our goal must be to secure the right of all children—and all people—to an improved and sustainable quality of life. This will require more equitable, accountable and genuinely participatory social structures.

An **Appendix** at the back of the book considers the position of UNICEF and the World Health Organization in terms of the world power structures and the sociopolitical determinants of health. This is followed by a short **Reading List** on the Politics of Health, extensive **Endnotes** and the **Index.**

Acknowledgements

Many people have helped in different ways with the various stages of this book: research, collection and organization of reference material, fact checking, critical review of the manuscript, content editing, copy editing, proofreading, artwork, graphics, and selection of illustrations. The book has truly been a group effort, and we would like to give our heartfelt thanks to all who have assisted … especially those who have worked so hard and long as volunteers.

For help in the early stages of the book, we would especially like to thank Steve Babb for months of dedicated research, data checking, writing, and editing; to Irene Yen for organizing and cataloging a mountain of reference materials; and to Lisa de Avila for reorganizing the manuscript. For more than two years of untiring help in the later and final stages of the book, including research and writing, graphics and page layout, data collection, editing, computer trouble-shooting and entering endless changes into the "final" draft, we would like to express our deep appreciation to Jason Weston of Health-Wrights. And for the monumental task of content editing and condensing the entire manuscript, we are enormously grateful to Bill Rodriguez of Partners in Health and Tamitza Toroyan.

For providing critical review of part or all of the manuscript in different stages of completion, we would like to thank Robert Hogan and Elizabeth Mason of the World Health Organization; William Greenough III, Norbert Hirschhorn, and Charlene Dale of the Child Health Foundation; Pam Zinkin, Maria Hamlin Zuniga, Mira Shiva, Michel Chossudovsky, and David Legge of the International People's Health Council; Michael Tan and Mary Grenough of the Health Action Information Network; Martin Khor of the Third World Network; Paul Ekins of The Other Economic Summit; Katherine Hodgkins and Andrew Chetley of Health Action International–Europe. Others whom we thank for helping to review the manuscript and/or providing additional studies or references include Robert Moy, Richard Carver, Julie Cliff,

Joe Collins, Naomi Baumslag, Andrew Green, Carl Taylor, Walden Bello, Stina Almroth, Sue Fawcus, Meri Koivusalo, and the helpful staff at The Appropriate Health Resources and Technologies Action Group (AHRTAG). For help with copy editing and/or proof reading we warmly thank Trude Bock, Renée Burgard, Bruce Hobson, Barry Goldensohn, Mari Quihuis, Dorothy Weston, Ted Weston, Edward J. Weston, Lisa Wright, and Lela Bachrach. For work on the Politics of Health reading list we thank Bruce Hobson, Katherine Acevedo, and Pol de Vos. For other kinds of assistance including literature searches, copying and communications we thank Merlin Schlumberger, Efrain Zamora, and Dan Perlman.

For her fine drawings which she designed to set the tone for the four main parts of the book, as well as the cover drawing, we are deeply grateful to Alicia (Tattie) Brelsford, as we are for the artwork of Elizabeth Irwin and Molly Bang. For their invaluable contributions to the design of this book and its cover, we thank Renée Burgard, Trude Bock, and Jason Weston. For permission to use their illustrations and graphics we thank the many sources and publications cited below.

For funding assistance we thank Bread for the World in Germany and Carol Bernstein Ferry. We also thank the Hesperian Foundation for its support in the first stages of the manuscript. For the initial impetus to undertake this book we are grateful to Joe Collins and the Institute of Food and Development Policy. And for their overall support and backing our gratitude goes to our friends at HealthWrights (Workgroup for People's Health and Rights) and the International People's Health Council.

An especially warm thank you and deep appreciation go to Trude Bock of HealthWrights, who selflessly provided her home, meals, support, encouragement, endless editing and proofreading, and a hundred different forms of assistance to help the book, its authors and co-authors along the way. Without her, this book would never have been completed.

Photo, Cartoon, Graph, Table and Illustration Credits

We would like to thank the following people and groups for their invaluable contributions to this book. For drawing the cover graphic, the illustrations which begin each section (pp. 1, 9, 31, 73, 127) as well as the illustrations on pp. 10–12, 87, our warmest thanks go to Alicia (Tattie) Brelsford. For permission to use their excellent cartoons we thank Kirk Anderson (p. 147), Christopher Bing (p. 162), Bulbul (p. 126), Health for the Millions (p. 83), Gary Huck (p. 128, used with permission—Gary Huck, UE\Huck\Konopacki cartoons), Link—CAFOD Development Education Newsletter (p. 170), Southern Poverty Law Center (p. 148), and Nicolas Spinga via WHO (p. 94). For the use of their illustrations, we thank the Council for Health and Development, Manila (p. 130), Merck Corp. (p. 42), David Morley and the Institute for Child Health (pp. 14, 24, 43, 90 [top], 92, 141), Silvio Pampiglione (p, 134), Population and Development Rev. (122), The Sub Committee on the South of the Special NGO Committee on Development (p. 168), David Werner (pp. 23, 29, 36, 39, 44, 57, 58, 62, 65, 89 [bottom], 93, 131, 132, 164) and the World Health Organization (p. 45 [mother's card]). For the use of their photographs, we thank Health for the millions (p. 61), Silvio

Pampiglione (p. 135), David Werner, (pp. 55, 69, 89, 88, 122, 144–145, 157), UNICEF/Lemoyne (p. 52), and the World Health Organization (pp. 6, 18, 34).

We also thank Blackwell Scientific Publications (p. 76, fig. 3-2), Enyimeyew and WEMOS (p. 103), L.A. Fingerhut and J.C. Kleinman (p. 110), David Morley, Stephan, and the Institute for Child Health (pp. 45, 72, 76 fig. 3-3, 85, 118), David Morley and Jason Weston (p. 123), Nuffield Provincial Hospitals Trust (p. 76), UNICEF (pp. 3, 76 [New York City], 117), United Nations Development Program (p. 88), Jason Weston (p. 113), the World Bank (p. 106), the World Health Organization (pp. 3, 33, 38), and the Worldwatch Institute (pp. 7, 82) for the use of their graphs. For their maps, our appreciation goes to Walden Bello (p. 84), Alicia (Tattie) Brelsford (p. 150), Merlin Schlumberger (p. 119), and the Mozambique Support Network (p. 133). For the use of their tables, we thank Walden Bello (p. 110 [from his book, Dark Victory]), UNICEF (pp. 38, 75), the World Bank, (p. 105 all), Worldwatch Institute (p. 125).

TABLE OF CONTENTS

INTRODUCTION: UNFULFILLED PROMISE
THE FAILURE OF INTERNATIONAL HEALTH AND DEVELOPMENT
STRATEGIES TO PROTECT CHILDREN'S LIVES AND HEALTH

PART 1: THE RISE AND FALL OF PRIMARY HEALTH CARE

PART 2: ORAL REHYDRATION THERAPY
A SOLUTION TO DEATH FROM DIARRHEA?

PART 3: WHAT REALLY DETERMINES THE HEALTH OF A POPULATION?

PART 4: SOLUTIONS THAT EMPOWER THE POOR: EXAMPLES OF EQUITY-ORIENTED INITIATIVES

PART 4: CONTINUED

FIGURES, BOXES, AND MAPS

LIST OF FIGURES

LIST OF BOXES

LIST OF MAPS

ABBREVIATIONS USED IN THIS BOOK*

AIDS — Acquired Immune Deficiency Syndrome
ARI — Acute Respiratory Infection
ASAP — Alternative Structural Adjustment Program
BWRO — Bretton Woods Reform Organization
CB-ORS — Cereal-Based Oral Rehydration Salts
CB-ORT* — Cereal-Based Oral Rehydration Therapy
CBHP — Community-Based Health Workers
CHW — Community Health Worker
CIA — Central Intelligence Agency (US)
CPHC — Comprehensive Primary Health Care
DALY — Disability Adjusted Life Year
FB-ORT* — Food-Based ORT
FDA — Food and Drug Administration (US)
FRELIMO — Front for the Liberation of Mozambique
FSLN — Sandinista Front for National Liberation
    (Nicaragua)
GATT — General Agreement on Tariffs and Trade
GDP* — Gross Domestic Product
GE — Gini Coefficient
GNP* — Gross National Product
GOBI* — Growth Monitoring, ORT, Breast-feeding,
    and Immunization
GOBI-FFF — GOBI plus Family Planning, Female
    Literacy, and Food Supplementation
HAI — Health Action International
HIV — Human Immunodeficiency Virus
IBFAN — International Baby Food Action Network
ICCDDR,B — International Center of Diarrhoeal
    Disease Research, Bangladesh
ICORT — International Conference on Oral
    Rehydration Therapy
ICPD — International Conference on Population and
    Development
IMF* — International Monetary Fund
IMR* — Infant Mortality Rate

IPHC — International People's Health Council
IV — Intravenous
MINSA — Ministry of Health (Nicaragua)
NAFTA — North American Free Trade Agreement
    (Canada, US, and Mexico)
NCDDP — National Control of Diarrheal Disease
    Program (Egypt)
NGO — Nongovernmental Organization
NTAE — Nontraditional Agricultural Exports
ORS* — Oral Rehydration Salts
ORT* — Oral Rehydration Therapy
PCDD — Programme for Control of Diarrhoeal
    Diseases
PHC — Primary Health Care
PRI — Institutional Revolutionary Party (Mexico)
RENAMO — Mozambique National Resistance
RHF — Recommended Home Fluids
SAP* — Structural Adjustment Programs
SPHC — Selective Primary Health Care
SSS* — Sugar Salt Solution
STD — Sexually Transmitted Disease
TB — Tuberculosis
TNC — Transnational Corporation
U5MR* — Under Five Mortality Rate
UK — United Kingdom
UN — United Nations
UNDP — United Nations Development Program
UNESCO — United Nations Educational Scientific and
    Cultural Organization
UNICEF* — United Nations Children's Fund
UNO — United Nicaraguan Opposition
US — United States of America
USAID* — United States Agency for International
    Development
USSR — Union of Soviet Socialist Republics
WHO* — World Health Organization

---

*Abbreviations marked with an asterisk are discussed in the glossary.

GLOSSARY
Explanation of Measures, Acronyms, And Terms Used in This Book

MEASURES OF HEALTH AND WEALTH

Infant mortality rate (IMR) — The number of children out of every 1,000 born alive who die before reaching one year of age.

Under five mortality rate (U5MR) — The number of children out of every 1,000 born alive who die before reaching five years of age.

Maternal mortality rate — The number of women who die from complications of pregnancy per 100,000 live births.

Gross domestic product (GDP) — The total value of final goods and services produced within a country in a year. The three major components of GDP are consumer purchases, private investment, and government spending.

Gross national product (GNP) — The total value of final goods and services produced by a country in a year. A country's GNP differs from its GDP in that it includes income that individuals and companies based in the country earn abroad and excludes income foreign individuals and companies earn in the country. A country's GNP can also be viewed as its total earnings.

GNP per capita — A country's GNP divided by its population gives the average personal income of the country's population. However, it tells us nothing about how that income is distributed. The same is true of GDP per capita, which is a country's GDP divided by its population.

ACRONYMS

WHO — World Health Organization, the agency of the United Nations primarily concerned with health. WHO has a maternal and child health program, but apart from that does not have its own child survival program, nor does it focus specifically on children's health problems. WHO defines its central role as "provid[ing] technical support to national programmes" on health matters. To this end, WHO's Division of Diarrhoeal and Acute Respiratory Disease Control conducts research "aimed at identifying, developing and evaluating new or improved approaches to the prevention and treatment of diarrhoea...." It also produces and disseminates teaching materials on diarrheal management and prevention.

UNICEF — United Nations Children's Emergency Fund. UNICEF was established in 1946 by the UN General Assembly to coordinate assistance to children threatened by famine and disease in the wake of the Second World War. The initial intention was to dissolve the agency when this short-term problem subsided, but the General Assembly changed its mind and extended UNICEF's life and mandate in 1950 in recognition of the continuing needs of children world-wide, particularly in the Third World. In the years since, UNICEF has carried out a variety of activities, including vaccination campaigns, a drive to eradicate malaria, and an initiative aimed at providing villages with clean drinking water. Following its central role in the activities surrounding the "International Year of the Child" (1979), UNICEF launched its "Child Survival and Development Revolution" in 1983. This initiative is coordinated by the agency's headquarters in New York, but field offices in developing countries are allowed considerable autonomy. UNICEF works closely with Third World governments to implement this initiative, encouraging them to establish national child survival programs. UNICEF sees its chief function as promoting useful health knowledge to those who need it, such as mothers. For a fuller discussion of UNICEF's policies and factors influencing them, see the Appendix at the end of this book (see page 171).

IMF and World Bank — The International Monetary Fund and the International Bank for Reconstruction and Development (the World Bank) are powerful multilateral lenders. Both international institutions were conceived at the 1944 Bretton Woods Conference—which laid the ground rules for the post-war international economic and monetary system—and were created during the following year. In recent years an important role of both institutions has been to dictate the terms of loans to Third World countries. Beyond its direct loans, the IMF serves as a highly influential "gatekeeper": it certifies to other lenders that a particular Third World country is pursuing "responsible" economic and social policies and is therefore a good credit risk. To qualify for such a seal of approval, a country usually has to embrace free market economics and to implement structural adjustment policies (see definition below). Voting rights in the IMF and the World Bank are allocated among member countries in accordance with their donations to these bodies. This places control in the hands of its five major donors: the United States, Great Britain, Germany, France, and Japan. Many of the deliberations of the IMF and the World Bank are shrouded in secrecy.

USAID — United States Agency for International Development. An arm of the US government whose mission is to advance US foreign policy objectives (e.g., by promoting privatization, free market approaches, and an open door to US exports and investment). USAID operates its own child survival program, and has spent up to $150 million a year in this area.

GOBI — The four key interventions of "selective primary health care" and UNICEF's "Child Survival Revolution," consisting of Growth monitoring, Oral rehydration therapy, Breastfeeding, and Immunization. An expanded version is GOBI-FFF: the additional components refer to Family planning, Female literacy, and Food supplementation.

ORT — Oral Rehydration Therapy, the replacement by mouth of liquid and salts lost through diarrhea. It is now recognized that for optimal ORT a child with diarrhea needs not only *increased fluids* but also *foods*. ORT has been widely celebrated as "the medical breakthrough of the century" with the potential of radically reducing the staggering number of deaths from diarrhea, the world's second leading killer of children. But, as we will discuss in this book, the solution is not that simple.

ORS — Oral Rehydration Salts or Solution. As used by WHO, UNICEF, and also in this book, ORS refers specifically to the WHO full-formula glucose-based mixture distributed in factory-produced aluminum foil packets. This formula, strongly promoted by WHO and UNICEF, consists of a combination of glucose (a simple sugar), sodium chloride (table salt), potassium chloride, and trisodium citrate dihydrate (formerly sodium bicarbonate, or baking soda). (See page 60.)

SSS — Sugar-Salt Solution. A home-made rehydration drink formerly recommended by UNICEF as an alternative to ORS packets. Now UNICEF and WHO have stopped promoting SSS and instead simply recommend "home fluids" (teas, soups, etc.). However, in some countries and programs SSS is still widely used (see page 42).

CB-ORT and **FB-ORT** — Cereal Based and Food Based Oral Rehydration Therapy. In recent years it has been found that cereal or starch drinks can be more effective in combating dehydration than sugar based drinks (either ORS or SSS)(see page 66).

TERMS

Development — We use this term to refer to progress that improves the well-being and living standards of disadvantaged populations. The dominant school of thought holds that development can best be accomplished through "modernization" along Western lines of economic growth. Thus the Third World must follow the same path that the First World took. The concept of development has, to a large extent, been used by powerful First World interests to reshape the politics and economies of poor countries to their advantage. As a result, activists in poor countries sometimes object to the very concept of development as manipulative and neo-colonial.

Growth-oriented development — We use this term for the conventional development model that has dominated the North and largely been imposed on the South. According to this model, development is virtually synonymous with economic growth. Its goal is to improve a poor country's economic stability (i.e. market potential) by increasing its GNP (gross national product). Economic growth is pursued through a combination of industrialization and large-scale agribusiness.

Equity-oriented development — We use this term as an alternative to "growth-oriented development." It is an approach that places basic human needs before the lopsided pursuit of economic growth. It recognizes that the health and well-being of a population depend more on fair distribution of resources and power than on the total wealth of a country or increase in GNP. It builds from the bottom up, involving as many people as possible both in the process and the fruits of production. People participate strongly in the decisions that affect their lives. Society makes sure all people's basic needs are met, and encourages people to organize to defend their rights. Terms such as "real development" and "sustainable development," used by institutions ranging from UNICEF to the World Bank, often give at least lip service to the concept of equity and elimination of poverty. However, they generally place strong emphasis on economic growth without insistence on structures or regulations that will ensure more equitable distribution of wealth and basic services.

Underdeveloped countries — In this book we use the term "underdeveloped" to refer to countries which are relatively poor, dependent, and often heavily indebted to the rich (industrialized or so-called developed) countries. We prefer the term *underdeveloped* to *developing* because it more accurately reflects what is happening. Contrary to becoming increasingly developed (in terms of more fully meeting everyone's needs), many of the poorest countries are being systematically underdeveloped in the name of development (see above). There is an increasing net flow of wealth from the poor to the rich, both within countries and between them. To ensure that they can keep servicing their debts, poor countries have been obliged to cut public spending on health and education, to reduce the earning power of the poor, and to deplete (or decimate) natural resources (such as forests, topsoil, and groundwater).

Third World — This term is used, on occasion, to refer to underdeveloped countries as a group. In comparing underdeveloped to industrialized or "developed" countries, we also sometimes speak of the former as *the South* and the latter as *the North.* Or, for the sake of simplicity, sometimes we simply refer to *rich countries* and *poor countries.* We recognize that none of these terms is completely satisfactory.

Intersectoral — Relating to a combination of various sectors or disciplines. For example, an "intersectoral approach" to health care might include the ministries of health, education, agriculture, and social welfare.

Military-industrial complex — Originally coined by former US President Dwight Eisenhower, this term refers to the array of powerful economic entities—ranging from giant multinational corporations and to arms producers military contractors, and the Pentagon—whose influence and lobbying do much to determine national and international policies. Often we use this term (or the terms "power structure," "powerful interests," or "entrenched interests") to refer to the elite minority of persons and groups who dominate and direct the present political and economic world order, shaping major economic and development policies to their own advantage.

Structural — When we speak of the "structural causes of poor health" or the need for "structural change," "structural" refers to the structure or composition of society, especially the prevailing power structure. It includes the dominant social, economic, and political forces. It embraces the body of laws, social control mechanisms, and economic policies—typically enforced by government— which often determine and perpetuate the balance (or imbalance) of wealth and power within a nation or community.

Structural Adjustment Programs (SAPs) — Economic policies imposed on Third World countries by the International Monetary Fund and the World Bank. These policies, which have had a devastating impact on poor people in many countries, derive their name from the fact that they are designed to "adjust" the economic structures of poor countries to ensure that they keep making interest payments on their foreign debts. Key structural adjustment measures include:

- cutting public spending on health, education, and other social services;

- removing subsidies for and lifting price controls on staple foods and other basic commodities; and

- shifting from production for domestic consumption to production for export.

(For a discussion of structural adjustment and its impact on health, see page 83.)

⌘

NOTE: The spelling used in this book is that used in the United States (home to four of the authors). However, there are many differences in the spelling of English in different regions of the world, and there are many instances where we have quoted individuals whose spelling differs from ours. In these cases we have retained the original spelling of the author. This has resulted in spelling inconsistencies (for example, paragraphs which include both *diarrhea* and *diarrhoea*). Hopefully the reader will not find this too confusing.

INTRODUCTION

Unfulfilled Promise

The Failure of International Health and Development Strategies to Protect Children's Lives and Health

A Rude Awakening:
Cholera Makes a Deadly Comeback

The most terrifying and deadly of the diarrheal diseases is making an alarming comeback. During most of the twentieth century, cholera was largely confined to Asia.[1] In Latin America it was considered a plague of the past. But in January 1991 a few cases of cholera were discovered in Peru.[2] Within two months 70,000 people were infected. The outbreak swiftly spread as far as Brazil in the east, Chile in the south, and Mexico in the north. By late 1991 all but seven nations in South and Central America were affected.[3] By the end of 1992 more than 730,000 cases of cholera had been reported, with over 6,300 deaths.[4] Despite massive control and education efforts, sporadic outbreaks still occur, mostly in the rapidly growing "septic fringe" of towns and cities. In Mexico, where the 1994 peso crash caused a sharp decline in living standards, cholera cases doubled in 1995.[5] The World Health Organization (WHO) predicts that in Latin America cholera will become *endemic* (there to stay).[6]

The Latin American cholera outbreak is part of a global resurgence of the disease that began in Indonesia in 1961 and that has spread through much of the Third World within the last few years. Ominously, the present pandemic has lasted much longer than its nineteenth century predecessors. Today cholera remains a major problem throughout much of Asia, Latin America, and Africa.[7] In 1991 Africa reported over 150,000 cases and 14,000 deaths from cholera—until then the highest figures ever recorded for that continent. The numbers continue to rise. The 1994 cholera epidemic among refugees from Rwanda is one of the most disastrous outbreaks to date.

Far from approaching the proclaimed global goal of "Health for All by the Year 2000," the Third World is now fighting a losing battle against a scourge once considered a disease of the nineteenth century.[8] Health workers and citizens throughout much of the Third World are asking in bewilderment: *How·could this happen? What went wrong?* The resurgence of cholera can be directly linked to deteriorating living conditions for increasing numbers of people. It starkly illustrates that prevailing health and development strategies are grievously flawed.

Cholera is not the only disease of poverty on the rise. Malaria, which in the 1970s was thought to be largely under control, is also making an alarming comeback in many countries, despite major efforts to fight it.[9] An upsurge of tuberculosis is ravaging much of the Third World, as well as the mushrooming inner city neighborhoods of the United States and other rich countries.[10] And AIDS—which is fueled by conditions of poverty and inequity[11]—is spreading like wildfire, especially in Africa, Southeast Asia, and parts of Latin America.[12]

As the year 2000 approaches it is increasingly clear that the ambitious programs mounted by WHO, UNICEF, USAID, the World Bank, and other institutions to address problems of disease, hunger, and poverty in the Third World have fallen far short of their goals. In many countries progress toward health has stagnated during the last decade. In others, the living conditions and health status of growing numbers of impoverished people have actually been deteriorating.

In particular, these global programs have failed to adequately reduce the continuing high rates of malnutrition, illness, and death among Third World children. The substantial gains achieved by the narrowly focused "child survival" campaign (using technological interventions such as immunization) have, to a large extent, been offset by a worsening standard of living for much of humanity. According to UNICEF's latest calculations, 12.5 million of the world's children under age five still die each year.[13] The agency asserts that without its Child Survival Revolution, the number of children dying yearly would have risen to 17.5 million by 1990 as a result of Third World population growth. Although the percentage of children dying has dropped, it is deeply disturbing that approximately the same number of children are dying today as were dying ten years ago.[14]

A persistent high death rate among children is widely considered to be the most telling indicator of unmet health needs in a population. In the world today, one in five people (more than 1 billion) lives in absolute poverty—earning less than one dollar a day—and 1.5 billion are unemployed.[15] One in four people lacks clean drinking water, and never sees a trained health worker.[16] In the Third World alone, at least 780 million people are undernourished. This is pertinent because malnutrition is an underlying cause of most child deaths. Every day some 40,000 children die from causes related to hunger.[17] As a result of chronic undernutrition, 190 million children in the Third World suffer from poor health, often accompanied by delayed mental and physical development.[18] Overall, one in four of the world's children is malnourished.[19]

The first years of the 1990s have shown ominous reversals in some of the earlier gains toward widespread coverage of protective health measures. This is true even of the so-called "twin engines" of the Child Survival

Revolution: immunization and oral rehydration therapy (ORT). In spite of a global campaign to improve immunization coverage, and the remarkable increase in coverage which occurred throughout the 1980s, from the start of the 1990s the percentage of the world's children protected by immunization began to decline. This decline is evident on the graph in Fig. I–1, adapted from UNICEF's 1994 *State of the World's Children Report*.[20] In the 1995 edition of the report, UNICEF claims that such reversals have been at least partially corrected; for example new cases of polio, which rose substantially in 1992, began to drop again by 1993. However, Zaire, which has immunized only 29% of its children against polio, experienced the worst polio epidemic in its history in June, 1995.[21] Globally the number of child deaths from measles has been rising steadily since the beginning of the 1990s.[22] And the number of newborn children dying from tetanus is sharply increasing (see Fig. I–2).[23]

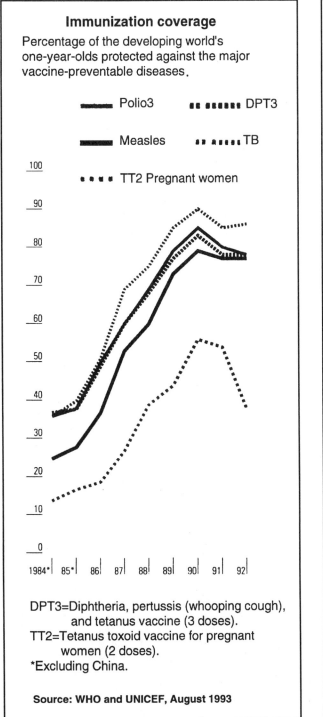

Fig. I–1 Global immunization coverage.

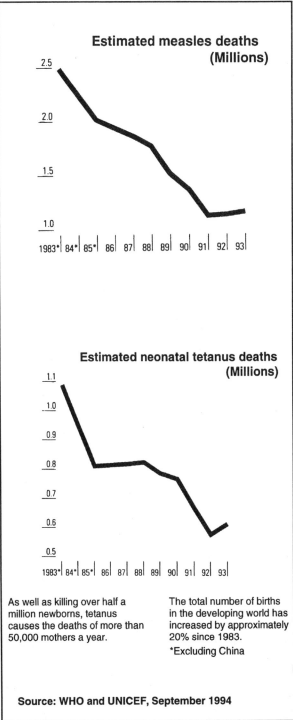

Fig I–2 Global deaths from measles and tetanus (millions).

Previous health gains from the use of oral rehydration therapy as the primary treatment for diarrhea in children appears to be backsliding since the start of the 1990s. Such reversals include the showcase success story in Egypt, where ORT usage rates have declined alarmingly.[24] (See Chapter 7.) The risk of child death from malnutrition and diarrhea is compounded by the fact that increasing numbers of the world's mothers are bottle-feeding their babies instead of breastfeeding them.[25] (See page 89.)

While considering the direct and indirect causes of hunger, disease, and death among the world's children, we must not overlook the swelling tide of social unrest, crime, and violence, including armed conflict. One example is the cholera outbreak in 1994 among refugees from the war in Rwanda which took the lives of thousands of children and orphaned thousands more.

The optimistic goal of "Health for All" is increasingly remote. The purpose of this book is to investigate the reasons for the failure of prevailing strategies to improve health, especially in children, and to explore more promising alternatives. As a focal area for in-depth study, we will examine the continuing high child death rate from diarrhea. Specifically, we will explore the case of oral rehydration therapy (ORT), the major intervention of the Child Survival Revolution which has been promoted to combat death from diarrhea.

ORT is a method for combating dehydration, the most common immediate cause of death in children with diarrhea.[*26] Simply put, ORT consists of giving *increased fluids* (and *food*) to a child with diarrhea. This book's critical analysis of the approach UNICEF and WHO have taken to promoting ORT helps explain its limited success in reducing child death rates from diarrhea. It also sheds light on the larger issues of why the Child Survival Revolution, Primary Health Care, and ultimately, international development have not done more to safeguard children's health and lives.

The resurgence of cholera in the Third World starkly illustrates the central flaw of current health and development strategies. Instead of working to resolve the root causes of poverty and poor health, policy-makers have settled for promoting stopgap technological interventions. ORT is a prime example.

It is clear that if ORT were promoted in ways that would make it quickly and readily available—even in emergen-

cies—it could help to prevent deaths from cholera. But ORT does nothing to check the spread of this dreadful disease. *Vibrio cholerae*, the cholera bacterium, is spread through contaminated water and food, and thrives on unsanitary conditions. WHO attributes the resurgence of cholera in Latin America and Africa to a "decline of living standards."[27] Many of the various factors that contribute to this decline—migration of destitute peasants to large cities, overcrowding in shantytowns, rising unemployment, falling wages, and cutbacks in public spending—are direct consequences of current development and structural adjustment policies.

It has been said that "sanitation is the only cure for cholera."[28] The UN designated the 1980s as the "International Drinking Water and Sanitation Decade."[29] But high hopes have proved wishful thinking for much of Latin America and the Third World. In many poor communities, sanitation and water supplies have deteriorated as a result of the economic recession and cutbacks in public spending during the 1980s.[30] According to UNICEF, "by the end of the century … the number of people without adequate sanitation will have increased to approximately 1.9 billion." Given that one out of three human beings lacks adequate sanitation, it is hardly surprising that cholera is making a global comeback. The World Bank's 1993 *Investing in Health* report claims that, although water and sanitation projects provide "substantial health gains," they are not cost effective.[31] Latin American countries have a vast foreign debt, and their limited resources have largely been earmarked for interest payments and grandiose development projects, not basic sanitation and primary health care.

WHO Director-General Dr. Hiroshi Nakajima sums up the lesson of the cholera epidemic of the 1990s:

> Improvement of water supplies and sanitation is the ultimate solution to the problem, and action to this end must commence immediately. What must be faced, however, is the reality of increasing poverty and widespread underdevelopment around the world. Today, we live in a world where the gap between rich and poor, north and south is painfully apparent, and even more sharply illustrated by this current outbreak. We know how to control cholera, but the disease can easily get out of control when economic, social and health infrastructures fail. Cholera is but one dramatic symptom of the failure of development. In combating cholera, and many other health problems as well, we are combating underdevelopment as well as striving for better health.[32]

---

[*] According to UNICEF, dehydration is now responsible for almost half of the deaths from diarrhea among children under five years old. Malnourished children are especially vulnerable to dehydration.

The 1994 Rwanda-Zaire Cholera Outbreak: The Tragic Cost of Not Promoting a Local Solution

The high mortality rates experienced by Rwandan refugees in eastern Zaire were almost unprecedented in refugee populations, and the world must take note of the lessons from this disaster. The immediate, medical cause of most of the deaths was diarrhoeal disease, but the underlying causes were the historical, ethnic, demographic, socioeconomic, and political factors that led to the collapse of Rwandan society and to this mass population migration.[33]

— *The Lancet,* February 11, 1995

The 1994 cholera epidemic that ravaged the Rwandan refugee camps in Goma, Zaire provides compelling support for some key points we are trying to make in this book.[*] One of these is the importance of promoting ORT (and other potentially life-saving solutions) in ways that place control in the hands of users. Another more basic point is that tragedies such as that among Rwandan refugees—and the inequities which precipitated such massive displacement—must be prevented. To achieve this, local and global power structures need radical rethinking and revision. First, let us consider the question of ORT.

The major symptom of cholera is severe watery diarrhea, which can drain the life out of a person within a number of hours. Until the 1970s the main way that doctors used to combat dehydration from cholera was with intravenous solutions (IV drips). Although highly effective for those it reached, this approach was so costly and impractical that in major cholera epidemics mortality rates sometimes ran as high as 30 to 40%.[34] Then in 1971, during a huge cholera outbreak among refugees of a civil war in East Pakistan (now Bangladesh), ORT was introduced for the first time on a major scale. Amazingly, mortality dropped to as low as 1%. This discovery—heralded as a great breakthrough in public health—should have made it possible to achieve low death rates in cholera epidemics from then on.

Why then did the death rate from cholera among Rwandan refugees reach between 24% and 50% (according to varying reports) of severe cases, with as many as 2,000 deaths a day?[35] What happened to the life-saving potential of ORT?

When the sudden outbreak of cholera began striking thousands of people, neither the refugees nor the health personnel on the scene were sufficiently informed or prepared to cope with the epidemic. As cholera and other forms of acute diarrhea ravaged the camp, thousands of people rapidly became dehydrated and many died without receiving any kind of rehydration. A cry went out internationally. After a flurry of faxes and meetings, relief agencies rallied to respond.

Within two weeks a massive supply effort was launched. First, over 10,000 liters of IV solutions were flown in, only to find too few health personnel to administer them. Then US President Bill Clinton promised 20 million packets of oral rehydration salts. But delivery of goods was delayed by logistical problems. Airplanes released their loads from too high up. Some of the relief packages landed on grounded helicopters, and others so far from the camps that trucks that were needed to deliver clean water lost time hunting for the missing supplies. In short, for thousands of dehydrating men, women, and children, ORT was made available too late. An effort was made to save those who were most severely dehydrated by providing them with intravenous solutions. But many were too far gone. Mothers with I.V. drips in their arms died while breastfeeding their babies.[36]

The Child Health Foundation reports that when cholera experts were finally brought to Rwanda from Bangladesh, "they observed the use of inadequate amounts and the wrong solutions of intravenous fluids, poor assessment of the need for ORT and improper composition of the solution, and the use of antibiotics to which the strain of cholera was resistant."[37] After treatment centers and rehydration posts were set up, personnel trained, and an adequate supply of packets of Oral Rehydration Salts (ORS) shipped in, the situation improved dramatically. Within 10 to 12 days the mortality rate from cholera dropped from around 24% (WHO's estimate) to less than 2%.[38] Some epidemiologists consider this another success story for ORT.

But for the 20,000 men, women and children who died of dehydration during the first days of the outbreak, there was no success story. Could this enormous loss of life have been avoided? And if so, how?

Some observers say that during the first days of the crisis—as hundreds of thousands of uprooted, desperate

[*] The July, 1994, cholera outbreak among Rwandan refugees was complicated by a simultaneous epidemic of especially virulent shigella dysentery, which also caused thousands of deaths. Although the causal organism in the vast majority of deaths was not identified, the cholera death toll has been estimated at between 10,000 and 20,000.

people poured into the refugee camp—the degree of chaos made it impossible to set up any kind of functional treatment centers or rehydration posts. These observers also point to shortages of clean water and of adequately trained health care personnel. One WHO official explained that in such crises there is always considerable lag time before achieving successful management of the extraordinary fluid loss associated with severe cholera; inexperienced health personnel only seem to "learn through a number of deaths." Like many other observers, he contends that it would have been virtually impossible to have prevented the initial high death toll from cholera.

Some health activists disagree. They suggest that had a different approach to oral rehydration been taught in Rwanda prior to the crisis, many lives might have been saved. Rather than teaching people to depend on manufactured packets of ORS—which are often unavailable when and where they are needed—it would have been more practical to teach people (during peace time, before the crisis occurred) to prepare effective rehydration drinks from local ingredients. In the refugee camps such ingredients could have consisted of the maize and other foods the refugees were cooking on their campfires. (Indeed, research has shown that home drinks made from a local grain can reduce fluid loss from cholera up to twice as effectively as can the standard ORS formula. See Chapter 10.)

Clearly, once the cholera epidemic hit the Rwandan refugee camp, it was too late to teach people how to effectively prepare their own rehydration drinks. But if in recent years, WHO's and UNICEF's international ORT campaigns had placed more emphasis on teaching about effective home fluids, and less on marketing ORS packets as a magic wonder drug, perhaps more lives could have been saved.

This is, of course, debatable. We have encountered different opinions—even among those present at or knowledgeable about the Rwandan disaster—as to whether self-made rehydration drinks would have been feasible under those circumstances. Were sufficient water and food available? Some say no, claiming that there was an acute water shortage. Others, however, observed streams of people trekking back and forth from Lake Kivu with pots of lake water. (The refugees initially settled in a town located right on the lake shore, but were subsequently relocated out of town and further from the lake; for some refugees the distance to water—other than that which was trucked in—was several kilometers.) Whatever the case, it appears that at least some firewood, food, and water were available. News reports mentioned that it was difficult to breathe in the camps because of all the smoke from 50,000 cooking fires. Evidently, people were cooking cereal gruels and other foods which might have been diluted to form life-saving rehydration drinks.

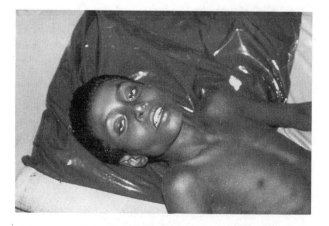

What the refugees and the on-site health care personnel lacked was the know-how.

Some experts argue that even if the refugees had been taught ahead of time about home-mix ORT, it would have been extremely difficult for families—even in more amenable circumstances—to have coped with the extraordinary fluid loss associated with cholera. These experts contend that only specially trained personnel would have been able to assure fluid replacement in sufficient quantities to prevent fatal dehydration. Others argue, however, that there is nothing magical or sophisticated about this treatment. What is needed is 1) an understanding that *what comes out must be replaced*, no matter how large the amount, and 2) the persevering concern (or love) required to coax the sick person to drink the huge amounts of fluid required. Often the person most qualified to make sure that the sick child drinks enough is the mother, so it is important that she learn about these concepts and be empowered to use them.

Dr. William Greenough, co-founder of the International Child Health Foundation who has conducted research on oral rehydration therapy over the last 25 years, makes the following comment on the Rwandan cholera outbreak:

> I could not agree more that had Rwandans learned how to make effective ORT solutions from ingredients at hand and used lake water, however contaminated, many lives would have been saved. Disaster planners and executors simply have not learned the lessons of 1971 from the Bangladesh refugee experience.[39]

⌘

These continuing tragedies in cholera outbreaks are appalling. More appalling still, however, is the continuing high death rate of children from ordinary (non-cholera) diarrhea. Indeed, for every child who dies from cholera, more than 100 die in the silent emergency of fatality due to commonplace watery stools. UNICEF has stated that oral rehydration therapy—if it were promoted in such a way that people could understand it, prepare it, and give it using local resources—could prevent many of the 3 million child deaths from diarrhea that occur each year.[40] And we suggest that if ORT were integrated into a comprehensive, empowering health care strategy, that the child death rate from diarrhea and other diseases of poverty could be substantially and sustainably reduced.

Unfortunately, however, high-level health and development policies have done discouragingly little to address the root causes of widespread poor health. Despite WHO's global campaign for Health for All, many millions of people are worse off today than ten years ago in terms of living conditions, nutrition, health status, and overall quality of life.[41] What went wrong? Why have international health strategies not had greater impact? It is essential that those of us concerned with the rights and well-being of children take a fresh look at the causes of high child death and sickness rates, and place them in the context of poverty and underdevelopment.

⌘

The second major point we will explore in this book is illustrated by the Rwandan experience. Even if ORT had been applied in a more effective and timely manner, any amount of suffering and death would have been unacceptable. Prevention of the disaster—which would have required taking steps to avert the tide of violence that drove over two million refugees out of their country—is the larger issue. Timely action to address Rwanda's underlying sociopolitical and economic problems were the missing keys.

Rwanda was not always a country at war with itself. Before Christian missionaries from Germany arrived in 1880, the indigenous people of Rwanda, Hutu and Tutsi, were not divided into ethnic groups as we now think of them. After the Belgians took over Rwanda in 1919 under the terms of the Treaty of Versailles, they assigned the Tutsis (the herders), who tended to be taller and more "European-looking," superior status over the Hutus (the farmers).[42]

The Belgians imposed colonial ideology and stripped the Rwandan people of their culture and wealth, sowing the seeds of ethnic resentment. Tensions became especially acute after the Roman Catholic Church reversed the roles of the Hutus and Tutsis, paving the way for the Hutus to prosper at the Tutsis' expense. The increasing economic polarization that occurred during the colonial period further exacerbated these tensions, especially when set against the backdrop of overcrowding and land scarcity. (Rwanda is the most densely populated country in Africa.)[43]

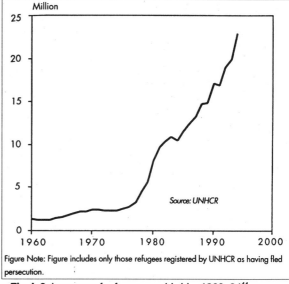

Figure Note: Figure includes only those refugees registered by UNHCR as having fled persecution.

Fig. I–3 Increase of refugees worldwide, 1960–94[44]

In November of 1990 the government devalued the Rwandan franc by 50 percent at the insistence of the International Monetary Fund (IMF). The devaluation coincided with the commencement of civil war and was coupled with a sharp increase in the price of fuel and other basic consumer goods. It destabilized the economy. Real earnings plummeted, child malnutrition soared, and health and education services all but disappeared.[45]

The Hutu's politically inspired genocidal attack on the Tutsis took the lives of more than one million people in three months. Clearly, not all of the blame can be placed on Rwanda's colonial history of ethnic and economic destabilization. However, these factors set the stage for Rwanda's downward spiral and political unrest. Alarmingly, Rwanda's dire situation is not unique. As we will explore in Part 3, a number of countries around the world share Rwanda's colonial history and are being systematically sundered by transnational corporations and the economic policies of the global power structures and financial institutions.

The resurgence of cholera is a dramatic symptom of development gone amok. However, a far more pervasive symptom is the unyielding high rates of child malnutrition and death. Until health and development policies effectively confront the problems of increasing poverty and deteriorating living conditions millions of children will continue to die from preventable diseases. In order for health workers to achieve lasting gains in the health of their communities, they must address short-term health needs in ways that lay the groundwork for the more far-reaching changes that promote basic human rights and fairer social structures. In the following pages we will attempt to show why this is true and how it can be accomplished.

PART 1

The Rise And Fall of
Primary Health Care

INTRODUCTION TO PART 1

In Part 1 of this book we review briefly the evolution of Third World health systems from colonial times to the present. In particular, we focus on events during the last three decades that have led to the rise and decline of Primary Health Care.

While the concept of Primary Health Care in its comprehensive form holds promise for the well-being of the world's poor, the application and misapplication of its principles have failed to fulfill this promise. Examining both social and technical factors, we explore reasons why.

In the first chapter, so as to start with our feet on the ground, we relate the true story of a poor woman and her children in a village in India. We look at the chain of causes that leads to one child's death, at the courageous attempts of the child's mother to save his life, and at her powerlessness to interrupt the deadly march of events.

In the second chapter we look at the Western medical model as implemented in the Third World since colonial times. We see how it has been—and often still is—used as a tool of domination.

In Chapter 3 we discuss the attempt of the Alma Ata Declaration to meet the health needs of all people through the potentially revolutionary concept of Primary Health Care. The convention at Alma Ata looked far beyond the customary boundaries of curative and preventive medicine and tried to address the underlying social causes of poverty, hunger, and poor health.

In Chapter 4 we see that the dominant social class, including the medical establishment, quickly stripped Primary Health Care of its social-change promoting features and introduced more conservative versions known as Selective Primary Health Care and the Child Survival Revolution, which attempt to lower mortality rates through a few technological interventions.

In Chapter 5 we take a closer look at some of the concepts and methods of the Selective Primary Health Care approach. In particular, we examine its similarity to the colonial approach to health care as a form of social control, converting the empowering concept of participation into disempowering compliance. The burden of responsibility for child survival is put on mothers, thus blaming the victim, rather than seeking to correct the crushing social and economic inequities that lead to poverty, undernutrition, and high child mortality. As a result, in spite of the global campaign for child survival, millions of children continue to die from the diseases of poverty.

When looking at the larger picture we must try not to lose our human perspective. Of the millions of children who die, each death is a personal tragedy. Each child, in his or her short life-span, and each child's family, has a heart-rending story. Each death marks a saga of struggle, courage, and desperation, of a battle to survive in the face of overwhelming odds, of parental or sibling love: often the final fragile life-line in the absence of food and justice.

To connect our readers to this personal struggle, and to reflect on how high-level decisions in the arena of health and development may affect the lives and deaths of real families, let us first listen to one mother's story.

The Life and Death of One Child: Rakku's Story

CHAPTER 1

The Chain of Causes

The account below is drawn from *Rakku's Story,* a book by Sheila Zurbrigg based on a true incident that took place in a village in India.[1] (We have condensed and somewhat modified the original version.) The story vividly illustrates how a child's death—in this case from diarrhea—is the final outcome of a long chain of interrelated causes. Links in the chain included severe diarrhea and dehydration; extreme malnutrition; crowded, unsanitary living conditions; and lack of clean water. These, in turn, had many underlying causes. Rakku's story points to some of the many links in the causal chain.

RAKKU'S STORY

Rakku had wanted to only breastfeed her baby. This had long been the tradition of women in her village. However, in order for her family to survive, Rakku had to work in the land owner's fields from dawn to dusk. With the long hours of separation from her baby, she had little choice but to give her baby other foods. Soon she no longer could produce much breast milk.

As both a landless peasant and a woman, Rakku was doubly disadvantaged. For long hours of exhausting work, she was paid too little to adequately feed her family. Since the age of seven, her older son, Kannan, had been helping make ends meet by taking the cattle of several landowning families out to graze in the scrub.

While she was working in the distant fields, Rakku left her baby in their wattle hut in the care of her five-year-old daughter, Ponnu. Each morning before dawn, Rakku would haul water from the distant water hole. She would pound a few handfuls of *ragi* (millet) and cook it into a gruel for the family to eat. Although there was often not enough *ragi* to fill all their stomachs, Rakku would always leave a little on the plate, instructing Ponnu to feed it to the baby while her mother was at work in the distant fields.

Even with the older children also working, the family's earnings could scarcely buy enough food. The baby, like the rest of the family, often went hungry. Worsening malnutrition and repeated bouts of diarrhea soon became a vicious cycle. Sometimes Rakku took the sick baby to a traditional healer, who gave him rice water and herbal teas.

The baby would usually get better for a few days, but soon Rakku's baby became thinner and thinner. One day he developed such severe diarrhea that did not get much better even when Rakku gave him the traditional remedies of rice water and herbal tea. His "runny stomach" continued for several days, until the baby was as limp and shriveled as a rice paddy in a drought.

In desperation, Rakku decided to take her baby to the hospital in the city. This was a hard decision, as Rakku had to miss a day's work and a day's pay. At best, this meant a day without food, for the family had no reserves. At worst, Rakku might lose her job—the consequences of which she was afraid to think about. She knew that a wiser mother would let her sick baby die to preserve the rest of the family. But Rakku's love for her baby was too strong.

Rakku sold a bronze pot she had inherited from her mother—the last of her remaining possessions of any value—to pay for bus fare and medicine, and took her baby to the city hospital. She had to pay a bribe to the guard to let her in the hospital gate. After hours of waiting in long lines, at last her baby was seen. By then the baby was on the verge of death.

The doctor scolded Rakku for waiting so long, and for not taking better care of her baby. He referred her to a nurse, who carefully explained to her the importance of breast-feeding and something the nurse called "hygiene." Above all, the nurse emphasized, her baby needed more and better food. Rakku listened in silence.

Meanwhile, the doctor put a needle into a vein in the baby's ankle and connected it by a thin tube to a bottle of glucose water. By evening the baby's shrunken body filled out a bit, and he seemed more alert. The diarrhea had stopped, and the late night nurse removed the needle from the baby's leg.
The next morning a doctor gave Rakku a prescription for medicines to buy in the pharmacy and sent them home. On the way home the baby's diarrhea began again.

Arriving back home, Rakku had neither food, nor money, nor anything left to sell. Her baby died a short time later.

One characteristic portrayed in the story as told by Sheila Zurbrigg, but lost in our short summary, is Rakku's deep love for her baby: the enormous courage of her struggle to save his life, and her clear perception of her baby's basic needs. What also comes across strongly is Rakku's powerlessness to do anything about the inescapable underlying causes of her baby's death.

What Caused the Baby's Death?

If someone were to ask *What caused Rakku's baby's death?*, what answer or answers might be given? The

death certificate—had there been one—would probably have listed "gastroenteritis" (diarrhea), or possibly "dehydration" (water loss). But, clearly, diarrhea and dehydration—and even "severe malnutrition"—were only the final links in a long chain of causes: physical, biological, cultural, economic, and political.

Most doctors, like the doctor in Rakku's story, would probably define the baby's life-endangering problem primarily as a medical one, and fail to fully take into account the crucial underlying social and economic factors. This narrow viewpoint made the doctor's medical intervention in some ways counterproductive—even deadly. As we could see, the expenses Rakku incurred to obtain this medical intervention worsened her economic plight, aggravated her baby's already weakened state, and became one more link in the chain of causes contributing to her baby's death.

Similarly, the nurse in the story at once recognized that poor nutrition contributed to the baby's illness. But instead of exploring the situational causes and helping Rakku find ways to address them, she put the blame on Rakku. The nurse's health messages—aimed at solving a problem defined as behavioral and educational—were more humiliating than helpful. They did little either to empower Rakku or to avert her baby's death.

As *Rakku's Story* documents, it is essential that those of us concerned with the health needs of Third World children take a fresh look at the causes of high child mortality and morbidity—death and sickness rates—within the context of poverty and underdevelopment. As Carl Taylor (a pioneer of primary health care) and William Greenough point out, "Few health problems are influenced as much by multi-causality as the diarrheal diseases."[2] Typically, a child who is healthy and well-nourished recovers quickly from a bout of diarrhea; the illness is messy and unpleasant, but not life-threatening. In communities where children's health is already compromised by malnutrition, poor sanitation, and repeated infection, diarrheal diseases become a major killer.

In this book, we will discuss in detail a whole network of factors that contribute to the unacceptably high death rates of children, focusing particularly on childhood death from diarrhea. The list of causes ranges all the way from specific disease agents (bacteria, viruses, parasites) in the individual child, to environmental conditions in the home and community (such as lack of sufficient food, clean water, and toilets), to social and political factors at the local, national, and global levels.

In trying to explain the poor state of health of the world's children, different observers tend to focus on different causes. Which causes capture our attention, and which we tend to overlook, depends to a large extent on our own social background and world view. *And yet, the way we define the causes of human ills often determines the solutions we seek.*

The Historical Failures and Accomplishments of the Western Medical Model in the Third World

The evolution of health policies and different approaches to health care occurs within the larger context of social and economic development. Changing perspectives of development strongly influence prevailing models of medical and health services and affect who benefits most and who benefits least or is harmed in some way. We discuss the processes of development and underdevelopment in detail in Part 4, but here provide a brief summary as background to the discussion on changing approaches to health care.

The Development Debate

Since colonial times, the "development" of the so-called "undeveloped," "less developed," or "developing" colonized lands in the South has been defined and directed by the more powerful nations of the North. The net transfer of wealth from the South to the North has always been the bottom-line of the development process. As we will explore further in Part 3, the persistent high incidence of illness, death, and developmental delay in the world's children is inseparably linked to the increasingly globalized forces of under-development—carried out in the name of development. (For this reason, we usually use the term "underdeveloped" rather than "developing" countries.)

In the course of the twentieth century, the concept of development has become synonymous with *economic growth*. To this end, during the 1950s development planners urged Third World governments to invest in (and accept giant loans for) large-scale agribusiness and industrialization. Although the planners recognized that this model of *growth-oriented development* would concentrate wealth in the hands of a small, more affluent sector of the population, they maintained that the benefits would eventually trickle down to the poor. In the subsequent two decades, however, it became increasingly clear that this trickle down theory did not work. Overall economic growth was frequently accompanied by expanding poverty.

As poverty and consequent social unrest became more acute during the late 1960s and early 1970s, development planners came to emphasize—at least in their rhetoric—

the importance of eliminating poverty through measures such as increasing employment and promoting fairer income distribution. This led to the concept of providing *basic services* in response to *basic needs,* which became dominant in health and development thinking.

However, this progressive trend was reversed by the economic crisis that began in the late 1970s. Combined with a political shift to the conservative right in a number of major industrialized countries, this caused a drastic regression in mainstream development policy that prevails today. In response to their huge foreign debt burden, debtor countries of the Third World were forced to accept Structural Adjustment Programs (SAPs) imposed by the World Bank and International Monetary Fund (IMF) as a condition for receiving bailout loans. These adjustment policies—which lowered real wages, reduced food subsidies, and slashed budgets for public health and education— harmed, rather than benefited, the poorest people. (See chapter 11.)

Thus, during the 1980s policies for providing poor people with more adequate incomes and services were deprioritized. As wages fell and unemployment rose, the basic needs of a large and growing sector of humanity remained unmet. At the time they were needed most the social programs designed to serve as a safety net for the poor were systematically cut back. Development strategies in the 1990s have begun to show gaping contradictions which undermine their credibility. Despite the World Bank's pledge to prioritize the elimination of poverty, its big-business promoting policies remain firmly in place, and the gulf between rich and poor continues to widen. These macro-economic trends—which we will look at in more detail in Part 3—have a profound influence on changing patterns of both health systems and health.

The Evolution of Third World Health Policies: Western Medicine as a Tool of Colonial Domination

Throughout the Third World, traditional healers (shamans, herbalists, witch doctors, bonesetters, etc.) have for centuries been the major providers of health care. Even today, in many countries they still offer an alternative to Western medicine, often serving as the principal care-givers for the majority of people in rural and poor urban areas.

Prior to the nineteenth century, colonial medical services—provided by Western doctors linked to trading companies—served their European employees almost exclusively. Throughout the colonial period, public health activities were initiated either to combat diseases that affected the European populations (e.g., malaria and sleeping sickness) or as attempts to maintain a healthier work-force and so ensure healthy profits.[3] For example, the Colonial Development Advisory Committee of Britain in 1939 noted that:

> If the productivity of the East African territories is to be fully developed, and with it, the potential capacity of those territories to absorb manufactured goods from the United Kingdom, it is essential that the standard of life of the native should be raised and to this end the eradication of disease is one of the most important measures.[4]

By the end of the colonial period, the pattern of health care which had developed in most of the Third World was largely modeled on the system in the industrialized countries. It emphasized expensive high-technology and urban-based curative care in large hospitals, with Western-trained care-providers. Its services were almost wholly confined to the larger towns and, to a lesser extent, to plantations and mines.

The few public health services that existed were rudimentary and urban-based. The needs of people living in rural areas and urban slums were largely neglected. This situation continued with little change until the middle of the twentieth century.

Attempts to reform the Western medical model

The 1950s and 1960s saw most of Asia and Africa win independence from colonial rule. Most of the newly independent states drew up plans to expand adequate health services into underserved areas. Although on paper these plans often emphasized prevention and gave priority to rural areas, most government and international funding continued to go to curative, urban services. Some poor countries spent over half their national health budgets maintaining one or two huge, urban, tertiary care hospitals.

These "Disease Palaces"* were equipped with the latest, most expensive, imported medical equipment. Their

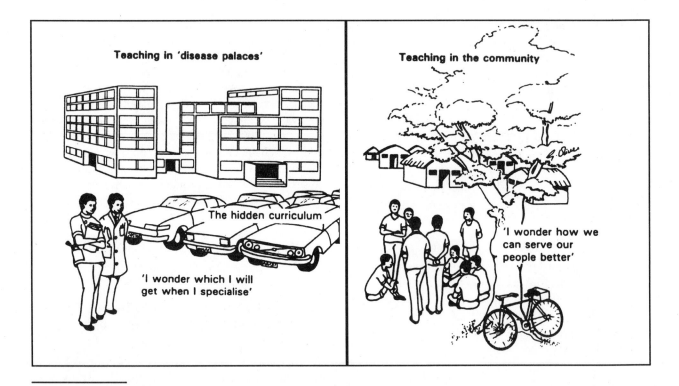

Teaching in 'disease palaces'

The hidden curriculum

'I wonder which I will get when I specialise'

Teaching in the community

'I wonder how we can serve our people better'

---

* This term was coined by David Morley, public health pioneer and author of *Paediatric Priorities in the Developing World* and *See How They Grow*. During the 1950s and 1960s, Morley, Maurice King (author of *Medical Care in Developing Countries*) and other researchers advocated the redesign of medical services to meet the needs of the poor.

western-trained specialists and researchers focused their attention on the diseases of the affluent while neglecting those of the poor majority. For example, Imelda Marcos built The Lung Center of the Philippines at great cost but the Center would not take tuberculosis patients because it did not want to deal with infectious diseases.

Tuberculosis, at the time the Lung Center was built, was the third leading cause of death in the country. (It is, today, still the fourth leading cause of death.) For many years, the Lung Center's operations had to be heavily subsidized. Meanwhile the Quezon Institute, an older establishment for tuberculosis patients, had its budget slashed each year.[5]

The public health campaigns during this time tended to be quite narrow. They were designed to eradicate specific diseases such as yaws, smallpox, or malaria. These campaigns were often "vertical" (specific to a single disease): each had its own administration and budget and operated autonomously, rather than being integrated into the larger health care system. Often these narrow campaigns absorbed more resources than did all the rest of the country's rural health services. As we shall see, international promotion of narrow, vertical campaigns has continued to this day, despite attempts to introduce more comprehensive health strategies.

Probably the most significant development of the 1950s and 1960s was the creation of the *rural health center* staffed by paramedical workers or auxiliaries, called *medical assistants* and *health assistants.* This approach—promoted by the Indian Bhore Commission and later outlined in Maurice King's book *Medical Care in Developing Countries*—has come to be known as the *basic health services* approach.[6] Although it did improve coverage somewhat, the approach was still very service-oriented and medicalized, with little community involvement.

During the late 1960s and early 1970s health and development planners became more aware of the social and economic dimensions of poor health. A growing social consciousness that health—and health care—was a basic human right led to international support for a *basic needs approach* to national health services. Rethinking their priorities in the light of this budding social ethic of basic health services for the entire population, some major funding agencies began shifting their funding emphasis from huge urban hospitals to community health programs. They calculated that the funds spent on a single teaching hospital could maintain hundreds of health centers or clinics staffed by auxiliary health workers, and could provide basic services to many times the number of people.[7]

By the mid1970s, although access to health care for many people in rural parts of underdeveloped countries had been improved through the use of auxiliaries, their expected potential was still far from fully realized. This was partly because medical assistants and other auxiliaries, like their professional mentors (doctors and nurses), had little attachment or accountability to the communities they served. Frequently, they either migrated upwards in the medical hierarchy or dropped out altogether.

The negative effects of the Western medical model

The most serious shortcoming of the Western health care model—which even today remains the dominant model in the Third World—is the way it almost entirely ignores the underlying socio-economic and political causes of health problems. The health professions have helped spread the idea that the ill health of people living in poor countries is largely due to ignorance and overpopulation, rather than to the systematic underdevelopment of the Third World by the First World.

The transfer of Western medicine to the Third World has had other negative effects. In poor countries, as in rich, most physicians come from the higher social classes. Frequently they ally themselves with local and international business interests, particularly medical ones. Invoking the principle of "professional autonomy," doctors insist on their unlimited right to acquire and use sophisticated, costly technology and to prescribe expensive, often ineffective and/or dangerous drugs. Above all, most insist on their right to private practice. Their vested interests have often led them to resist social change, whether at the national or international level. For example, in Chile during the presidency of Salvador Allende, many doctors obstructed efforts to democratize health care institutions. Similar professional opposition occurred in Nicaragua following the overthrow of the colonial regime in that country.

The germs of reform

The disappointing performance of auxiliaries, coupled with growing interest in the *basic needs approach* during the 1970s, led to growing critique and rethinking of Third World health care strategy. This was spurred by the remarkable progress in health attained in China, as well as by the achievements of many small grassroots initiatives in Third World countries, undertaken mostly by nongovernmental organizations.

From these alternative approaches emerged the concept of *community-based health care.* Key to this concept were *community health workers* or *health promoters:* persons selected from and by their own communities and given brief courses showing them how to help their neighbors meet their most important health needs. Self-reliance and the use of low-cost, local resources were encouraged. Emphasis was placed on preventive measures, health education, and involvement and leadership by members of the community.

Throughout the 1960s and 1970s concerned groups of health workers and community organizers began to pioneer what became known as "Community-Based Health Programs," or CBHP. These participatory, awareness-raising grassroots initiatives arose in a number of regions, including Nicaragua, Costa Rica, Guatemala, Honduras, Mexico, South Africa, India, Bangladesh, and the Philippines.

Most of these programs started as a humanitarian response to enormous unmet needs, with a humanitarian rather than a political agenda. But institutionalized exploitation and routine violation of poor people's basic rights so clearly contributed to ill health and high death rates (especially of children) that many of these community-based programs evolved strong sociopolitical components. In some regions (the Philippines, Central America, and South Africa) a wide diversity of small, isolated, community-based health programs began to form loose alliances which gradually grew into broad-based movements, linking health, social justice, and basic human rights.

In Nicaragua (under Anastasio Somoza), the Philippines (under Ferdinand Marcos), and South Africa (under apartheid rule), enormous social inequities and systematic violations of human rights contributed to the abysmal health status of a marginalized majority. And in each of these countries, a strong community-based health movement played a crucial role in "awareness raising" and the development of problem-solving and organizing which enabled people to finally stand up and oust the despotic regimes.

Community-based health initiatives in different parts of the world developed different methods for helping health workers, mothers groups, farm workers, and others learn to analyze their health needs and take organized action. In Latin America, the awareness-raising methods of Paulo Freire's renowned adult literacy program in Brazil (out of which grew his classic book *Pedagogy of the Oppressed)* were adapted to health education. (See page 132.) A "Discovery-Based Learning" model was developed in Central America and Mexico and described in David Werner and Bill Bower's *Helping Health Workers Learn.*[8] At the same time in the Philippines, a group process of "situational analysis" or "structural analysis" was like-

wise used to help people diagnose the underlying causes of poor health. These methodologies for empowerment became important tools in helping groups of disadvantaged people conduct a "community diagnosis" of their health problems, analyze the multiplicity of causes, and plan strategic remedial actions in innovative and creative ways.

The biggest and probably most highly acclaimed community-based health initiative was the barefoot doctors program in China. This grew out of a national liberation movement and was subsequently incorporated into the national health system of the victorious People's Republic. As an integral part of a revolutionary development process it sought to ensure that the people's basic health needs were met. To this end the campaign was remarkable in that it promoted a decentralized process in a country that has always had a strongly centralized government. Each barefoot doctor was accountable to members of the community, although the central government was backing the program. In this way the local community acquired more influence in the nature and quality of the health service provided; millions of people were mobilized to become involved. In addition, the campaign was unique in its commitment to ensuring comprehensive improvements in food, housing, and environmental sanitation. As a result, a number of diseases were virtually eliminated, while child mortality dropped significantly. (China's achievement of "Good Health at Low Cost" is further discussed in Chapter 17.)

Adapting Community-Based Approaches to National Health Systems

In the mid 1970s, a number of top scholars and development planners—observing the failure of the imposed Western model of health care to improve health statistics in many Third World countries—decided to look closely at models that appeared more successful.

The impressive health gains in China and by community-based health programs in the Philippines and elsewhere stood out in stark contrast to the disappointing results of most western-oriented national health programs. Despite criticisms dismissing them as "non professional" or "second rate," health planners began to examine the potential of using the principles of CBHP for national health services. This would entail a revolutionary shift from the existing medical establishment to strong community participation, with emphases on prevention, prioritization of rural areas, and an approach which put disease in its social context. This meant literally turning the system upside down, from a top-down system to a bottom-up approach.

Nonetheless, reforms proceeded cautiously, due in part to increasing tensions over social issues affecting health. Large top-down governments began to co-opt some of the new ideas while prestigious Western academic institutions began to use the rhetoric of bottom-up alternative approaches. Terms like "self determination" and "community participation" entered the vocabulary of professors and graduates under the new doctrine of "Health by the People."

At last, in 1978 in Alma Ata, Kazakhstan (then the Soviet Union), a grand meeting of health ministers from around the world led to the formulation of a plan whereby basic health services would be available to all people. In the next chapter, we look at the Alma Ata Declaration, an unusually progressive document with far-reaching structural and economic implications. If fully implemented, it could have substantial benefits for poor and disadvantaged people the world over.

Alma Ata and the Institutionalization of Primary Health Care

A potential breakthrough in global health rights took place at the International Conference on Primary Health Care, held in 1978 in Alma Ata, USSR (Kazakhstan). The conference, sponsored by WHO and UNICEF, was attended by ministers of health from more than 100 countries. Virtually all of the 134 nations represented subscribed to the goal of "Health for All by the Year 2000."[9] Furthermore, they affirmed the WHO broad definition of health as "a state of complete physical, mental, and social well-being."[10] This was articulated in the Alma Ata Declaration, the conference's final document, which is reproduced in full on pages 21–22.

To achieve the ambitious goal of Health for All, the world's nations—together with WHO, UNICEF, and major funding agencies—pledged to work toward meeting people's basic needs through a comprehensive and remarkably progressive approach called *Primary Health Care* (PHC).

As we mentioned at the end of Chapter 2, many of the principles of Primary Health Care were garnered from China and from the diverse experiences of small, struggling, nongovernmental Community-Based Health Programs (CBHP) in the Philippines, Latin America, and elsewhere. The intimate connection of many of these initiatives to political reform movements explains to some extent why the concepts underlying PHC have received both criticism and praise for being revolutionary.

The Alma Ata Conference in Kazakhstan in progress

The Social and Political Implications of Primary Health Care and the Alma Ata Declaration

As proposed at Alma Ata, the concept of PHC had strong sociopolitical implications. First, it explicitly stated the need for a comprehensive health strategy that not only provided health services, but also addressed the underlying *social, economic, and political causes of poor health*. Specifically, as conceived in the Alma Ata Declaration, such a strategy must promote a more equitable distribution of resources:

> Political commitment to Primary Health Care implies more than formal support from the government and community leaders.... For developing countries in particular, it implies the transfer of a greater share of health resources to the under-served majority of the population. At the same time, there is a need to increase the national health budget until the total population has access to essential health care....
>
> Also, an explicit policy is required whereby the affluent countries commit themselves to a more equitable distribution of international health resources to enable the developing countries, and especially the least developed, to apply primary health care.[11]

PHC also emphasized the close link between health and development of the poorer sector of the community. (Unfortunately, in order to make the declaration palatable to the politically diverse governments represented at the gathering—ranging from Mozambique to Zaire, from China to South Korea, and from the US to the USSR—a precise statement of just how development was to be achieved was left out.) Thus:

> Any distinction between economic and social development is no longer tenable.... Indeed, social factors are the real driving force behind development. The purpose of development is to permit people to lead economically productive and socially satisfying lives....

Since primary health care is the key to attaining an acceptable level of health by all, it will help people to contribute to their own social and economic development. It follows that primary health care should be an integral part of the overall development of society.[12]

The Declaration of Alma Ata also maintains that in order to plan and implement PHC effectively, strong participation of the people affected would be essential. Strong consumer participation had clearly been a common feature of the successful community-based programs which had been studied in the process of formulating the Declaration. It asserts that "self-reliance and social awareness are key factors in human development," and emphasizes the importance of "community participation in deciding on policies and in planning, implementing, and controlling development programmes."[13]

The participants at Alma Ata also recognized that PHC itself can contribute to development and serve as an arena for awareness-raising and organized action. At the same time, they realized that the dynamic unleashed by greater awareness and mobilization was potentially revolutionary, and was therefore likely to meet with opposition from those wanting to maintain the status quo:

> It can be seen that the proper application of primary health care will have far-reaching consequences, not only throughout the health sector but also for other social and economic sectors at the community level. Moreover, it will greatly influence community organization in general. Resistance to such change is only to be expected....[14]

Because UNICEF and WHO represent world governments, they have to be careful not to word revolutionary proposals too blatantly. As health activist Vincent Navarro has pointed out, this indeed may be the Achilles heel of the Declaration. Much of the language used leaves enough room for interpretation that oppressive governments can translate it as they see fit. This undermines the essence and muffles the power of Alma Ata's call for "Health for All" and the sweeping changes in power structures and economic systems that it requires.

Resistance to Primary Health Care

In the wake of Alma Ata, health ministries of underdeveloped countries—prompted by international funding agencies and consultants—began to launch national programs based on Primary Health Care. It was foreseeable that in countries whose leadership was less than fully accountable to the people (that is to say, most countries),

the liberating component of PHC soon resulted in resistance to its implementation.

As a result, many national programs were launched and attracted funding under the PHC banner. But in practice, they tended to treat Primary Health Care as an extension of the same old top-down, Western medical system and extend it into under-served areas. To maintain the new image, the progressive language of Alma Ata was co-opted; expressions such as *"people's participation," "decision-making by the people,"* and *"empowerment"* became part of the new, official jargon. Central control, however, remained intact. While community participation was encouraged, it was generally the participation of weak compliance, rather than the strong participation of decision-making control.

Community health workers (CHWs) were trained, but rather than being the most important members of the health team, they were relegated to the lowest, most subservient position in the existing health hierarchy. The services that they were allowed to provide, especially the curative ones, were usually so limited that it was difficult for the CHWs to earn people's respect. Far from being the envisaged agent of change, the community health worker's role became that of civil servant: lackey, not liberator.[15]

In sum, the transformative potential of Alma Ata remained largely on the drawing board.

The use of the Alma Ata Declaration to neutralize successful community-based health work

As mentioned in the previous chapter, many of the Community-Based Health Programs which provided the inspiration for PHC were not just health initiatives. They were part of a larger struggle by marginalized people for their well-being and their rights. As such, they often ran into serious opposition. Even programs which may not have explicitly put social change on their agendas posed a threat to entrenched interests with their emphasis on addressing root causes of poor health and "putting the last first."[16] The awareness raising and community organizing they conducted to this end was often seen as stirring up trouble by local authorities.

Grassroots efforts to put health into the hands of the people posed a serious threat—not only to elites and governments—but also to the medical establishment, who for so long had maintained a powerful monopoly on the knowledge and power of healing. Their reluctance to relinquish control, combined with government's bureaucratic procedures placed major obstacles in the path of these new programs.

Some opposition to these progressive health programs was overt; in some authoritarian countries, CHWs were harassed or arrested. More often, however, the projects were thwarted by more insidious methods. To make community-run health programs redundant, they introduced costly government-run health posts into the same communities (while often completely neglecting areas that had no health services at all).[17] Staffed with uniformed, well-paid and credentialed health workers, these government posts were accountable directly to the government. They were stocked with a supply of colorfully packaged but nonessential drugs which they were encouraged to distribute liberally —in complete contrast to the PHC ethos of the community-based programs which attempted to encourage responsible and limited use of medicines. Thus, these new government-sponsored programs were instrumental in undermining the potentially progressive thrust of community-based initiatives.

Ironically then, the Alma Ata Declaration, which built its philosophy of PHC on the grassroots "struggles for health" of Community-Based Health Programs, was soon used by authoritarian governments as a pretext for getting rid of these more truly community-based programs. On the grounds that all community outreach in health should be standardized under the national PHC banner, they proceeded to assimilate, co-opt, or close down the autonomous, community-run programs.

Now, nearly two decades after the Alma Ata Declaration, many critics have concluded that PHC was an *experiment that failed.* Others argue that, in its full, empowering sense, Primary Health Care has never been tried.[18] Despite efforts aligned against them, however, there are some success stories—or stories of at least temporary success. During the 1980s, the governments of both Mozambique and Nicaragua carried out comprehensive PHC initiatives very much in line with the Alma Ata protocol. Both countries were lauded by WHO for expanding their PHC coverage and greatly improving their health statistics. The keys to these accomplishments appeared to be: (1) the presence of the political will to meet all citizens' basic health needs; (2) active popular participation in the effort to realize this goal; and (3) increased social and economic equity.

Unfortunately, the early successes in both Mozambique and Nicaragua were short-lived. The governments of South Africa and the United States, respectively—concerned about the alternative model these countries might be setting for their neighbors—launched destabilization campaigns designed to halt their progress. Health workers in both countries were singled out for elimination by proxy terrorist forces sponsored by the regional and global superpowers.[19] When the two countries were unable to sustain their early progress, opponents of PHC (and of equity-oriented development) used this to argue that the successes of these people-supportive alternatives were transitory and unsustainable.

The biggest assault on PHC, however, came from within the international public health establishment itself. The powerful global health institutions launched an international effort to strip PHC of its comprehensive and potentially revolutionary components, and reduce it to a narrow approach with which the national and global power structures could feel more comfortable. This disembowelment of PHC will be the subject of the next chapter.

THE DECLARATION OF ALMA ATA

I. The Conference strongly reaffirms that health, which is a state of complete physical, mental and social well being, and not merely the absence of disease or infirmity, is a fundamental human right and that the attainment of the highest possible level of health is a most important world-wide social goal whose realization requires the action of many other social and economic sectors in addition to the health sector.

II. The existing gross inequality in the health status of the people—particularly between the developed and developing countries as well as within them—is politically, socially and economically unacceptable and is, therefore, of common concern to all countries.

III. Economic and social development, based on a New International Economic Order, is of basic importance to the fullest attainment of health for all and to the reduction of the gap between the health status of the developing and developed countries. The promotion and protection of the health of the people is essential to sustained economic and social development and contributes to a better quality of life and to world peace.

IV. The people have the right and duty to participate individually and collectively in the planning and implementation of their health care.

V. Governments have a responsibility for the health of their people which can be fulfilled only by the provision of adequate health and social measures. A main social target of governments, international organizations and the whole world community in the coming decades should be the attainment by all peoples of the world by the year 2000 of a level of health that will permit them to lead a socially and economically productive life. Primary health care is the key to attaining this target as part of development in the spirit of social justice.

VI. Primary health care is essential health care based on practical, scientifically sound and socially acceptable methods and technology made universally accessible to individuals and families in the community through their full participation and at a cost that the community and country can afford to maintain at every stage of their development in the spirit of self-reliance and self-determination. It forms an integral part both of the country's health system, of which it is the central function and main focus, and of the overall social and economic development of the community. It is the first level of contact of individuals, the family and community with the national health system, bringing health care as close as possible to where people live and work, and constitutes the first element of a continuing health care process.

VII. Primary health care:

A. Reflects and evolves from the economic conditions and sociocultural and political characteristics of the country and its communities and is based on the application of the relevant results of social, biomedical and health services research and public health experience;

B. Addresses the main health problems in the community, providing promotive, preventative, curative, and rehabilitative services accordingly;

THE DECLARATION OF ALMA ATA, CONTINUED...

C.   Includes at least: education concerning prevailing health problems and the methods of preventing and controlling them; promotion of food supply and proper nutrition; an adequate supply of safe water and basic sanitation; maternal and child health care, including family planning; immunization against the major infectious diseases; prevention and control of locally endemic diseases; appropriate treatment of common diseases and injuries; and provision of essential drugs;

D.   Involves, in addition to the health sector, all related sectors and aspects of national and community development: in particular agriculture, animal husbandry, food, industry, education, housing, public works, communications and other sectors; and demands the coordinated efforts of all those sectors;

E.   Requires and promotes maximum community and individual self-reliance and participation in the planning, organization, operation and control of primary health care, making fullest use of local, national and other available resources; and to this end develops through appropriate education the ability of communities to participate;

F.   Should be sustained by integrated, functional and mutually-supportive referral systems, leading to the progressive improvement of comprehensive health for all, and giving priority to those most in need;

G.   Relies, at local and referral levels, on health workers, including physicians, nurses, midwives, auxiliaries and community workers as applicable, as well as traditional practitioners as needed, suitably trained—socially and technically—to work as a health team and to respond to the expressed health needs of the community.

VIII. All governments should formulate national policies, strategies and plans of action to launch and sustain primary health care as part of a comprehensive national health system and in coordination with other sectors. To this end, it will be necessary to exercise political will, to mobilize the country's resources and to use available external resources rationally.

IX.   All countries should cooperate in a spirit of partnership and service to ensure primary health care for all people since the attainment of health by people in any one country directly concerns and benefits every other country. In this context the joint WHO/UNICEF report on primary health care constitutes a solid basis for the further development and operation of primary health care throughout the world.

X.   An acceptable level of health for all the people of the world by the year 2000 can be attained through a fuller and better use of the world's resources, a considerable part of which is now spent on armaments and military conflicts. A genuine policy of independence, peace, détente and disarmament could and should release additional resources that could well be devoted to peaceful aims and in particular to the acceleration of social and economic development of which primary health care, as an essential part, should be allotted its proper share.

⌘

The International Conference on Primary Health Care calls for urgent and effective national and international action to develop and implement primary health care throughout the world and particularly in developing countries in a spirit of technical cooperation and in keeping with a New International Economic Order. It urges governments, WHO and UNICEF, and other international organizations, as well as multilateral and bilateral agencies, nongovernmental organizations, funding agencies, all health workers and the whole world community to support national and international commitment to primary health care and to channel increased technical and financial support to it, particularly in developing countries. The Conference calls on all the aforementioned to collaborate in introducing, developing and maintaining primary health care in accordance with the spirit and content of this Declaration.

The Demise of Primary Health Care and the Rise of the Child Survival Revolution

CHAPTER 4

From Comprehensive to Selective Primary Health Care

For reasons we have discussed, the Alma Ata formulation of Primary Health Care came under attack almost from its inception. This attack came even from within the public health sector itself. As early as 1979, before the debt crisis and structural adjustment programs were used as arguments against it (see Part 3), Julia A. Walsh and Kenneth S. Warren of the Rockefeller Foundation argued that the comprehensive version of Primary Health Care (Comprehensive Primary Health Care, or CPHC) formulated in the Alma Ata Declaration was too costly and unrealistic.[20] If health statistics were to be improved, they argued, high risk groups must be "targeted" with carefully selected, cost-effective interventions. This new, more narrow approach became known as Selective Primary Health Care (SPHC).

This new approach stripped PHC of many of its key concepts. The emphasis on overall social and economic development was removed, as was the need to include all other sectors that related to health in the focus of the programs. Furthermore the keystone of involving communities in the planning, implementation, and control of PHC no longer existed. This selective, politically sanitized (and thus unthreatening) version of PHC was thus reduced to a few high priority technological interventions, determined not by communities but by international health experts. Thus Selective, Primary Health Care was quickly embraced by national governments, ministries of health, and many of the larger, mainstream international organizations.

Governments that cater to a privileged minority—with vested interests in preserving the inequities of the status quo—had been especially reticent to implement the comprehensive Alma Ata version of Primary Health Care. While no one quite dared say publicly that the Alma Ata model of PHC was subversive, almost from the time of its conception there were choruses of important voices proclaiming that it would not, could not, and did not work. These were the same governments and voices that were so quick to support Selective Primary Health Care.

Another Setback to Comprehensive Primary Health Care: the Global Recession of the 1980s

As we will discuss in greater detail in Part 3, the 1980s brought a combination of global recession, suffocating foreign debt, devastating adjustment policies, escalating military spending, worsening poverty, and massive environmental destruction, each exacerbating the others in a vicious cycle. The underdeveloped countries, and in particular their poorest citizens, were especially hard hit—so much so that UNICEF dubbed the 1980s the "decade of despair."[21] In *The State of the World's Children, 1989,* UNICEF reported that:

- In much of Africa and Latin America, average incomes fell by 10% to 25% during the 1980s. Hardest hit were families who, even before the fall in income, did not earn enough to adequately feed their children.[22] The number of malnourished children increased in many countries.[23]

- In the poorest 37 countries, public spending per capita on health was reduced by 50%.[24]

- In these 37 countries, spending on education dropped by 25%.[*][25] And in almost half of the 103 countries reviewed, the proportion of six- to eleven-year-olds (especially girls) enrolled in primary school fell.[26] This has special significance for health, as the average level of female education is often correlated with child mortality.

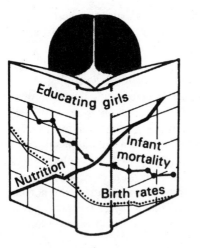

Confronted by these escalating obstacles to the goal of Health for All, in the early 1980s UNICEF faced some difficult decisions. One of the hardest was whether to promote Comprehensive or Selective Primary Health Care. Should UNICEF continue its uphill battle for a broad, empowering approach, as advocated at Alma Ata? Or should it ride with the conservative winds of the decade by endorsing the more selective approach that could more easily win support from powerful governments, institutions, and funding sources? This was a difficult and a crucial choice.

Painfully, UNICEF began to back away from its advocacy of a comprehensive, equity-oriented approach to health care. Rather than renewing its 1970s call for a more just international economic order, expressed in the Alma Ata Declaration, UNICEF began to speak of the "opposing force … affecting the world's children—the continuing economic recession" as if the socially regressive policies imposed on poor countries were an inescapable force of nature.[27] UNICEF's refusal to "question the need for adjustment policies leading to a restoration of economic growth,"[28] was tantamount to accepting inequity and poverty as unalterable facts of life.

---

[*] In some Third World countries, cutbacks in spending on health and education have been even more drastic. For example, in 1991 Peru spent roughly $12 per capita on health and education, one-fourth what it had spent a decade before—and half the amount it was spending on debt payments to Western banks.

By accepting the thesis that the global conditions increasing inequity and poverty could not be corrected, it became easier to argue that the Alma Ata goal of "health for all" was unrealistic. Clearly, "complete physical, mental, and social well-being" was out of the question for the growing millions of people living in dire poverty. And even the medical goal of "absence of disease and infirmity" was unattainable given the mandated cutbacks in health services and increasing levels of hunger and poverty.

Since *health for all* was no longer a viable goal, UNICEF opted for *survival of children*.

The Child Survival Revolution: An adjustment policy for health

In 1983 UNICEF announced that it was adopting a new strategy designed to achieve a "revolution in child survival and development" at a cost that poor countries could afford.[29] Falling clearly within the paradigm of Selective Primary Health Care, the Child Survival Revolution was presented as a streamlined, cheaper, more feasible version of Primary Health Care designed to shelter children from the impact of deteriorating economic conditions. Aimed principally at children under five years old, its goal was to cut Third World mortality of young children in half by the year 2000.[30] To this end, it prioritized four important health interventions, together bearing the acronym "GOBI:"

- Growth monitoring;

- Oral rehydration therapy;

- Breastfeeding; and

- Immunization.

In response to concerns that GOBI might be too selective, UNICEF the following year recommended an expanded version, "GOBI-FFF," adding Family planning, Food supplements, and Female education. Although the response to the limited version of GOBI had been enthusiastic, the expanded version of GOBI-FFF made little headway among health ministries and donors. In fact, in actual practice GOBI was often trimmed further. Many nations limited their major child survival campaigns to Oral Rehydration Therapy and Immunization, which UNICEF began to call the "twin engines" of the Child Survival Revolution. Some countries even put most of their resources into one of these "engines" while neglecting the other.

At face value, UNICEF's argument for GOBI appears compelling. It has been summed up by Ben Wisner, a strong critic of GOBI, in four steps:

1) Financial and human resources for primary health care in poor countries are scarce and growing scarcer due to the persisting international economic crisis;

2) Simple, low-cost, widely accessible technologies for saving children's lives exist;

3) A method for popularizing these technologies at low cost (i.e., "social marketing") also exists;

4) Therefore, GOBI should be implemented as a priority now.[31]

If funding and government support are used as the determining indicators, the Child Survival Revolution can be seen as an almost instant success. Business-friendly governments in both hemispheres which had shown little support for Comprehensive PHC welcomed GOBI enthusiastically. USAID and the World Bank both pledged major financial support; the Holy See (the headquarters of the Catholic church) and Rotary International also jumped on the bandwagon. By the mid 1980s virtually every underdeveloped country had launched a campaign promoting some or all of the GOBI interventions.

However, not everyone has been happy with the Child Survival Revolution. GOBI has been criticized for giving high priority to a few selected health interventions. Indisputably, immunization and oral rehydration therapy are effective, low-cost interventions that can help to save many children's lives, if sometimes only temporarily. Many social activists and community health workers, however, argued that the shift from Comprehensive to Selective Primary Health Care and GOBI was a way for governments and health professionals to avoid dealing with the social and political causes of poor health, and thus to preserve the inequities of the status quo. As one author noted, "The effect of this [sort of] promotion of SPHC under the PHC umbrella is to keep health interventions firmly within medical control and to detract from the need for long-term social, economic and political change."[32]

UNICEF has received some strong criticism for its silent acceptance of government imposed "adjustment policies" (see page 83) and its self resignation to narrow approaches to health care. George Kent, author of *The Politics of Children's Survival,* notes:

Such resignation is not the only possible response. Even while adapting to an economic squeeze by developing low-cost health care techniques, it is possible to resist and fight that squeeze. Instead of asking only how citizens and public health workers can adapt, one can also ask how they might become vigorous advocates of their cause, cultivating a power base of their own and making their demands felt.[33]

Because it represents a compromise away from the potentially more empowering Comprehensive Primary Health Care to a more limited and conservative Selective Primary Health Care, some critics have called the Child Survival Revolution "the revolution that isn't."[34] One thing is certain: UNICEF's endorsement of Selective Primary Health Care via the Child Survival Revolution represented a major policy shift with profound political implications.

UNICEF's defense to this criticism is to insist that the Child Survival Revolution is compatible with Comprehensive Primary Health Care, suggesting it represents the leading edge of PHC. However, Child Survival measures have too often been implemented in the manner of the medical care given by the doctor in *Rakku's Story*, with predictable results: the treatment was successful (or successfully implemented) but the patient died. Because the measures of the Child Survival Revolution do not adequately combat the underlying social causes that contribute to children's deaths, they are much less "life-effective" than they would be if posited in a more comprehensive strategy. In its writings, UNICEF continues to address societal causes of poor health, but the actual health measures it promotes carefully avoid them. This may put UNICEF in a position of lower political risk. But what of the children?

We believe that the health measures included in the Child Survival initiative could do more to save children's lives. But for this to happen, these priority health measures need to be implemented in a comprehensive, empowering way. When it is controlled by consumers, health work can be an important component of, and even a leading edge for, social development and change. Indeed, this is one of the central points of this book. But the process is not as simple as UNICEF suggests. There are as many approaches to health interventions as there are to development.

As with development strategies, health interventions are never politically neutral: they can promote self-reliance and empowerment or they can foster dependency and passivity. They can support either a just or an unjust form of governance. They can pave the way for an equitable social order or they can bolster an inequitable and despotic one. Health planners must be careful to formulate and implement interventions in ways that facilitate progressive social change rather than obstruct it. UNICEF's unwillingness (or inability) to embrace the political dimension of health interventions is largely responsible for the inadequate and often unsustainable results of its various child survival strategies.

Health Care as if People Mattered

CHAPTER 5

Concepts That Need to Be Challenged

In this chapter we will briefly raise the following issues, in the hope that readers will keep them in mind as we proceed in Part 2 of this book with an in-depth analysis of the global campaign to control childhood diarrhea:

1. Technological solutions to social problems: Can they succeed?

2. Survival versus quality of life: Is survival enough?

3. After Alma Ata: What happened to community participation?

4. Health through behavioral change and female education: Blaming the victim.

5. Social mobilization: UNICEF's shift from bottom-up to top-down.

6. From awareness-raising to brainwashing: "Social marketing."

1. Technological Solutions to Social Problems: Can They Succeed?

The story of Rakku in Chapter 1 is an example of how medical technology failed to save a child's life because planners and providers failed to take into account the economic, political, and social factors leading to a child's death. The journals of health and development policy are replete with attempts to solve the problems of the poor through technological "magic bullets." Sometimes the results are positive, but just as often the proposed technological solutions seem to backfire, placing the very people whom they were intended to help at an even greater disadvantage.

A good example is the introduction of tube wells in rural Bangladesh.[35] In villages with long dry seasons and severe water shortage, UNICEF provided tube wells hoping that the increased water supply would help poor families to grow more food and improve their hygiene and health. But repeatedly, big landholders volunteered to install the wells on their land, and subsequently took control of water distribution. They charged prohibitively high rates and denied water to those who either could not afford to pay or resisted such exploitation. The net result

of the new technology was to increase the wealth and power of the rich landholders, while making the poor poorer, more dependent, and more exploited.

Not until Gonoshasthaya Kendra (The People's Health Center) began to organize groups of poor farmers to analyze their situation, and to put in and maintain their own tube wells (still donated by UNICEF), did the wells begin to effectively meet the water needs of poor families. At the same time, the people gained confidence in their ability to work collectively for change.

The lessons from this experience— and many others like it—are apparent: any technology, however appropriate it appears, can be used either for or against those in greatest need, depending on who controls it and how it is implemented. Moreover, when technological solutions are promoted to resolve problems in isolation from their social context, they often backfire.

2. Survival Versus Quality of Life: Is Survival Enough?

Millions of children like Rakku's baby die every year. But what happens to the far greater number of children in similar circumstances who somehow manage to survive? They enter health statistics as successes, but at what cost?

If we recall the story of Rakku's baby, we remember that most children at high risk of dying from diarrhea are undernourished and live in very difficult or even devastating conditions. Thus, efforts that focus on saving children's lives without adequately combating the causes of the poverty and malnutrition may result in decreases in mortality, but may also increase both the number and proportion of malnourished, sickly, and developmentally delayed children. There is evidence of this happening in several areas of the Third World, for example, the Philippines, Chile, and the state of São Paulo in Brazil.[36]

This approach is unacceptable on two counts. First, high levels of hunger and sickness mean that children's quality of life is deplorable; second, in situations where children remain hungry and sick, or living standards are deteriorating, it is unlikely that progress in reducing mortality can be sustained. Already, in some countries where child survival interventions have resulted in reduced child mortality rates, economic recession and structural adjustment measures have slowed or even reversed these gains.[37]

Almost no one would argue that children's lives should not be saved wherever possible. *But survival is not enough.* As George Kent points out,

> Improved children survival rates are not very meaningful if children reach their fifth birthdays but are doomed to lives of misery.... Successful child survival programs improve the survival rate not as an isolated phenomenon but as part of overall improvement in the quality of life.... Child survival is an integral part of development and should not be separated from it.[38]

3. After Alma Ata: What Happened to Community Participation?

The Alma Ata Declaration emphasizes the importance of *strong community involvement* and *self-determination*; the signatories of the Declaration recognized that all health initiatives must possess these features if they are to succeed. There are three main reasons for this.

First, good health is not a product that can be delivered in discrete packages. It results from a process over which people themselves need to take charge. Indeed, for individuals, families, communities, and nations alike, direct involvement in the decisions that influence their well-being is part of what it means to be healthy. Health and self-determination are inextricably intertwined.

The second reason is pragmatic. There may never be enough professionally trained doctors, nurses, or even health workers to meet everyone's health needs. Therefore, in order for improvements in health to be sustained, the community itself needs to become involved in maintaining its own health.

Third, health is determined to a large extent by levels of equality and social justice. Better health depends on improvements in living conditions, nutrition and other basic needs. In order to address the underlying social and political determinants of health, the Declaration calls for accountability of health workers and health ministries to the common people, and for social guarantees to make sure that the basic needs—including food needs—of all people are met. recognizing that socially progressive change only comes through organized demand, it calls for strong popular participation.

Although the Alma Ata Declaration stresses the importance of *strong community involvement* and *self-determi-*

nation to the successful implementation of Primary Health Care, these essential elements have too often been undermined or ignored. The relative success of those programs and policies which have maintained this community-oriented approach, and the failures of those programs and policies which have not, only underscore its importance in attaining health for all.

4. Health Through Behavioral Change and Female Education: Blaming the Victim

The ill health and high death rates of poor children necessitate that far reaching changes be made. But change what? The debate around this issue centers on whether what is needed is social change or behavioral change. This in turn depends on whether the situation is viewed from the perspective of those at the top or those at the bottom. We will use Rakku's story again to illustrate these perspectives.

A top-down perspective tends to blame the situation on the behavior of the poor. So, in Rakku's situation, the health workers entering Rakku's hut would note the unsanitary conditions of the floor, water, etc. They would blame Rakku's "unhealthy behavior" (resulting in her child's death) on her lack of education. They would then try to educate her in how to change this, for example, by instructing her on a few priority health measures that would "empower" her to take care of her baby. They may instruct her on how to breastfeed, where to buy packets of ORS, and when to take her child for vaccination. Or they might encourage her to take her children, especially her girls, to school, so that future generations might make more informed health decisions. If, in spite of these instructions and assistance, the mother's behavior and living conditions remained unaltered, they would blame her for inadequate effort, or possibly ignorance. This paternalistic approach puts the onus on the victim, rarely examining the responsibility of the larger players in the picture—big landowners, politicians or development agencies.

In contrast, a bottom-up perspective analysis starts from a different premise and arrives at a different conclusion. It recognizes that the poor are more adept at coping with life-threatening circumstances than most health experts, and thus usually know best what it takes for them to survive. In this view, the unhealthy living conditions result not from ignorance, but from powerlessness. To combat this predicament, health promotion should aim to equip the poor with the skills and confidence they need to change the system that is stacked against them—that is, to work toward removing the underlying social causes of poor health and poverty.

An example of the first approach, a top down perspective, can be seen by looking at the new "Communications Strategy" of the Child Survival and subsequent "Safe Motherhood" initiatives. These focused on bombarding the "target audience" with essential health messages. UNICEF's publication *Facts for Life* begins:

> A Communication Challenge. The health of children in the developing world could be dramatically improved if all families were empowered with today's essential child health information. That information has now been brought together in *Facts for Life* . . . *Facts for Life* is a challenge to communicators of all kinds—politicians, educators, religious leaders, health professionals, business leaders, trade unions, voluntary organizations, and the mass media. It is for all those who can help to make its contents part of every family's basic stock of child-care knowledge.[39]

At first glance all this sounds quite palatable. But a closer reading reveals some disturbing assumptions:

1) Children's poor health is blamed on parents' (especially mothers') *lack of knowledge*;

2) Therefore, the knowledge that parents need most is about *technical interventions* and *behavior in the home*. Nothing is said about poor people's need for *knowledge about their rights, grassroots organizing, and strategies for social change;*

3) The proper role for persons in positions of power (politicians, religious leaders, etc.) is to *benevolently help remedy the ignorance of the poor*. Rather than making it clear that the powerful are a major part of the problem, *Facts for Life* portrays them as part of the solution; rather than calling on them to share their power and wealth, it invites them to help lift their less fortunate fellow citizens out of their ignorance and self-created misery. This has the effect of legitimizing the dominant position of social elites. It deflects any moral demand that they relinquish some of their privileges (and assumed superiority) as a step toward a more equitable, healthier society.

UNICEF's emphasis on female education is another example of a message that has the potential to be victim-blaming. (Recall that female education is one of the three F's in the expanded version of GOBI.) Numerous studies have supported the assertion that female education is one of the factors most closely correlated with reduction in child mortality.

The point is valid, as far as it goes. As Kent states,

> Maternal education is clearly and strongly associated with children's mortality, in that a child's probability of dying is inversely related to the mother's years of schooling. Maternal education is one of the strongest socioeconomic factors associated with children's survival.[40]

But why? True, literacy permits women to access written information. But it may well be that it benefits women even more by better equipping them to defend their rights. Education—especially the learner-centered, problem-posing type—can be an important stepping stone toward empowerment and change.

Nonetheless, stressing female education as a solution to child mortality reinforces the victim-blaming idea that women's ignorance is its principal cause. A more positive approach might be to emphasize women's empowerment rather than female education. This way the fault-finding finger would shift from ignorance (blaming the victim) to powerlessness (holding the powerful responsible). It would make clear that technical information is not enough: that what is needed is to give women, children, and other disadvantaged groups a stronger, more equal position in society. As Kent puts it: "the more fundamental issue may be women's autonomy rather than education."[41]

5. Social Mobilization: UNICEF's Shift from Bottom-up to Top-down.

Mobilization no longer means what it used to. It was once a politically loaded term used by social activists for mass action in a popular struggle: a grassroots process of achieving popular power. But high-level health and development strategists have co-opted this and other terms like *community-based, participation,* and *empowerment,* stripping them of their progressive political content.

Today social mobilization is not aimed at activating the poor, but at recruiting the powerful. As the term is now used in the promotion of Child Survival initiatives, it signifies the courting and enlisting of prominent decision makers, opinion leaders, funding agencies, schools of public health, etc. It solicits movie stars, sports heroes, politicians, and other popular idols to promote the products of Child Survival with the same seductive advertising gimmicks used to sell cigarettes. George Kent draws the distinction between this current concept of mobilization and empowerment:

> While *mobilization* commonly refers to recruiting people to act on someone else's agenda,

empowerment means increasing people's capacities to pursue their own agenda (italics in original).[42]

The most disturbing aspect of this meaning of mobilization is that it reflects a shift in solidarity on the part of agencies like UNICEF from those at the bottom to those at the top. In the 1960s and 1970s UNICEF took some important stands in defense of the disadvantaged. It even went so far as to call for changes in unjust structures. On several occasions the positions UNICEF took angered the US government, which retaliated by threatening to stop funding the agency. Faced with the conservative climate of the 1980s, UNICEF became more cautious. In 1983 it introduced a new, watered-down strategy for protecting children. This strategy replaced *participation* with *compliance*—in practice, if not in rhetoric. It interpreted *equity* to mean nothing more than *universal coverage with health services*. And it transformed *social mobilization* into the manipulative, top-down technique called *social marketing*.

In 1986, David Werner asked one of the authors of UNICEF's *The State of the World's Children* Reports why UNICEF did not take a stronger position and call for member governments' action to end suffocating debt, devastating adjustment mandates, unfair trade policies, and other root causes of poverty and poor health in the 1980s. He replied, "UNICEF'S goals are the same as yours. We are just more realistic than you are. We recognize our limitations and work within them."

6. From awareness-raising to brainwashing: "social marketing."

In a 1984 article called "Marketing Child Survival," UNICEF's late Executive Director, James Grant, complained that, "in a world where information technology has become the new wonder of our age, shamefully little is known about how to communicate information whose principal value is to the poor."[43] In response to this call, the commercial sector helped adapt advertising techniques to create the new health promotion technique of "social marketing." Glenn Wasek, Director of the Marketing Services Group of John Snow Inc. (a private public health consulting firm), in a book called *Child Health and Survival,* describes social marketing as "a specialty within the management discipline of marketing, [which] incorporates an entire approach to planning, executing, and advancing ideas, concepts, behaviors, services, and/or products to reach the objectives of international public health programmes." He goes on to present "the powerful tools, techniques, and overall approach of social marketing."

This approach was in sharp contrast to the bottom-up, awareness-raising approach widely used in previous decades. The methodology of informal learner-centered education for health and community action in the 1960s and 1970s— strongly influenced by Paulo Freire, the controversial Brazilian educator—promoted "awareness-raising" (or "consciousness-raising"), along with "structural analysis" (analysis of the social causes of people's problems). These became the watchwords of the community-based health and development movements. (For a fuller discussion of Paulo Freire's innovative teaching methodology, see page 132.)

In the 1980s, however, social marketing quickly became the norm. This technique resembles the "banking" approach to education described by Freire. It involves winning the hearts and minds of the people in order to persuade them to accept a pre-designed health care package. Preliminary studies are made, with interviews of the prospective "target population" to determine what sales strategy and product packaging will be most seductive. Then a blitz of advertising is launched through the mass media: radio, television, and village loudspeakers. Movie stars, popular singers, and other public figures (including, in the case of the Child Survival campaign, the Pope and the United States President) are recruited to bolster mass enthusiasm. Unlike Freire's open-ended, problem-posing approach promoted in the 1960s and 1970s, social marketing does not give people the opportunity to make their own decisions and take autonomous action. It often comes closer to brainwashing than awareness-raising.

CONCLUSION TO PART 1

Structural Adjustment Programs (SAPs), privatization of health services, and the World Bank's powerful new role in shaping health care policy have ushered in the demise of primary health care. Later, in Part 3, we will examine in greater detail how economic policies instituted by international financial institutions and global power structures are widening the gap between rich and poor, and stalling or reversing improvements in children's survival and quality of life. We will explore how these policies violate not only the guidelines and spirit of the Alma Ata Declaration, but also of the United Nations Declaration of Human Rights and the more recent Declaration of the Rights of Children.

One of the clearest examples of how global economic policies have adversely influenced the potential of health promotion can be found in the field of diarrheal disease control. Despite a concentrated global effort focusing on prevention and treatment of diarrhea, the diarrheal diseases remain a leading killer of children.[44] How can it be—despite an all-out effort by WHO, UNICEF, and global public health leaders—that common diarrhea continues to claim millions of children's lives each year? This is the subject of Part 2.

PART 2

Oral Rehydration Therapy

A Solution to
Death From Diarrhea?

INTRODUCTION TO PART 2

When examined in its historical context, the story [of oral rehydration therapy] lends itself to discussion of many of the themes which perplex medical historians: the conflicts between 'high' and 'low' technology, between laboratory and clinical science, and between public health and medical research. Furthermore, it demonstrates how the prejudices of the medical establishment and its reverence for advanced technology can postpone life-saving discoveries.[1]

—Joshua Nalibow Ruxin, Wellcome Institute for the History of Medicine, 1994

In the first part of this book we looked at the history of health services in the Third World and at the rise and fall of primary health care (PHC). We saw how health and development policies have long been influenced by social and political factors, often in ways that favor the strong at the expense of the weak. And we noted how attempts to reach Health for All through selected "magic bullet" technologies have limited success because they do little to address the inequities perpetuating poverty and poor health.

In Part 2 we now examine one of the key technologies of the global Child Survival campaign: Oral Rehydration Therapy (ORT). We analyze why this life-saving technology—although it has helped to save countless lives—has fallen short of expectations. Of the many contributing factors, two are outstanding: (1) global promotion of ORT as a factory-made product rather than as a home-made solution, and (2) commercialization of ORT, causing families to spend their limited food money on a remedy they could prepare cheaper, faster, and possibly better at home.

Part 2 includes five chapters. Chapter 6 looks at historical events leading up to ORT, and notes how the medical establishment is perennially resistant to change. Chapter 7 explores the science and politics behind decisions to promote commercial packets, home-made ORT solutions, and/or less clearly defined "home fluids." Chapter 8 discusses the obstacles and controversies surrounding ORT (including the incorrigible overuse of pharmaceuticals). Chapter 9 emphasizes the importance of food as part of ORT and of breastfeeding in preventing death from diarrhea. And Chapter 10 stresses the advantages of rehydration drinks made with cereals rather than sugars.

In the last analysis we conclude that although ORT is an important stop-gap measure, it alone will never reduce child death from diarrhea to acceptable levels. That can only be done by making sure that all children's basic needs are met, and above all else, that they have enough to eat.

Diarrhea: A Leading Killer of Children

The only 'immunization' against diarrhea is for us to find a way out of poverty and under-development.[2]

— Dr. Fernando Silva, Nicaragua

Introduction

Diarrhea, known medically as *gastroenteritis*, is a major cause of children's death in the world—second only to acute respiratory infections (ARI). One out of every four childhood deaths is from diarrhea,[3] which drains the life out of at least 3 million infants and young children every year.[4] Of these deaths, 99.6% occur in the Third World,[5] where one in ten children dies of diarrhea before the age five.[6]

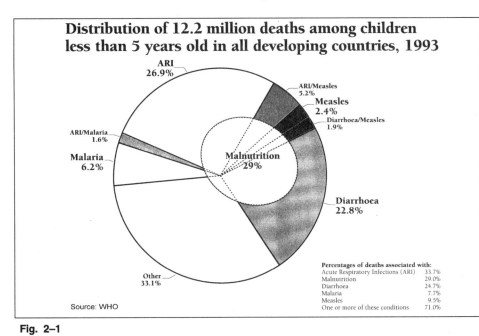

Distribution of 12.2 million deaths among children less than 5 years old in all developing countries, 1993

ARI
26.9%

ARI/Measles
5.2%

Measles
2.4%

Diarrhoea/Measles
1.9%

ARI/Malaria
1.6%

Malaria
6.2%

Malnutrition
29%

Diarrhoea
22.8%

Other
33.1%

Percentages of deaths associated with:
Acute Respiratory Infections (ARI)   33.7%
Malnutrition   29.0%
Diarrhoea   24.7%
Malaria   7.7%
Measles   9.5%
One or more of these conditions   71.0%

Source: WHO

Fig. 2–1

In poor countries and communities most diarrhea— frequent, watery stools (runny bowel movements)—is caused by infectious agents (viruses or bacteria, or less often, intestinal parasites). It is especially common and dangerous in young children, whose developing bodies often lack resistance to effectively combat these infections. Babies who are under-nourished or bottle-fed (or not exclusively breast-fed) are at a higher risk of death from diarrhea.

Most children who die from diarrhea die because too much liquid drains out of their bodies, a process called *dehydration*. A child who loses large volumes of liquid through frequent watery stools can become dehydrated very quickly; the smaller and thinner the child, the more quickly she is likely to dehydrate and die. Life can drain from a baby within hours.

During the last few decades a major international effort has been made to reduce the high death rate from diarrhea among Third World children. *Diarrheal Disease Control* has become a high priority of the World Health Organization (WHO) and is a key component of UNICEF's Child Survival Revolution. The primary strategy for reducing child mortality from diarrhea has been—and remains—Oral Rehydration Therapy (ORT). But, as we shall see, the definition of what ORT is, and consequently the methods by which it is implemented, remain questions of intense debate.

It has long been recognized that fluid replacement—or *rehydration*—in a child with watery diarrhea can prevent or correct dehydration, and can often be life-saving. While this simple concept is at least two thousand years old, Western medicine has in the past century increasingly brought to light the *scientific* principles underlying dehydration and rehydration. This knowledge, however, has not in and of itself always led to effective treatment, as is evidenced by the 12,500 children who continue to die from diarrhea each day.

The history of medicine is replete with examples of the medical establishment's resistance to change and reluctance to admit mistakes. For the management of diarrhea, as with other disease entities, stubborn concern for scientific proof has often been a pretext for rejecting an approach that would bring greater benefits to the sick and fewer benefits to the doctor. Fluid replacement therapy, in particular, has been characterized by these types of obstacles, where professional resistance has repeatedly delayed transitions to safer, more effective therapies.

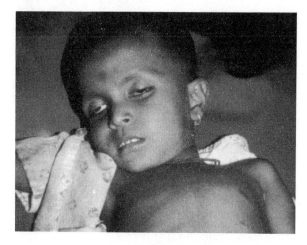

This child is severely dehydrated

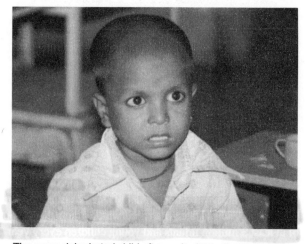

The same dehydrated child after oral rehydration therapy

Diarrhea management has traveled a varied and convoluted path since the early 20th century. Early methods of using calomel, purgatives, and therapeutic bleeding were phased out of use as intravenous (IV) drips became the accepted method of treatment. The next shift was from these drips to similarly formulated oral rehydration salts (ORS) in the 1960s and 1970s. Considered unnecessarily medicalized and costly, the next move was to more simple and accessible home solutions. Currently, and still in a struggle for acceptance, is a transition from sugar-based drinks to safer home-made cereal drinks and gruels. The shift from a precisely standardized formula to the promotion of "increased fluids and foods" has been fraught with difficulties and it is this area that we will now explore.

The Evolution of Diarrhea Management: Old Wine in New Bottles

As a home remedy for diarrhea, "the return of liquid lost" has been a standard part of traditional healing in many cultures for centuries. One of the earliest references—prescribing "profuse quantities" of water with molasses and salt—can be found in a document of the Ayurvedic healer Sushruta from about 1500 B.C. in India. Since that time, special drinks, herbal teas, soups, and broths are found to be part of the traditional treatment of diarrhea in many parts of the world.

References to this form of home therapy can be traced through the Western tradition as well. In 1793 Benjamin Franklin printed an edition of William Park's book, *Everyman His Own Doctor: Or the Poor Planter's Physician.* The book recommends that a person with "Purging [diarrhea] ... forthwith make two Gallons of thin Broth [of chicken cooked in water] and drink it all within the Space of two Hours." It warns that "... Some of this will come up, Some go down, and cleanse Your Stomach in such a Manner, as to make You well before You expect it."

In the nineteenth century, Western medicine introduced a new approach to replacing lost fluids: intravenous (IV) therapy. One of the first recorded uses of fluid replacement directly into the bloodstream was in the 1830s in Moscow when, during a worldwide cholera pandemic, scientists at the *Institute for Artificial Waters* tried to treat dehydrated cholera victims through intravenous therapy.[7]

However, it was not until 1908, in Calcutta, India, that a British doctor, Sir Leonard Rogers, demonstrated that the death rate from cholera could be cut in half through the use of an IV saline (salt) solution. Despite initial problems caused by the solution—such as toxically high salt levels and blood acidity—over the next few decades physicians tinkered with the salt composition of these IV solutions in ways that increased their effectiveness in lowering death rates due to cholera. However, it was not until the 1940s—following the inclusion of potassium in these solutions which resulted in dramatic reductions in hospital death rates—that IV fluid replacement became routine treatment for severe diarrhea and dehydration.[8]

[Diarrhea victims are to be] given to drink a profuse quantity of tepid water in which rock salt and molasses have been dissolved; or clarified water combined with rice gruel.
 	
    —*Sushruta Samhita III,* verse II 1500 B.C.
	The discovery that sodium transport and glucose transport are coupled in the small intestine so that glucose accelerates the absorption of solute and water was potentially the most important medical advance of this century.
	
	    —Lancet A.D. 1978

Today IV treatment is still standard therapy, despite serious limitations to its use. Studies have clearly demonstrated that oral rehydration combined with early feeding, is at least as effective and often safer than IV fluids in treating mild to moderate dehydration.[9] Even into the 1960s there were difficulties in keeping the rubber delivery tubes sterile, and if boiled, they often accumulated endotoxic pyrogens which regularly caused rigors and high fever.[10] Also, there is a danger of giving too much IV fluid. For example, following the 1993 cholera outbreak in Zimbabwe, in one location (Nyangombe) one out of three deaths in young children was caused by over-hydration (administering too much IV solution).[11] None of these concerns arises with oral rehydration.

However, the biggest drawback to IV therapy is logistical. The relatively high cost and level of skill required to administer it makes it simply inaccessible to most of the 1 billion cases of diarrhea occurring annually among children.

Nonetheless, into the 1970s, Western medical professionals continued to advocate IV therapy as the best way to prevent death from diarrhea. Oral rehydration therapy was at last "discovered" by health professionals during the late 1970s. Although oral rehydration actually represented a rediscovery of ancient traditional practices, the introduction of this concept into the modern medical world was to have revolutionary implications. Within a few years, ORT was internationally proclaimed as the "simple solution" to the high child death rate due to diarrhea, and as we saw in Chapter 4, was soon promoted as one of the "twin engines" of UNICEF's Child Survival Revolution.

Discovery of ORT

ORT, simply put, means making sure a person drinks enough fluids, and eats enough foods to replace the water, salts, and nutrients which are lost through diarrhea. The first scientific reports of using oral sugar/salt solutions to treat cholera were published in the early 1950s and an ensuing series of events precipitated a gradual breakthrough in their use. Researchers at Western academic institutions began to understand the cellular mechanisms of water and salt absorption in the intestines. Perhaps the most important finding was that the simple sugar (monosaccharide) glucose is a critical ingredient in transporting salt and water across the cells that line the gut and into the bloodstream. The addition of glucose (or another more complex sugar or starch which can be broken down into glucose) to ORT can greatly speed up the rehydration process. Dr. Norbert Hirschhorn, who facilitated this landmark research on ORT, remarked on the phenomenon:

Even while bacteria [that cause diarrhea] can block sodium chloride absorption, the sugar glucose continues to stimulate sodium absorption. Water and other salts follow along ... at a rate 3 to 10 times greater than normal salt absorption without glucose.[12]

Thus the addition of glucose (or a more complex sugar or starch that gut enzymes break down into glucose) to the solution can greatly speed up rehydration.

This research was followed in the 1960s by clinical work applying these findings to save lives. Much of this was done at the Cholera Research Laboratories in Dhaka, Bangladesh, the Johns Hopkins University International Centers for Medical Research and Training in Baltimore, Maryland, USA, and the All India Institute for Tropical Medicine and Hygiene in Calcutta, India.[13]

Also, by 1955 the "barefoot doctors" throughout China were already treating diarrhea with a sugar and salt ORT drink, or with herbal teas to which mothers traditionally added sugar.[14] According to Carl Taylor, emeritus Professor of International Health at Johns Hopkins School of Public Health and subsequently a former senior advisor to UNICEF, the successful use of a home-brewed form of oral rehydration continues up to the present in rural China.[15]

Despite such reports, it was not until the huge cholera epidemic which hit East Pakistan (now Bangladesh) in 1962 that ORT got wider recognition for its potential. The limited use of IV therapy for just a fraction of the epidemic's victims led desperate doctors in one hospital to begin administering the same solutions that were in the drip by mouth. In this way they were able to rehydrate a far greater number of people, with spectacular results. They reported a death rate of near zero, compared to 27% and 47% in other hospitals.[16]

Physiological studies of how oral rehydration works were carried out in the late 1960s, which led to WHO's declaration of its official approval of the therapy in 1969.[17] Soon after, in 1971, the Bangladeshi war for Independence led to an influx of refugees from East Pakistan into India. Diarrhea was rampant, with a mortality rate of over 30%. In desperation, relief doctors from the US began to package table salt, baking soda, and sugar into plastic bags, to be dissolved in water in the camps. As a result, the death rate from diarrhea dropped to under 3%, and the rate in some camps fell to as low as 1%.[18] Thus, oral rehydration finally established itself as the primary therapy for cholera and acute diarrhea. These hand-packaged plastic bags used in the refugee camps were the forerunners of the ORS packets that are now in worldwide use.

In 1978 the British medical journal *The Lancet* put the final seal of approval on ORT, declaring it to be "potentially the most important medical advance of this century."[19] But the big "breakthrough" heralded by the *Lancet* was not the discovery of ORT, which had happened long before. Rather, it was the grand event of partially breaking through professional resistance to the use of a simpler, more practical alternative.

Despite decades of mounting evidence, it took nearly 30 years to prove the effectiveness of oral rehydration to the medical establishment. Finally, with growing support from the international public health community, in the early 1980s ORT was promoted on a large scale.[20] Nevertheless, the medical establishment in the West (where trends tend to be set) has been slow to fully accept the concept of ORT. For example, a recent article in a US medical journal ill-advisedly recommends no ORT for children under three months old, and *gradual* refeeding in young children.[21] But the main problem is that US physicians prescribe clear, sugary solutions with little or no salt (sodium).[22] Their training in diarrhea management needs updating.

ORT—The Magic Bullet for Child Survival

Once the resistance of the medical establishment had been at least partly overcome, oral rehydration became widely accepted by health policy-makers as the mainstay of treatment for diarrhea. With major international promotion and economic support, by the late 1980s national

without
water

with
water

ORT programs had been launched in 90 countries.[23] WHO's Diarrheal Disease Control Programme took the lead in coordinating the worldwide ORT effort, with UNICEF and USAID playing key roles.[24]

Suddenly, ORT's potential seemed limitless. UNICEF, in its 1986 *The State of the World's Children* report, called ORT technology "an incredibly cheap, simple, safe, and effective method by which parents themselves, however poor, can protect the lives and growth of their children against one of the most common causes of child malnutrition and child death in the modern world."[25] USAID estimated that ORT could save the lives of 4 million children who die every year from diarrheal dehydration.[26] Yet with all the high powered and costly promotion, it is unclear to what extent ORT has realized its much-touted potential.

ORT proponents herald its efficacy in reducing diarrhea-induced child mortality. At the Third International conference on ORT in 1988, representatives from UNICEF and USAID focused on ORT's success; they estimated that it was saving as many as 2 million children's lives per year, thereby reducing the estimated annual child mortality from 5 to 3 million. Recently these estimates have been more conservative: since 1993 UNICEF has reported that ORT is saving 1 million lives per year,[27] resulting in the demotion of diarrheal disease to second place [after pneumonia] among the causes of child death.[28]

There is no question that ORT has contributed substantially to reducing child deaths from dehydration. However, it is becoming increasingly clear that despite its significant impact, it has not lived up to its predicted potential.[29] ORT's performance has been disappointing on two counts: its usage rate and its impact on child mortality.

Access rates, use rates, and effective use of ORT

Several different indicators have been used in trying to determine the progress made in programs promoting ORT. These include "access rates," "use rates," and estimates of "effective use." Unfortunately, the definitions of these indicators are vague, and—apart from the difficulties in getting actual counts or even reliable estimates—allow a wide range of interpretation.

Access rates. Access rates are defined as "the proportion of the population with reasonable access to a provider of ORS."[30] The rate is one of the principal indicators which WHO uses to monitor ORS progress,[31] and applies only to manufactured oral rehydration salts and not to home solutions. In the past few years the figures on access rates have been contradictory. Although accessibility to ORS in the Third World was reported to have increased to 72% by 1992 and nearly 80% by 1994,[32] production of ORS packets has reportedly dropped. From 1991 to 1992, production fell from 410 million to 390 million packets. And in several countries—Afghanistan, Albania, Somalia,, and Sudan—packet production has been suspended. (This apparent discrepancy may be due to faulty data; WHO describes the estimates of ORS access rates through 1993 as "based on reports, many invalidated ... or extrapolated from ORS production figures." In describing its new, more reliable 1994 figures WHO states that, although its "surveys cannot support a global estimate" that "access to ORS is approaching, if not exceeding, ... 80%."[33]) But as prices of commercial ORS products steadily climb, in some countries the ORS use rate has dropped, in some cases to less than half its peak rates. (See discussion of ORS in Egypt, page 49.)

Use rates. "ORT use rates" currently refer to use of ORS and/ or Recommended Home Fluids (ORS/RHF), and are defined as the "proportion of children under five years with diarrhoea who receive increased fluids and continued feeding." At the 1990 Global Summit on the Rights of Children, a goal was set that 80% of families "should be empowered to use ORT by 1995." The 1995 *State of the World's Children Report* states that "the most recent figures (1993) on progress toward this goal suggest that the ORT use rate was at that time approximately 44% for the developing world as a whole."[34] A still more recent table provided by UNICEF—also using 1993 data—indicates the "global ORT use rate" at 57%.[35] (See figure 2–2, page 38.)

The estimates in Figure 2–3 look fairly good: a global ORS access rate of 75%, a global ORS/RHF use rate of 51%, and an ORS use rate of 25%.[36] All estimates show a modest rise since 1989. However, these figures cannot be taken at face value. First, the global estimates exclude China, and if China were included, they would be considerably lower. In 1993, China, where more than a quarter of the world's children live,[37] reportedly had an ORS+RHF use rate of 22%, and an ORS use rate of only 3%.

The biggest problem with interpreting "ORS/RHF Use Rates," however, is the possibly misleading nature of the figures. The apparent increase in use rates may be due, at least in part, to a redefinition of recommended home fluids (RHF). Around 1989 the definition of RHF was expanded to include everything from unsweetened tea to plain water.

Some country reports show a wide gap between knowledge and use. For example, a 1989–1990 survey in the Philippines found that while 73% of mothers surveyed could demonstrate how to prepare ORS correctly, only 14% used ORS for treating diarrhea in their children under age 5. (By contrast, 30.3% of the cases involved use of drugs.)[38]

Over the last several years, there has been growing concern about the validity and implications of reported ORT use rates. In 1990, the WHO Programme for Control of Diarrhoeal Disease (PCDD) reported that when more reliable data sources were used, the estimates of ORT use rates in India, Bangladesh, Indonesia, and a number of other countries dropped.[39] UNICEF, in its 1994 *State of the World's Children Report,* acknowledged that "in some parts of the world ORT utilization rate is slipping."[40] In February, 1994, UNICEF and the International Centre for Diarrhoeal Disease Research in Dhaka, Bangladesh, acknowledged concern about declining use rates in proclaiming the need "to refocus attention on the continued underutilization of ORT throughout the world."[41]

Low effectiveness of ORT use

If the "ORT use rate" is difficult to assess, the "effective use rate" is even more problematic. It is widely recognized that ineffective use of ORT—whether packets, home mix, or home fluids—is a major stumbling block. Norbert Hirschhorn, a leading pioneer in ORT, agrees that "... it is abundantly clear that many [children] do not receive what they need even when packets and home fluids are known and available."[42] Estimates of effective use vary greatly, but on the average it is thought that only about one third of current usage is done correctly.

Correct use of ORT involves at least 3 aspects: (1) correctly prepared or balanced drink(s), (2) increased fluid intake, and (3) continuation of feeding. In a WHO sponsored meta-study of 76 surveys in 36 countries, conducted between 1990 and 1993, it was found that 58% of households used ORS and/or Recommended Home Fluids.[43] However, only 32% of households increased the amount of fluid given to the child, and only 20.5% both increased fluids and continued feeding. Thus, fully effective use of ORT occurred, at the most, for only one of five children.

The problem of error in preparation of rehydration drinks is quite prevalent. Studies carried out in six countries showed that between 23% and 73% of mothers prepared sugar and salt solution (SSS) drinks with "dangerously high salt solutions."[44] This led to WHO discouraging the use of home-made SSS rehydration drinks on the grounds that they are often not safely and correctly prepared. However, high rates of incorrect use also occur in preparing the ORS packets, often as a result of adding insufficient water. For example, in studies in Brazil[45] and Kenya,[46] many children's caretakers were unable to prepare ORS correctly (39% and 50% respectively).

Global ORT Use Rates 1994

Region	Population < 5 Yrs (thousands)	Under 5 Deaths (thousands)	Total Episodes (thousands)	Diarrhoeal Deaths (thousands)	ORT Use 1993 (percent)
East Asia and Pacific	185500	2530	481650	281	79
Middle East and North Africa	54000	997	188400	283	61
Eastern and Southern Africa	48585	1970	216770	578	60
Americas and the Caribbean	54300	590	192425	153	58
South Asia Region	161040	4955	507320	1309	44
West and Central Africa	51494	2335	267927	658	36
GLOBAL	**554919**	**13377**	**1854492**	**3262**	**57**

Fig. 2–2. The ORT use rate is defined as proportion of children under five years with diarrhea who receive ORS/RHF. Source: Fax sent to the authors from UNICEF, May 1995.

WHO's Programme for the Control of Diarrhoeal Disease (PCDD) most recent ORS/RHF use rate—*at 51%*—falls midway between those of UNICEF. The PCDD's *Ninth Programme Report 1992–1993* (the latest report available at the time of this writing) presents its calculations of both ORS access rates and ORS/ RHF use rates.[47]   (See Figure 2–3).

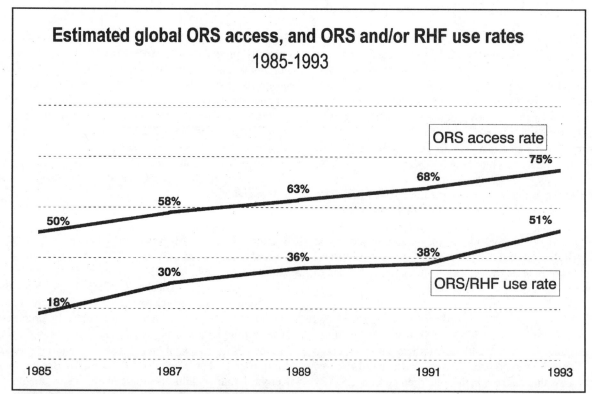

Fig. 2–3. Programme for the Control of Diarrhoeal Disease: Ninth Programme Report 1992–1993, World Health Organization, 1994 p. 36. As explained in the text, this global estimate excludes China, which pulls true global estimates down considerably (the ORS and RHF use rate in China for 1993 was estimated at 22%).

One of the most common reasons for failure of ORT to adequately combat dehydration is that too little fluid is given. A child with severe watery diarrhea (especially cholera) can sometimes lose a liter or more of liquid a day. With vomiting the loss can be still greater. To prevent death, all the volume of fluid that is lost must be replaced. Caretakers need to understand why such large quantities of liquids are required, and learn to give the drink often—sometimes every few minutes—day and night. Even if the child vomits, some of the liquid stays down, particularly if small quantities are given frequently. WHO and UNICEF, with good reason, have put increasingly strong emphasis on *increased fluid intake*. But the problem of giving too little persists.

In the whole of the Third World, how many children are effectively reached with ORT? If we accept the average estimate that the global use rate for all forms of ORT (ORS and RHF) is around 50%, and estimate that one third of ORT use is effective, then ORT effectively reaches around 17% of the children who need it. Even this figure may be an overestimate.

"Resting the Gut"—A Harmful Practice Introduced Mainly By Western Doctors

In the early days of the big push for ORT, many health authorities criticized traditional remedies, asserting that mothers frequently withheld food and drink when their children had diarrhea. They were said to do this based on the belief that to stop what goes in would slow down what comes out. However, assessments in Bangladesh, Saudi Arabia, India, Peru, Mexico, Kenya, Swaziland, and Lesotho have shown that *traditionally most mothers continue to feed their children during diarrhea, and that nearly all continue breastfeeding.*[48]

In fact, the idea of "resting the gut" seems to have been promoted mainly by qualified (Western-style) doctors. In several countries, mothers who withheld food and milk during their children's diarrheal episodes often said they did so because "My doctor told me not to feed my child when he has diarrhea."[49] Although food and milk, especially breast milk, are now considered an essential part of ORT, many physicians (in both the North and the South) still tell mothers not to give food, or at least not milk, when their children have diarrhea. Such advice can, and often does, prove fatal, especially for undernourished children.[50]

Does ORT Prevent Child Death?

Toward the end of the 1980s it was becoming clear that the impact of ORT on child survival, while substantial, was less than had been euphorically predicted. In 1988, USAID, while still extolling ORT as a "major breakthrough," conceded (rather oxymoronically), that a "continuing breakthrough" is needed.[51]

Robert Moy—a well-known researcher on diarrheal disease—in response to a draft copy of this book wrote:

> I agree that the effect of ORT on mortality is disappointing. The claims of UNICEF about millions of lives being saved each year by ORT … are of course a load of wishful thinking and only mathematical models that bear little reality to the real world. Maybe fewer children die of acute dehydration these days …but they still will die later of persistent diarrhoea, malnutrition, bloody diarrhoea or now diarrhoea associated with HIV for which ORT alone would be ineffective. It is of course highly misleading for UNICEF/WHO/USAID to peddle the notion to the general public that all the world's problems will be solved by a consignment of packets of ORS …[52]

Moy and others have raised the question as to whether ORT—when introduced in isolation from efforts to combat poverty and unhealthy living conditions—actually prevents child death or merely postpones it. In analyzing the situation, we must be careful not to confuse the impact of rehydration on an individual child who has diarrhea—a proven therapy for an acute illness—with overall child mortality in a population.

In many countries, figures on mortality from diarrhea are sketchy and often misleading, largely because many children's deaths are never recorded. As Carl Taylor and William Greenough, III—two highly respected ORT experts—point out, original estimates of deaths caused by diarrhea came from extrapolations from local field studies in areas of high prevalence, and deaths averted are calculated by projecting results from some of the best programs. In both instances there are questions about whether the numbers are representative of global reality.[53]

Some critics argue that, even though an ORT program permits a certain number of children to survive one bout of diarrhea, there is a good chance that many of them will die of a subsequent diarrheal episode or another of the diseases of poverty.[54] Data suggest that, in some circumstances, ORT programs that have been judged successful

according to reported access or use rates have failed to significantly reduce overall child mortality.[55]

One study from Honduras found that although diarrhea death rates declined as a result of an ORT campaign, no change in overall death rates could be detected. Even more disturbingly, perhaps, a 1992 study in a rural community in Bangladesh found that *infant* mortality from acute watery diarrhea actually increased significantly during the implementation of an ORT program.[56] This is of special note because ORT has been strongly and (according to many reports) effectively promoted throughout Bangladesh. The study blamed the program's disappointing results on inadequate education of families about correct use of ORT.[57] However, the Bangladesh Rural Advancement Committee has conducted one of the world's most extensive and well monitored ORT education campaigns, reaching virtually every mother in the country.[58] Therefore, it seems more likely that the study's results showing no decline in children's deaths with the introduction of ORT may stem from worsening poverty, related in turn to deteriorating social policies, foreign debt, and structural adjustment programs. Even the best ORT initiative cannot offset the harmful effects of these macro-economic trends.[*/59]

⌘

In the final analysis, UNICEF's official "guesstimate" of one million children's lives saved annually by ORT must be seriously questioned. Such questioning, however, is by no means intended to denigrate the accomplishments of ORT initiatives or the commitment of those who have worked so hard to make them a success. On balance, it is safe to say that in the face of difficult circumstances ORT is saving the lives of large numbers of children—at least temporarily. The fact remains, however, that of the 3 million or so who die from diarrhea every year, roughly 2 million children still die from dehydration.

By comparing Third World diarrheal death rates with those of children growing up in better living conditions, we know that nearly all deaths from diarrhea and dehydration are preventable. Clearly, the current Child Survival interventions are not enough. Too often, as we discussed in Part 1, ORT has been promoted and funded as a vertical intervention, separate from the basic needs

---

*Hirschhorn points out that this study in Bangladesh was done in an area where most of the diarrhea mortality is from dysenteric or persistent diarrhea for which ORT is not the primary therapeutic need. However, if over-emphasis on ORT led to underuse of more urgently needed forms of treatment, in a paradoxical way this could have contributed to the recorded increase in mortality.

and rights of children, and consistent with the child survival strategy of selective primary health care. Might not more children's lives be saved if ORT were integrated into a broad primary health care approach?

Part of the problem of low effectiveness may relate to the fact that promotion of ORT has been more product— than process—oriented. It has been based more on convincing people to buy and use packets than on helping them to acquire conceptual understanding and basic problem-solving skills concerning the child's food and fluid needs and overall well-being. Information-sharing has been weak. Health facility surveys in several countries show that "the proportion of mothers correctly advised by health workers ranges from 1% to 10%."[60] Much more emphasis needs to be placed on education and enablement, especially of women and girls. WHO is now giving this higher priority.[61]

The Oral Rehydration Debate: ORS Packets or Home Fluids

CHAPTER 7

"A terrific polemic with ideological color has been raging over whether ORT should be delivered as WHO 'full formula' packets or by teaching mothers to make salt and sucrose solutions at home."[62] So wrote Dr. Norbert Hirschhorn in a chapter on ORT he contributed to a 1987 book titled *Child Health and Survival: The UNICEF GOBI–FFF Program.*[63] On the surface, the differences between packets and home-made rehydration solutions may not seem to warrant such heated debate. And many experts claim that it is a debate that has been resolved. But as we shall see, the key issues are still at stake. This chapter will examine the divergent forms of oral rehydration therapy, and consider the pros and cons of manufactured ORS packets and of homemade solutions.

Oral Rehydration Salts (WHO's full formula ORS) usually come in factory-produced aluminum-foil packets, or *sachets* containing exact measurements of salts and a simple sugar. The current standard WHO/UNICEF ORS formula, designed to be mixed with one liter of water, consists of:

Glucose (a simple sugar)	20.0 grams
Sodium chloride (table salt)	3.5 grams
Potassium chloride	1.5 grams
Trisodium citrate, dihydrate	2.9 grams
(formerly sodium bicarbonate, 2.5 grams)[64]	

Although the standard WHO/UNICEF ORS formula is mixed with one liter of water, commercial products exist which require different amounts of water, from 200 or 350 milliliters to one liter. Formula also vary, and some products add flavoring. Apart from ORS in packets, in some countries a corresponding formula is fabricated as tablets to be dissolved in a glass of water. Ready-mixed ORS and similar drinks also come in bottles or in cans as a costly commercial product. However, this discussion will be limited to the packet form of ORS, which—with strong promotion and investment by major institutions like UNICEF and USAID—has by far the widest distribution.

In the early years of ORT campaigns, packets of ORS were manufactured in industrialized countries and shipped to the Third World. They were delivered to health ministries, distributed to clinics and health posts, and mostly given to mothers free of charge. But with passing years and cutbacks in health budgets, production and distribution have increasingly become commercialized. Currently, about 400 million ORS packets are produced annually, 2/3 of which are locally produced in 60 developing countries.[65] UNICEF still provides about 80 million packets annually, most of which are produced in industrialized countries and exported, primarily to Africa.

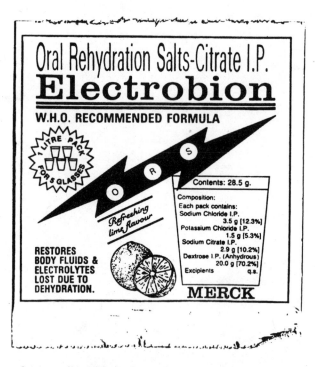

Commercial ORS packets often use medicalized and mystifying terminology and flashy promotional gimmicks.

Home-made ORT drinks, unlike ORS packets, are prepared in the home using ingredients that most poor families already have on hand. Less standardized than the factory-produced ORS packets, they can be adapted to utilize local low-cost staples and traditional methods of measuring foodstuffs.

One of the first, still widely used home mix formulas—called SSS (sugar & salt solution)—consists of ordinary sugar (sucrose) and table salt, in roughly the proportions of the WHO formula. Although the formula recommended varies considerably, a safe and effective ORT drink can be made by mixing 8 teaspoons of sugar and half a teaspoon of salt in a liter of water.[66] Raw sugar, molasses, or honey can be used instead of refined sugar. Where locally available, baking soda (sodium bicarbonate) is sometimes added, but not considered essential. To provide flavor and potassium (both of which may help restore the sick child's appetite), citrus, tomato, and other fruit juices may be added, or the child can be encouraged to eat bananas. When fruits are unavailable, ashes (potash) from the cooking fire can provide potassium. Water poured through ash in a cloth can be added to the home mix.[67]

Food as a part of ORT. Before continuing our debate, it is essential to stress the importance of *continuing to feed a child who is suffering from diarrhea.* Food is now considered a key part of any method of oral rehydration. Not only does the food help to maintain the child's nutritional level and ability to fight the infection, but foods help to transport water from the gut into the bloodstream, hastening rehydration. Frequent feeding should be encouraged as soon as the sick child is able to take food. *Breast milk* is an excellent rehydration drink; women who breastfeed their babies should always try to breastfeed prior to administering an ORT drink.

Now recognized as an effective form of home-made ORT, *food-based* or *cereal-based* rehydration drinks are increasingly encouraged, especially by community-based programs. They can be made as a thin gruel of rice, maize, potato, or whatever staple low-cost grain or root crop the family has in the home. Studies show that drinks made with rice powder (and a little salt) not only rehydrate effectively, but in some cases (mainly cholera) reduce both diarrhea and vomiting better than either standard ORS packets or homemade sugar-salt solutions.[68] The role of food and food-based drinks in oral rehydration is discussed more fully in chapters 9 and 10.

Which Groups Favor Packets and Which Favor Home-made Drinks?

The debate over what approach to ORT is best, and why, has evolved during the last decade. Controversy is growing about the relative precision or simplicity of home fluids, the content of full formula ORS, and home-preparation versus commercialization of food-based drinks. But the core debate continues to rage between those who continue to promote ORS packets for home use, and those who champion home-made solutions.

The packet promoters. With few exceptions, the strongest proponents of ORS packets, including for formulated for home use, tend to be large national and international institutions. These include WHO and UNICEF, and most ministries of health. USAID has been one of the most consistent and aggressive champions of packets and has strongly promoted their commercial production and distribution. Following USAID's lead are the hundreds of government programs, university extension projects, and nongovernment organizations (NGOs) financed by USAID's deep pocket.

In general, the institutions which strongly favor ORS packets over home-made solutions are those which promote health and development more from a technological than a social perspective: from the top down rather than the bottom up. They argue that the packets are safer because their scientifically formulated contents are precisely measured and controlled. They quote studies showing that mothers often prepare home-made ORT incorrectly.

From the perspective of policy-makers and bureaucrats, ORS packets are more sharply defined and fit more easily into centrally packaged plans than do fuzzier and more adaptable home-made solutions. However, even among the packeteers, there may be different rationales for their choice. A long time veteran in the international promotion of ORT comments on divergent reasons for promoting ORS packets comments:

> It is interesting to consider why UNICEF and USAID have put nearly all their emphasis on packets, and I think the motivations are different. UNICEF needs to be able to say that it has made progress over the short term, to maintain its financial support; and progress, they believe, depends on having an intervention based on a simple discrete countable item, such as vaccines, vitamin A, or packets. USAID, on the other hand, has a social policy based on willingness to pay. Paying for things is what life is all about for them.[69]

A RANGE OF REHYDRATION METHODS FOR CHILDREN WITH DIARRHEA

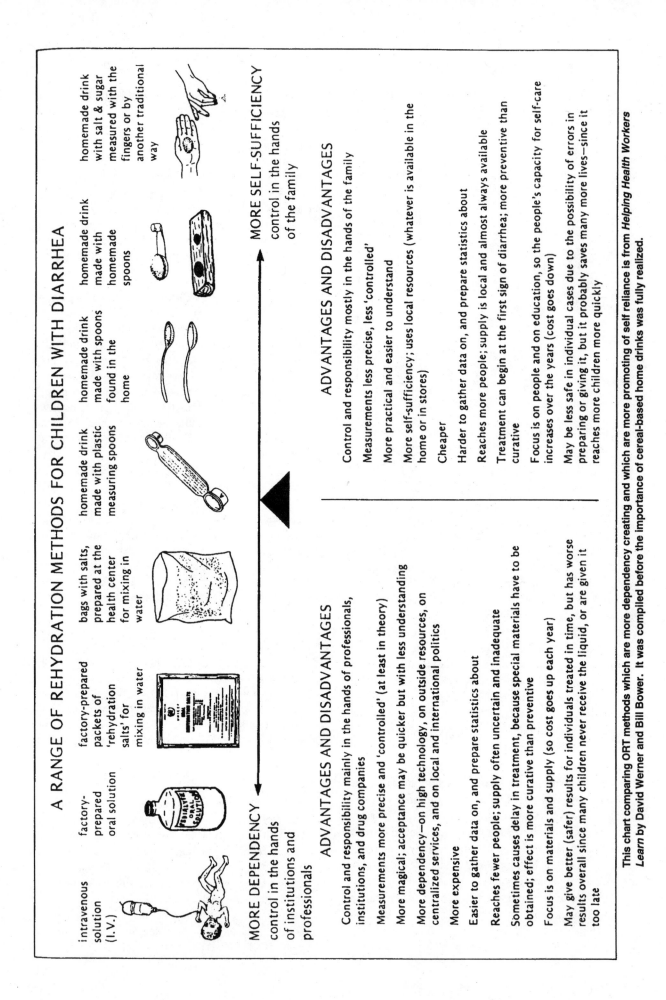

| intravenous solution (I.V.) | factory-prepared oral solution | factory-prepared packets of 'rehydration salts' for mixing in water | bags with salts, prepared at the health center for mixing in water | homemade drink made with plastic measuring spoons | homemade drink made with spoons found in the home | homemade drink made with homemade spoons | homemade drink with salt & sugar measured with the fingers or by another traditional way |

MORE DEPENDENCY
control in the hands of institutions and professionals

MORE SELF-SUFFICIENCY
control in the hands of the family

ADVANTAGES AND DISADVANTAGES

Control and responsibility mainly in the hands of professionals, institutions, and drug companies

Measurements more precise and 'controlled' (at least in theory)

More magical; acceptance may be quicker but with less understanding

More dependency—on high technology, on outside resources, on centralized services, and on local and international politics

More expensive

Easier to gather data on, and prepare statistics about

Reaches fewer people; supply often uncertain and inadequate

Sometimes causes delay in treatment, because special materials have to be obtained; effect is more curative than preventive

Focus is on materials and supply (so cost goes up each year)

May give better (safer) results for individuals treated in time, but has worse results overall since many children never receive the liquid, or are given it too late

ADVANTAGES AND DISADVANTAGES

Control and responsibility mostly in the hands of the family

Measurements less precise, less 'controlled'

More practical and easier to understand

More self-sufficiency; uses local resources (whatever is available in the home or in stores)

Cheaper

Harder to gather data on, and prepare statistics about

Reaches more people; supply is local and almost always available

Treatment can begin at the first sign of diarrhea; more preventive than curative

Focus is on people and on education, so the people's capacity for self-care increases over the years (cost goes down)

May be less safe in individual cases due to the possibility of errors in preparing or giving it, but it probably saves many more lives—since it reaches more children more quickly

This chart comparing ORT methods which are more dependency creating and which are more promoting of self reliance is from *Helping Health Workers Learn* by David Werner and Bill Bower. It was compiled before the importance of cereal-based home drinks was fully realized.

The home mixers. In marked contrast to the packet promoters, the most vocal proponents of home-prepared rehydration drinks tend to be small community organizations. These groups typically take a comprehensive approach to primary health care that includes working for social change. Instead of implementing ORT programs in isolation, they try to integrate them into broader initiatives that encompass health care, education, and empowerment.

Proponents of home-solutions argue that it is safer for children if families learn to make a reliable drink from ingredients they have on hand. This fosters self-reliance in the family and the community and avoids unnecessary dependence on products whose supply may be outside the consumer's control. They point out that when a mother learns to manage diarrhea with home staples, she does not have to delay treatment while she goes to the village store. Nor does she spend family food money on something she can prepare more cheaply and quickly at home.

These organizations are often highly critical of the packet-centered approach. They quote studies showing that people often mix ORS with too little water, which can be dangerous. In addition, the cost of ORS and its presentation as a medicine frequently results in mothers (and even health workers) giving the sick child too little ORS to be effective. They insist that more emphasis is needed on communication of basic principles, and less on product marketing.

Top-down and bottom-up policies for ORT

Spokespersons for WHO and UNICEF tell us that the polarized debate over ORS versus home fluids now has little substance: that they have been unfairly accused of promoting commercial ORS packets over local alternatives. WHO public statements for several years have recommended "home fluids" as the first-line of home management for diarrhea. For example, the 1990 *"WHO Guidelines: Selection of Home Fluid"* states that, "Where ORS is not available, other fluids should be used to prevent dehydration."[70] However, it places ORS at the top of its list of recommended forms of rehydration for the early home treatment of diarrhea. More recently, in its 1993 booklet, *The Management and Prevention of Diarrhoea, Practical Guidelines*[71] WHO promotes both "home fluids" and ORS, as follows:

How to treat diarrhoea at home (mother's card)

1. AS SOON AS DIARRHOEA STARTS, GIVE YOUR CHILD MORE FLUIDS THAN USUAL:

GIVE:

- ORS solution

- Food-based fluids, such as soup, rice water and yoghurt drink

- Plain water

- If the child is under 6 months old and taking only breast milk, give only ORS solution or plain water, in addition to breast milk.

GIVE AS MUCH OF THESE FLUIDS AS YOUR CHILD WANTS.

Thus, in their formal recommendations, WHO and UNICEF support the use of home fluids for the early home treatment of diarrhea. But do they practice what they preach? If we look at where they have invested the bulk of their money, personnel, and research, these agencies have clearly placed their primary emphasis on packets. This bias is reflected in both their national programs and their official documents.

As we shall discuss in Chapter 10, the above prioritization of ORS as a 'home fluid' must be questioned. Sometimes food-based drinks and even sugar-salt solutions may, *in community settings,* be as effective or more effective than ORS—partly because packets are often unavailable (or unaffordable) where and when needed. The choice is often *not* between home-made drink or ORS, but between home-made drink or *nothing.*

One critic has suggested that the recent laxity about home fluids—the list of which now includes "plain water"—reflects a need to 'massage the statistics' of ORT use rates in order to hit some arbitrary target (such as UNICEF's goal of 80% accessibility to ORS).[72]

Although WHO has modified some of the details in the last few years, its basic recommendations have changed little. In its 1993 "The Selection of Fluids and Food for Home Therapy to Prevent Dehydration from Diarrhoea: Guidelines for Developing a National Policy," WHO has eliminated sugar-salt solution from its RHF (recommended home fluids) list. But it still favors ORS:

> "When possible, a fluid should be promoted that contains salt. The possibilities include:
> - ORS solution
> - a salted drink
> - a salted soup
> ORS solution is very effective for home therapy to prevent dehydration. It should be promoted if ORS packets are readily available and affordable, and mothers know, or will be taught, how to mix and give ORS solution."[73]

These 1993 guidelines wisely stress the importance of giving *increased quantities of fluids, together with foods.* They also place even stronger emphasis on home fluids. But the fact that the list of RHFs is still headed with ORS continues to give this commercial product top priority in the minds of both health planners and consumers. The mild admonition to promote them "if ORS packets are readily available and affordable" may be sound advice, but is scarcely strong enough to reverse the decade of social marketing which promoted ORS as a wonder drug that poor families should procure irrespective of distance and cost. The bias in favor of packets is deeply entrenched, both at national and community levels. In Jamaica, for example, anthropologists found that nurses explicitly warned guardians of children with diarrhea never to use traditional home drinks, and that they "must only use the packets mixed with water."[74]

"Irrational use of ORS." In an article in the March, 1995 issue of *Lancet* entitled "Rational Home Management of Diarrhea," Almroth and Latham challenge the rationale for strongly promoting ORS packets for home use, comparing it with irrational drug use:

> Irrational use of drugs for treatment of diarrhea, according to WHO, is associated with problems such as diversion of attention from appropriate treatment, unnecessarily high treatment costs, and adverse reactions. Would this list not be an equally appropriate description of the consequences of the promotion of irrational use of ORS at home?

> As failures of ORS at home have become apparent, more rational guidelines for the use of ORS have emerged. However, a programme for home management of diarrhoea will remain fundamentally irrational if built on the premise that ORS is the ideal therapy that should be used if at all possible. ORS is not needed for most cases of diarrhoea at home. Home-based fluids and foods may be at least as effective, and are simpler and cheaper. Rational use of ORS at home implies that it should be limited.[75]

We agree. Unfortunately, throughout most of the Third World, commercial ORS continues to be aggressively marketed to poor families, not only for the treatment of dehydration but as "the first medical response" to diarrhea. This is partly explained by USAID's funding of packet-centered ORT programs.

In the early 1980s, UNICEF India's "Health and Nutrition" program participated with the Health Ministry and nongovernment organizations in launching a nation-wide ORT program based on home fluids (mainly SSS). The main ingredient was the traditional raw sugar (jaggery) found in most Indian households. The national campaign, perhaps the world's largest, achieved a modest degree of success and deserved wide attention. Yet at the Second International Conference on Oral Rehydration Therapy (sponsored by WHO, UNICEF, and USAID) there was no opportunity to report on India's exceptional (but nonconforming) program. The UNICEF India team (and many of us present) felt that the conference was loaded in favor of ORS, and that its organizers deliberately excluded from the platform any reports that might question the appropriateness of packet-based programs.[76]

Subsequently, in the late 1980s, the India program changed radically. SSS was discredited, ostensibly as a result of mothers' inability to retain the accurate formula, as well as due to problems with access to sugar and salt. Rather than addressing these issues, for example by improving health education, the program shifted to an emphasis on ORS promotion. Justification for this decision was published in 1990 by UNICEF in a book entitled *Diarrhoea in Rural India.*[77] Based on a study of difficulties and misconceptions of the National Diarrhea Control Program, it set out recommendations for a revised plan. These gave credit to the importance of using home fluids and breast milk in diarrhea treatment.[78] But far greater emphasis was placed on the need for aggressive promotion of ORS packets, even at the household level:

> A major strategic effort is needed to promote the ORS packet as the most important and first medical response to think of for a child with diarrhoea. While widely recognized by medical practitioners, paramedical workers, and to some extent mothers, as a treatment for advanced diarrhoea with signs of dehydration, ORS is not yet widely viewed as a first response for all cases of diarrhoea requiring treatment. The draft National Diarrhoea Management Plan now envisions a major social marketing effort with the recent deregulation of ORS packets making it available as an over-the-counter … product, available in any retail outlet reaching far beyond the current network of chemists and drugstores. Coupled with wide scale aggressive distribution of the packet should be a major public marketing effort conducted along the lines of other private sector products reaching far into the rural areas.[79]

The same packet-based, social marketing approach can be found in many other national diarrhea control programs that have received the Midas touch of USAID. For example, Egypt's national diarrhea control program, at first heavily funded by USAID, has focused almost exclusively on the large-scale, aggressive distribution of ORS packets. Once USAID withdrew its funding for ORS packets, their price skyrocketed and their use rate plummeted (See page 49).[80]

The Problem of Not Getting ORS Packets When They Are Needed

In its Ninth Programme Report (1992–1993), WHO's PCDD reports that ORS packets are now available to 75% of Third World communities worldwide. This figure may be exaggerated. For millions of people in rural areas, packets remain hard to come by, either because of distance, cost, or because the supply has run out.

The tragic losses that can result from dependency on ORS packets are described in this true account from rural Africa:

An instructor of health workers in a community health program in Kenya told one of us (David Werner) how she became convinced that it was better to teach people about home mix ORT rather than to encourage the use of packets. One day when she was visiting a rural health post, a young mother arrived, exhausted from the long walk in the scorching sun. On her back she carried a thin baby wrapped in a shawl. She had come on foot from an isolated hut in the savannah, nearly five miles away. She explained to the health worker that she had come as fast as she could, because her baby had 'running stomach' and was very ill. She begged the health worker for the lifesaving medicine in the silver envelope that her radio said was available at the nearest health post.

When the mother unwrapped her baby from the shawl, she discovered her child was dead. His shriveled body made it clear he had died of dehydration. The long trip in the hot sun had been too much for him.

'I felt partly responsible,' said the instructor. 'If we had only taught that mother about making a rehydration drink at home, instead of telling her she needed to go to the health post for a magic drug, her baby might still be alive.

'All this talk about packets being safer and more effective is nonsense,' grumbled the aging instructor. '*What is safest is what will save most lives. And what will save most lives is what mothers can do easiest and without delay, in their own homes.* In our circumstances a homemade drink is safer. If you ask me, *ORS packets are downright dangerous!*'

She looked at me piercingly. 'What I mean is that making folks believe that ORS packets are somehow better than or superior to what they can provide in their own homes is dangerous. And that's exactly what the big government programs are doing. We used to do it ourselves, until we learned the hard way. Do you understand what I mean?'

We do. Our communications with scores of small community programs in many poor countries indicate that a majority have reached a similar conclusion and have chosen to promote homemade drinks while discouraging the use of packets. But with the international Child Survival network churning out 400 million packets a year, it is an uphill battle. We cite another example, from South Africa:

> In the 1980s, in the urban black townships of South Africa, the government launched an ORT program based on ORS packets made available through health centers and hospitals. In April 1988, one of us (David Werner) visited a 'day clinic' in a black township on the outskirts of Durban. Hundreds of people were waiting for consultation. The average waiting time was from three to five hours. The pediatrician, who told me he saw more than 100 children a day, acknowledged that—although the staff had a *triage* system to try to spot and provide earlier care for severely ill children—several children had died of dehydration while waiting in line to be seen.

> Had mothers been encouraged to prepare a rehydration drink at home, many deaths might have been prevented. In addition, the lines at the health center would have been shorter, and the few children who failed to respond to home management could thus have received treatment more quickly.

Even in some areas where ORS is aggressively marketed, the lack of availability of ORS packets is a major problem. A USAID-funded study confirmed that shortages of packets are common even in countries where it supports large-scale programs.[81] A study in Honduras, for instance, revealed that while the country's central warehouse was overstocked with packets, irregular deliveries led to widespread shortages at the community level.[82] Similar shortages were reported by mothers in Afghan refugee camps in Pakistan.[83] A study in rural Bangladesh showed that diarrheal mortality was directly related to the distance from children's homes to the nearest clinic; children living over 5 miles from the clinic were 3 times more likely to die than those within this radius. The authors concluded that diarrheal mortality rate could be reduced in one of two ways: by building treatment centers every 4 miles throughout Bangladesh or, more feasibly, by making ORT available at the household level.[84]

Economic Perspectives in the ORS-ORT Debate

USAID's big push for "…promoting private sector production and distribution of ORS packets" is no surprise.[85] Former USAID Director Alan Woods stated at the Third International Conference on Oral Rehydration Therapy that "The goal for sustainability of ORT is private-public sector collaboration, and that such collaboration 'is not happening fast enough.'" For better or worse, it has now happened. Today the vast majority of ORS packets are produced and distributed commercially.

The economic impact of ORT is a concern to representatives from both sides of the debate. Home-drink advocates worry about the costs to poor families which can decrease ORS use and increase poor nutrition. These costs include the expense of the packets and of traveling to the nearest point of distribution, as well as time lost and wages foregone.* [86]

By contrast, the packet promoters worry more about costs of packet production and distribution. These costs particularly affect Third World governments obliged to cut spending as part of structural adjustment (see page 83). High-level planners have thus opted for commercialization of packets and *cost recovery schemes*. Such measures are criticized by home ORT advocates (and even some promoters of packets) because user charges for packets both decrease ORS use rates and increase the economic and nutritional toll to families of high risk children. In many countries privatization of ORS has pushed prices out of reach of the poorest families. As WHO cautiously notes, "The price of locally produced ORS is often viewed as excessive in comparison with the world market price or that of UNICEF-supplied ORS."[87]

The impact of commercial ORS on the poor

How does involving the private sector in marketing ORS affect the poorest families? Cost of commercial ORS packets in different countries ranges from about 5

---

*In a recent case study in Jamaica, "63% (165) of guardians spent between 1 and 10 Jamaican dollars in transport to come to the clinic, 57% (149) spent between 1 and 10 dollars on snack food as they traveled and waited, and others lost their wage for the day or had to pay for a minder to look after other children left at home. Given these costs there was quite a good economic reason for the guardian to nip into a nearby shop and buy a look-alike packet of Epsom Salts instead."

to 40 US cents per liter; the average is 15 to 20 US cents.[88] While to some of us 15 cents is not much, we must remember that over one billion people earn less than one dollar a day. These are, of course, the people whose children die from diarrhea. In Bangladesh during times of floods and famine—when diarrhea is most prevalent—landless peasants may earn as little as 7 to 13 US cents a day.[89] Not surprisingly, many families surveyed in a nationwide study in Bangladesh said that ORS was too expensive for them.[90]

In several countries for which we have information, the low wages paid to farmworkers and 'unskilled' laborers mean that many poor families—who already earn too little to adequately feed their children—have to spend from 1/4 to 3/4 or more of their day's wages for a single ORS packet.[91] In India ORS packets cost as much as 7–8 rupees (50 US cents), and the minimum wage is 10 rupees a day. Many workers earn as little as 4 rupees daily, when they can find work.

Even in the United States, the high prices of oral rehydration products place them out of reach of low-income people. The *Journal of the American Medical Association* reports on an infant who died because its mother could not afford to spend 5 to 6 dollars a liter for the bottled ORS solution prescribed by the child's pediatrician.[92]

The problem of the cost of ORS to families is compounded by the fact that diarrhea strikes children so often. Diarrhea is not only a leading killer of children, but also *the illness that children in poor families have most often.* According to some estimates, Third World children under five years experience from 2 to 5 diarrhea episodes annually.[93] Those under three living in areas where sanitary and hygienic conditions are poor may have from 4 to 8 episodes a year, each lasting an average of a week.[94] It has been estimated that Third World children under age three have diarrhea over 10% of the time.[95] In some areas this figure is higher. According to the Pan American Health Organization, Bolivian children under 5 years old have "9 to 12 diarrheal episodes each year."[96] A study in rural Bangladesh found that children under two years old may have diarrhea 16% to 17% of the time—or up to 60 days a year.[97] This means a family with three young children may be treating a child with diarrhea half the days of a year. A five year old with severe watery diarrhea may need two liters or more of rehydration fluid a day. To try to meet this enormous need with ORS packets would be exorbitant. If a poor family were to spend one-tenth of its daily wages on each ORS packet, it would create a staggering economic burden.

Poor families are damned if they do and damned if they don't. The high price of commercial ORS means they often simply cannot afford to buy packets for their children, at least not in sufficient quantities to make a life-saving difference. And if they *do* buy packets, the cost may adversely affect their children's nutrition and even survival.

Certainly, for the poorest families, the cost of ORS may be a contributing cause of under-utilization. Yet UNICEF seems blind to this point. In its 1994 *State of the World's Children* report it comments:

> Progress on promoting ORT has also been too slow. A quarter of a century has now passed since its discovery.... *The technique is virtually cost free.* Yet it is still known to only about one third of the developing world's families." (italics added)

Far from being virtually cost-free, for poor families ORS packets can be prohibitively expensive. A study in Bangladesh found that the cost of a commercially produced ORS packet was seven times greater than that of a liter of a home ORT solution made with unrefined cane sugar and table salt.[98] If the energy and funds that UNICEF and WHO have invested over the years in promoting ORS packets had been put into popular education about effective home solutions, nearly every Third World family could truly have access to ORT. Once information becomes "common knowledge," shared and passed on from family to family, the technology and its transfer could become virtually cost free.

Is Egypt's Costly Success Story Sustainable?

Egypt's National Control of Diarrheal Disease Program (NCDDP), which ran from 1981 to 1991, has often been cited as the world's most successful large scale ORT initiative. Indeed, the results were remarkable. Before the program began, diarrhea was the leading killer of Egypt's children. Within a 5 year period (1983–1988) diarrhea mortality dropped by 58% for infants and 53% for children aged 1–4.[99] During this same period (1982–1987) overall infant and child mortality rates also dropped substantially (by 36% and 43% respectively). Most of this drop reportedly was due to the fall in diarrheal deaths, which were said to account for 82% of the overall decline in infant deaths and 62% of the overall decline in young children's deaths.[100] A recent monograph of the program provides detailed evidence that (1) the mortality decline—and in particular the diarrheal mortality decline—were actual events, (2) case management improved sufficiently to account for most of the diarrheal mortality decline, and (3) changes in other factors that might contribute to mortality decline, such as host resistance or diarrheal incidence, do not plausibly account for the magnitude of the reductions seen.[101]

Although the results of Egypt's NCDDP are impressive by any measure, a large study published in 1994 questions the extent of the claimed project impact on mortality, pointing out that "deaths from other causes have declined almost as much as those from diarrhoea, and most importantly, diarrhoea remains the main cause of death among children."[102]

The Egyptian program was funded by a ten year $32 million grant from USAID, which collaborated with the Egyptian Ministry of Health in designing the project. Central to the project was the use of ORS packets, including for home treatments of diarrhea. The program received a blitz of media attention: posters, megaphones, radio, and TV spots hammered home basic messages to a wide sector of the population. In addition, for 10 years USAID heavily subsidized the price of the ORS packets; a 'ten-pack' of mini-packets (theoretically enough to manage the average case of child diarrhea) cost a family less than half an Egyptian pound (EP) (up to one quarter of a day's wages for some families).

However, the subsidy ended when USAID withdrew its support in September 1991, a time when the Egyptian Health Ministry was already having difficulties in shouldering the program's costs. The shortfall resulted partly because Egypt—in spite of being a middle income country and the recipient of the second highest amount of US foreign aid—is saddled with a huge foreign debt. Consequently it has been subjected to structural adjustment programs (SAPs) which include cutbacks of the health budget. So the Health Ministry (in compliance with the World Bank's call for cost recovery) decided to make its diarrhea control program 'sustainable' by selling ORS packets at cost.

Shortly before USAID withdrew, one of us (David Werner) visited Egypt and discussed the situation with the programs directors. They conceded that ending the subsidy on ORS packets and selling them at cost posed a dilemma. Some of them questioned whether promoting the packets might not have been a mistake, which led to the difficulties with cost, sustainability, and dependence on a product that may not always be available.[103]

Predictably, when USAID cut back its funding from the program in 1991, the price of the ORS ten-pack jumped to 1.50 EP, an unrealistic cost for Egyptian families earning as little as 2 EPs per day.[104] As expected, the use rate of ORS packets dropped from over 50% to 23% and the use rate for ORT of any kind (ORS or home fluids) fell to 34%.[105] From 1992 to 1994, the percentage of children receiving inappropriate drug treatment for diarrhea jumped from 54.2% to 76%.[106]

Maintenance of supply also became a problem. In the province of Beni Suef, for example, it was reported that ORS packets had not been available for a year because the local health officer had not reordered them. This leads us to ask, "how sustainable is a selective health intervention within a deteriorating socioeconomic environment?" Hirschhorn argues that, although the use of ORS has declined sharply, the educational component of the program—which reached virtually the entire population, including health professionals—will have long-lasting effects. However, might not the long-term effects have been even greater if the investment had been put into teaching people a more self-reliance-building alternative, as part of a comprehensive effort to combat poverty and undernutrition?

The sad state of children's nutrition in Egypt brings into focus another stumbling block to sustaining the success of its ORT program. Although child mortality from diarrhea dropped significantly during the years of the program, the high rates of malnutrition and growth stunting in children remained almost unchanged, as they had for the last decade. (Hirschhorn cites a modest improvement in growth stunting during the program period, and suggests this may be due to better management of child diarrhea—including continued feeding.)[107] Since adequate nutrition is a key factor in eliminating diarrhea as a major cause of child death, can it be expected that Egypt's diarrhea control program, which had focused so selectively (and expensively) on ORS, will have a lasting impact?

A report delivered at a conference sponsored by the World Bank and USAID[108] contends that the claims of success even at the height of Egypt's ORT program may have been overstated. Most importantly, perhaps, the study notes that the lowering of child mortality has not been accompanied by substantial improvements in children's health, nutritional status, or quality of life. It concludes that "the utilization of infant or child mortality as outcome measures, biases the conclusions drawn. Measures of health must be brought to the forefront."[109]

Dr. Norbert Hirschhorn, who headed the John Snow advisory team to the program, does not refute observations of an overall deterioration of support services and the economy as a whole during the program period. Indeed, he points out that from 1984–85 onward, public spending by government (including food subsidies) declined, real wages decreased, and families living in absolute poverty rose from 23% to 34%.[110] Some critics have argued that the success of the program is questionable because child mortality had been falling steeply during the previous 30 years. However, the economic setbacks in the 1980s might well have interrupted that positive trend (as they did in many countries). Given the deepening poverty in Egypt during the 1980s, the success of the program is even more remarkable.

To put the relative success or failure of Egypt's diarrheal control program into perspective, it is important to draw comparisons with countries such as Cuba and China, both of which have much lower diarrhea mortality rates in children (and lower child mortality in general). There seems little doubt that the most effective program for reducing deaths from diarrhea is not to focus selectively on ORT, but to meet all children's nutritional and other basic needs. Whether this is possible in a poor country in the absence of an over-all commitment to equity, is doubtful. Approaches based on a commitment to equity will be discussed in Part 4.

The Need for Studies Correlating Family ORS Expenditures with Child Malnutrition

We have seen how the cost of ORS packets—whether borne by governments or by families—can compromise both the effectiveness and sustainability of ORT initiatives. We have discussed the possibility that strong promotion of commercial packets for home use may be indirectly contributing to children's deaths by leading families to spend on packets what they might otherwise spend on food. The question of whether—and to what extent—this is happening merits serious investigation. This is particularly important given that packets are increasingly being commercially marketed and 'user financed.'

However, at all three International Conferences on ORT, to our knowledge, the main speakers made no reference to the impact of family ORS expenditures on children's nutrition and, ultimately, their survival. By contrast, numerous studies have been done showing the negative impact on children's health and survival due to family expenditures on infant formula, junk food, cigarettes, vitamin tonics, unnecessary medicines, and even antidiarrheal drugs (see page 92).[111] But, of more than 1,000 papers published on ORT,[112] not one (that we know of) compares prices of ORS packets to minimum wages in different countries, or researches the ways in which the aggressive marketing of ORS packets may in fact contribute to child malnutrition and death. There is a need for such studies.

Does the End Justify the Means?

Despite its gradual drift toward home fluids, WHO still encourages home use of ORS packets. It recognizes, however, how hard it can be for families to obtain ORS quickly enough to prevent dehydration. So WHO now

stresses that when health centers give mothers ORS packets, in addition to teaching them how to use them, they should also teach them about the use of home fluids. (It would be helpful if WHO would insist, and governments require, that ORS manufacturers print instructions for use of home fluids on every packet.)[113]

Studies in several countries confirm that mothers often give their children ORS in quantities that are inadequate to prevent dehydration.[114] A common problem is that health centers tend to give mothers only a single packet of ORS at a time. This is a mere token, since the average case of diarrhea lasts 5 to 7 days[115] and a child with severe diarrhea may require one or more liters of rehydration per day. This practice of one packet per visit, along with the pharmaceutical image of ORS (in slick aluminum-foil packets) helps explain why mothers often give it like medicinal tonic: in small doses a few times a day.[116] In such situations, ORS packets may sometimes cause more dehydration than they prevent.

There is some indication—from within WHO's Program for the Control of Diarrheal Disease—that the weakness of a packet-centered approach was not entirely unanticipated. In a private discussion at the Second International Conference on Oral Rehydration Therapy (ICORT 2), a senior officer of the WHO program criticized one of us (David Werner) for overstating the differences between WHO's approach and that of community-based programs. He conceded that planners of ORT strategy were aware of the financial, practical, and sustainable advantages of home-based rehydration over ORS packets. But, he argued, in order to win the medical establishment's support for ORT, it would first have to be promoted in a way that left the professionals a certain amount of power and control. As the problems of a packet-based approach became evident, home-based therapy would gain precedence.

This official's startling argument comes down to saying that *the end justifies the means*. The strategy he laid out—whereby ORS packets pave the way for home-made ORT, and dependency-creation becomes a stepping stone to self-reliance—is not only ethically problematic, but doomed to backfire.

And backfire it did. What the strategy overlooked was the fact that diarrheal disease control programs (including WHO's) would develop a major stake in the packet approach. Over the years these programs have invested large amounts of money in the infrastructure of packeteering; careers and reputations are wedded to it. Moreover, the privatization of ORS marketing has transformed a "simple solution" into a multi-million dollar business.

One fallout from the over-zealous promotion of ORS packets has been to undermine people's confidence in home solutions. Now that WHO and UNICEF are trying to place more emphasis on home fluids and healthworkers are trying to promote them, people complain about "a second-rate solution for second-class citizens." Poor people want the best for their sick children and are prepared to make sacrifices. So they continue to walk long distances and spend their food money to obtain the magic packets with the silver lining. And their children continue to die.

The "Success" of Marketing

Most health planners agree that the main objective of ORT should be to stop dehydration before it starts. So mothers should begin oral hydration before dehydration sets in. They should start by giving their children home fluids and food, and turn to ORS packets only when children show signs of dehydration. By logical conclusion, the real measure of an ORT program's success, i.e., prevention of dehydration in the home, would be seen in a reduced demand for ORS packets. Hence the more successful the program, the more the production and distribution of ORS packets would decline. In practice, this contradicts the market perspective held by WHO; in this view, the more packets are produced, the more effective the program. And as long as commercial interests have their say, they will flood the market with as many packets as poverty can bear.

Unfortunately, successful marketing strategies and successful health initiatives are founded on very different principles. For example, as a result of India's "Revised

Social Marketing: Using people's religious and cultural beliefs to promote the use of ORS packets

National Diarrhea Management Plan," marketing consultants appear to have designed the plan based on consumption.[117] So a study showing mothers' demand for medicines for diarrhea and health workers' zealous promotion of antidiarrheal drugs was interpreted as a need for more ORS promotion, rather than a need for more effective education of mothers and health workers about sensible and limited use of medicines. In a classically opportunistic approach, the authors of the study suggested making use of these misguided popular beliefs by promoting ORS as a medicine. As part of this ploy, the authors recommended reinforcing the incorrect belief held by many mothers that ORS stops diarrhea. After all, they argue, "Wider promotion of ... [ORS'] healing properties could be expected to lead to not only wider use, but also wider satisfaction."[118] Instead of correcting poor people's misconceptions, this strategy takes advantage of them. Rather than correcting the notion that medicines and commercial products are always needed to cure their children, this approach reinforces and profits from harmful ideas.

The latest argument in defense of the aggressive promotion of ORS points to the "success" of marketing efforts; studies now show that mothers of sick children want

---

Handwashing Campaign Opens New Market for Soap Producers

BASICS and the Environmental Health Project (EHP) have been catalysts for creation of an alliance among soap manufacturers in Central America. At a meeting convened in Guatemala in March, these competing firms agreed on a broad strategy and common objectives for a joint campaign throughout Central America to promote handwashing with soap to prevent disease.

in children und⟨
America.

Most of these s⟨
tion their produ⟩
toilet/cosmetic ⟨
enthusiastic abo⟩
to expand their ⟨
their products w⟨
and reducing di⟨
cholera.

"This is a good ⟨
public and priva⟩
to reach comm⟨
explains Camill⟨
Technical Offic⟩
Social Marketin⟩
benefits corpora⟨

This announcement in USAID's *Basics* newsletter promoting its social marketing campaign captures the essence of its marketing approach to health care.

medicine and are not satisfied until they get it. Mothers tend to regard other treatment options (especially home remedies) as second-rate, and are more likely to accept ORS—presented as a medicine—than home-based rehydration drinks. Though ORS costs more, the marketers argue, it is better that mothers spend a little on ORS than spend a lot on ineffective or dangerous antidiarrheal drugs.

This argument, however, suffers from the same flaws as the one advanced by the authors of *Diarrhoea in Rural India*. It tries to justify a strategy that capitalizes on poor peoples' misconceptions rather than helping to dispel them. Instead of helping break the habit of wasting food money on unnecessary products, it encourages it.

If, however, poor people were helped to understand the real needs of children with acute diarrhea, they would be more able to meet those needs with their own resources at almost no cost. The knowledge and confidence they would gain by doing so might empower them to grapple with other issues and, ultimately, to attack the root causes of their poverty and poor health. As part of a larger process of standing up for their rights, people need to demand that health officials and other authorities stop misleading them and start telling them the truth. In the long run, this sort of assertive action is more effective in promoting the health and well-being of their children than ORT alone can ever be. Health workers (and institutions) can either help this process or hold it back.

Unless social marketing strategists radically alter their mind-sets, health planners should think twice before recruiting them. One of the drawbacks of commercial marketing tactics is that they often sacrifice or distort the truth. We believe that the goals of enhancing child survival and quality of life cannot be advanced through deception; awareness-raising is ultimately more effective than brainwashing.

Zimbabwe's Lone Stand for Self-reliance

Zimbabwe is one of the few poor countries that has refused to follow the WHO/UNICEF guidelines for ORS packets. Planners in the new Health Ministry, committed to greater equity of services, foresaw some of the difficulties we have already discussed, and refused to promote the use of factory produced ORS packets, even in health facilities. They argued that *if mothers are to become self-reliant in home management of diarrhea, one of the best places for them to learn to prepare and give a home mix solution is in the health facility. More lives can be saved if health facilities use the same home mix methods that mothers are encouraged to use in the home.* Thus the mother's visit to a health post becomes a teaching oppor-

The current formula used in Zimbabwe is 6 level teaspoons of sugar and a half a level teaspoon of salt in a 750 ml bottle.

tunity for home methods, rather than undermining the mother's confidence in home methods by exposing her to a medicalized, more costly, less accessible alternative.

WHO and UNICEF have pressured Zimbabwe to bring its policy into line with their pro-packet stance.[119] The agencies have even sent unsolicited shipments of ORS to several community hospitals. Fortunately, the hospitals refused them. Accepting them would not only have undermined Zimbabwe's more effective approach, it might also have endangered children's lives with solutions that were too salty, since the packets were meant to be mixed with one liter while the standard container used to mix ORT in Zimbabwe is a 750 ml. bottle.

Even WHO has had to admit that Zimbabwe's diarrhea control program has been unusually successful; its 1992 evaluation found the program had achieved "unusually high ORT use rates."[120] The evaluation attributed this success in large part to Zimbabwe's emphasis on home mix.[121] However, the debate continues, and it appears Zimbabwe is giving in to the pressure. A recent review by the Zimbabwe CDD Programme recommends full-formula—made up as a liquid by the hospital pharmacy—for ORS for hospitalized dehydrated persons.[122]

Controversial Issues Affecting the Success of ORT Initiatives

In the last chapter, we reviewed some of the major issues that affect the policies and practice of oral rehydration. We focused on the debate between the use of ORS packets and home-based ORT. Now, in order to further reveal how top-down, centralized decision-making undermines programs designed to benefit marginalized groups, in this chapter we will briefly examine some additional, controversial issues of oral rehydration therapy. These include:

- Underuse of ORT and overuse of drugs

- What's in a name? Mystification versus demystification.

- A simple solution or a magic medicine

- "Boil the water" and other misguided health messages

- Blunders in the formula: how much salt?

In looking at each of these issues, we will show that the positions which commercial interests and/or mainstream policy-makers have taken have often been inappropriate and counterproductive. And we will explore how and why policy-makers arrived at some of these positions.

Underuse of ORT and Overuse of Drugs

The medicalization and mystification of simple therapies for purposes of personal financial gain is common in poor countries as well as rich. In some cases, doctors may continue to overuse IV therapy in the management of diarrhea because they are unwilling to re-examine their entrenched beliefs; the inadequate discussion of ORT in many medical textbooks is also an important contributing factor.[123] In other cases, doctors' resistance to change may relate to considerations of power, prestige, and profit. By continuing to use a relatively sophisticated technology and to prescribe unnecessary medication, they hang on to their monopolistic control over one of the world's most common ailments. Joshua Ruxin has this to say about doctors' low use of ORT in the United States:

> The formidable and persistent ignorance of the Western Medical establishment ... of ORT is phenomenal. While its refusal to advocate ORT

may be due in part to the notion that ORT is only necessary in the developing world, its actions appear to be driven also by financial considerations. Most hospitals do not train physicians in the use of ORT since they have no financial reason to do so. The use of intravenous therapy, which often involves keeping a dehydrated child overnight, assures maximum insurance reimbursement. Sending children home with ORT would destroy these profits.[124]

In Latin America overuse and misuse of IV therapy is not limited to treatment of diarrhea. Many doctors (both government and private) plus a motley army of "*médicos practicantes*" (self-taught quacks) still routinely administer IV dextrose solution for a variety of ailments ranging from anemia and asthma to aging. In Mexican villages, people reverently speak of these misused IV solutions as *vida artificial* (artificial life). A poor family whose breadwinners are weak from malnutrition will often pay two weeks' wages to have a half liter of IV sugar water dripped into their veins, in the belief that this will renew their energy and health. In some instances it does give them a transient lift—but at considerable cost and risk. This practice is so common that the village health team in Project Piaxtla, Mexico, has used farmworkers' theater to demystify *vida artificial* and warn the public against its use. (For more information on Project Piaxtla, see Chapter 19.)[125]

Overuse and misuse of medicines for diarrhea

Medical practitioners' persistent overuse of IV therapy in the treatment of diarrhea is paralleled by their continued overuse and misuse of medicines.[126] Both WHO and UNICEF clearly state that for most cases of diarrhea no medicines are needed and many do more harm than good. WHO estimates that antibiotic treatment is necessary in only one in twenty cases of childhood diarrhea episodes.[127]

Yet the world over, drug therapy is still the treatment most prescribed by doctors and most demanded by consumers. In many countries antibiotics—often sold over the counter—are part of the standard treatment of virtually all cases of diarrhea. Multinational drug companies exploit this misuse of drugs by placing on the market hundreds of irrational products (see page 92). Drugs are used two to four times more often than is ORS, and a

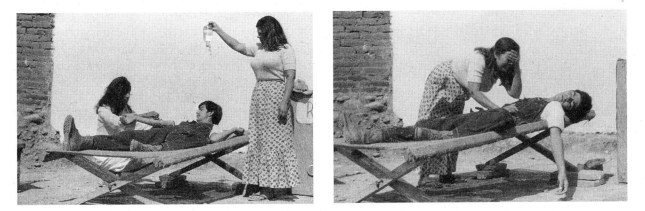

In a Farmworkers Theater skit titled *Useless Medicines that Sometimes Kill* healthworkers show that the misuse of IV solutions ("vida artificial") can be dangerous.

prescription of four or more drugs is common.[128] A recent WHO survey in Egypt—whose anti-diarrheal program has been held up as a model for success—shows ORS was used in 23% of diarrhea cases while drugs were prescribed in 54%.[129]

Antibiotics are ineffective against many common causes of diarrhea (including viral infections), and can seriously upset the normal bacterial flora of the gut, often exacerbating or prolonging the diarrhea. Infectious diarrheas that require antibiotics or antiparasite drugs (for example, those caused by *Shigella and amoeba)* represent only about 10% of cases of children's diarrhea.

The drugs misused for diarrhea also include antidiarrheals, or "motility agents." Antidiarrheals such as diphenoxylate hydrochloride with atropine sulfate *(Lomotil)* and kaolin with pectin (e.g., *Kaopectate),* slow down the activity of the gut or thicken stools. While often used to ease the discomfort of diarrhea, such remedies can actually prolong infection and mask the signs of dehydration.[130]

To its credit, WHO has recently taken a stand against the irrational use of antidiarrheal drugs. In 1990 it published a manual on *The Rational Use of Drugs in the Management of Acute Diarrhea in Children,[131]* recommending that certain of the more useless and harmful drugs have their availability reduced or be withdrawn from the market altogether.[132] WHO now advises that drugs commonly used for diarrhea—including diphenoxylate hydrochloride, kaolin and pectin, loperamide, streptomycin, neomycin, hydroxyquinoline, nonabsorbable sulfonamide, activated charcoal, attapulgite, and smectite—"have no role in the management of acute diarrhoea in children."[133] The WHO guide states flatly that "antidiarrheal drugs ... should never be used" since "none has any proven practical value and some are dangerous."[134]

Even more harmful is the danger that arises from what poor people spend on these medicines—often in lieu of food. Many of the medicines are sold to poor parents who are willing to spend their last pennies to keep their children from dying of diarrhea. According to WHO, "over one billion dollars a year is currently being spent on anti-diarrhoeal drugs, most of which are useless or harmful, while all that is needed in the vast majority of cases, is simple and inexpensive ORT."[135]

In response to this mounting criticism of inappropriate anti-diarrheal medicines, a few pharmaceutical companies have withdrawn some of their most indefensible products. Nonetheless, the pharmaceutical industry continues to do a highly profitable business in most Third World countries where scores of brand name anti-diarrheals remain on the market. Exploiting the fact that diarrhea remains a widespread, life-threatening health problem in developing countries, doctors, pharmacists, and street vendors there sell some 150 million dollars worth of over 400 different antidiarrheal drugs each year.[136] Some 350 million dollars worth of antidiarrheal drugs are sold each year by major Western manufacturers alone, with one third of them going to the Third World.[137] In general, the poorer the country (as measured by GNP per capita), the higher the per capita spending on such drugs.[138]

UNICEF acknowledges that:

> Even among doctors who have started using ORT, 'kicking the drug habit' is hard. Far too many prescribe both ORT and drugs, thus diverting the mother's attention from the need to give the child fluids and food, and undermining the credibility and effectiveness of oral rehydration. Good therapy has not replaced bad therapy; it has simply been tacked on to it.[139]

The continued overuse by doctors of IV fluids and pharmaceuticals in the management of acute diarrhea is one of the major obstacles to the successful promotion of ORT.[140]

What's in a Name? Mystification Versus Demystification

We live in an age of high-tech information; yet, as noted earlier, the late Executive Director of UNICEF, James Grant, lamented the fact that "shamefully little is known about how to communicate information whose principal value is to the poor."[141] Nowhere is bungling in communication more obvious than in the language with which experts first chose to popularize ORT. Even the three Latinized medical terms in the name itself—*oral, rehydration,* and *therapy*—are words unfamiliar to people with limited formal education (in any language). Might not people grasp the idea more easily, and make it their own, if we adapted our language to *theirs?* Instead of making people feel ignorant and inferior by introducing an unfamiliar term like Oral Rehydration Solution, could we not simply speak of a "special drink to return liquid?"

But rather than simplify, the pundits of public health further muddied the "simple solution" by introducing a whole set of abbreviations: ORT for *oral rehydration therapy*; ORS for *oral rehydration salts/solution* (designating specifically the WHO "full formula" packets); SSS for homemade *sugar and salt solution*; CB-ORT for *cereal-based oral rehydration therapy*; and so on.

To top it all, experts in Geneva started calling the aluminum foil envelopes of ORS salts *sachets*. This French term was used in English language instructions that were printed for care-givers, many of whom are only marginally literate in English. Grassroots educators complained for years about this snobbish and unnecessary linguistic barrier, until at last WHO and UNICEF began to speak of the envelopes as "packets."

Anthropologists C. MacCormack and A. Draper, in a study in Jamaica, found that the mystification of ORT was an important obstacle to the understanding and proper use of rehydration procedures:

> Nurses validated their professional status by using words such as 'electrolytes' when explaining the therapy, and it is therefore not surprising that 52% of the guardians who had just heard the nurse's talk did not have any idea—correct or incorrect—of what the [rehydration] 'salts' were.… People were being told never to use the traditional therapies they understood and could make at home, and therefore were being made dependent upon medical services provided by 'qualified' personnel who commanded secret knowledge.[142]

A Simple Solution or a Magic Medicine?

The use of mystifying, medicalized language in introducing ORT to the general public may not have been altogether accidental. As we have seen, the medical profession resisted the shift from intravenous to oral fluid replacement. This shift represented a move toward demystifying and demedicalizing the management of diarrhea. It was a move towards health care in the hands of the people, a relinquishing of physicians' control. One way for doctors to retain control over the new treatment was to cloak it in medical mystique.

For instance, many doctors have argued for a highly medicalized approach to ORT, insisting on a strictly controlled product with precise measurements and pure ingredients. But this emphasis on absolute, precise measurements makes little sense. After all, experts differ greatly on the ideal formula for oral rehydration solution; some recommend that it contain twice as much sugar or salt as do others. This is not, of course, to say that relative accuracy of measurements is not important. Although there is a wide range of acceptable proportions, too much salt or sugar can be dangerous, as we will discuss in item 4 below.

In addition, ORT strategists have debated heatedly about whether oral rehydration solution should be promoted as a simple food (or special drink) or as a medicine. Social marketing experts point out that parents want "strong medicine" for their sick children.[143] It is not easy to convince parents (or doctors) that ordinary salt, sugar, and foods in their homes can be as effective as factory-packaged medicine. In order to sell ORT, they argue, present it as medicine. Package it in shiny little packets, and call them *sachets*. Call the ingredients by their chemical, not their common names—*sodium chloride* for table salt, *sodium bicarbonate* for baking soda, and *glucose* for simple sugar. Keep people in awe. Portraying ORS as a powerful new wonder drug, these experts argue, is the quickest way to get people to buy the idea.

The Piaxtla wonder drug: a big mistake

I (David Werner) am embarrassed to say that the above line of reasoning was more or less the one that my fellow health workers and I took 28 years ago in Project Piaxtla, Mexico, when we first began promoting what was later to become known as oral rehydration therapy. Finding mothers reluctant to simply give their sick child a drink made from common household ingredients, we decided to trick them: "You want medicine, we'll give you medicine!" We began to package measured quantities of sugar, salt, and baking soda into little plastic bags. We even added a pinch of strawberry Kool-Aid to color it red, so it would look medicinal. And we promoted it as the *"Piaxtla Wonder Drug."*

Only slowly, working closely with the local people, did we begin to realize our mistake. The population served was scattered over hundreds of miles of rugged mountainous terrain. During the rainy season (when more children die from diarrhea), rivers flood and access to health posts is often cut off. By leading people to believe that oral rehydration works best with a "special medicine," we were keeping from them the knowledge and ability to manage diarrhea effectively in their own homes. We were making them dependent on our services and products, rather than encouraging them to be self-sufficient. Gradually it dawned on us that, although the Piaxtla Wonder Drug was technically safe and effective, in the social context within which we worked it became dangerous. The misconceptions and dependency it created were costing children's lives. We needed an alternative that would demystify the technology and place it in the people's hands, so that they could manage most cases of

child diarrhea in their own homes, without having to depend on medicines and services beyond their control.

Making the shift was not easy. But fortunately we were a small program that had no major investment, economically or politically, in our new "wonder drug." Our primary motive was to help people meet their needs, so we gathered courage and openly admitted that our gimmick for promoting ORT had backfired. We told people what was in the plastic bags, and apologized for tricking them with the Kool-Aid. Over the next several years we collaborated with them to develop simple methods and teaching aids to help parents and school children clearly understand about dehydration and rehydration. We tried to demystify the whole process, so that families would fully realize the importance of giving children with diarrhea plenty of drink and food. We helped them to understand why a simple homemade solution usually works better than losing time and money by going a long way for unnecessary medicines.

For parents who could read and write, or who had children who could read and write, we began to make simple, illustrated sheets explaining how to prepare and give a special drink for diarrhea right in the home. These instruction sheets were eventually included in our villagers' health care handbook, *Where There Is No Doctor.* A variety of hands-on, discovery-based teaching aids were also developed. (These and other ORT-related teaching methods and aids are depicted in more detail in *Helping Health Workers Learn.*[144])

Around the world, many community-based programs have come to the same conclusions as we did in Project

Piaxtla and have tried to demedicalize and demystify oral rehydration, placing the technology as much as possible in the people's hands. However, many large government programs still favor presenting ORT as a pre-packaged "medicine." This "pharmaceuticalization" of a simple solution has led to a great deal of misunderstanding and incorrect use.[145] For instance, mothers who have been led to think that ORT is a medicine often give it to their children in "doses" that are much too small and infrequent to be effective.[146]

The mystification of oral rehydration by calling ORS packets "oral rehydration salts" has, in Jamaica, led to confusion which can cost children's lives. Traditionally, some people have used Epsom Salts or Andrews Salts (both laxatives made of magnesium sulfate) to wash out the gut of persons with diarrhea—a dangerous practice that had gradually lost popularity. However, the promotion of "oral rehydration salts" led people to return to using Epsom Salts and Andrews Salts as substitutes for ORS. People preferred buying the laxative salts at the corner shop to making a long trip to the health post and then waiting for hours in line for a single packet of ORS. Perhaps if the medicalized name *oral rehydration salts* had been replaced by a term like "special drink for diarrhea" and otherwise demystified, mothers would have been less likely to confuse it with medicines and laxatives—and fewer children might have died.[147]

"Boil the Water" and Other Misguided Health Messages

One reason why those who formulate health education messages often miss the mark is that they live in a different world from those whom their messages address. They tend to take a narrowly medical/scientific/technological approach to problem solving and neglect the actual situations people live in and the overwhelming constraints they face.

A good example of this is the advice to mothers to *always boil the water* they use for making oral rehydration drinks. This message used to be standard advice—until some of the "experts" listened to what mothers had to say about it. They then realized that the message to boil the water may actually cause more infant deaths than it prevents, for two reasons:

- *Boiling water takes time.* Women must often walk for hours to collect the firewood or cow manure they use for fuel. Time is also required to actually heat the water, and finally, the water must be cooled, which takes still more time. However, a child with severe diarrhea needs liquid *now*. The delay entailed in boiling the water *increases* the risk of dehydration and as such may far outweigh the benefit of boiling. After all, the child with diarrhea has probably already been exposed to whatever infection he might get from the unboiled water. Thus, in many cases boiling is unnecessary and may be dangerous.[148]

- Boiling water costs money. In many poor communities, fuel is expensive relative to the incomes of the poor. Because of the time and expense involved, some mothers will simply not make the special drink if told they must boil the water. Others may spend food money for the extra fuel, at the expense of their children's nutrition.[149]

Instead of telling mothers that they must always boil the water they use to make the rehydration drink, it is usually better to advise them, "Prepare the drink fast! Use the cleanest water you have on hand. If you have water that has already been boiled or filtered, use that. But *don't lose time boiling water* when your baby has severe diarrhea." (There are, of course, exceptions to this recommendation. For example, in some squatter camps where all of the water comes from sewage systems, *all* water should be boiled first.)

Although this new advice to "use the cleanest water you can" is now fairly widely accepted, including by WHO and UNICEF, in many countries health educators and instructional material still tell mothers they must "always boil the water." For millions of families whose children are at the greatest risk, this advice can be deadly.

Other erroneous messages Examples abound of well-intentioned health education messages that prove ineffective or even counterproductive in practice. For example, in the November 1992 issue of *The Prescriber*—published by UNICEF in cooperation with The United States Pharmacopoeial Convention—in an article titled "Management of Acute Diarrhea: The Appropriate Way," a prominent sidebar displays in large letters: "ORS Solution: The recommended fluid for diarrhea and its prevention."[150] What is meant of course is "… for *dehydration* and its prevention." Such dangerous carelessness is unconscionable. Adding credence to this error, the article with this sidebar is credited as having been "prepared by the Programme for the Control of Diarrheal Diseases—The World Health Organization—Geneva."[151] Mistakes such as this are often amplified by other normally reliable sources such as when the Worldwatch Institute, in its April 1996 report on infectious disease, reported that "ORS is useful to prevent and treat diarrhea."[152] Thus it comes as no great surprise that Arturo Quispe, a pediatrician in Ecuador, reports that poor families were giving ORS to their healthy children to *prevent* cholera.

Overzealous marketing of ORS as a "wonder drug" in Pakistan led to a situation where more mothers (15%) were giving ORS to children who did not have diarrhea than to children who had diarrhea (11%). The reason given by mothers was that "ORS is good for a child's health, especially in summer."[153] If poor families spend their limited money on ORS rather than food, ORS—far from being good for a child's health—could contribute to the child's undernutrition, and hence to the increased incidence and severity of diarrhea, and the risk of death.

When to use other drugs for diarrhoeal diseases: The vast majority of patients visiting a health centre or a hospital can be successfully treated by using Oral Rehydration Therapy (ORT) and continued feeding. Antibiotic treatment or antiparasitic treatment should never be given routinely. The diseases for which antimicrobials should be given are listed below, and the recommended drugs can be found in Table 1 and Table 2.

ORS Solution: The recommended fluid for diarrhoea and its prevention

Inaccurate information like this from *The Prescriber* (a UNICEF publication) can lead poor families to waste money by giving their children ORS to prevent diarrhea—which it does not do.[150]

Blunders in the Formula: How Much Salt?

Even solutions that are technically accurate can be socially disastrous—as we have seen with the bacteriologically sound advice to boil water. However, there are times when the technology itself has shortcomings that arise from not looking at critical factors from a community perspective. ORS is a case in point. The WHO formula was developed and tested by highly qualified doctors, chemists, and physiologists. Yet the standard WHO ORS formula—at least for community use—may be less safe and less effective than some alternative formulas now being used. One of the drawbacks of the standard WHO formula is its *relatively high salt content*. Even WHO admits that this can be risky for certain small, undernourished infants.[154] Although reducing the salt content of standard "full formula" ORS could result in safer, more effective oral rehydration, WHO has long delayed changing the "standard formula." (A WHO-sponsored multi-center trial with a lower sodium content is now underway. See page 60.)

Originally, the salt content for ORS was based on that needed for intravenous solutions. In such solutions—which go directly into the bloodstream, the concentration of molecules (osmolarity) of salt plus other ingredients needs to be close to that of the blood (isotonic). For oral rehydration solutions, however, such a high amount of salt is usually unnecessary—and carries additional risks. Drinking a solution with a higher concentration of salt than is in the blood (a hypertonic solution) would, through the process of osmosis, draw water from the blood back into the gut, thus increasing both the diarrhea and dehydration. Such a hypertonic salt solution also tends to provoke vomiting. For these reasons, considerable care needs to be taken not to exceed the amount of salt recommended in the WHO formula (and not to mix the ORS packet with too little water).

Another reason the salt in ORS is higher than is usually needed or desirable is that ORS was originally developed for rehydrating persons with cholera.[155] With cholera, salt loss tends to be much higher than in other forms of diarrhea. Therefore, to avoid sodium depletion, scientists put as much salt in the ORS formula as they considered to be physiologically safe. While a relatively high salt content may have been appropriate for cholera (and even this is now being questioned), it has become evident that for most types of diarrhea less salt is required.[156] Solutions containing as little as one-third of the amount of salt in the WHO formula appear to work just as well when rehydration is begun before dehydration sets in.[157] Since cholera accounts for relatively few cases of diarrhea in children, by the mid 1980s many health advisors had begun to recommend using a smaller amount of salt.[158]

WHO ORS Formulas

Current full formula WHO/UNICEF ORS (In millimoles per liter)		Proposed new low-osmolarity ORS formula (In millimoles per liter)	
glucose	111	glucose	75
sodium (Na)	90	sodium (Na)	75
chloride (Cl)	80	chloride (Cl)	65
potassium (K)	20	potassium (K)	20
citrate	30	citrate	10
total	331	total	245

Fig. 2–4 From 25 Years of ORS: Joint WHO/ICDDR, Consultative Meeting on ORS Formulation

A pragmatic argument for a lower salt content is that, as studies in a number of countries have shown, *mothers often do not mix ORS packets with enough water,* leading to an even saltier solution.[159]

In contrast to WHO, many programs working close to the community have adjusted their home mix formula to allow for a wide range of error. For the same reason, in the villager's health care manual *Where There Is No Doctor* we recommend half a teaspoon of salt per liter—roughly half the amount of salt in the standard WHO formula.[160] This low-salt content was initially criticized by medical experts, but an increasing number of studies bear out its effectiveness and added safety.*[161]

It was then postulated that a lower salt concentration might make ORS more effective in terms of reducing stool volume and duration. To investigate this, a multi-center clinical trial was conducted in four countries (Brazil, India, Mexico, and Peru) comparing the standard WHO ORS formulation (311 millimoles/liter) with a low osmolarity ORS (225 millimoles/liter). It was found that rehydration took place faster with the less concentrated solution than with the standard ORS and that the mean duration of illness was 18% shorter.[162]

Reducing the salt content and osmolarity of the WHO-UNICEF "standard formula ORS"

Finally, in response to the growing concern that the salt content (or osmolarity) of standard formula ORS is too high (and in response to increasing interest in cereal-based ORT, see page 66), WHO, together with the International Center of Diarrhoeal Disease Research, Bangla-

desh (ICDDR,B), held a consultative meeting on ORS formulation. In December 1994, in Dhaka, Bangladesh, an international team reviewed seven controlled trials in underdeveloped countries, and found that:

- A solution with a reduced amount of sugar (glucose) and salt was significantly more effective than standard ORS.

- In treatment of cholera, the less concentrated solution reduced stool output by 15% and decreased the need for IV fluids (i.e. the occurrence of advanced dehydration) by 33%.

- In treatment of acute noncholera diarrhea, stool output was reduced by 25% in the first 24 hours, and need for IV fluids was reduced by 33%.

- In non-breastfed children the lower concentration ORS reduced the risk of severe dehydration (need for IV fluids) by 50%.

WHO concluded that the results were convincing enough to recommend that a single "reduced osmolarity ORS formulation" be selected and evaluated. The new formulation will reduce both the glucose and salt content of ORS by about 25%, bringing the osmolarity from 331 mmls/l down to 245 mmls/l.[163]

It remains to be seen how long it will be until WHO and UNICEF officially revise the standard formula so that ORS can combat dehydration more effectively and save more children's lives. A question which is still unanswered is whether the standard home-mix sugar-and-salt solution (SSS), when made with less salt than the standard ORS formula, is more effective in combating dehydration and in reducing stool volume than is standard (high-salt) ORS. Research on this is needed, but to our knowledge has not been initiated.

---

*There is limited empirical evidence that food-based drinks which contain no added salt may rehydrate people effectively (though probably less effectively than food-based drinks containing salt), or at least prevent dehydration. This deserves further study, since salt is unavailable in certain remote areas (for example, in parts of northern Mozambique).

Principles of fluid and food management of diarrhoea in the home

Several fluids should be identified that are readily available, considered acceptable by mothers, and that do not have adverse effects for children with diarrhoea. If possible, one selected fluid should normally contain salt. Some examples are: salted rice water, a salted soup, and ORS solution. Mothers may also be taught to add salt (about 3 g/l) to an unsalted soup or drink, but this requires a substantial and sustained educational effort, which may not be cost-effective.

Salt-free fluids should also be selected. These include common drinks such as weak tea (plain or slightly sweetened), rice water, yoghurt-based drinks, and plain water. Certain fluids should be avoided, such as soft drinks, coffee, or those with diuretic or purgative effects.

The fluids selected above should be given in increased amounts up to as much as the child wants to drink, and along with continued feeding. Breastfeeding should be maintained. Children taking infant formula, or animal milk should continue to receive it at full strength. Children eating solid foods should continue to take them, including, if possible, one that normally contains some salt.

When this approach is followed, the child will receive enough carbohydrates and protein to promote the absorption of ingested salt. This together with increased water taken in drinks, will prevent dehydration in most episodes of diarrhoea.

From Programme for the Control of Diarrhoeal Disease: Ninth Programme Report 1992–1993 World Health Organization, 1994, p. 14

WHO's latest guidelines for home fluids

In its most recent guidelines for early home management of diarrhea, WHO has completely changed tack. Specially prepared rehydration drinks are de-emphasized, and in their place WHO recommends simply that children with diarrhea be given "more fluids than usual" and "plenty of food."[164] An assortment of "recommended home fluids" (RHF) is suggested, with more stress placed on quantity than quality.

While WHO's move away from emphasizing packets is laudable, many critics feel the new recommendations have gone too far. They suggest WHO is giving up the search for a highly effective and reliable home mix, as evidenced by the imprecise list of RHF's; this includes a pot luck assortment of both salted and unsalted local home drinks, with or without sugar and/or starches. Little attempt is made to make sure the salt and carbohydrate content is

conducive to effective rehydration. Dr. William Greenough (who has for years spearheaded research on ORT), on comparing home-made cereal-based rehydration drinks with ORS, asserts that

> Clearly, properly constituted home fluids (not what WHO calls home fluids) are equally effective [to ORS] when controlled trials have been done... The critical issue is to insure that any solution has adequate substrate (cereals preferred) and the right amount of salt — 40–120mEq/L is a safe range and can be achieved by crude measurement methods (hands or spoons). Proper education and understanding are the key.[165]

Where people are accustomed to using their hands and fingers for measurements of food and condiments, home solutions can often be reliably prepared in this way.

Many child health advocates feel that WHO's new stance is as unacceptable as its old one. The agency must not be allowed to settle for a complicated second-rate home solution when a simple first-rate home solution is attainable. The WHO guidelines are summarized in the box on this page. These may be followed by a village mother to produce an effective rehydration drink for her child to drink along with foods. However, they may also be followed to produce drinks which fill her child's belly with a combination of salted rice water and unsweetened tea—a nonrehydrating drink deficient in both fluid transfer ability and nutritional content. The problem is that some fluids on the RHF list will only have a rehydrating effect when taken with food. Since children often refuse food when they are dehydrated, the ability of these fluids to rehydrate is compromised. If dehydration is already present, WHO of course recommends its full-formula ORS, reserving home fluids for nondehydrated children. But in reality early dehydration and loss of appetite may begin almost as soon as watery diarrhea does; in such cases a well-formulated home solution (cereal or sugar based) will rehydrate quickly and appetite will begin to be restored. Unfortunately many of WHO's RHFs simply do not provide adequate rehydration during the very critical initial hours before the child accepts food.

Food as a Key Part of ORT

When oral rehydration was first heralded as a major breakthrough, doctors thought of it primarily as a low cost means of fluid replacement: a simple substitute for IV therapy. It was promoted as a drink and as a medicine. Its purpose was to save lives by combating dehydration, or loss of water and salts. Nobody thought much about oral rehydration in relation to food or children's nutritional status. Nor did they consider food as a vital part of rehydration therapy.

Yet the relation between nutritional status and death from diarrhea is clear. It has been known for decades that most of the children who die from diarrhea are undernourished.[166] While the onset of infectious disease is largely determined by environmental factors (including sanitation and hygiene), child mortality rates are linked even more strongly to nutritional status, which affects the body's ability to resist infection.[167] Although WHO and the principal ORT researchers emphasized the nutritional component of ORT from the early 1970s, in practice this was often lost. In fact, one of the reasons why ORT and immunization were so popular with many governments was that these simple technologies held the promise of lowering child mortality without having to resolve the more difficult underlying problems of malnutrition and poverty. As observed in Part 1, the Child Survival interventions were seen as a way to improve health (or at least survival rates) without addressing the inequities of the existing social order. As James Grant, UNICEF's Executive Director, put it: GOBI is a set of "low cost, low-risk, low resistance people's health actions which do not depend on the economic and political changes which are necessary in the longer term if poverty is to be eradicated."

Diarrhea contributes to malnutrition in four ways. First, children with diarrhea have markedly reduced appetites, resulting in significantly reduced food intake. Second, food passes through the gut more quickly than normal, allowing less time for digestion. Third, the injured walls of the intestines cannot digest and absorb food as well as they normally do (although they can always absorb some of it). Fourth, when children are ill their nutritional requirements increase as the body's rate of metabolism increases.[168] This means that to combat both malnutrition and infection a child with diarrhea needs more food, more often.[169]

In a child, each episode of diarrhea causes further weight loss. As he grows thinner and weaker, the episodes of illness—including diarrhea—tend to be longer and more severe. Advanced protein-calorie malnutrition (marasmus

and kwashiorkor) often appears after a severe illness such as measles or persistent diarrhea. Finally, the child goes over the edge. Though the final cause of death may be dehydration, pneumonia, or tuberculosis, often this was preceded by repeated bouts of diarrhea, common infections, and increasing malnutrition.[170] The death of a child living in poverty usually does not result from a single episode of illness, but rather from a whole series of assaults.[171] As Carl Taylor and William Greenough, III put it:

> The diarrheal diseases and acute respiratory infections interact with malnutrition so that most of the deaths occur not because of an event but from a downward spiraling sequence of multiple synergistic combinations.[172]

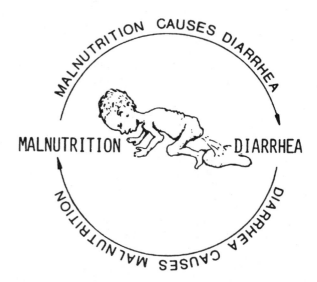

Which Causes Malnutrition: Infection or Lack of Food?

The proponents of Selective Primary Health Care look for ways to combat malnutrition through technological fixes rather than by correcting its root causes. In support of this position, they insist that the primary cause of malnutrition in children is not a shortage of food, but rather repeated infections.

UNICEF in its *State of the World's Children* report for 1988 asserts that:

> ...although not having enough to eat is still a fundamental problem in some of the world's very poorest communities, the major cause of

undernutrition in the world today is not a shortage of food in the home. It is rather a lack of basic services and a shortage of information about preventing infection and using food to promote growth. Making sure that all parents know they can protect their children's nutritional health by such means as birth spacing, care in pregnancy, breastfeeding, immunization, preventing illness, special feeding during and after illness, regularly checking their child's weight gain—and supporting parents in putting that knowledge into action—can overcome most, though not all, cases of malnutrition and poor growth in the world today.[173]

In its 1992 *The State of the World's Children* report UNICEF flatly states that "child malnutrition is caused more by the frequency of infection than by the lack of food."[174] And the 1993 edition of the report goes even further, asserting that "diarrhoeal disease is also a major cause—perhaps even the major cause—of malnutrition among the developing world's children."[175]

Thus, it is proposed that the answer to child malnutrition is to fight debilitating infections (diarrhea, pneumonia, measles) with cost-effective technological interventions (ORT, antibiotics, and immunizations). These interventions—while they indeed deserve high priority—are often introduced as selected technological interventions without an accompanying strong emphasis on actions to address the root causes of these diseases. The effect of this approach is to divert attention and resources away from the underlying causes of hunger, ill-health, and poverty.

We must question not only the politics behind this line of argument but also its biological basis. Recent evidence supports the view that malnutrition predisposes children to more severe and frequent bouts of diarrhea. The most rigorous studies on the subject suggest that malnutrition is a more significant risk factor for diarrhea than is diarrhea for malnutrition.[176] A recent study in rural Zimbabwe found that:

> The pattern of growth of children with infrequent diarrhoea was identical to that of children with very frequent diarrhoea, and equally poor. Analysis of child growth during three month intervals showed that the weight and height increments were less during intervals with diarrhoea, but this effect was only transient as catch up occurred within a few weeks. Our findings … indicate that *it is the lack of food rather than frequent diarrhoea that is the cause of the poor nutritional status of this community.*[177] (Italics added)

Another study done in Bangladesh corroborates this finding. In two villages studied, child growth faltering and undernutrition were "almost universal." In the study group of 70 children aged 5 to 18 months the average caloric intake was only 70% of the WHO recommendations. The study found that:

> The effect of caloric intake … on growth is greater than the adverse effect of diarrhea and fever combined. Specifically, if all children had energy intakes at the recommended WHO value and had even average amounts of diarrhea and fever, their weight gains would be predicted to be more than those children who had no diarrhea or fever but had median energy intakes for this population. These results suggest that, from the standpoint of children's weight gain, nutrition-intervention programs deserve as much attention as prevention and therapy of diarrhea or control of fever-inducing diseases.[178]

The graph on the following page (adapted from the study report) shows that the monthly weight gain of children is influenced more by adequate calorie intake than by presence or absence of diarrhea and fever. [179]

The fact that malnutrition probably does more to aggravate infection than infection does to aggravate malnutrition is also borne out by a study in China. The study found that, despite a high incidence of child diarrhea, child mortality from diarrhea was relatively low. It attributed this low death rate in part to the good nutrition enjoyed by Chinese children—a result of the country's equitable socio-economic policies.[180] Conversely, the fact that high diarrhea morbidity did not translate into poor nutritional status tends to confirm that infection may not be as major a determinant of poor nutritional status as has been asserted. It will be important to study whether diarrhea mortality rises as China's recent shift toward a free market approach takes effect and widens the gap between rich and poor.

These studies concur that *malnutrition over time is a major cause of increase in the incidence of, severity of, and mortality from diarrhea.* To lower child mortality from diarrhea, one study concludes that rather than focusing on technological fixes, "Efforts could be better directed to ensure that the poor have more access to food."[181]

The Changing Concept of ORT: Food-based Therapy.

Although oral rehydration initially focused on fluids, getting enough to eat is such a key factor for child survival that it could not be left out of the equation for long. It was inevitable that the nutritional component of diarrhea management gradually came to the fore. Food is recognized as an essential part of effective oral rehydration, and ORT is currently considered to be a process of providing increased fluid *and* food to a child with diarrhea.[182]

Giving food in frequent feedings to a child with diarrhea is vitally important for two reasons: *promoting rehydration and maintaining an adequate level of nutrition.*

1) *The contribution of food to rehydration.* As we touched on earlier, food intake in conjunction with oral rehydration speeds up the absorption of water through the gut.[183] When the starch and protein in food reaches the intestine, digestive juices (acids, alkalis, and enzymes) break them down into tiny molecules of sugars and amino acids. These are then carried through the lining of the gut into the bloodstream, taking water and salt with them. The greater the variety of molecules that carry the water in, the faster the total absorption. Therefore, by providing foods together with oral rehydration drinks, hydration is more effective. Thus food is essential for more efficient rehydration.[184] Hirschhorn suggests that improved feeding during diarrhea may have as much or more to do with mortality reduction as use of ORS. He considers that one of the most important functions of rehydration is to help the child feel well enough to eat (and the mother to respond by feeding).[185]

2) *Nutrition and resistance to infection.* Children need plenty of food to grow well and to resist infection. Adequate food intake during diarrhea has both an immediate and extended impact on survival. In the short term, it helps to prevent death during the immediate episode by preventing increased weakness and weight loss. In the longer term, it helps sustain the child's nutritional status and defense system, decreasing both the frequency and the severity of future illnesses, including diarrhea.[186]

There is accumulating evidence that many micronutrients—certainly Vitamin A and possibly others—independently influence mortality and severity of symptoms caused by infectious diseases. These effects are mediated by improved immunity and, in some cases, such as Vitamin A, enhanced integrity of epithelial tissues, including the gut lining. A number of studies have shown significantly reduced mortality (average 23%) from diarrheal diseases and acute respiratory infection after Vitamin A supplementation to young children in populations where some clinical

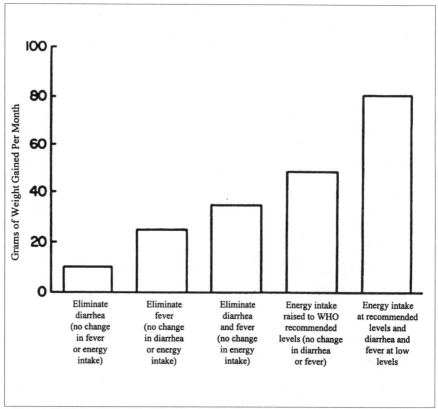

Fig. 2–5 Effect of different health measures on children's increase in weight.[179]

deficiency exists.[187] Many micronutrient deficiencies are also associated with reduced appetite and slower rates of catch-up growth after episodes of infection.[188]

Clearly, for children who are undernourished or at risk of becoming so, every effort must be made to encourage better nutrition. WHO and UNICEF quite rightly place strong emphasis on continuing to give food during diarrhea as a part of ORT, and on giving the child extra food after recovery, in order to catch up. They also correctly point out that giving a rehydration drink to a dehydrated child who refuses food will often allow the child to begin feeding again more quickly—thereby minimizing the child's nutritional deficit.[189]

It is becoming increasingly apparent, however, that taking care to meet the child's nutritional needs only during and immediately after he has diarrhea, while it helps, is not enough. To have an optimal chance of survival, *the child needs adequate food all the time.*

Breast milk — an ideal rehydration drink

One of the best ways to prevent death from diarrhea is to promote breastfeeding. This is because *breast milk is the most nutritious food for a baby,* yet it's fluid and contains a lot of water. Breastfeeding protects infants against diarrhea, not only by helping prevent dehydration once diarrhea occurs, but also by actually warding off infection.[190] Thus, unlike most rehydration drinks, the promotion of breastfeeding helps to both prevent diarrhea and to cure it. It enhances not only child survival, but nutrition, growth, and the child's overall state of health.[191]

Thirty-five studies conducted in fourteen countries found that breastfeeding was "one of the most effective ways of reducing diarrhea morbidity and mortality."[192] By contrast, bottle–fed infants get diarrhea five times as often, and die from diarrhea up to 25 times as often as exclusively breast-fed infants.[193]

Margaret Bentley (a consultant for WHO) and others have helped to focus attention on the importance of *maintaining adequate nutrition during the weaning period,* which is a time when many children become undernourished and die from diarrhea.[194] Good weaning practices are very important. But in emphasizing them, too often health educators only teach mothers about the technical aspects of weaning. Good weaning instructions are not enough. We also need to help mothers find ways to earn sufficient wages, gain rights to sufficient land, and secure sufficient status in their communities so that they can care for and feed their children adequately and achieve a satisfactory level of health themselves.

Maternal and child health are closely linked.[195] A recent article by Mosley and Chen contends that malnutrition in young children "is as much dependent on maternal health factors and infections as it is on the child's nutrient deficiency."[196] Trying to combat malnutrition by simply combating infection, without confronting the underlying socio-economic problems, is like trying to cure diarrhea with Kaopectate. Like putting a finger in the dike, it may help partially and temporarily, but it does not resolve the underlying problem. We will return to the question of breastfeeding when we discuss the unscrupulous promotion of bottle feeding in Chapter 12.

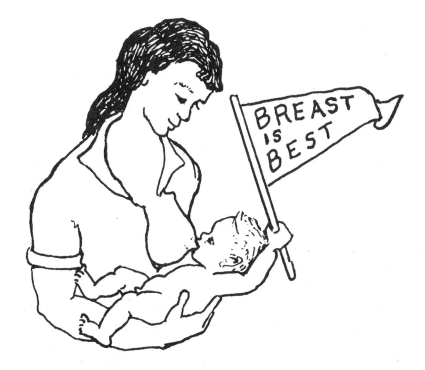

BREAST MILK—A TOP QUALITY LOCAL RESOURCE—BETTER THAN ANYTHING MONEY CAN BUY!

Food Based ORT

Researchers have devised a rice-based ORT solution that matches one the Chinese had for thousands of years. The glucose in [ORS] comes from rice, a starch. Rice happens to be a food staple in Bangladesh. In other developing countries, the food staple may be maize, wheat, or another grain. Instead of sending grain to the factory to process it, why not use it directly?

— William Greenough III, International Child Health Foundation[197]

Cereal-based Versus Sugar-based ORT

In recent years an important new dimension has been added to the debate over the use of packets versus home mix ORT. A completely different kind of oral rehydration solution is being explored: cereal-based (or food-based)* oral rehydration therapy. In many ways this is the most promising ORT approach yet. Studies in various countries over the last several years have confirmed that cereal or food-based liquids (with a little salt) are at least as effective and often more effective than sugar-based solutions in preventing and treating dehydration.[198] Thus the debate over packets versus home drinks has taken a new turn.

In addition, the fact that cereal or gruels are traditional foods in many parts of the world also makes them more familiar and acceptable. In many societies a drink or gruel made with a cereal or starchy food has long been a common home remedy for diarrhea. For example, rice water has long been a favorite folk remedy for diarrhea in South-East Asia.[199] Soaked rice in one form or another, often with salt or sugar, has been used to treat diarrhea in Bangladesh and many other Third World countries for hundreds of years.[200] And rice gruel, often with a little salt and lemon, is still a traditional home treatment for diarrhea in many regions.[201]

Gruels or porridges for treating diarrhea are traditionally made from other grains or starch foods, including millet or maize (Mozambique), wheat (Egypt), quinoa (Bolivia), and cassava (Colombia). Porridges, as well as rice water, are also traditional folk remedies for diarrhea in China and Indonesia.[202] Similarly, in Nicaragua corn flour gruel (along with rice water) is commonly given to children during diarrhea episodes.[203] And gruels made from fermented maize or cassava are a traditional home remedy for diarrhea in many parts of Africa.[204]

It was not until the early 1980s, however, that Molla, Mahalanabis, Greenough, Patra, and others carried out studies showing conclusively that in a hospital setting cereal-based oral rehydration is as effective as sugar-based oral rehydration.[205] Subsequent studies have found that solutions made from rice flour or any of a number of other cereals reduce the volume, frequency, and duration of diarrhea.[206] When rice drinks are used in the management of cholera, stool volume is reduced by an average of 35%.[207] By contrast, sugar-based drinks—including ORS—do not reduce stool volume.[208] Cereal-based ORT (CB-ORT) has also been shown to speed up the resumption of solid food intake and to increase the amount eaten.[209]

In its 1994 Interim Programme Report, WHO's Programme for Control of Diarrhoeal Diseases (PCDD) acknowledges that "in cholera, rice-based ORS solution significantly reduces stool output compared with WHO ORS solution. The use of rice-based ORS solution for cholera patients can be recommended for any situation where its preparation and use are practical."[210] With the debate over cereal-based ORT intensifying, WHO together with the International Center of Diarrhoeal Disease Research, Bangladesh (ICDDR,B) held a Meeting on ORS Formulation in Dhaka, Bangladesh, in December, 1994. A stated objective of the meeting was to:

> determine from completed clinical trials whether there is an ORS formulation that is sufficiently more effective than the current WHO/UNICEF ORS to justify exploring the many non-clinical issues involved in recommending that it replace WHO/UNICEF ORS.[211]

A meta-analysis of many studies reconfirmed that rice-based ORS is superior to standard ORS for adults and children with cholera, reducing stool output by 35%, and again concluded that "rice ORS may be used to treat such [cholera] patients wherever its preparation is convenient."[212]

Nevertheless, WHO has resisted endorsing cereal-based ORT, either as a manufactured product (CB-ORS) or as a

---

*While we will refer primarily to "cereal-based" drinks, studies have shown that other foods such as potatoes, yams, and even lentils and chicken soup are also effective.

specially formulated home solution (CB-ORT). Although some of its published guidelines include rice water and/or porridges in their list of recommended home fluids (RHF), these do not provide sufficient information about the concentrations of starch or salt needed to make an optimal rehydration drink. For years, WHO's PCDD has been reluctant to officially fully endorse rice-based ORS, insisting that "further studies are required before any recommendation can be made concerning its use in acute non-cholera diarrhoea in children."[213] (For experimental reasons, however, in 1989 it quietly became involved with the baby-food corporation, Galactina, in starting what was to become commercial production of rice-based ORS. See page 97).

But what about diarrhea other than cholera? The meta-analysis of six studies of children with noncholera diarrhea showed that with CB-ORS, stool output was 18% lower than with standard ORS. Subsequent studies have shown that when food was given soon after rehydration, the reduction of stool output with CB-ORT was only 3.4%, a difference not considered significant.

Notwithstanding the above, WHO has until now decided to stick with its standard glucose-based ORS, which is tested, proven, and familiar to health workers and families world-wide. It argues that, since standard ORS is nearly as effective as cereal-based ORS, there is no justification for promoting the latter. This decision may be partly based on justifiable concerns about flooding the market with yet another confusing array of costly and redundant CB-ORS products. (Alas, this is already happening within the private sector.)

Many researchers, including those at the International Child Health Foundation, argue that, even though the physiological advantages of cereal-based over glucose-based drinks may not be great, there are also nonclinical advantages. They object to WHO's position (stated in the objectives of the Dhaka meeting) that an alternative formulation needs to be "sufficiently more effective than the current WHO/UNICEF ORS" in order to "justify exploring its nonclinical advantages." They point out that the nonclinical advantages would deserve exploration even if there were *no* physiological advantages. And if substantial, they could justify preferential promotion of CB-ORT.[214]

The biggest nonclinical advantages of cereal-based rehydration are associated with home-prepared CB-ORT (as distinct from pre-packaged CB-ORS which has many of the same disadvantages as standard ORS). In many countries, excellent food-based rehydration drinks can be made by building on local traditions. Health workers can help people understand why it is important to add cooked rice to the traditional rice water home remedy to make it somewhat thicker, and how much salt is desirable. Almost any local grain or starch-rich food can give good results.[215] These include *maize, wheat, millet, and sorghum,*[216] *gram, lentils, plantain, bananas, potatoes,* and certain local *tubers.*[217] In short, people can usually make an effective ORT drink out of their locally-available, low-cost food staple.

Why Cereals Work Better

The reason that starch works better than sugar for rehydration has to do with its molecular composition and the principle of *osmosis*. Put simply, osmosis is the pull of water through a membrane from a less-concentrated to a more-concentrated solution (of sugar and/or salt), resulting in more equal concentrations on both sides. (In a sense, osmosis is the struggle for equity at the molecular level.) Sugar molecules are very small, while starch molecules, although made up of many long chains of sugar molecules, are individually relatively large. The osmotic force that pulls water into sugar or starch solution is affected, not by the size of the molecules, but by how many molecules are in the solution. So sugar solutions, consisting of lots of small molecules at a high concentration, have more "osmotic pull" than starch solutions.

Sugar has been used in rehydration drinks because it helps the active transport of water and salt through the lining of the gut into the body. In addition, it provides needed calories, especially in the early stages of diarrhea when the child has no appetite. But there is a problem with sugar that decreases its effectiveness. In a concentrated sugar solution such as ORS (or SSS), the millions of tiny sugar molecules create an osmotic pull that can draw water back out of the bloodstream into the gut. So at the same time that sugar helps transport water and salt into the bloodstream, its high osmotic pull tends to draw part of that water back out. For this reason, a sugar-based solution—whether in packet form or home mix—does nothing to slow the flow of diarrhea. If the sugar solution is sufficiently dilute, more water is carried into the blood than is pulled back, and rehydration takes place. But if the sugar solution is too concentrated, it can increase both the diarrhea and dehydration. Therefore, too much sugar can be dangerous.[218]

Cereals on the other hand, are composed of large starch molecules with a low osmotic pull. With a cereal based drink the osmotic flow is in the opposite direction, pushing water from the gut into the bloodstream, rather than pulling it back. Where the starch molecules come into contact with the gut lining, enzymes break them down into simple sugars which are immediately absorbed, carrying with them water and salt. But since the starch solution does not have the opposing osmotic pull of a sugar solution, much more water passes into the body from the gut than comes out. This helps to explain why a cereal drink slows down dehydration and diarrhea more efficiently.

Summary of arguments in favor of cereal-based ORT

In addition to the biological advantages, there are also strong psychological, socio-economic, and other practical arguments in favor of cereal-based ORT as compared to sugar-based ORS, and especially as compared to the standard, high-sugar, high-salt WHO formula. Some of these are listed below.

- **Physiological:** Cereal-based drinks reduce dehydration and also the volume, frequency, and duration of liquid stools (especially with cholera) by up to 40% or 50% more than sugar-based (glucose-based) ORS.[219] They also reduce vomiting more quickly and effectively.[220]

- **Nutritional:** Cereal-based drinks—because of their low osmotic pull—can be prepared with up to three times the number of calories as sugar or glucose drinks, without any risk to the child. It is now recognized that a contributing cause of malnutrition in children of poor families is that the food they are given often has so much water in it that their stomachs fill up before they get enough calories.[221] Similarly, large quantities of rehydration drink (or any fluid) take up volume, and hence limit the amount of food a child can consume. Therefore it helps if the drink itself is rich in calories. Also, with a cereal solution, the faster passage of water out of the gut into the bloodstream could mean that space for additional food becomes available more quickly. (Better control of vomiting with cereal-based drinks is another strong nutritional advantage.)

- **Safety:** As with the amount of salt, the amount of sugar (glucose) in the WHO formula is close to the upper limit of safety. If mothers prepare an ORS packet with too little water, which often happens, the ORS drink itself can contribute to dehydration. By contrast, no such danger exists for cereal drinks unless too much salt is used. Even if made more concentrated than usual, it is still safe (and is nutritionally richer). The drink will be useful as long as it remains liquid and the child accepts it.

- **Acceptability to the children:** Children are often already used to cereal gruels as weaning food and accept them more readily than the standard ORS solution. Also, most mothers (who usually taste anything before giving it to their child) prefer the taste of a

cereal porridge to a solution of sugar and salt. Many say that ORS tastes bad.[222]

- **Practicality and cost:** For the family that does not have enough money to feed its children adequately, the cost of a few ORS packets, together with that of the travel and time lost from work involved, can be nutritionally devastating. Even sugar is a luxury that is beyond the means of many poor families. However, virtually every family has some basic low-cost or home-grown grain that is their main staple. Thus cereal drinks may improve nutrition not only because they contain more calories than ORS, but also because the very low cost leaves families with more money to buy food. Moreover, by reducing the frequency and duration of the diarrhea, cereal-based ORT reduces another key cost—the amount of time poor mothers must spend administering ORS solution to (and cleaning up after) their sick children. As one author points out,

> a sick child with a common rota virus infection, who has diarrhoea, vomiting, and is peevish with fever, will require an enormous amount of mothering time if oral rehydration fluid in sufficient quantity is coaxed into its mouth, spoonful by spoonful.[223]

Considering the Demands on Mothers

There are many competing demands on these mothers' time: caring for other children, cooking, cleaning, hauling water, collecting fuel, tending gardens, fields, animals, and often long hours of fatiguing work to earn money. Studies have suggested that one of the major reasons mothers fail to treat their children's diarrhea with ORS is that they lack the time to do so.[224] Thus the shorter the episode of diarrhea, the better chance a poor child has of receiving adequate care, and therefore of surviving.[225]

A study in Jamaica found that the time lost in travel to the health center and waiting in line for ORS packets was one of the main reasons why mothers preferred to buy (inappropriate) medicines in local shops.[226] In considering home management of diarrhea it is important to pay greater attention to the constraints on mothers and to look for solutions that meet their needs as well as the children's. One way to partially relieve the time burden for mothers is by teaching the sick child's older siblings to prepare and give ORT. Because less precision is needed in preparing cereal based drinks, (and because they taste better than ORS) they lend themselves to this Child-to-child approach.[227]

First and foremost, mothers must be consulted and be more fully informed of the issues and choices, so they can be more involved in the strategies and programs that affect them. We need to learn to listen before we begin to advise.

A Poorly Considered Warning: "Do not use weaning foods to make ORT"

As cereal-based ORT becomes more widely appreciated, a new warning has been sounded by the "experts" regarding its preparation and use. For example, the following admonition appeared in the June 1990 issue of *Dialogue on Diarrhoea*:

> It is most important that cereal-based ORT solutions are not confused with food, and that mothers *do not dilute the child's usual foods to make home fluids.*[228] [italics added]

The first part of the above warning makes a lot of sense; the second must be questioned. Nutritionists stress that parents must realize that no rehydration drink is a substitute for other food and that, in addition to the drink, regular foods should be given in frequent small feedings as soon as the child will accept them. Although cereal drinks can provide more calories (energy) than sugar or glucose based drinks, no rehydration drink—because of its necessarily high water content—provides enough calories to meet the child's energy requirements. Worded more accurately, cereal-based drinks alone do not provide enough food to meet a sick child's needs.

However, advising mothers not to use the child's usual foods which are already in the home to make a rehydration drink could cause more child deaths than it prevents. It could deny many families the chance to use the easiest, quickest, safest, most effective, most nutritious, most economical, best tasting, culturally most appropriate, most consistently available, and most self-reliance-promoting ORT alternative available to them: a cereal-based drink.[229] As we have discussed, in many poor homes around the world, traditional weaning foods can be diluted to form an excellent rehydration drink. Since they are already prepared each day for babies in the home,

with no additional time or cost they can be converted for ORT almost instantly, simply by adding water and a bit of salt (if they do not already have it).

Yet certain experts warn us that, if mothers are taught to prepare ORT by diluting weaning foods, they may give this dilute drink as food, thereby leading to low energy intakes and malnutrition. The implication is that mothers are too stupid to understand that the child with diarrhea needs more solid foods in addition to the diluted drink. (To build up a child's strength, it is important for mothers to realize that, in general, weaning foods should be prepared THICK—and if possible with added oil to increase calories.)

Our own experience shows that mothers can readily understand two simple messages: 1) that children should be given food regularly at all times, even when they have diarrhea, and 2) that children with diarrhea should be given lots of liquid, preferably a "special drink" (appropriate to their local situation), which may or may not be prepared from conventional foods.

Our confidence in mothers' ability to care for their children is backed by a WHO report which stated that "children given rice-based solution were not given less rice or rice porridge to eat than children given other types of ORS."[230] Also, a study by Hirschhorn and others (still unpublished) "shows no confusion of wheat/rice-based ORS with regular food; the children actually ate better, gained more weight, and ended diarrhea sooner than did those on ORS packets."[231] We hope that WHO will reconsider, and begin

A child with diarrhea requires love and patience, along with ORT.

to encourage the use of home-made CB-ORT by building on local traditions.

Additional objections to cereal-based ORT

Opponents of cereal-based ORT stress the disadvantages that their use entails: the "added cost of fuel," the "extra work," and the "delay caused by the need to cook the mix."[232] However, *in the homes of poor families in many societies, cereal gruels are the standard weaning food of babies.* They are already cooked and ready for use on a daily basis. All the mother has to do is to scoop some out of the common pot, add a bit of water if it is too thick or salty, and every few minutes give as much to her child as she will take.

Critics also cite the inability of very young infants to digest starch completely, and possible allergic/ immunological reactions in such infants to proteins contained in some cereals. Some authorities advise against use in infants less than three months old. But as far as we can determine their arguments are more theoretical than factual. A recent study sponsored by the PCDD found that a rice-based solution was digested and absorbed efficiently in a group of severely malnourished children and infants under six months, and was at least as effective as sugar-based ORS in correcting dehydration and maintaining hydration.[233]

Perhaps the biggest real disadvantage of cereal based rehydration drinks is that they do tend to spoil faster than sugar based drinks—sometimes within 6 or 8 hours (under some conditions within as little as two to three hours). However, when cereal gruels are the traditional weaning food, families often know how to prevent spoiling, either by periodically reheating the gruel or through "souring" or fermentation. This latter process opens up some exciting possibilities for an improved cereal-based rehydration drink.

Building on Local Traditions: "Soured Porridges" as Homemade ORT

One of the most promising possibilities for cereal-based ORT is the use of soured gruels or fermented porridges, which are traditional weaning foods in much of Africa, the Middle East, and in some other parts of the Third World.

Until recently, nutritionists in Southern Africa discouraged mothers from giving fermented or soured millet or maize porridges to their children because they thought these traditional weaning foods were disgusting,

bad-smelling, and presumably unhealthy. But in fact, studies have shown that these traditional soured gruels are excellent weaning foods.[234] The increased acidity that comes with the non-alcoholic fermentation of cereal porridges by lactic acid-producing bacteria (as in yogurt) delays spoilage. Therefore, soured gruels can be kept safely for up to a week. The fermentation process is also said to make the grain easier for young children to digest. And there is some evidence that the bacteriostatic effect of the acidified gruel may help to combat the infectious agents causing the diarrhea.[235]

In Mozambique mothers traditionally use soured porridges for treatment of their children's diarrhea, often with excellent results. There is growing interest in conducting further research on this. They are ready and waiting in most homes with young children and, since these are the traditional weaning foods, sick children tend to accept them more readily than ORS.

Kishk neshif—a traditional CB-ORT with a storage life of months[236]

An Egyptian equivalent of the soured gruels of southern Africa is *"kishk neshif."* A popular home remedy for diarrhea, *kishk* is a traditional food made with wheat and the whey of water buffalo milk. The whey is separated from the curd by placing it for a while in the stomach removed from a young goat. In the process the whey becomes fermented and develops a sharp smell and acid taste, similar to yogurt. The wheat grain is then washed, pounded just a little (not enough to destroy the form of the grains), boiled, and then mixed with the fermented whey. The resulting *kishk* is rolled into little spheres the size of golf balls and dried in the sun. This *kishk neshif* (dried *kishk*) can be kept for up to a year without spoiling. As a village health worker explained, "The wheat alone will spoil. The whey alone will spoil. But put together and dried they do not spoil." For the treatment of diarrhea, the rock-hard *kishk neshif* is ground up and boiled in water to form a thin gruel, and a little salt is added.

Kishk is widely recognized by villagers as a good treatment for diarrhea. A taxi driver in Cairo, hearing us talk of *kishk neshif,* commented that it is "good for an upset stomach." And a Lebanese health worker confirmed this by saying that he had given *kishk* to his child as a weaning food and for diarrhea. However, nutritionists and diarrhea control researchers in Egypt have apparently overlooked *kishk neshif* because educated persons—even in areas where it is traditionally used—look down on it as primitive and disgusting. When one of us first mentioned it to the staff of the National Control of Diarrheal Diseases Project in Cairo, everyone laughed.

The application of soured porridges and *kishk neshif* both, as weaning foods and for oral rehydration, deserves serious study. In the areas where they are traditionally used, they could possibly provide a cheaper, more effective, more sustainable solution for oral rehydration—one that not only combats dehydration but also reduces the problem of child malnutrition, which is the underlying cause of the high death rate from diarrhea.

In summary, soured cereal-based porridges may well answer the major objections often posed concerning cereal-based mixes. They have the following advantages (for much of Africa, the Near East, India, and other parts of the world where they are traditionally used):

Advantages of soured (fermented) cereal-based porridges

- They are traditionally used both as weaning food and as a preferred food for sick children, including children with diarrhea. Thus poor people already believe in their value and are familiar with their preparation and use.

- According to mothers, sick children like and accept soured porridge better than other food, and they say it combats diarrhea.

- In homes where soured porridges are part of the daily diet, or are the standard weaning foods, there are no additional costs—in money or time—for preparing the drink or for obtaining fuel. From the pot that has already been prepared, all the mother has to do is add enough water to make the porridge fairly liquid (and add a small pinch of salt if not already included and if salt is available)[*] and give it to the child.

- Soured porridges can be kept safely (without risk of breeding diarrhea-producing organisms) for days at room temperature, thus making them safer than other porridges.[237] They are also biologically safer (less contaminated) than the unboiled water used to make sugar-based ORT solutions or to mix ORS packets.[238] (Even if the water added is somewhat contaminated, the acidity and the beneficial microorganisms of the fermented gruel may help to reduce any pathogens present.)

---

[*]Less salt is probably needed in cereal-based than sugar-based mixes, because the cereals already contain some sodium and because reduced diarrhea permits better absorption of salt from the gut. By recommending less salt, there is much less risk that mothers will add dangerously large amounts. There is also some evidence that cereal-based mixes without any added salt may be effective (although probably less effective than mixes including salt) for the prevention of dehydration in most cases of diarrhea. Mothers in Mozambique report successful results from treating diarrhea with cereal mixes without salt.

- Souring of cereal mush gives the child a head start on the digestive process.[239] (The fermentation process breaks down some of the carbohydrates into sugars, and may also increase the body's ability to make use of proteins, vitamins, and minerals.[240]) For the same reason, the consistency of the soured porridge is smoother. These soured porridges appear to be more easily digested and handled by a small child than are the non-soured porridges.[241]

- Perhaps most importantly, fermentation decreases the gruel's viscosity (thickness), which permits making a drink that is more energy-rich without becoming thick. This is important because with non-fermented cereal gruels—especially the more watery ones—a child's stomach fills up before she eats enough to provide the energy (calories) her body needs for adequate nutrition. Soured gruels, with proportionately more calories for the same viscosity than non-soured gruels, partially overcome this problem.[242] (It is, of course, important that the oral rehydration drink not be seen as a substitute for more solid food—and that mothers, while giving the drink, are encouraged to also give food as soon as the child will accept it. See the discussions on pages 63 and 69.)

Adding germinated flour for higher energy ORT

Another possibility for an improved rehydration drink is the use of germinated flour (flour made from grain that has begun to sprout). As with the fermentation process, the addition of germinated flour (which is rich in the enzyme amylase) to a cereal drink substantially decreases its viscosity. This means that the drink can be made more concentrated (energy-rich) without becoming too thick.[243] Adding a little germinated flour to a cereal ORT mix (fermented or otherwise) results in a drink that provides more calories per unit volume and thus helps to minimize the nutritional deficit during the period when the sick child with acute diarrhea is accepting little or no (other) food.[244]

In some African countries (e.g., Uganda and Rwanda), as well as some Asian ones (e.g., India), weaning foods are traditionally prepared using both fermentation and germinated grain.[245] This offers the possibility of promoting improved low-viscosity, high-energy ORT by building on local customs: a "Super-ORT" based in local tradition. To date most of the research on fermentation and germination has focused on their use in weaning foods. Research on their potential use in ORT is greatly needed and holds exciting promise.

CONCLUSION TO PART 2

Official explanations for the disappointing impact of prevailing ORT initiatives include: poor user compliance, weak health education, inadequate social marketing, difficulties of maintaining production and supply of ORS packets, etc. But as we have seen, the problems are more fundamental.

One problem is the idea that a technological fix can solve an illness so deeply rooted in social and economic inequities. Another problem has been prioritization of product over process: to market ORS packets rather than to facilitate informed, intelligent use of local solutions. The product has been packaged and promoted as a "wonder drug," thus creating false expectations and undermining efforts to encourage cheaper, home-made, and potentially more effective alternatives. Families are enticed to misspend their limited food money on a fancy, medicalized, and (for most diarrheas) unnecessary product. Thus Oral Rehydration Therapy—when introduced in a disempowering way—can result in additional nutritional deficit to already undernourished children. Last but not least, the ORS technology—like the other Child Survival interventions—was developed in a selective, top-down way. Little effort has been made to link it to any comprehensive approach to resolve to underlying causes of death from diarrhea: malnutrition and extreme poverty.

It is our thesis that ORT's failure to fulfill its promise stems largely from the fact that ORT policy-making is concentrated in a few hands. Despite much good will on the part of many, the conservative social climate and deteriorating economic conditions of the 1980s led many international health policy-makers to switch from challenging the unjust world order to trying to mitigate its effects.

Involving disadvantaged people meaningfully in the planning and implementation of health and development initiatives that affect them is not just an ethical imperative, but a pragmatic one. It is a crucial step in the process of empowerment, democratization, and equity that is the key to true development and health for all.

In Part 3 we will try to place in historical perspective the current political atmosphere that dictates health policies and patterns of poor health. We will also look at the ways in which three multinational industries—the producers of breast milk substitutes, pharmaceuticals, and arms—contribute to poor health in the Third World, and particularly to high child death rates from diarrhea.

PART 3

What Really Determines the Health of a Population?

INTRODUCTION TO PART 3

In considering what determines the health of a population we must not only analyze the causes of poor health, but also identify factors that lead to improvements in the health and well-being of populations. In Part 3 we compare populations that have achieved relatively good health with others that have not, and ask why. What are the salient features or circumstances—medical, environmental, social, economic or political—which have been determinants of improved health?

It is often assumed that either medical breakthroughs or systematic improvements in health services are the key determinants of health. But, as we see in the next chapters, both historical and current evidence tend to refute this assumption.

In Chapter 11, we compare the health status in developing and developed countries, past and present. We examine historical and recent evidence which shows that major long-term improvements in health and survival are due less to medical breakthroughs than to changing social, economic, and political factors.

In Chapter 12 we explore some of the powerful forces and interest groups that stand in the way of sustainable development and improved levels of health. Specifically, we look at the role of transnational industries, which in the last two decades have played an increasingly dominant role in promoting a development model that places corporate greed before human need. Here we focus on the manufacturers of breast milk substitutes and the transnational pharmaceutical companies—whose unscrupulous practices directly contribute to the high child death rate from diarrhea. We also discuss the impact of the arms industry on health.

In Chapter 13 we examine what is emerging as one of the biggest threats to comprehensive Primary Health Care:

the intrusion by the World Bank into Third World health care policy-making. We see how the policies of the World Bank and the market-oriented development paradigm have reversed much of the progress made in recent decades toward a society which regards health and the meeting of all peoples' basic needs as fundamental human rights.

In Chapter 14, we compare contrasting models for meeting a nation's health needs. To provide an extreme example of *poor health at high cost* we look at the United States which, despite enormous wealth and huge health expenditures, has the worst health status of all industrialized countries. Next, for examples of *good health at low cost,* we look at a Rockefeller Foundation study of four countries (Costa Rica, China, Sri Lanka, and Kerala State of India) and we also examine health care in Cuba. From this comparison we see that extreme inequity leads to an unhealthy society, regardless of national wealth, while a strong commitment to equity is conducive to a healthy population, even in a poor country.

In Chapter 15 we explore two areas of widespread concern when considering questions of sustainable development, child survival, and the prospects of health for all—namely *AIDS* and *population growth.* Once again, we see that high-level attempts to control both AIDS and population growth rates have used mainly technological interventions (such as condoms, etc.) without getting to the root social causes of these conditions. We see that for AIDS and population growth, as for diarrhea control and *health for all*, social equity may be the key to any long-term solution.

Let us begin by taking a look at the historical process which led to improvements in health in the developed (industrialized) countries.

Health Status in Different Lands at Different Times in History— A Comparative Perspective

Health Indicators in Populations

To compare differences between and changes within the health of populations, it is helpful to agree upon some sort of standard health indicators. Mortality rates and life expectancy are the ones most commonly used.

For many years, UNICEF and others considered *the infant mortality rate* (IMR) to be the best indicator of a population's overall health level. IMR is the number of deaths per 1000 live births in children under one year of age. Not only are infants especially vulnerable to the ravages of ill health, but their survival depends on a diversity of factors ranging from biological and environmental to economic and cultural. Although IMR is still a widely used indicator, UNICEF now regards the *mortality rate of children under age five* (U5MR) as a truer measure of a population's well-being. Clearly, no death statistics entirely reflect the health or quality of life of survivors. However, if we accept IMR and U5MR as rough indicators of a population's health, we can observe striking differences in different countries at different times. This allows us to correlate economic, social, and political conditions with levels of children's health.

COUNTRY	U5MR 1993	IMR 1993	Total population in millions 1993	GNP per capita (US $) 1992	Life expectancy at birth 1993	Total adult literacy rate 1990	% share hold of household income 1980–1991 Lowest 40%	highest 40%
MOZAMBIQUE	282	164	15.3	60	47	33	—	—
NIGERIA	191	114	119.3	320	53	51	—	—
GABON	154	93	1.3	4450	54	61	—	—
NEPAL	128	90	21.1	170	54	26	22	40
BANGLADESH	122	94	122.2	220	53	35	23	39
INDIA	122	81	896.6	310	61	48	21	41
LIBYA	100	67	5.1	5310	63	64	—	—
SOUTH AFRICA	69	53	40.8	2670	63	76	—	—
BRAZIL	63	52	156.6	2770	66	82	7	68
PERU	62	43	22.9	950	65	85	14	51
EGYPT	59	46	56.1	640	62	48	—	—
BOTSWANA	56	43	1.4	2790	61	74	11	59
IRAN	54	42	63.2	2200	67	54	—	—
VIETNAM	48	36	70.9	240	64	88	—	—
CHINA	43	35	1205.2	470	71	78	17	42
MEXICO	32	27	90.0	3470	70	88	12	56
SRI LANKA	19	15	17.9	540	72	88	22	39
COSTA RICA	16	14	3.3	1960	76	93	13	51
JAMAICA	13	11	2.5	1340	74	98	16	48
CUBA	10	9	10.9	1170	76	94	—	—
UNITED STATES	10	9	257.8	23240	76	—	16	42
UNITED KINGDOM	8	7	57.8	17790	76	—	15	44
HONG KONG	7	6	5.9	15360	78	77	16	47
SINGAPORE	6	5	2.8	15730	75	83	15	49
SWEDEN	6	5	8.7	27010	78	—	21	37

Fig. 3–1 Under-five mortality rate (per 1000 live births), GNP per capita, and distribution of wealth (defined as the proportion of household income going to the wealthiest 20% of the population relative to that going to the poorest 40%) (Source: UNICEF, *State of the World's Children, 1995*, pp. 66–67.)

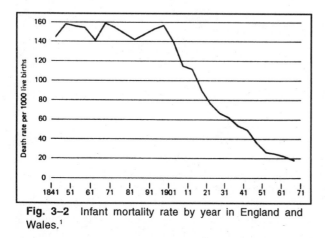

Fig. 3–2 Infant mortality rate by year in England and Wales.[1]

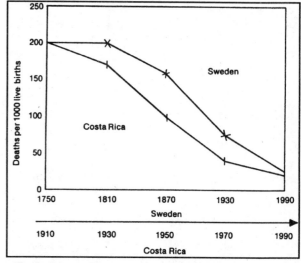

Fig. 3–4 A comparison of infant mortality rates in Sweden and Costa Rica[3]

For instance, the economic status of a country often appears to correlate, more or less, with its health status. Figure 3–1 shows us that the U5MR can be up to sixty times higher in poor than in rich nations, while the IMR is as much as forty times higher. However, as we will discuss later, a country's total wealth is not the most important determinant of its people's health.

To offer some insight into how the health indicators of a country change it develops, we can compare current mortality rates against some historical reference points.

Figures 3–2 to 3–4 show the trends of IMRs in selected countries, North and South, in the past and present. Note that in Great Britain, Sweden and New York City, even at the close of the nineteenth century, more than 100 of every 1000 babies were dying. This represents a higher infant mortality rate than in many underdeveloped countries today. Moreover, the main causes of death in 19th century England and Wales were essentially the same infectious diseases that are killing children in underdeveloped countries today: diarrhea, measles, and respiratory infections such as pneumonia, tuberculosis,

and whooping cough. Even the diseases we now refer to as tropical, such as malaria and leprosy, were once problems as far north as Scotland and Ontario, Canada. Cholera was formerly a dreaded scourge in Europe.

What caused Europe's and the United States' IMRs to drop to their present levels? This dramatic decline is sometimes credited to medical breakthroughs, such as the discovery of antibiotics and vaccines. However, the evidence suggests otherwise. Studies have found that in England and Wales the drop in IMR was mainly due to fewer deaths from infectious disease, but this decline in infectious disease occurred well before the discovery of antibiotics and vaccines.[4]

Figure 3–5 shows that the death rate from tuberculosis, the single biggest killer in 19th century England and Wales, fell sharply before the development of any effective drug

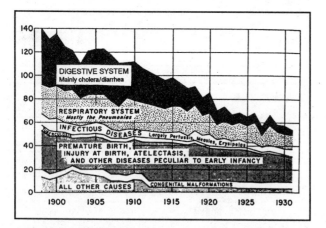

Fig. 3–3 Infant mortality by prominent causes in New York City. (Rates per 1000 live births)[2]

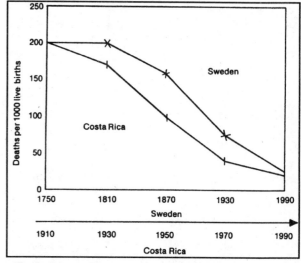

Fig. 3–5 Decline in TB in England and Wales before drugs.[5]

treatment or a vaccine. Similar patterns exist for the decline of measles, whooping cough, and others of the current major killers of children in developing countries.

Development in the "Developed" World

To understand whether today's underdeveloped nations can hope to duplicate the health improvements of the developed countries, we must first examine what brought about these improvements. Historically, the declining death rates in the North coincided with improvements in nutrition and the living and working conditions of working class and poor families. Because the circumstances of how this happened in England and Wales are particularly well-documented, we will use them as a case study.[6]

The improvement in the living standards and health of the English people is often traced to the Agricultural Revolution of the eighteenth century and the Industrial Revolution of 1750–1850. However, these revolutions were a mixed blessing. While the shift toward large-scale agriculture and industry increased production of food and goods, it also resulted in widespread landlessness, migration to the cities, unemployment, unsanitary conditions, and malnutrition—all of which took a devastating toll on the health of working and poor people. The misery unleashed by such inequities triggered another kind of revolution: a revolution of the working class, which galvanized the downtrodden into creating a unified, organized struggle. It was this class struggle, the demand of disadvantaged people for their rights, that ultimately led to a redistribution of resources and widespread improvements in living conditions and health.

In sum, the agricultural and industrial revolutions did not bring about better health *per se*, but because of the cruel hardships they brought to millions of people, they triggered an organized popular demand for a fairer, more equitable society.

One of the first steps toward large-scale capitalist production which typified the Agricultural Revolution was the Enclosure Movement, which peaked in the years between 1760 and 1812. Large landholders, eager to make huge profits by selling food to Great Britain's rapidly growing population, swept aside the "commons" or open-field system of land tenure which had prevailed for almost one thousand years.[7] These land barons appropriated, consolidated, and fenced in both land that had previously been cultivated by small individual subsistence farmers, as well as land that had been used in common by all members of a community to graze their cattle or collect firewood.[8] In essence, the Enclosure Movement replaced small-scale subsistence farming with large-scale commercial agriculture. This led to more food output, but it also forced many small farmers off their land, most of whom migrated to the cities and became the factory workers of the Industrial Revolution. The seeds of the ensuing class struggle is vividly captured in the desperate words of a participant in a rural riot that took place in 1816:

> Here I am between Earth and Sky, so help me God. I would sooner lose my life than go home as I am. Bread I want and bread I will have.[9]

The migration of displaced rural families to the cities, known as "urban drift," persisted throughout the agricultural and industrial revolutions. The shanty towns these families flocked to had deficient housing and grossly inadequate water and sanitation. The overcrowding and poor hygiene in these urban ghettos mirrors Third World squatter settlements today.

In the early days of the Industrial Revolution, malnutrition was the norm. This is evidenced by the recorded growth-stunting of English schoolchildren, which highlights the link between malnutrition and poverty. In the 1870s, children over 11 years old in working class schools were, on average, from three to five inches shorter than their counterparts in upper class schools. Today, although Third World children are, on average, shorter than those in developed countries, those children from affluent Third World families are as tall as First World children.[10]

Similar disparities in health indicators between rich and poor were noted by Frederick Engels in his path-breaking 1845 work, *The Condition of the Working Class in England*. He found that the death rate in lower-class streets was up to twice that in upper-class streets.[11]

In nineteenth century England hunger, poverty, and unemployment led first to widespread discontent, then to strikes and riots. The state responded with brutal repression; in fact, the British police force was created in 1829 precisely in order to counter such unrest. Popular misery and discontent led to the formation of labor unions, whose basic demand was that employers pay workers enough to feed their families. The awareness-raising induced by these demands, together with the writings of Dickens and other social activists, eventually had an effect. Some influential figures among the middle and upper classes began to call for measures to improve the situation of the poor, either out of compassion (especially for poor children) or out of a pragmatic desire to head off widespread revolt.

Over a period of decades, pressure from labor organizations and reformers led to better wages and working conditions. Growing public outrage over high death rates from infectious disease—and in particular over four major cholera epidemics that occurred between 1830 and 1866—forced Parliament to pass the Public Health Acts of 1848, 1866, and 1875.[12] The 1875 Act created local committees responsible for sanitary measures. Health initiatives included environmental regulations governing the water supply, sewage disposal, housing standards, livestock slaughtering, quarantine hospitals, and the creation of parks and other open spaces, as well as a move for more universal education.[13]

Monster Soup, commonly called Thames Water—an engraving of 1828

In sum, the profound health gains in the English population were the result of improvements in living and working conditions and nutrition. More broadly, they were the direct result of gains in social equity. These improvements were not automatic by-products of economic growth. Rather, poor people had to fight for them against the resistance of the entrenched interests of the privileged. Similar processes took place in the other industrialized countries.

Changes in the social order which benefit the disadvantaged tend to be resisted by the ruling elite, and require organized demand from the bottom up. As Frederick Douglass, a leader in the struggle to abolish American slavery, put it:

> If there is no struggle there is no progress ... Power concedes nothing without a demand. It never did and it never will ... People may not get all they work for ... but they must certainly work for all they get.[14]

Another important lesson from history is that social changes that benefit the disadvantaged, once won, must be vigorously and continuously defended; Thomas Jefferson said that *revolutions must be re-fought every 20 years.*

Today, London once again is faced with rising levels of poverty, slums, street children, and inequity, as is New York City. Under the conservative leadership of Britain's Margaret Thatcher, the standard of living of the lower classes unquestionably deteriorated. Nevertheless, when compared to the situation as it was in the 19th century, the rights and wages of today's English working people are much improved, as are their nutrition, living conditions, water supply, and sanitation. Labor unions remain relatively strong. Education is nearly universal. And although the National Health Service has been partially dismantled and privatized by conservative administrations, basic health services are still available to most citizens at public expense.

The plight of many Third World children today is comparable to that of poor children in nineteenth century England whose tragic lives and deaths are vividly depicted by Charles Dickens in *Oliver Twist* and other novels. With minor changes, Dickens' London street urchins could pass for the "untouchable" children in Dominique Lapierre's *The City of Joy* (based in the slums of Calcutta, India), or for the homeless boy, Pixote, in the Brazilian film of that title, or Krishna in the Indian film *Salaam Bombay.*

The creators of all these heart-rending novels and films, past and present, bring vividly to life the extent of personal tragedy and suffering that is too often lost when we talk of "under five mortality rates" (U5MR) in the millions. They make it clear that hunger, poverty, high unemployment, inadequate wages, miserable living conditions—largely the consequence of routine exploitation of the weak by the strong, and the powerlessness of the poor majority—are the key factors behind ill health and early death.

Having looked at some of the events and confrontations that led to improvements in living standards and health in the northern industrialized countries, can we realistically expect today's Third World countries to follow a similar path of economic and social development? Before assessing this question we must briefly examine the reasons for these countries' current state of underdevelopment.

The Development of Underdevelopment

To a large extent it was the ruthless exploitation of the non-European world that made the industrial revolution possible. Mushrooming colonization decimated indigenous populations in Africa, Asia, and the Americas. Their subsistence economies, cultural patterns, and whole ways of life were violated. The introduction of infectious diseases, such as smallpox and measles, virtually wiped out entire populations which had previously been unexposed. Furthermore, it was wealth plundered from the southern colonies that fueled industrialization in many northern countries. This was particularly true in Great Britain, where foreign trade was a main source of new capital. The cotton textile industry, for example, was instrumental in providing capital for the development of the country's iron, steel, and engineering industries. The story was the same in other European countries, including Spain, Portugal, France, and the Netherlands. To make matters worse, many colonized countries of the south became victims of the slave trade, another major source of capital for the colonizing nations. After the first slaves were shipped to Virginia in 1619, tens of millions of Africans were abducted to the Americas in a human market that continued until 1867. Thus the onset of private, profit-driven market economies (i.e., capitalism) that accompanied the agricultural and industrial revolutions was made possible at the considerable expense of poor people within the northern countries, as well as their colonies in the south.

By the 1860s, the market forces and free competition which had stimulated the development of European industry had unquestionably resulted in increased production of goods. But mechanized production began to replace workers, leading to rising unemployment and falling wages, triggering the first serious economic depression in Europe. In an attempt to generate economic recovery, many industries merged, leading to a shift away from relatively competitive conditions to more monopolistic ones with concentrated economic power.

This transition from small competitive production units to large monopolistic industries has accelerated during the 20th century with profound repercussions on the Third World. Business interests in the North turned increasingly to the nonindustrialized South as a lucrative outlet for investing their surplus capital. By exporting their large scale, monopolistic form of production and technology to the underdeveloped countries, the industrialized nations stifled indigenous economic development. In this way powerful business interests in the North transformed the Third World into a field ripe for investment.

The trends toward monopoly, growing concentration of economic power, and increased investment in the Third World have culminated during the twentieth century in the formation of giant transnational (multinational) corporations (TNCs).[*] Today the combined sales of the 350 largest TNCs exceed the individual gross national products of all Third World countries.[15] Many TNCs have diversified, investing in industries far removed from their original lines of business. TNCs do about two-thirds of their business in developed countries, and the remaining one-third in Asia, Africa, and Latin America. Initially, their Third World operations emphasized mining and agriculture. However, in recent decades TNCs have begun moving their manufacturing plants to Third World countries with adequate infrastructures (such as Mexico, South Korea, Taiwan, and South Africa) in order to take advantage of their less organized, cheap labor. (The negative impact of TNCs on health is discussed in Chapter 12.)

Underdevelopment of the Third World as an Ongoing Process

We have briefly outlined the process by which the First World has colonized and taken advantage of the Third. Grasping this historical dynamic is crucial to assessing whether the Third World is now capable of repeating the process which led to European social and economic development and corresponding improvements in health.

Today, giant monopolies, with their advanced technology and sophisticated marketing prowess, have penetrated most of the Third World. As happened in feudal England, wealthy interests (both foreign and domestic) have appropriated large tracts of land from small farmers in order to grow cash crops. The introduction of large scale agribusiness—promoted by foreign aid as a form of development—has left millions of Third World rural inhabitants landless. One study estimates that "at least 1 billion rural people in the third world (or roughly one in three) have been deprived of farmland."[16] The change in land tenure has also undermined traditional subsistence agriculture, leading to a sharp decrease in food production for local consumption and an increase in malnutrition. (Land scarcity has also been cited as a contributing cause to the recent genocide in Rwanda.)[17]

Some small farmers who have been driven off their land find jobs as farmworkers for large landowners or foreign-owned agribusiness. However, such jobs become scarce as manual labor is replaced by machines. So the majority of landless peasants migrate to urban shantytowns in search of work in a disturbing repetition of the urban drift of nineteenth-century England. Today, nearly 45 percent of the world's people (some 2.6 billion) live in cities, and the Worldwatch Institute estimates that by the year 2025, approximately 60 percent (about 4 billion) will reside in urban areas.[18] Once there, the migrant workers discover that foreign-dominated, mechanized industry can absorb only a fraction of them. The widespread unemployment resulting from the so-called *jobless growth* of big industry translates into weak labor unions and falling wages.

---

[*]The first transnational corporations were formed early in this century, and their numbers increased rapidly after the Second World War.

The resourcefulness of the poor who migrate to the cities has given rise to the so-called informal sector. (This refers to people earning income outside the wage economy through improvised activities such as odd jobs, vegetable-hawking, refuse collection, basket-making, shoe repair, water-selling, and guiding tourists—not to mention stealing, prostitution, drug peddling, and begging.)[19] Meanwhile, dirty, overcrowded shantytowns and slums are expanding at an alarming rate in Latin America and Southeast Asia (and to a lesser extent in Africa, which has traditionally been more rural). The *septic fringe* of many cities today hosts higher rates of sickness and death than many rural areas.[20] Because of poor sanitation and crowding, diarrheal diseases in children are especially devastating.

From *trickle down* to *trickle up*

During the 1950s, mainstream development thinkers saw national economic growth through big business and international trade as a panacea which would eventually "trickle down" from Third World elites to the poor majority. Over the next two decades, however, it became evident that more trickled up than trickled down. Economic growth was often accompanied by increasing poverty. Rising unemployment and falling wages led to growing social and economic inequality.[21]

A stark example of this is Brazil's "economic miracle" of the late 1960s and early 1970s. The 1964 military coup in Brazil was followed by a high rate of economic growth. In his study of the city of São Paulo, Charles Wood shows that this miracle was based on the intensive exploitation of the working class, which resulted in a substantial decline in the wages and standard of living of the majority of the population. Similarly, the Philippines experienced an increase in gross national product (GNP) per capita during the first half of the 1970s, yet the number of Filipinos living in poverty increased over this period. [22]

This correlation of economic growth in the industrial sector with increasing misery for the poor prompts George Kent in *The Politics of Children's Survival* to advocate using children's survival rates instead of economic growth as the gauge of a society's level of development.[23] Kent acknowledges that this would be "a biased indicator, one that is particularly sensitive to the conditions of the poor," but argues that the "more conventional measure of development, gross national product per capita, is also a biased indicator, one that favors the interests of the rich."[24] One could argue that a still better gauge of development would include quality of life indicators such as illness and malnutrition rates, and not merely survival rates.

As we have seen, the situation of the Third World today resembles that of the First World in the eighteenth and nineteenth centuries, but is in some ways quite different. Faced with similar circumstances, the now-industrialized countries achieved improvements in health primarily through widespread gains in nutrition, sanitation, living and working conditions, and education. These were achieved through a combination of factors, including pressure through the union movement for improved wages and working conditions, concern in elite circles about social stability, and pressure from social movements such as the Health of Towns movement. Industrial growth had created many of the new threats to health but also contributed to improved living conditions and new social programs. The impact of more effective preventive strategies and treatments on population health status came much later and was less significant than improved living conditions. (It is difficult to differentiate the impact of new prevention and treatment technologies from the impact of increasing health literacy across the population which often comes with widespread access to medical care.)

Today's underdeveloped world may be able to attain advances in health, in part through a similar process. But the task of improving health and overcoming underdevelopment is more complex than simply retracing the path of development of the industrialized countries. The paths of development of individual countries must be contextualized within the wider global economy. Several exploitative development mechanisms utilized by the North cannot be reproduced by present-day developing nations. These include (1) the plundering of the other nations' human and material riches, (2) the slave trade, and (3) the export of surplus capital and import of raw materials from weaker, more dependent countries under exploitative terms of trade.*

Much of the capital needed for the industrialization of the northern countries came from the exploitation of "their" colonies. The underdeveloped countries of today are not in a position to exploit any colonies of their own; on the contrary, they continue to be exploited through a financial and trading regime which is structured to serve the interests of the elite and middle classes of the North. Third World economies have become increasingly dominated by First World transnational corporations which have formed alliances with Third World elites. Given all these factors, the First

---

*Some of the more recently developed countries—notably Japan and the oil producing countries—have approximated this colonial (or neocolonial) pattern of plundering poor countries. (The slave trade has, of course, been replaced by the import of low paid servants, sex workers, etc.) However, the fact that a few former colonies have "succeeded" makes it all the more difficult for remaining countries to follow suit.

World's path to development is simply not available to most developing countries.

In addition, growing numbers of citizens in both the First and Third Worlds are reevaluating the path of Northern (or Western) development, and deciding that it no longer appears desirable, ethically acceptable, or even feasible. They see that conventional development encompasses stark and growing inequities. Further, even if the Western development paradigm were to prove successful in many more countries, the global environment could not sustain the exorbitant use of resources and massive production of waste.

If our current development paradigm failed to achieve sustainable economic growth for many Third World countries, it had even less success in producing genuine socio-economic and human development for those countries' poor majorities. For millions of people, gains in income, nutrition, living conditions, health care, and education have been marginal at best, and for many the overall quality of life has worsened. More than one billion people continue to live in absolute poverty.[25]

Third World Development— of Massive Foreign Debt

In its 1989 *State of the World's Children* report, UNICEF blamed the reversals in progress in health and development in the 1980s on the "financial prison" of "rising debt repayments and falling commodity prices."[26] The series of blunders which led to this continuing debt crisis was caused primarily by irresponsible lending by large commercial banks based in the US, Europe, and Japan.[27] Let us look at the events which led Third World countries into this debt trap.

During the 1970s, the Organization of Petroleum Exporting Countries (OPEC) quadrupled the price of oil. These oil-rich countries deposited much of the resulting revenue in Northern banks. Glutted with money, the banks decided to invest in Third World development, the terms of which were largely determined by the Northern lenders. Massive loans were given for large scale agribusiness and big industry which would produce goods for export and thereby generate the foreign exchange needed for servicing the debt.

These loans were distributed generously without serious assessment of the ability of the recipient nations to ever pay them back. Indeed, in many cases they were being paid to take the loans through negative interest rates (interest rates lower than the current inflation rate). An aura of optimism led bank officials to believe that the

indebted nations would move steadily toward economic prosperity, and that their loans would yield handsome returns. Thus, between 1970 and the early 1980s, the Third World's foreign debt increased from $68 billion to $596 billion.[28]

However, the situation has changed dramatically since 1981. President Reagan came to power on a platform of tightening the monetary supply to control inflation and reducing domestic taxes while simultaneously outspending and forcing bankruptcy on the USSR by a renewed arms race. The combination of high interest rates and massive borrowing reversed the flow of petrodollars (which were drying up anyway following the fall in oil prices toward the end of the 1970s).

The debt trap was sprung with an abrupt rise in interest rates worldwide (to as high as 18%); Third World debtor countries were well and truly trapped. By the early 1980s it was becoming clear that some countries were in danger of defaulting on their debts. The banks adopted a new conservative stance: tight credit, high interest rates, and a freeze on new loans. At the same time, underdeveloped countries were suffering declining returns for their exports (associated with the recession) and growing inflation. Mexico, in 1982, was the first country to announce that it simply could not pay.

By the early 1980s this rapidly mounting debt burden was causing stalls and setbacks in the economic growth of many Third World countries. It was also slowing down or halting gains in people's health and child survival. While the elite in the poor countries got richer (as did the experts and merchants of development in the North) Third World governments did not have enough in their coffers to pay the salaries of teachers and nurses and to maintain basic social programs.

It should be stressed that Third World governments and national elites who eagerly sought these loans must also bear a share of the blame for the economic stagnation that resulted. It was reckless of them to borrow amounts they had no realistic hope of repaying, and to wholeheartedly embrace the Western growth-oriented development model. In many cases the borrowed funds were used for grandiose, top-down " development" projects, such as giant dams, elegant international airports, high-risk entrepreneurial schemes, arms imports, and other activities designed to advance their own political and economic fortunes. However, given their powerful positions and their ability to set the terms of the world economy, the banks and the northern governments/ universities/industries that promoted the development-through-debt paradigm must be seen as the biggest culprits.

Current Threats to Health —
The Debt Crisis, Recession and Adjustment

Structural adjustment programs imposed by the International Monetary Fund and World Bank have consistently undermined economic and social progress by suppressing wages, undermining the contributions of small producers, and placing social services—particularly health care and education—out of reach of the poor.

—from the *Alternative Copenhagen Declaration* at the UN Summit for Social Development, March 1995[29]

The debt crisis of Third World countries—which continues to this day—has also contributed to the world-wide economic recession. The recession started in the industrialized countries in 1981–83, ending the long post-World War II economic boom. It was precipitated by the stringent financial policies that were adopted by the Northern countries (in particular the US and the UK) from the early 1980s, involving tight credit, high interest rates and cutbacks in government spending.

The resulting growth slowdown was immediately passed along to the underdeveloped countries through reduced US and European demand for Third World exports (leading to a decline both in the volume of exports and their prices) and cuts in foreign aid.[30] This led to a reduction in the funds flowing into Third World countries, as well as rising interest payments on their foreign debts and continued deterioration in their terms of trade (prices of imports increasing relative to prices for exports). The net result was a reversal in the flow of capital between the First and Third World. *The underdeveloped countries went from being net importers to net exporters of capital.* In 1979, there was a net flow of $40 billion from the rich countries to the poor.[31] By 1989, there was

a net flow of at least $20 billion a year from the poor countries to the rich.[33] If we take the deteriorating terms of trade faced by developing countries into account, this flow approaches $60 billion per year.[34] Moreover, at the same time that they were exporting capital to the developed countries, the underdeveloped nations saw their debts continue to grow.

These events have had a devastating impact on the Third World. From 1980 to 1985, three quarters of the developing countries experienced a decline in gross domestic product per capita. In Africa, 84% of the population experienced negative economic growth. The number of Latin Americans with incomes below the poverty line increased by 27% between 1980 and 1990, with minimum urban salaries falling 74% in Peru, 58% in Ecuador, and 50% in Mexico.[35] Perhaps most telling of all, the number of Third World countries classified as "least developed countries" by the UN increased from 31 to 42 during the 1980's.[36]

The debt crisis and recession of the 1980s hit poor families in underdeveloped countries especially hard, particularly the children. These can be directly linked to the slowdown in the rate of decline in child mortality in several countries, including Chile and the Philippines. In countries as diverse as Brazil, Ghana, and Uruguay, infant mortality rates actually *increased* significantly.[37] UNICEF stated that

> It is children who have paid the heaviest price for the developing world's debts. Fragmentary evidence ... has shown a picture of rising malnutrition, and in some cases rising child deaths, in some of the most heavily indebted countries of Africa and Latin America.[38]

When we grasp the full impact of the debt crisis, such reversals are understandable. Today, many countries owe more in debt principal and interest than they earn from exports.[39] Many spend as much as 40% of their export

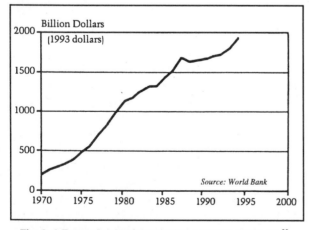

Fig. 3–6 External debt of developing countries, 1970–94.[32]

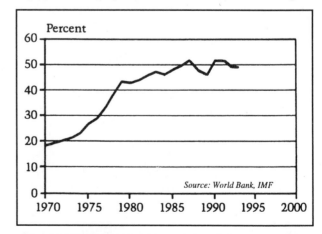

Fig. 3–7 Third World debt as share of Gross Domestic Product, 1970–93.[40]

earnings just to meet their interest payments.[41] And most poor countries spend more on debt payments than they receive in new loans and foreign aid. In Sub-Saharan Africa (excluding South Africa) collectively the region's debt amounts to $180 billion—three times the 1980 total, and 10 percent higher than its annual output of goods and services.[42]

As cynically as in the days of colonialism, the rich are living off the backs of the poor. US economist John Kenneth Galbraith describes the debt crisis as an "astounding process of impoverishment of the poor for the sake of further enrichment of the rich."[43]

Structural Adjustment Policies: Rescuing the Rich at the Expense of the Poor

> They no longer use bullets and ropes.
> They use the World Bank and the IMF.
> —Jesse Jackson[44]

At the peak of the debt crisis, in the early 1980s the International Monetary Fund (IMF) and World Bank came to the rescue of the Northern banks. In order to prevent Third World nations from defaulting on their huge debts, the IMF and the World Bank began to offer them bail-out loans. But not without strings attached. To qualify for IMF loans, poor countries had to agree to accept austere Structural Adjustment Programs (SAPs). These programs, in brief, require debtor countries to adjust the structure of their economies to ensure that they (1) keep servicing their foreign debts and (2) comply with the requirements of the Northern market system.

The debtor nations have had little choice but to accept the dictates of the international financial institutions. Beyond the loans they make directly, these powerful institutions also serve as gatekeepers to Northern assistance. Thus, other big lenders, both private and governmental, look to the IMF and the World Bank to certify that a given Third World country is pursuing responsible (read "free market adjusted") policies and is therefore deserving of further loans. An IMF rebuff is the kiss of death for a country's prospects of foreign financing.[45]

Many progressive analysts agree that the structural adjustment policies imposed by the IMF and the World Bank are the opposite of what is needed to promote health and equity-oriented development. Instead of helping Third World governments to move beyond emergency interventions to broad social change, they force governments to drastically slash public services and assistance. As Jonathan Cahn argues in the *Harvard Human Rights Journal*:

> The World Bank must be regarded as a governance institution, exercising power through its financial leverage to legislate entire legal regimens and even to alter the constitutional structure of borrowing nations. Bank-approved consultants often rewrite a country's trade policy, fiscal policies, civil servant requirements, labor laws, health care arrangements, environmental regulations, energy policy, resettlement requirements, procurement rules, and budgetary policy.[46]

Components of Structural Adjustment

In general, SAPs require poor countries to redirect capital in order to continue to service their foreign debts to Northern banks. Components include:

- sharp cuts in public spending on health, education, and other social services;
- removal of subsidies and lifting of price controls on staple foods and other basic commodities;
- freezing of wages;
- a shift from production of food and goods for domestic consumption to production for export;
- liberalization of trade policies (through tariff elimination and restrictions on imports);
- efforts to attract foreign investors by providing them with incentives such as lax regulations and tax breaks;
- privatization of public services and state enterprises;
- devaluation of the local currency.

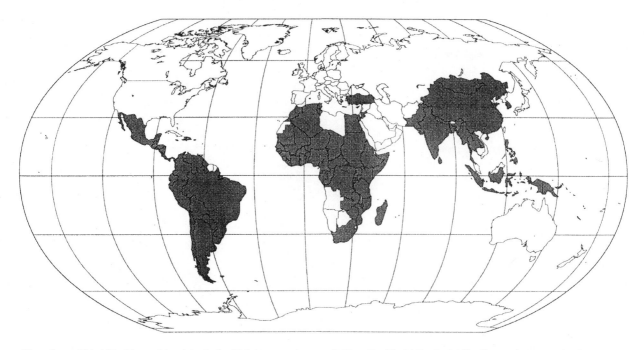

Map shows Third World countries (shaded) which have undergone IMF and/or World Bank stabilization and structural adjustment programs in the period 1980–1991.

In general, SAPs require that national economies conform to the free market, private sector and foreign (Northern) business paradigm.

The World Bank argues that there is no proof that SAPs have had an adverse effect on the health and living standards of the poor, but reports from many countries testify to the contrary. The Bank claims that although poverty has worsened in most of the countries that have been subjected to structural adjustment, no one knows if their condition might have deteriorated as much or more without structural adjustment; thus, there is no basis for the charges that SAPs have hurt the poor. (This claim by the Bank is reminiscent of the tobacco industry's insistence that there is no proof that smokers who die of cancer and heart disease wouldn't have died even if they hadn't smoked.) There is, however, a wealth of evidence indicating these policies have had a devastating effect on poor families, often pushing them over the brink into complete destitution.

Structural adjustment hurts the poor in a number of interrelated ways:

- By lifting price controls while freezing wages, and by devaluing the local currency, it diminishes purchasing power. This reduces the ability of the poor to buy food, health care, and other basic necessities.

- SAPs intensify economic inequities. In countries with adjustment policies, the majority of citizens have seen their real earnings cut in half, while the consumption of the wealthiest citizens has increased.[47]

- The social programs designed to protect the most vulnerable groups (such as food subsidies for the hungry and feeding programs for underweight babies) are being sharply scaled back as the need for them increases.

- Public health services have been severely retrenched, privatized, or subjected to user financing. This puts poor families in a no-win situation: either they forgo the health care they need in order to feed their children, or they let their children go hungry to pay for health care. Either way their children suffer.

- Gearing agriculture to production for export rather than for domestic consumption creates scarcity of local foods and drives up prices.

Given these effects, it is little wonder that the rates of child malnutrition and mortality have increased in a number of the countries that have adopted SAPs. Some experts contend that if these policies continue, it will require 30 years to attain the living standards of 25 years ago.[48]

Brazil provides a graphic example. With one of the world's highest foreign debts of over $100 billion, its interest payments exceed $30 million a day. The country has had little choice but to adopt structural adjustment in exchange for further IMF loans. UNICEF reports that in Brazil "cuts in the health budget led to delays in immunizing children, with later outbreaks in communicable diseases."[49]

Since the late 1980s Brazil's infant and child mortality rates have reportedly improved (according to data from UNICEF's *State of the World Children* reports). The most outstanding improvements have been in the state of Ceara, which has put a good deal of investment into a primary health care initiative, complete with a network of paid community health workers. In spite of some recent gains, however, Brazil as a whole continues to have a disturbingly high child mortality rate (U5MR of 63) in view of its relatively high GNP per capita. The problem, in large part, lies in the gross inequality with which that GNP is distributed.

In Mexico, which has a debt burden and adjustment program similar to Brazil's, minimum urban salaries fell by 50% from 1980 to 1990.[50] In 1987 the Mexican National Institute of Nutrition reported that "80% to 90% of [Mexican] children pass through a period of early malnutrition, from which they suffer irremediable losses in mental and physical capacity."[51] The 1994 North American Free Trade Agreement (NAFTA) and the collapse of the peso at the end of 1994 are causing even more unemployment and hardships for the poor as wages continue to fall while prices skyrocket.[52] (See page 147.)

Why does structural adjustment not slash military budgets instead of health and education?

> *The World Bank has to accept that its real instrument of torture is its insistence on growth, its economic theorizing at the expense of human welfare...*
>
> *The sooner debtor nations realize the political nature of the World Bank, the sooner they will be able to face the bogus economic theories of the Bank with an equivalent weapon—people's power.*
>
> —Ken Saro-Wiwa, Nigerian dissident and environmentalist, hanged by the Nigerian military dictatorship[53]

The IMF and World Bank's SAPs have targeted the so-called nonproductive (i.e. nonprofitable) sectors of national economies, such as health and education, for budget cuts. Yet, until recently, they have almost never called for cuts in military spending ... even though the military budgets of Third World countries are today an

average of seven times higher than they were in 1960, and in many countries the military budget is larger than the budgets of the health and education sectors combined. Clearly, such high expenditure on weaponry is not in the best interests of either the development or economic recovery of poor countries. Nor is it in the interests of children, who suffer inordinately from the ravages of armed conflict.[54] It is, on the other hand, of great economic interest to governments and the powerful arms industry in the North. Additionally, as structural adjustment and other neo-liberal policies drive larger sectors of the population into poverty and hardship, a strong and well-armed military becomes increasingly useful for quelling riots and keeping countries stable for foreign investment. (Decisions governing cuts in military spending clearly have an ideological agenda. It is noteworthy that one of the few countries where the IMF has required reduction of military spending has been Nicaragua, where the military is still largely controlled by Sandinistas.)

In some countries, structural adjustment policies have, indeed, been associated with repression. The deep suffering they cause often sparks popular protests, which in turn frequently lead to government crackdowns.[55] The IMF, World Bank, and USAID contribute to this social unrest by encouraging the governments of developing countries to show "resolve" in pursuing structural adjustment policies and not to relent in the face of public resistance.[56] In practice, resolve often translates into repression.

In sum, structural adjustment mandates are fundamentally unfair. As George Kent puts it,

> the rich got the loans and the poor got the debts.[57]... It is the poor countries that are called upon to do the adjusting because they are weak and vulnerable to the pressures of the more powerful developed countries. The structural adjustment policies of the international lending agencies in effect blame the victims; they do not consider that it might be the structure of the world economy itself that is in need of adjustment.[58]

The paradigm of structural adjustment "holds that the weak must adjust to a system governed by the strong."[59] While millions of poor people in the Third World have suffered and died from the harsh austerity and adjustment measures imposed by the World Bank and IMF, the commercial banks have flourished. Between 1982—when Mexico came close to defaulting on its debt—and the end of 1985, banking profits showed healthy gains, and the nine largest banks increased the dividends they paid stockholders by over a third.[60] Since then they have continued to prosper as they have made new loans, assuring the continuation of the status quo. According to a 1995 report by the Worldwatch Institute, "US banks ... posted a 17 percent increase in developing-country loans over the year ending March 1994 and a 33-percent increase since 1990."[61] David Korten writes in *When Corporations Rule the World*:

> If measured by contributions to improving the lives of people or strengthening the institutions of democratic governance, the World Bank and the IMF have been disastrous failures — imposing an enormous burden on the world's poor and seriously impeding their development. In terms of fulfilling the mandates set for them by their original architects—advancing economic globalization under the domination of the economically powerful—they both have been a resounding success.[62]

The wealth, power, and global reach of many TNCs is now so extensive that they have a strategic influence in determining economic and development policies at both national and international levels, and in steering policies in ways that put corporate profit before the needs of people and the environment. Indirectly they have strong influence on the decisions of the World Bank, IMF, and international trade agreements, and help to push through the conservative growth-at-all-costs global agendas which are exacerbating the crises of our times. Furthermore, some TNCs, through unscrupulous marketing practices, contribute directly to the poor health, malnutrition, and high death rates of Third World children. In the next chapter we look at three industries whose practices increase child mortality from diarrhea.

Healthy Profits in A Dying World:

Three "Killer Industries" and Their Impact on Children's Health And Survival

Two points of view at the World Social Summit March 1995:[63]

The market system unlocks a higher fraction of human potential than any other form of economic organization, and has the demonstrated potential to create broadly distributed new wealth.
    —US Vice President Al Gore

Are we really going to let the world become a global market without any rules other than those of the jungle and with no purpose other than … maximum profit in the minimum time?
    —France's late President Mitterand

Corporate Greed Versus Human Need

> *Wealth, not scarcity, makes people hungry.*
> —Dinyar Godrej, *New Internationalist,*
> May, 1995[64]

Of the 13 million children who die each year, the vast majority live (and die) in conditions of dire poverty. Today, more people live with life-threatening deprivation than ever before.[65] The United Nations Development Program (UNDP) estimates that one quarter of the world's population, or more than 1.3 billion men, women, and children, live in absolute poverty with an income of less than one dollar per day.[66]

Some people blame growing poverty and hunger on the increasing global population (see Chapter 15). But the planet—though stressed—still provides enough food and renewable resources to adequately meet the needs of considerably more than the current population. (In some countries farmers are still subsidized *not* to grow food!) As we will discuss later, it is the high consumption rates in rich countries that contribute most to the depletion of non-renewable resources and the deterioration of the global environment.

The chasm between rich and poor, both within countries and between them, has been widening to record extremes. In its 1993 Human Development Report, the UNDP disclosed that the richest 20% of the world's people own and control 83% of the earth's resources. The poorest 20% own and control less than 1.5 percent of resources. This disparity is rapidly growing: the share held by the richest fifth of humanity rose from 70.2% in 1960 to 82.7% in 1989, and to 84.7% in 1991. So 4 billion people must share the remaining 15% of global income, surviving on an average monthly income of US$70. According to UNDP Administrator J. G. Speth:

> The gap between the rich and the poor has not narrowed over the past 30 years, but has in fact widened greatly. In 1962 the richest 20 percent of the world's population had 30 times the income of the poorest 20 percent. Today the gap has doubled to 60 fold.[67]

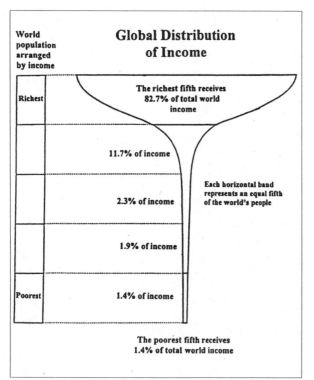

Fig. 3–8 Global distribution of income.

By the same token, today the world's 358 billionaires have a combined net worth of $760 billion—equal to the total assets of the poorest 45 percent of the world's population: about 2.5 billion people.[68] Many of the world's "filthy rich" are owners/proprietors of the world's biggest businesses and transnational corporations (TNCs). As a group, TNCs control 70% of world trade and 80% of all land growing export crops.[69] Yet the TNCs employ only 3% of the world's paid labor.[70] Their huge profits go mainly to a handful of owners. Thus with their emphasis on large-scale industry, nonrenewable energy, and labor-saving technology, TNCs significantly contribute to jobless growth which has increased global unemployment to a crisis level. As David Korten observes: "We are ruled by an oppressive market, not an oppressive state."[71]

The TNCs have enormous power. The clout of these private economic fiefdoms is so great that they threaten the sovereignty of independent governments. They influence international economic and development policies (including health policies) to satisfy their hunger for profits. They do this by sinking millions of dollars into *political action committees* (PACs) and lobbies which can either make or break influential politicians. In addition, they maintain a near-monopoly over the mass media (and thus, public opinion) which assists their ability to structure socioeconomic development in ways which feed their insatiable appetite for profit. Washington journalist William Greider writes in *Who Will Tell the People? The*

Betrayal of American Democracy: "Corporations exist to pursue their own profit maximization, not the collective aspirations of the society. They are commanded by a hierarchy of managers, not the collective aspirations of the society."[72]

This chapter examines three particularly blatant examples of TNCs that have a large and direct causal relationship to child death from diarrhea. These are the infant formula industry, the pharmaceutical industry, and the arms industry.* Although our discussion is limited to these three industries, keep in mind that they are only part of a market-oriented economic order: the so-called *neoliberal* global system, which many critics believe perpetuates global poverty, environmental demise, and poor health. (This is the thesis of the Alternative Copenhagen Declaration at the World Summit on Social Development, held in March, 1995. The Alternative Declaration was signed by over 600 nongovernmental and popular organizations.)**

The three TNCs discussed here are not the only killer industries. A number of other multi-billion dollar, worldwide enterprises manufacture and market products that harm the health of Third World citizens. The list includes the alcoholic beverage industry ($170 billion a year), the tobacco industry ($35 billion a year), the illicit narcotics industry ($100 billion a year), and the pesticide industry ($14 billion a year). All of these adversely impact the world's environment and its people, both directly and indirectly. We have chosen to focus on the infant formula, the drug, and the arms industries because they have such direct bearing on child health and survival. After all, two keys to combating diarrhea (and to the promotion of child health in general) are breastfeeding and avoidance of the unnecessary use of medicines. Both of these lifesaving measures are dangerously sabotaged by these three industries.

Like many of the other killer industries, the infant formula, pharmaceutical, and arms businesses (along with the tobacco industry) have increasingly turned to the Third World as their new and most vulnerable market. The US government and World Bank have stood firmly behind the TNCs by pressuring for free

---

*We lack space to fully chronicle the abuses of even these three industries. We refer readers seeking more information on these or other killer industries to the sources cited in our endnotes, to the suggested reading list at the end of this book, and to David Werner's paper *Health for No One by the Year 2000*, which has an extensive appendix on all of the killer industries mentioned above.

**The Alternative Copenhagen Declaration, March, 1995, is available through the Development Gap, 927 15th Street NW, Washington D.C., 20005, USA.

market and free trade—even when their "rights" to profit have been at the expense of children's health or survival. A number of nongovernmental organizations, more progressive governments, and UN agencies have attempted to limit industry-caused damage to people's health. But these institutions are no match for the industries, which wield enormous power thanks to their colossal wealth and global reach. Although corporate codes of conduct have been introduced, their teeth have been extracted before birth. Big industries can often get away with simply ignoring or riding roughshod over attempts at regulation.[73] Their powerful lobbies have spearheaded the market-friendly (people-and-environment-unfriendly) model of development by establishing a trend of deregulation and by weakening organized labor.

When all else fails, the killer industries know they can always rely on the US government to defend their interests. Corporate executives and Washington officials justify the TNCs' promotion of dangerous substances to the Third World by arguing that it is the responsibility of governments to safeguard their citizens' health. However, this is hypocritical because the companies often choose to export their products to these countries precisely because of their lax regulatory policies. To make things worse, the corporations, the US government, and often the international financial institutions apply relentless pressure on poor nations whenever they do try to crack down on the TNCs. The attempt by Bangladesh to regulate pharmaceuticals is a good example (see page 95).

Unfortunately, the unscrupulous health-damaging corporate actions we describe in these chapters are not isolated abuses committed by a handful of corporate outlaws. They are the norm. The problem is not merely a few unethical individuals (though such individuals certainly exist), but a fundamentally unethical system which leads ordinary, well-intentioned people who are "just doing their jobs" or "acting in the interest of their stockholders" to take unethical actions. Today the composite of such actions jeopardizes not only the health and survival of vast numbers of children, but ultimately the health of the global environment and all of humanity.

The Infant Formula Industry: High Profits and Dying Babies

The United Nations has estimated that health problems associated with bottle feeding result in at least one and a half million infant deaths in underdeveloped countries each year.[74] Similarly, UNICEF states that 1 million children's lives could be saved each year if mothers worldwide would exclusively breastfeed their babies until they are four to six months old.[75]

In the US and other developed countries, many parents are becoming aware that breastfeeding is healthier for their babies than bottle feeding. During the last two decades the number of First World mothers—particularly middle and upper class women—choosing to breastfeed their babies has steadily increased. In both developed and underdeveloped countries, women's activist groups such as the International Baby Food Action Network (IBFAN) and La Leche League (The Milk League) have lobbied for policies that would make it easier for working mothers to breastfeed their babies, including longer maternity leaves, more day care centers, breastfeeding breaks, and areas for breastfeeding in workplaces.

Breast milk is superior to infant formula in several ways. First and foremost, it is the most complete, nutritious food for an infant. As a result, it helps them grow healthy and strong. Breast milk also protects children from infection in two important ways. First, breast milk contains antibacterial substances that help the baby fight off infections until the baby's own immune system is fully functional. Second, breast milk is usually free of infectious agents, whereas substitutes given in a baby bottle are often contaminated the time they reach the baby. This

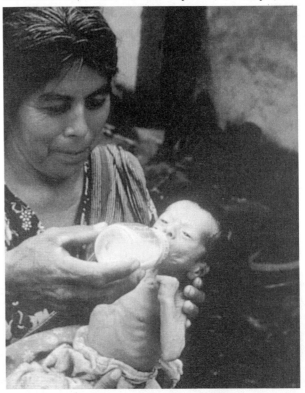

is common in the Third World, where clean water is often not easily accessible and sanitary conditions are poor.[76]

Another major advantage of breast milk over infant formula is that it is free. Infant formula is expensive relative to the incomes of poor people in the Third World. As we have mentioned earlier, the poorest fifth of the world's people earn less than one dollar a day. As a result, many mothers spend money on formula that is desperately needed for food. Because it is so costly, they often over-dilute the formula to make it last longer.[77] The money spent, the diluted drink, and the infections resulting from contamination all make it more likely that their babies will become malnourished. Malnutrition in turn lowers the babies' resistance to diarrhea and other infections. And not only the bottle-fed baby is affected. The drain on family income may adversely affect the nutrition of older siblings and of the mothers themselves. (Conversely, breastfeeding not only protects the baby, but also reduces the mothers' risk of contracting breast and ovarian cancer.[78])

Breastfeeding —
The Best Protection against Death from Diarrhea

Every day, between 3,000 and 4,000 infants die from diarrhoea and acute infections because the ability to feed them adequately has been taken away from their mothers.

—"Take the Baby-Friendly Initiative," UNICEF, 1992[79]

Recently, some big foreign companies came to China and took it as a big market for them to sell their substitutes. This is one of the key factors for the decline of breastfeeding.

—Dr. Wang Feng-Lan, Head of Maternal and Child Health, Ministry of Public Health, Beijing, 1990[80]

There is a wealth of evidence that in poor communities breastfed babies have a substantially better chance of survival than bottle-fed babies. Studies have shown that, holding socio-economic conditions and other factors con-

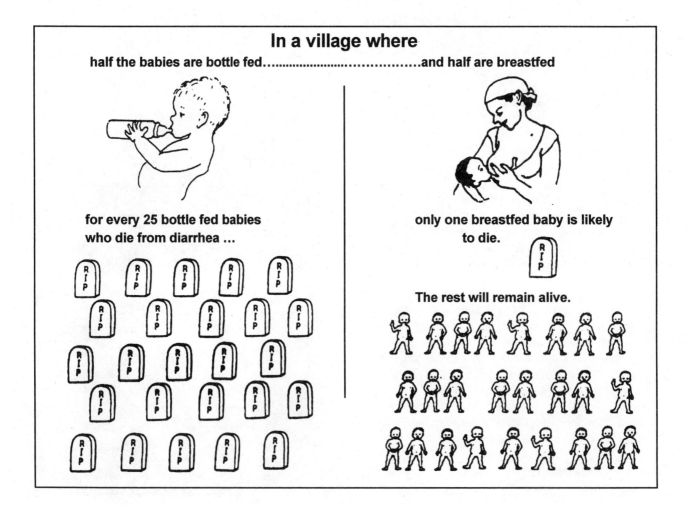

In a village where
half the babies are bottle fed...and half are breastfed

for every 25 bottle fed babies who die from diarrhea ...

only one breastfed baby is likely to die.

The rest will remain alive.

stant, the death rate from infant diarrhea is much lower in breastfed babies than in bottle-fed ones. For example:

- A study in Bangladesh found that mortality from diarrhea was up to 70% lower in the breastfed babies.[81]

- A study in Brazil found that infants who received no breast milk were 14 times more likely to die of diarrhea than those who were given only breast milk.[82]

- A WHO review of published research from various parts of the Third World found that infants who received no breast milk were 25 times more likely to die of diarrhea than those who were exclusively breastfed.[83]

- UNICEF estimates that in communities without clean drinking water, bottle-fed infants are 25 times more likely to die of diarrhea than breastfed ones.[84]

- Studies in the Philippines found that bottle-fed babies are up to 40 times more likely to die of all causes than breastfed ones.[85]

As one author puts it,

> Millions of babies have died from inadequate nutrition where an adequate food supply was no farther than the mother's breast.[86]

Breastfeeding is considered so critical to the health and survival of children that UNICEF included its promotion as one of the four key measures of the Child Survival Revo-

lution. In 1981 the agency launched an international campaign to educate mothers that "breast is best."[87]

However, the infant formula industry has become a huge, profitable business, dominated by TNCs. The leading TNC in this case is Nestle, the largest food company in the world,[88] which controls between 35 and 50% of the world baby milk market. Like several other killer industries, the infant formula business has increasingly targeted the Third World. Its aggressive promotion of bottle-feeding has contributed to a sharp decrease in breastfeeding among Third World women, especially in Latin America and Asia. A 1986 study in five Third World countries found that some 40% of the mothers surveyed used infant formula.[89]

When UNICEF and nongovernmental organizations mounted campaigns to encourage breastfeeding in developing countries, Nestle and other manufacturers of infant formula countered by stepping up their promotional campaigns. They gave medical students and doctors misleading literature and free samples of infant formula, often complete with bottles. They had employees dressed as "milk nurses" make the rounds of hospital maternity wards handing out starter packs of baby bottles and infant formula to new mothers.[90] This unethical practice gives mothers the impression that the medical establishment approves of bottle feeding. Also, providing bottle feeds for the first several days causes the mother's breasts to go dry, leaving them dependent on the commercial substitute. (Mothers can often get back their breast milk by drinking lots of fluids and letting their baby suck at their breasts very frequently, but few mothers know or are taught this.)[91]

SUMMARY OF THE INTERNATIONAL CODE OF MARKETING OF BREAST MILK SUBSTITUTES[92]

1. No advertising of breast milk substitutes to mothers.
2. No free samples to mothers.
3. No promotion of products in health care facilities, including no free supplies.
4. No company "mothercraft" nurses to advise mothers.
5. No gifts or personal samples to health workers.
6. No words or pictures idealizing artificial feeding, including pictures of infants, on the labels of products.
7. Information to health workers should be scientific and factual.
8. All information on artificial infant feeding, including labels, should explain the benefits of breastfeeding, and the costs and hazards associated with artificial feeding.
9. Unsuitable products, such as sweetened condensed milk, should not be promoted for babies.
10. All products should be of a high quality and take account of the climatic and storage conditions of the country where they are used.

Gradually, growing numbers of ordinary citizens in Europe and the US became aware of Nestle's abuses. Outraged, they formed grassroots groups to educate others about the issue and to organize a boycott of Nestle products aimed at *ending unethical promotion of infant formula*. These groups linked up with each other and with Third World groups to mount a massive international campaign, which spearheaded the Nestle boycott. This campaign was coordinated by the International Baby Food Action Network (IBFAN) which is comprised of some 100 groups in 65 countries.[93]

Largely in response to this campaign, UNICEF and WHO developed a nonbinding "International Code of Marketing of Breast Milk Substitutes" to put an end to these abuses. When the World Health Assembly voted on the Code in May, 1981 it was approved by 118 countries. Only the United States voted against it because of concern "that the Code might have a detrimental effect on US business."[94]

However, continued vigilance has been necessary to keep Nestle and other baby food companies in line. In 1988 the watchdog group, Action for Corporate Accountability, charged that the Nestle Corporation and American Home Products were still violating and undermining the code in many countries. Nestle was accused of promoting its infant formula in Third World health facilities and pharmacies through "posters, advertisements, free and low cost supplies, bribes, competitions, and sales representatives."[95] Nestle has also subverted the code by pressuring Third World governments not to enforce it stringently, reportedly convincing them that the baby food industry can be trusted to regulate itself.[96]

Action for Corporate Accountability has responded to these bad faith actions by reviving the boycott.[97] The goal of the new boycott, which has spread to fourteen countries, is to force Nestle to stop promoting bottle feeding altogether.[98] But Nestle is showing no signs of changing its ways. In August, 1994 IBFAN released its *Breaking the Rules* report, chronicling the marketing activities of 74 infant formula companies in 62 countries.

Nestle was responsible for about 30% of complaints (twice as many as any other company). The report details how Nestle has continued to systematically violate the Code in more than 40 countries.[99] In response, Nestle defiantly published a brochure entitled *Marketing of Baby Milk* which stated that "In 1994, Nestle investigated 455 allegations made against them. Three required corrective action."[100] The pictures of fat, healthy babies on Nestle's infant milk products are still powerful product advertisements that reach even illiterate village mothers.

In the Third World, bottle feeding has taken deep root and in many countries is becoming more prevalent. The number of infants who die as a result is steadily increasing. Some estimates place the number of bottle feeding related deaths at 1½ million per year—up 50% from estimates just a few years ago.[101] If this trend is to be reversed, watchdog groups such as IBFAN must keep up vigilance and pressure on the baby food multinationals. A massive education campaign is needed in the Third World to raise awareness of the importance of breastfeeding and of how TNCs—often aided and abetted by big government—use every trick they can to increase their profits, regardless of the human suffering they cause.

A cartoon from "Pan," a paper produced during the Rome World Food Conference, illustrates the pressure of Western advertising.

The Pharmaceutical Industry:
Unscrupulous Promotion of Useless and Dangerous Drugs

Global pharmaceutical sales have been skyrocketing in recent years, from $22 billion in 1980 to $195 billion by 1991, and reaching $259 billion in 1994 (the latest year for which figures are available).[102] With an average annual profit of 18% since 1958, and estimated excess annual profits of $2 billion in 1991,[103] the pharmaceutical industry is the third most lucrative business in the United States. The drug companies have a powerful lobby with which to buy the support of politicians. The US government helps to guarantee their high rate of return by giving drug companies substantial tax benefits and subsidies for research (the priorities of which, as we will see, are

skewed). It also gives 22–year patent protection that assures the companies monopoly control and almost unrestricted pricing rights over new products. Profits of the drug companies rose sharply under the Reagan and Bush Administrations, which relaxed regulations on them, especially for exports overseas.

Like the infant formula industry, the tobacco industry, and many other killer industries, the pharmaceutical industry has targeted the Third World as a prime market because of its lax regulations and paucity of product information. In the case of the drug industry, a further factor that makes developing countries attractive is their abundance of pressing health problems, which creates an enormous demand for medicines.

Many Third World countries import or produce domestically 15,000 to 20,000 pharmaceutical products. These nations often spend up to half of their health budgets on these drugs.[104] Yet most of these medicines are unnecessary. Out of some 270,000 pharmaceutical products on the global market, WHO has compiled a list of about 270 essential drugs that are needed for the management of virtually all human ailments.[105] Most experts agree. Health Action International (HAI), a Netherlands-based watchdog group that monitors the abuses of drug companies, estimates that 70% of the medicines the drug companies sell to the Third World are nonessential. If underdeveloped countries were to stop buying these unnecessary drugs, they could cut their spending on medicines by over half, freeing more than $7 billion that could be used to purchase essential drugs and fund preventive measures and Primary Health Care.[106]

Some pharmaceuticals sold to Third World countries are unnecessary because they duplicate other medicines already available. But many others are completely ineffective or harmful. Antidiarrheal drugs are a prime example. As we saw in Chapter 8 (see page 55), WHO has stated that these drugs have no legitimate role in the treatment of diarrhea.[107] Yet the drug companies continue to aggressively promote and market them, and sales of these products are increasing sharply.[108] In Kenya, for example, the most widely used medicine for diarrhea is ADM, a kaolin-pectin mixture whose use the American Medical Association calls "unwarranted" and which, according to a British drug guide, has "no part to play in the treatment of infantile gastroenteritis."[109]

Even worse, many of the medicines the drug companies market in the Third World are dangerous. For example, during the 1980s a local subsidiary of Janssen Pharmaceuticals marketed the antidiarrheal Imodium in Pakistan despite a 1980 WHO warning that the medicine should not be used because it can paralyze a child's intestines. In 1989–1990, the drug was responsible for the death of several Pakistani infants. The subsidiary continued to sell the product for six months after the first deaths occurred. Only after British television ran a graphic exposé on the affair did the company agree to withdraw Imodium from the market, still refusing to acknowledge that the drug was unsafe.[110]

The drug companies treat poor countries as a dumping ground for pharmaceuticals that are banned or restricted in the parent countries because they can cause serious side effects.

For example:

- Winthrop and Carter-Wallace Inc. continued to market the painkiller Conmel (the brand name for dipyrone) in Mexico and other Third World countries through overseas subsidiaries fourteen years after the US Food and Drug Administration (FDA) banned its domestic use because it was linked to a fatal blood disorder.[111] Neither company informed Third World consumers of this ban, and Carter-Wallace didn't even include warnings of this potential side effect.[112]

- After the FDA severely restricted Upjohn's antibiotic Lincocin for being less safe and effective than cheaper equivalents, the company began promoting the drug heavily in Latin America. It was so successful in this regard that by 1978 Lincocin had become the second best-selling drug in Mexico,[113] where village stores sold it for coughs, colds, and diarrhea.

High cost of medicine can be deadly

In marketing their products in the Third World, drug companies often downplay or completely fail to mention their side effects while overstating their benefits.[114] Perhaps the most dangerous side effect of the medicines the drug companies market in the Third World has to do with their cost. As Virginia Beardshaw of HAI notes, poor Third World families "will mortgage their land, sell their cattle and sell their seed to buy medicines which they mistakenly think will save their children."[115] This leads them to spend on unnecessary medicines money sorely needed to buy food for their children.[116] As in the case of infant formula (and ORS packets) this misguided expenditure may contribute to greater child malnutrition, which lowers children's resistance to disease. As mentioned in Chapter 8, Third World families spend over $1 billion per year on useless and often harmful medicines for diarrhea.

The economic burden that medicines impose on poor people in the Third World is increased by the fact that they are often overpriced there.[117] For widely used drugs such as Tetracycline, drug companies sometimes charge three to four times as much in Third World countries as they do in First World Countries.[118]

Because of these excessive prices and the fact that poor people get sick more often than wealthier ones, poor families often spend a substantial share of their budgets on medicine. The Makapawa community-based health program, located on the outskirts of Tacloban City in the Philippines, offers an example both of the economic burden that medicines often impose on poor families, and of how people can work together to lighten this burden. The health workers there found that the money local poor families were spending on costly medicines instead of on food contributed to the undernutrition (and high death rate) of their children. When families began to cooperatively prepare their own herbal medicines for common ailments—including a sweetened herbal drink for diarrhea—they spent less on pharmaceuticals and had more money left to buy food. With more to eat, their children gained weight, and became sick and died less often. The community health workers proudly showed one of the authors (David Werner) records demonstrating this.[119]

Like the manufacturers of infant formula, the drug companies bombard the Third World with well-funded, slick, and often dishonest advertising campaigns. For example, in Bangladesh, detail men (drug company salesmen) outnumber doctors seven to one (as compared to three to one in the US).[120] Joel Lexchin relates a story of a Hoechst detailer in that country trying to persuade a doctor that Lasix (furosemide, a diuretic) was a good drug to use for children who had kwashiorkor (swelling from severe malnutrition). "When it was pointed out to the detailer that the swelling might go down if Lasix was used but the child would be killed, the detailer responded 'Well, the child is going to die anyway.'"[121] Equally shocking, the Merck company's 1980 Bangladesh marketing plan called for two of its products to be promoted to "fresh graduates and potential quacks."[122]

In 1991 the pharmaceutical industry spent $10 billion on advertising and promotion, as compared to $8 billion on research and development.[123] It's also worth noting that little of the money the drug companies *do* earmark for research is invested in developing medicines for the diseases of poverty. Instead, the bulk of this money is spent on finding cures for the diseases of the First World and Third World elites, and on turning out "me-too" drugs which offer no therapeutic advantage over products already on the market.[124] In their zeal to push their products, many drug companies often go so far as to offer Third World health officials bribes to buy large quantities of medicines that are unnecessary, overpriced, or banned in their parent countries.[125] Despite being repeatedly found out and penalized, many companies continue this practice.

The drug companies are not the only culprits. Third World pharmacists also contribute to the problem of unnecessary, dangerous, and overpriced medicines. As UNICEF notes, "private pharmacists and unqualified druggists have taken over the role of primary providers of health care in many regions."[126]

These pharmacists—along with shop keepers and street vendors who play the role of pharmacists in thousands of Third World villages—often have a strong incentive (the profit motive) to prescribe drugs whether or not they are appropriate. In areas where UNICEF's Bamako Initiative or similar cost-recovery schemes are being implemented, health workers—who rely on the sale of medicines to cover their costs and pay their salaries—also have an incentive to over-prescribe.

The result is a plague of over-prescription and overuse of medications which has reached epidemic proportions. The economic burden this "pharmaceuticalization of health care" places on already impoverished families is staggering. Privatization and user-financing schemes which shift the burden of costs from under-funded health ministries to poor families only compound the problem.

Taking all this into account, it can be safely argued that the Third World's over-reliance on commercial medicines for treating common childhood illnesses—especially diarrhea—contributes significantly to high child mortality.

Transnationals' and the World Bank's attack on essential drug policies

Some Third World countries that have adopted essential drug policies in keeping with WHO guidelines have sought to regulate the pharmaceutical companies themselves. In the early 1980s, one of the world's poorest countries, Bangladesh, took a daring step when it prohibited the import of a long list of nonessential drugs. The multinational drug companies were furious. They did everything in their power to pressure the Bangladesh Health Ministry into abandoning the policy. The companies even refused to sell essential medicines to the country, thus jeopardizing

millions of lives. Predictably, the US government threw its weight behind the pharmaceutical industry, threatening to cut off foreign aid to Bangladesh if it did not rescind its health-protecting laws.[127]

Thanks in part to the support of Sweden and several other progressive European countries, Bangladesh managed to stand its ground until it could step up its domestic production of essential drugs. One crucial step in this process was the creation of the Gonoshasthaya People's Pharmaceutical Company. This nongovernmental, nonprofit factory produces several essential drugs at prices 33 to 60 percent less than those of the multinationals. Committed to empowering and improving the economic situation of the least privileged members of society, Gonoshasthaya trains and employs mainly poor single mothers.[128]

But recently Bangladesh's National Drug Policy has come under renewed attack, this time by the World Bank. The Bank's *structural adjustment policies* have already forced Bangladesh to cut spending on health care, education, and food subsidies for the poor. And recently the Bank has been putting pressure on Bangladesh to make "detailed changes" in its National Drug Policy to bring it closer into line with a "free market" approach. The Bank insists that the current global orientation toward "free market" and "free trade" make it imperative that the country permit the multinational drug companies unrestricted markets in their country. Unfortunately the Bangladesh Medical Association—which has strenuously opposed the essential drug policy—has from the start sided with the World Bank. Bangladesh's new government also took steps to dismantle the national drug policy.

Similar stories can be told for many other countries. When Sri Lanka introduced a policy similar to that of Bangladesh, the American Pharmaceutical Manufacturers Association again responded by halting drug sales to the offending country. Sri Lanka ultimately gave in and watered down the policy.

Health rights activists have often criticized WHO, UNICEF, and other UN agencies for not taking a stronger stand against the economic policies and development strategies that permit TNCs to profit at the expense of poor nations and disadvantaged people. But, to a large extent, the hands of these agencies are tied. It is very hard, for instance, for WHO to take steps to regulate the unethical conduct of the multinational drug companies. The pharmaceutical industry, like the other killer industries, can count on the support of the same First World governments that provide most of WHO's funding to make sure WHO toes the line. The US government, which provides about 25% of the WHO's budget is a consistent champion of big business. The US has threatened on several occasions to stop funding WHO if it becomes "too political"[129]—that is, if it defends the interests of the poor when they conflict with big business. Such pressure helps explain why WHO has yet to follow through on its essential drug list by drawing up a code regulating drug marketing practices.

These pressure tactics were blatantly illustrated at a November 1985 closed-door meeting in Nairobi, Kenya organized by WHO. The issue being discussed was whether the pharmaceutical industry should have the right to promote and distribute its products in the free of regulation Third World. The interests of the industry were defended by Roger Brooks* of the Heritage Foundation, an ultra–right-wing, pro-business lobbying organization with close ties to the Reagan Administration.[130] Brooks slipped a propaganda piece into the folders handed out to conference participants.[131] In this polemic, Brooks charged that the consumer activist groups advocating a marketing code were really advancing a hidden agenda of "redistributing the world's wealth by fiat."[132]

After (then) WHO Director General Halfdan Mahler threatened to have him arrested, Brooks apologized for his action. However, the powerful forces that Brooks represented apparently succeeded in intimidating WHO. Under pressure from drug company delegates attending the conference, Mahler abruptly moved to cancel a scheduled premiere of *The Pill Jungle,* a film about pharmaceutical industry abuses that WHO had cosponsored with Radio Nederland TV.[133] Mahler also prevailed on the Kenyan government to cancel a scheduled airing of the film on local television. At the Kenya conference, WHO was frustrated once again in its efforts to formulate an effective marketing code.[134]

At the World Health Assembly in 1986, when the question of codes came up, the United States delegate stated that "it has been our strong position that the WHO should not be involved in efforts to regulate the commercial practices of private industry."[135] In 1986 and 1987 the US withheld its contribution to the WHO budget, allegedly because it disapproved of WHO's policies on breast milk substitutes and essential drugs.[136]

---

*Two years later Brooks, who was the head of the Foundation's UN Assessment Project, was appointed to a US State Department position in the policy planning branch of the Assistant Secretary for International Organizations, where he was responsible for "help[ing] formulate overall US policy towards the UN."

Today the prospects for a strong code appear even less promising. In 1988 WHO's Director-General Mahler—who at least was committed to such a code, was replaced by Hiroshi Nakajima, who was expected to be more amenable to the viewpoints of the US, Japan, and the drug industry. One of Nakajima's first actions was to replace the head of the Action Programme on Essential Drugs, Dr. Lauridsen—who had courageously fought for an Essential Drug Code—with more conservative personnel. In light of the constraints on WHO's action and the negative role played by the US government, many observers agree with author Jacqueline Orr that:

> Currently, consumer critics, international public interest organizations, and grassroots activists offer the greatest hope for protection of people's health against the [pharmaceutical] industry's aggressive pursuit of healthy profits.[137]

It is encouraging, however, that in the early 1990s—in part, perhaps, in response to encouragement and pressure from below—WHO seemed to be taking a somewhat stronger position. In 1990 it published an important document titled, *The Rational Use of Drugs in the Treatment of Acute Diarrhoea in Children.*[138]

Ciba-Geigy's dark history with drugs for diarrhea—and its friendship with WHO

Ciba-Geigy, one of the world's largest pharmaceutical companies, has a long history of promoting unsafe and/or ineffective products and covering up their sometimes deadly side effects. For more than 50 years, the company marketed an ineffective and dangerous antidiarrheal drug, *clioquinol.* Long one of the best-selling diarrhea medicines worldwide, clioquinol reportedly "contributed to [Ciba's] development into one of the world's largest transnational pharmaceutical companies."[139]

From early on, there was evidence that clioquinol was both ineffective and unsafe. Yet as the evidence mounted, for decades, Ciba-Geigy stubbornly refused to withdraw the drug from the world market.[140] The following account is taken from *Inside Ciba-Geigy*, by Olle Hansson, a Swedish neurologist and pediatrician who fought for 25 years to force the company to stop selling this dangerous drug.[141]

The first reports of serious neurological damage caused by clioquinol were published in 1935, a year after the drug had been introduced under the brand name of Entero-vioform.[142] At that time Ciba promised to warn physicians of its dangers, but failed to do so.[143] Even as increasing reports of paralysis and blindness secondary to use of clioquinol began to pour in, Ciba-Geigy repeatedly dismissed them and assured doctors and users of the drug's safety.[144]

Finally, in 1970, events reached a crisis point. In Japan, researchers concluded that a mysterious disease called SMON (sub-acute myelo-optic neuropathy) was caused by clioquinol.[145] This disease had caused nerve damage and often blindness and paralysis in at least 11,000 persons starting in 1955,[146] Ciba-Geigy was taken to court, and—after fighting the charges every step of the way—was forced to pay some $776 million in damages to the victims.[147] Japan banned clioquinol in 1970.[148] In 1972 Ciba-Geigy removed it from the US market for "economic reasons."

However, Ciba-Geigy continued to market clioquinol in many countries.[149] Not until 1985 did the company finally stop producing and selling the drug.[150] (Even though Ciba-Geigy is no longer directly involved, clioquinol continues to be marketed in the Third World to this day. A 1990 survey by Health Action International found that 13% of the antidiarrheal medicines being marketed in eleven Latin American countries contained the drug.)[151]

In recent years Ciba-Geigy has tried hard to clean up its image. But with its track record involving 50 years of unethical marketing of a medicine for diarrhea, one might think WHO would be cautious in accepting this giant drug company as a major sponsor of its diarrhea control efforts. Yet for a decade Ciba-Geigy made generous donations to WHO's Programme for the Control of Diarrhoeal Diseases (PCDD), and from 1986 through 1989 increased its donations to more than one million dollars per year.[152] Ciba-Geigy contributed US$2,650,970 to the PCDD in the biennium 1988–1989, over 12% of its budget.[153]

It is hard to say what influence—if any—Ciba-Geigy's donations to the PCDD have had on WHO's continued heavy promotion of glucose-based ORS packets. A highly respected leader in ORT research—who prefers to remain anonymous—has commented in a letter to us that, "I think it will be hard to prove through any paper documents that WHO/PCDD has been directly influenced by the industries that package and process oral hydration solutions. As increasing amounts of their budget [came] from that source, however, we would expect that their policy would reflect this." Ciba-Geigy discontinued its contributions to WHO after 1989.

WHO's Relationship with Galactina S.A.

Ciba-Geigy is not the only big corporation that has had close ties to WHO's PCDD. Another is Galactina S.A., a multinational baby-food corporation which toward the end of the 1980s was collaborating with WHO to develop *commercial packets of cereal-based ORS*.

To many of us concerned with health policy, the revelation of this collaboration came as a shock. For many years WHO's PCDD has consistently declined to recommend wide use of any form of food-based ORT (except as non-specific "home fluids"). In conferences it has repeatedly down-played research documenting the effectiveness of CB-ORT, consistently calling for "more research." So adamant has been WHO's public skepticism toward food-based ORT that it refused to attend an *ad hoc* meeting on the subject at the Third International Conference on Oral Rehydration Therapy. Similarly, WHO was reluctant to participate officially in the International Symposium on Food-Based Oral Rehydration Therapy, a meeting organized by the International Child Health Foundation in collaboration with Aga Khan University that was held in Karachi, Pakistan in November 1989.

However, a WHO staff person did unofficially attend the Karachi Symposium accompanied by representatives from Galactina S.A. To nearly everyone's surprise a collaborative venture between WHO and Galactina was announced.[154] A film was shown that portrayed a new Galactina factory already beginning commercial production of cereal-based ORS packets (using rice powder as the main ingredient). Some conference participants expressed outrage at this liaison between WHO and Galactina S.A. However, PCDD staff have subsequently explained that WHO, although it has never fully endorsed cereal-based ORS, has long been involved in researching its possibilities. For this and similar research—often not possible within the restrictions of its budget—the PCDD has collaborated with pharmaceutical, food, and other corporations. (It is worth noting that corporations producing foods and/or baby-foods have financed most of the studies done on cereal-based ORS.)[155]

Ciba-Geigy and Galactina S.A. are not the only multinationals that want to get in on the ground floor of commercial ORS products. The listed sponsors of the Karachi food-based ORT symposium included Nestle and Gerber (baby foods).[156] In fact, many of the big pharmaceutical and baby food corporations had representatives at the symposium, as did Intermed (a non-profit charitable organization, sponsored by a collection of the big drug companies, which provides free health education materials and cut-rate medicines to Third World health programs). Nestle had two representatives present, one of whom claimed to work simultaneously for WHO.[157]

It is hard to know how much of the donations and charitable work of corporations such as Nestle and Ciba-Geigy reflect an effort to whitewash their tarnished image, and how much is aimed at winning favors or contracts from agencies and programs in the health field. Both the pharmaceutical and infant food industries have come under heavy criticism for their long history of influence-buying of politicians and of wooing health professionals through free samples, special conferences, scholarships, research grants, free literature, and a wide range of gra-

tuities.[158] The recent plethora of alliances between multinational corporations and international health and development agencies merits close scrutiny.

It should be noted that, despite its relationship with Galactina, WHO's courtship with cereal-based ORS appears to have been short-lived. At a meeting in Dhaka, Bangladesh in December, 1994, WHO concluded that there is no advantage to rice-based ORS, and so standard (glucose-based) ORS should be used as the preferred option. Nevertheless, in many countries several CB-ORS products, such as Rice-Lyte, are now on the market.

Arms And Military Equipment — a $750 Billion-a-year Industry

One of the reasons most often cited for poor health is lack of sufficient funds for basic health services. However, this seems like a poor excuse in a world that spends over $750 billion each year on the military.[159] Since World War II, the world has spent $30 –35 trillion on arms.[160] It is ironic that money desperately needed to provide services to children, women, and men is spent instead to deploy weapons and soldiers which either deprive those very people of their lives and health, or are so dangerous that they dare not be used. UNICEF estimates that during the last decade, child victims of war include 2 million killed, 4–5 million disabled, 12 million left homeless, more than 1 million orphaned or separated from their parents, and some 10 million psychologically traumatized.[161]

The aims of the arms industry are antithetical to good health. The wares it produces and promotes are nightmares of death and destruction, designed specifically to kill and maim. In addition to the direct physical violence that weapons inflict on their victims, the industry itself inflicts economic violence by diverting enormous sums of money and other resources from health and other social programs. The arms industry cynically promotes fear, distrust and conflict through suggestive advertising and by actively lobbying governments around the world to purchase their products.

Nowhere has the arms industry been more successful than in the United States, which spends over $250 billion annually on arms.[162] The military industry is one of the biggest, most profitable, and politically most powerful in the country. Although ten giant military contractors account for one third of all US weapons contracts, about 35,000 businesses receive Department of Defense contracts and about 150,000 subcontract for

these firms. The top military contractors—IBM, General Motors, Ford, Boeing, Lockheed, Rockwell, and General Electric— represent the backbone of American Industry.

In September 1987, the United Nations called a meeting of member states to discuss the theme of Disarmament and Development. The US was the only nation that refused to attend the conference—which it boycotted, claiming that disarmament and development are unrelated issues, and that the Soviet Bloc had instigated the conference to attack US policy.[163] Even today, with the Cold War over, US arms merchants, acting with the support of the Clinton Administration, continue to peddle their lethal wares abroad. (It should be noted that while the United States has historically been the chief exporter of death, France surpassed the US in arms exports in 1994 with $11.4 billion in sales.[164])

People in underdeveloped countries suffer greatly, directly and indirectly, from high military expenditures. Since 1960, Third World countries have increased their military spending over twice as fast as their living standards.[165] From 1972 to 1982, while developing countries' spending on health and education fell, their military expenditures soared from $7 billion to over $100 billion.[166] By 1986 the 43 countries with the highest infant mortality rates spent three times as much on defense as on health.[167] In that same year, the industrialized nations spent over twenty times as much on the military as on development assistance.[168] By 1988, military spending in the developing countries totaled $145 billion—an annual expenditure that would be sufficient to end absolute poverty around the globe within the next ten years, allowing people throughout the world to satisfy their own and their children's needs for food, clean water, health care, and education.[169] Former Costa Rican president Oscar Arias Sanchez, whose own country disbanded its armed forces in 1948 (and has ever since been realizing a peace dividend that he estimates came to $100 million for the year 1987), contends that in squandering such vast sums on the military these governments are guilty of "an act of aggression against the well-being of their peoples."[170]

And, as George Kent points out,

> The linkage between hunger [and poverty] and military expenditures is not simply in the budgetary allocations; it is also in the ways in which armed forces are used to sustain repressive regimes. More hunger and more children's deaths result from the structural violence of repression than from the direct violence of warfare.[171]

Ruth Leger Sivard has categorized third world countries for their repressiveness in terms of whether there is *no, some,* or *frequent* official violence against citizens. If we check these data against the infant mortality rates, we find that those countries which impose *no* official violence against citizens have an average infant mortality rate of 54, while those which impose *some* or *frequent* violence have average infant mortality rates of about 90.[172]

Defense budgets protect the interest of the powerful through the ways in which the arms are used, and also by the ways in which the money spent rewards political allies of the powerful. To some extent defense budgets constitute a form of welfare for the rich.

Governments suggest that defense establishments serve all of their people's interests, but defense serves mainly the rich, not the poor. Poor people are still trying to get, while the rich want to protect what they already have . . . [Poor people] don't have a stake in the status quo in the way the rich and powerful do. No wonder poor people are far more concerned with development than with defense. If the poor were the ones who allocated the world's resources, we could be sure that far less would be spent on defense and far more on child survival.[173]

Kent clarifies that the most important way militarization contributes to low levels of child health in the Third World is by perpetuating the institutionalized inequity which is the ultimate root cause of poor people's health problems. He notes that

> Grossly undemocratic societies are characterized by gross inequalities. They are inherently unstable unless they are held together by force and intimidation. Thus repression requires militarization. It would be a mistake to think that

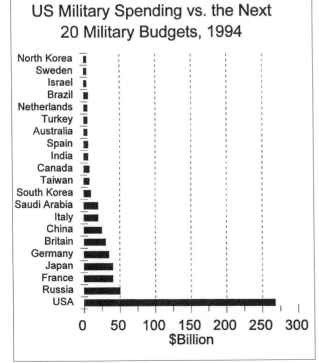

Fig. 3–9

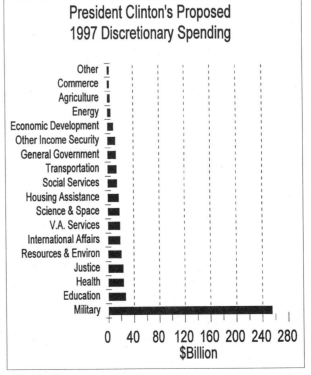

Fig. 3–10

ending active warfare would in itself lead to great gains in child survival. Structural violence must be ended as well.[174]

Thus in order to realize the goal of "health for all," we must not only demand an end to militarization, but also work to correct the inequitable distribution of wealth and power that it is designed to sustain. As Kent puts it,

> We should be concerned not only with negative peace, understood as the absence of warfare, but also with positive peace, understood as the presence of justice.[175]

Faced with huge foreign debts, many poor countries have been forced by the International Monetary Fund (IMF) to severely cut their budgets for health and education. Yet military budgets of Third World governments are today on average seven times higher than they were in 1960.[176] Curiously the IMF almost never requires that a developing nation reduce its military budget (see page 85).[177]

Like the pharmaceutical, infant formula, and tobacco industries, the arms industry has come to consider the Third World its most promising, fastest-growing market and is actively promoting its products there. Often this process is expedited by US foreign military aid. Arms sales under US government auspices during the 1970s were almost $100 billion, eight times greater than in the previous two decades combined.[178] During the 1980s, military aid became the largest category of US foreign aid.[179] And a disproportionate amount of US military aid has gone and continues to go to repressive governments with poor human rights records.[180] Examples include El Salvador, Honduras, Guatemala, Colombia, Peru, Israel, Egypt, Saudi Arabia, Pakistan, South Korea, the Philippines, Thailand, Taiwan, and Turkey. As part of its relentless drive to destabilize progressive governments and movements through the strategy of "low-intensity conflict," Washington also has supplied covert military assistance and training to a number of paramilitary groups which routinely commit human rights violations against civilians, including the Contras in Nicaragua, the death squads in El Salvador, Guatemala, and elsewhere in Latin America, UNITA in Angola, RENAMO in Mozambique, and the Khmer Rouge in Cambodia.

Massive supplies of arms from northern countries, armed violence, and militarization are increasing in the Third World. Not surprisingly, this increased violence is having an escalating impact on health. According to the Stockholm International Peace Research Institute, the number of major wars—those that kill at least 1,000 people—rose to 34 in 1993, after having dropped from 36 in 1987 to 30

in 1991.[181] Moreover, due to technological advances and changes in strategy, warfare has taken an increasing toll on the civilian population as this century has progressed. Whereas there were only a few noncombatant casualties in the First World War, civilians made up half the killed and wounded in the Second World War, and they account for 80%–90% of those killed, maimed, or traumatized in today's conflicts.[182] At least three times as many people are injured as are killed. Many more die or suffer as a result of secondary, indirect effects that make themselves felt after the fact.

One frightening trend in warfare is an increasing tendency to conscript children for active military duty, essentially using them as cannon fodder. One author reports that

> Thousands of children are currently bearing arms in at least 20 ongoing conflicts. Even children as young as nine years old are used as frontline combatants in unwinnable battles, as decoys to lure opposing forces into ambush and as human mine detectors to explode bombs in front of advancing adult troops.[183]

Those children who survive such ordeals often emerge physically and psychologically scarred.[184]

Rehabilitation International found that the war in Afghanistan has resulted in 100,000 disabled children, and that conflicts in Mozambique and Angola are responsible for 50,000 and 20,000 amputees, respectively, many of them civilians.[185] Many of the injuries in Afghanistan and Angola have been inflicted by land mines; fifteen million mines have been sown throughout the former country and hundreds of thousands in the latter.[186] They will continue to disable civilians long after the wars in these nations are officially over. Globally, land mines are responsible for killing or maiming more than 20,000 persons each year, many of them children.[187] Yet mines are still being laid 25 times faster than they are being removed, with up to 2 million new mines being planted each year.[188] Resisting international pressure to ban the use of mines, the United States and other countries insist that they need these indiscriminate killers.[189]

Another example of the impact of the arms industry is the effect of the Gulf War on Iraqi civilians. As devastating as the pounding that Iraq withstood was, it pales in contrast to the economic pummeling of Iraq's population in the years since. Iraq's infant mortality rate increased by some 330% in 1991, and its under–5 mortality rate rose 380%, from 27.8 to 104.4 deaths per thousand live births.[190] William M. Arkin, a former Army intelligence officer who works with Greenpeace International, estimates that 70,000–90,000 Iraqi civilians had died as of December 1991 as a result of conditions caused by the war.[191]

Even so, one could scarcely have guessed that by 1995, a study in Baghdad by the United Nations Food and Agriculture Organization (FAO) would reveal that severe malnutrition in 1 to 5-year-old children is rampant, with 28% stunting, 29% underweight, and 12% wasting as a result of food shortages due to prolonged sanctions. From 1990 to 1995 the mortality rate for children under five increased six times over pre-war levels. This can be regarded as the result of two major detrimental factors: malnutrition of mothers and children, and the widespread prevalence of infectious diseases, especially diarrhea, interacting with each other. According to conservative estimates, more than 1 million people, most of them children, have died in Iraq because of the sanctions. Today, 4 million people, half of them children, are starving to death in Iraq.[192] The US government's own Census Bureau reported that the war had reduced the life expectancy for Iraqi men from 66 to 46 years and the life expectancy for Iraqi women from 68 years to 57 years.[193]

Former attorney general Ramsey Clark calls the blockade

a crime against humanity … a weapon of mass destruction [that] attacks infants and children, the chronically ill, the elderly and emergency medical cases. Like the neutron bomb it takes lives, it kills people, but it protects property, it doesn't destroy property. So when you look at the effect of what we generally call the sanctions on Iraq, you see hundreds of thousands of deaths caused by those sanctions, far more than all the deaths caused by the military assault by the US, which included 110,000 aerial strikes in 42 days; one every 30 seconds night and day that dropped 88,500 tons of bombs, the equivalent of seven and a half Hiroshima bombs. But the sanctions have killed more than four times the number of people than the bombings killed.[194]

The United States' overpowering military might—largely the result of an overzealous arms industry promoting their products in a free market—seems to have engendered audacious cruelty on the part of its leadership while intimidating the rest of the world's leaders into a conspiracy of silence. How else can one explain carnage on this scale?

Conclusion to Chapter 12

This chapter has provided a glimpse into the ways in which interests and actions of three transnational industries can conflict with public interest and compromise the health and survival of children. Corporate power has grown to planetary proportions, too often placing aspirations of private profit before the common good. The powerful lobbies have spurred the free market paradigm of global development, with its trend to deregulate international trade and to champion unbridled pursuit of inequitable economic growth. As the triumvirate of big government, big business, and the international financial institutions (IMF and World Bank) increasingly find ways to maneuver the United Nations and other international agencies, the needs and wishes of common people are side-lined. It is now up to nongovernmental organizations, activists, watchdog groups, consumers unions, and grassroots movements to try to make the corporate world—and big government—more accountable.

Fortunately, around the world, watchdog and consumer organizations are helping to monitor and rein in the abuses of big industry. Actions and boycotts organized by IBFAN, La Leche League, and other networks have raised public awareness and put pressure on Nestle and other breast milk substitute producers to conform more closely to the Code of Conduct. Likewise, Health Action International (HAI)—with all its national and regional affiliates such as the Buko Pharma Campaign in Europe, Public Citizen in the US, and HAIN in the Philippines—has helped reduce the transgressions of the giant drug companies. But it is an up-hill battle. And the arms industry is thriving. In the present conservative world climate, new and more united grassroots efforts are needed to prevent backsliding.

Clearly, any serious attempt to enhance child survival and well-being must address the abuses committed by these unscrupulous businesses and by the other killer industries. But we must remember that beneath the health-damaging activities of transnational corporations lies an entire global economic system and power structure, of which the TNCs are only one part. In the last two decades the international financial institutions, whose lending policies and guidelines for economic development closely adhere to the interests of the corporate world, have gained overarching global power and influence. In the next chapter we will see how the World Bank has, to a large extent, taken over the role of the World Health Organization in health policy planning for the Third World, and how this has further weakened and distorted the implementation of comprehensive primary health care.

Turning Health Into an Investment:

The World Bank's Death Blow to Alma Ata

The World Bank's social reform efforts are an attempt to legalize, normalize, and even naturalize the fiscal neglect of the health sector.
—Dr. Javier Iguiñez, economist from the Instituto Bartolomé de las Casas, Peru

The "adverse economic climate" of the 1980s was accompanied by a conservative shift in domestic and foreign policies of the most powerful industrial countries, especially the United States and Great Britain. The new policies—dubbed *neoliberal* because they liberalized or freed major markets from government regulation—systematically put the growth of national economies before the basic needs and rights of the poor. Programs assisting poor people were cut back or dismantled, both in the North and the South.

One particularly insidious way in which the conservative policies of the 1980s undercut such programs was by introducing more vertical health and development strategies. Instead of promoting equity and social change, these top-down strategies tended to reinforce and legitimize the inequities of the status quo. To promote development of poor countries and communities, the empowering methodologies that had surfaced in the 1960s and 1970s were systematically replaced by strategies that—if not by design, certainly in effect—were disempowering. Although the rhetoric of participation and empowerment proliferated, in policy implementation emphasis shifted from encouraging the strong participation of decision-making control to the weak participation of compliance. At the same time, in high-level development planning there was a shift from social to technological interventions, from cooperatives to private enterprise, from process to product, from problem-posing learning to pre-charted training techniques, from critical analysis to social marketing, and—in health care goals—from a comprehensive vision of "health for all" to raising survival rates.

This conservative restructuring of development policy has permeated almost all aspects of foreign relations, but especially foreign aid. During the early 1980s the strategies and objectives of nearly every US government-run or government-sponsored charitable organization were redefined to favor the private sector. For example, the Peace Corps, which for years had focused on setting up community cooperatives, was told to redirect its energies toward setting up small private businesses and microenterprises. Even the Inter-America Foundation—which in the 1960s had been mandated by the US Congress to support grassroots initiatives for social change—had much of its top staff replaced and its objectives retargeted toward fostering private entrepreneurs.

Some of the most extreme examples of the use of development aid to further the political and economic interests of the donor country—often to the detriment of the poor in the recipient countries—can be observed in the agenda of the United States Agency for International Development. USAID, a largely political instrument of the US government, exhibits mixed and often contradictory motives. One of its stated aims is to promote private sector-dominated, profit-oriented national economies.[195] In practice, this often involves the undermining of equity-oriented economies and encouraging free market economies, most frequently dominated by powerful corporate interests in the North.

Privatization of Health Services

Health services in many parts of the world have been affected by the conservative development policies of the 1980s, especially by structural adjustment programs (SAPs) and the strong push for privatization. USAID's assistance to health ministries of poor countries with nationalized health systems has often been conditional: requiring steps toward privatization or "cost recovery" for services. For example, the US provided badly needed shipments of medicine to Mozambique on condition that the country compromise its egalitarian policy of "free medical service to all." Mozambique was forced to introduce user charges for both medicines and services.[196]

Bamako and other cost recovery schemes

UNICEF has also promoted user-financing of village health posts through the Bamako Initiative, now functioning in many African countries and elsewhere. While UNICEF has some reservations about the Bamako Initiative, it argues that in today's hard times it sees no better alternative. Cutbacks in health budgets during the 1980s resulted in the closure of many rural health posts, largely for lack of medicines. UNICEF, aware that poor people are usually willing to pay for medicines, advocates charging enough for drugs to keep the health posts stocked and functioning.

The Bamako Initiative is an attempt to address the problem of financing primary health care in the face of economic recession, SAPs, and cuts in public spending. It makes concessions to these socially regressive policy trends, while at the same time seeking to cushion their impact on the most vulnerable groups.[197] UNICEF has tried to make the Initiative user-friendly and community controlled, and the program does have a number of positive features. For one, only medicines included on WHO's essential drug list are used (although ORS packets are sold as an "essential drug" for home use). Also, in some of the Bamako community-run health posts, local participation has been active and enthusiastic.

But cost-recovery schemes often have serious—and perhaps life-threatening—drawbacks. Just because poor families are *willing* to pay for medicines does not mean they can *afford* to pay for them. As with ORS packets, poor families will often spend on medicine the last pennies they have, which they need to feed their sick children.[198] And because the poorest families get sick more frequently and tend to require more medication, they may carry more than their share of costs for the health post. While Bamako has provisions to charge less to *the poorest of the poor*, such safety nets work better on paper than in practice.

Studies in some countries have shown that *when cost-recovery has been introduced, utilization of health centers by high risk groups has dropped.*[199] For example, in Kenya the introduction of user fees at a center for sexually transmitted diseases caused a sharp decline in attendance and probably increased the number of untreated STDs in the population.[200] An editorial in *The Lancet* in November 1994 suggests that the introduction of user fees, along with other SAPs, may be contributing to the rapid spread of AIDS in Africa.[201] In Zimbabwe a study by the British aid agency, OXFAM, which reported negative effects from the introduction of user fees, led the government to threaten evicting the charity.[202] In the Upper Volta region of Ghana, health care utilization decreased by 50% when cost recovery was introduced.[203] When in 1981 China introduced user payment for tuberculosis treatment, between one and 1.5 million cases of TB remained untreated, leading to 10 million additional persons infected. Many of the 3 million deaths from TB in China during the 1980s might have been prevented.[204]

The Bamako Initiative has won support from major donors, especially the US, because it shifts much of the cost of primary health care from governments to consumers. Multi-national drug companies applaud the Initiative because it actively promotes and increases the sale of drugs to the poor. When health workers know that their salaries and health posts are financed through drug sales, the temptation to over-prescribe is almost irresistible.

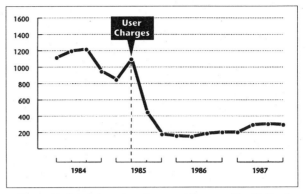

Fig. 3–11 Outpatient attendances at Dwease Health Post, Ghana, before and after introduction of user charges in 1985.[205]

Whatever their apparent impact, the introduction of these cost-recovery schemes has disturbing social and ethical implications. It is part of a far-reaching rollback of gradual progress toward a fairer, more democratic social order. This conservative shift is reflected in the recent reversals in the rates of child mortality after decades of gradual improvements in children's health.

The World Bank's Take-over of Health Policy Planning: *Investing in Health*

The World Bank and International Monetary Fund (IMF) were set up by the victorious Western powers in 1945. The role of the Bank was to assist in the reconstruction and development of European countries after World War II. The role of the Fund was to provide short term loans to trading nations to smooth out balance of payments fluctuations. The Bank and the Fund are often referred to as the "Bretton Woods institutions" after the town in New Hampshire where their establishment was agreed upon.

By the 1960s, Europe was finished with its post-war reconstruction phase and the bulk of World Bank development lending was going to large scale development projects in developing countries. Many of the projects supported by the Bank have been criticized for damaging the environment and adding to the burdens of the poor.

The role of the IMF was also changing as the private financial markets took over the role of smoothing out short term balance of payments fluctuations. By the 1960s the IMF was mainly lending to governments that were facing structural deficits rather than short term trading deficits and increasingly these were in developing countries. By the late 1970s the main role of the IMF was as a lender of last resort to severely indebted and out-of-credit Third World countries. The loans were tied to structural adjustment packages as referred to above. During the 1980s the Bank became more involved in structural adjustment lending, directing an increasing proportion of its development lending through structural adjustment packages negotiated by the IMF.

During the 1980s the IMF and the World Bank increasingly became the targets of criticism for the damaging effects of much of the Bank's development lending and for the disastrous effects of the conditions imposed as part of structural adjustment lending. But in recent years, the Bank claims to have learned from its mistakes, turned over a new leaf and committed itself to the "elimination of poverty." However, the Bank has so consistently financed policies that exacerbate the situation of disadvantaged people that it is difficult to avoid questioning its ability to change its course. A number of critics have suggested that perhaps the most effective step the World Bank could take to eliminate poverty would be to eliminate itself.[206]

As part of its effort to reposition itself, the Bank has become increasingly involved in questions of Third World health policy, both through lending for health sector programs and by including health policy reforms in the conditions of structural adjustment lending. The Bank's agenda for redirecting health policy and restructuring Third World health systems is spelled out in its 1993 World Development Report, entitled, *Investing in Health*. This report has had (and continues to have) a profound influence on health policy in developing countries. Countries willing to implement Bank-endorsed policies are regarded as appropriate candidates for aid and the Bank encourages other donor agencies to assist these compliant countries to finance the transitional costs of structural change in the health sector.

The report is based on propositions about the links between health and economic growth which are deliberately misleading. It asserts that economic growth will lead to good health and better population health will lead to more secure economic growth. The report does not acknowledge that industrialization has never been achieved without heavy human and environmental costs.

The report recognizes poverty as a threat to health but does not refer to the evidence linking economic inequality and poorer health standards. Indeed, underlying the whole report is an attempt to reconcile the goal of better health with the inequalities which are the pre-conditions for, and the consequences of, the Bank's model of economic development (see tables on page 105).

On first reading, the Bank's strategy for improving health status in developing countries sounds comprehensive, even modestly progressive. It acknowledges the links between poverty and ill health, and that improvements in social, economic and environmental factors are critical pre-requisites for improvements in health. It calls for increased family income, better education (especially for girls), greater access to health care, and a focus on basic health services rather than tertiary and specialist care. It quite rightly criticizes the persistent inefficiencies and inequities of current Third World health systems. Ironically, in view of its track record of slashing health budgets, the Bank even calls for increased health spending.... So far so good.

But on reading further, we discover that under the guise of promoting cost-effective, decentralized, and country-appropriate health systems, the report's key recommendations spring from the same sort of structural adjustment paradigm that has worsened poverty and lowered levels of health wherever it has been applied.

The Bank's three-pronged approach. According to the World Bank's prescription, in order to save "millions of lives and billions of dollars" governments must adopt "a three pronged policy approach to health reform:

1. Foster an enabling environment for households to improve health.

2. Improve government spending in health.

3. Facilitate involvement by the private sector."[207]

These recommendations are said to reflect new thinking. But from the "fine print" in the text of the Report, we can restate the policy's three prongs more clearly:

1. "Foster an enabling environment for households to improve health" is a return to "trickle down" development. Policies for economic growth must take priority. Family health will improve when household income starts to rise.

2. "Improve government spending in health" means trimming government spending by moving from comprehensive service provision to a number of narrow vertically planned programs, selected on the grounds of cost-effectiveness: in other words, *a new brand of selective primary health care*. It also means user charges, requiring disadvantaged families to cover the costs of their own health care, despite the fact that for many it will prohibit the use of health care services.

			Income per capita					
				Growth rate, 1975–90	Child mortality		Life expectancy at birth (years)	
Region	Population, 1990 (millions)	Deaths, 1990 (millions)	Dollars, 1990	(percent per year)	1975	1990	1975	1990
Sub-Saharan Africa	510	7.9	510	−1.0	212	175	48	52
India	850	9.3	360	2.5	195	127	53	58
China	1,134	8.9	370	7.4	85	43	56	69
Other Asia and islands	683	5.5	1,320	4.6	135	97	56	62
Latin America and the Caribbean	444	3.0	2,190	−0.1	104	60	62	70
Middle Eastern crescent	503	4.4	1,720	−1.3	174	111	52	61
Formerly socialist economies of Europe (FSE)	346	3.8	2,850	0.5	36	22	70	72
Established market economies (EME)	798	7.1	19,900	2.2	21	11	73	76
Demographically developing groupᵃ	4,123	39.1	900	3.0	152	106	56	63
FSE and EME	1,144	10.9	14,690	1.7	25	15	72	75
World	5,267	50.0	4,000	1.2	135	96	60	65

Population, economic indicators, and progress in health by demographic region, 1975–90

Note: Child mortality is the probability of dying between birth and age 5, expressed per 1,000 live births; life expectancy at birth is the average number of years that a person would expect to live at the prevailing age-specific mortality rates.
a. The countries of the demographic regions Sub-Saharan Africa, India, China, Other Asia and islands, Latin America and the Caribbean, and Middle Eastern crescent.

Fig. 3–12 Contrast the World Bank's optimistic table above which indicates universal improvement in health with figure 3–15 below which shows the widening gap in mortality between people in wealthy and poor countries (data drawn from same source).[208]

Age Group	1950	1980	1990
<5	3.4	6.4	8.8
5–14	3.8	6.5	7.0
15–59	2.2	1.8	1.7
60>	1.3	1.4	1.4

Fig. 3–13 Relative probability of people in developing countries dying (across the ages indicated) expressed as DDC/(FSE+ EME) (the ratio of Demographically Developing Countries to the combined Formerly Socialist Economies plus the Established Market Economies). Calculated from data in the World Bank's 1993 World Development Report by David Legge.[209]

3. "Facilitate involvement by the private sector" means turning over to private, profit-making doctors and businesses most of those government services that used to provide free or subsidized care to the poor ... in other words, *privatization of most medical and health services:* thus pricing many interventions beyond the reach of those in greatest need.

Disability Adjusted Life Years (DALYs) Many of the recommendations of *Investing in Health* are based on the concept of DALYs, or Disability Adjusted Life Years.

DALYs incorporate a number of very questionable assumptions about the value of life. The Bank assigns different values to years of life lost at different ages. The value for each year of life lost rises from zero at birth to a peak at age 25 and then declines gradually with increasing age. For the Bank, the very young, the elderly, and disabled people are less likely to contribute to society in economic terms; hence fewer DALYs will be saved by health interventions which address their ills. Therefore, asserts the bank, such interventions are less deserving of public support.

According to the Report, placing a dollar value on individual human lives, DALYs can be used to design more efficient health care. DALYs which might be lost through death, disease or injury may be saved, the Bank suggests, by selected health interventions. Inexpensive interventions which substantially reduce the number of DALYs lost are considered cost effective, and merit public support. Interventions which do not alter the future stream of disability-free years are not considered cost-effective, and are unworthy of support.

The Report compares 47 different public health and clinical interventions in terms of their cost-effectiveness, expressed in terms of the cost per DALY achieved. For example, leukemia treatment is not cost-effective, achieving only 1 DALY for every $1,000 spent, while vitamin A supplementation achieves 1 DALY for just under $1.

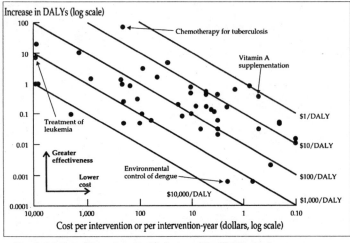

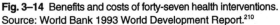

Fig. 3–14 Benefits and costs of forty-seven health interventions.
Source: World Bank 1993 World Development Report.[210]

The Report's contradictions and wider agenda

The World Bank's *Investing in Health* Report's most positive features are that it acknowledges that poverty and ill-health are causally related, and that improved health is likely to result from economic improvement and advances in non-health sectors. Also it urges countries to focus on basic health services rather than tertiary and specialist care. Nonetheless, as David Legge has pointed out, "there are ambiguities, selectivities and inconsistencies in the Report and it appears that the analysis and recommendations have been shaped by considerations from a wider agenda."[211]

According to this logic the overwhelming majority of nursing care would be judged to be of little or no value. As public health researcher David Legge puts it: "Caring activity which does not contribute to cure or prevention is rendered infinitely expensive, or infinitely ineffective by this methodology." This concept, which assumes that a disabled or chronically unhealthy person's life is less valuable than that of a non-disabled person, reflects the Bank's view that economic productivity is paramount.

Using DALY-based cost-effectiveness, the Report defines a minimum essential package of clinical and public health services. This package consists of a relatively small number of large-scale interventions which "cost-effectively" address those problems which are "among the largest afflicting developing countries." There is no consideration of how the community is to participate in or even understand this form of global health planning.

Many of the recommendations contradict the more progressive health objectives stated in the report. For example, the Report confirms that poverty which results in poor living conditions, unhealthy occupational exposures and maldistribution of household income is a health hazard. It then states that economic growth—particularly when guided by growth policies designed to benefit the poor—is a condition for health improvement, "including, where necessary, adjustment policies that preserve cost-effective health expenditures." Yet the Report does not address seriously the health consequences of unbridled economic growth, which has led in some countries to greater inequalities and widening health differentials, nor the negative impact of SAPs, particularly on the poor and vulnerable. Indeed, it claims that economic growth following adjustment has generally led to improved health. However, as we discussed in Chapter 11, a close examination of the data reveals that there is no basis for this conclusion.

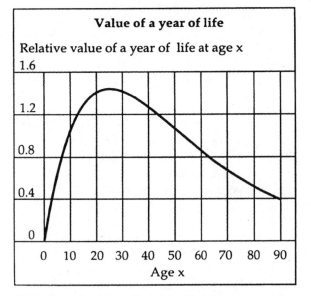

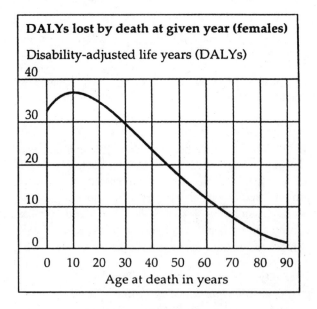

Fig. 3–15 Source: World Bank 1993 World Development Report

It is the almost total silence on SAPs that is especially telling and leads one to doubt the seriousness of the Bank's call for poverty reduction as a key to better health. For example, the Report singles out female education as a critical factor in health improvement. Yet it fails to acknowledge the many ways that SAPs have increased poverty and poor health: how cuts in education budgets and imposition of school fees have resulted in significant school dropouts, especially of girls, or how production of cash crops for export instead of production of traditional foods has led to higher food prices. The Report fails to address how SAPs have terminated food subsidies, leading directly to increased hunger, have promoted privatization and user fees which have placed health services out of reach of the neediest, and have "streamlined" public services resulting in increased unemployment.

With its call for "greater diversity and competition in the provision of health services, promoting competitive procurement practices, [and] fostering greater involvement by nongovernment and other private organizations" the Bank's new policy for the Third World sounds suspiciously like the health care model of the United States. It argues that private health care for individuals gives more choice and satisfaction and is more efficient. But there is little evidence to support this claim. The US health system, dominated by a strong profit-hungry private sector, is by far the most expensive in the world, yet US health statistics are among the worst among the Northern industrialized nations. Indeed, Washington DC, with its large low-income population, has poorer child and maternal mortality rates than Jamaica.[212] (The health situation in the United States is discussed in detail in Chapter 14.)

The Bank's new health policy is little more than old wine in new bottles: a rehash of the conservative strategies that have systematically derailed Comprehensive Primary Health Care, with elements of structural adjustment to boot.[213] It is a market-friendly version of Selective Primary Health Care, supplemented by privatization of medical services and user-financed cost recovery. As with other Selective PHC schemes, it focuses on technological interventions and glosses over the social and legislative determinants of health. David Legge observes that the World Bank Report is "primarily oriented around the technical fix rather than any focus on structural causes of poor health; it is about *healthier poverty*."[214]

The medical establishment in many countries has celebrated the Bank's 1993 World Development Report as a major breakthrough toward a more *cost-efficient* health care strategy. But many health activists see the Report as a disturbing document with dangerous implications. They are especially worried that the Bank will impose its recommendations on the countries that can least afford to implement them. With its enormous money-lending capacity, the Bank's financial leverage can force poor countries to accept its blueprint, as it has done with structural adjustment.

It is an ominous sign when a giant financial institution with such strong ties to big government and big business bullies its way into health care. Yet according to the British medical journal *The Lancet, the World Bank is now moving into first place as the global agency most influencing health policy*, leaving the World Health Organization a weak second.[215]

Despite all its rhetoric about the alleviation of poverty, strengthening of households, and more efficient health care, the central function of the World Bank remains the same: to draw the rulers and governments of weaker states into a global economy dominated by large, multinational corporations. Its loan programs, development priorities and adjustment policies have deepened inequalities and contributed to the perpetuation of poverty, ill health, and deteriorating living conditions for at least one billion human beings.

⌘

It is time to look for alternatives. Fortunately, there are many examples, small and large, of approaches to health and development that place the well-being of all members of society as top priority. Although none of these approaches is flawless, and many have run into powerful obstacles, we can still learn a lot from them. The next chapter examines some of these more promising alternatives. It shows that a society's level of equity (or inequity) is a key determinant of its health. Examples are provided from different countries, both of *poor health at high cost* and of *good health at low cost*.

A Look at the Situation Today: Equity as a Determinant of Health

Corporations have been enthroned... An era of corruption in high places will follow and the money power will endeavor to prolong its reign by working on the prejudices of the people... until wealth is aggregated in a few hands and the Republic is destroyed.[216]

—Abraham Lincoln

It is often the case that the people of rich nations are healthier than those of poor nations. But a comparative look at the world's countries—poor and rich—reveals some outstanding exceptions. A wealthy nation is not necessarily a healthy nation, nor is a poor nation necessarily unhealthy. This is evident if we compare the data in the "Basic Indicators" chart of UNICEF's 1995 *State of the World's Children Report* (see excerpt: figure 3–1 on page 75).[217]

For example, Vietnam, China and Sri Lanka are all countries with a gross national product (GNP) per capita of US$600.00 or less, yet each has achieved an under 5 mortality rate (U5MR) under 50 (in other words, fewer than 50 out of 1000 children die before age 5). By contrast, Gabon, Libya, South Africa, Brazil, Botswana and Iran are all countries with a GNP per capita of over US$2000, yet all have a U5MR of 56 or more. Gabon, despite its relatively high GNP per capita of $4450 has an appalling U5MR of 154! Compare this with Jamaica which, with a GNP per capita of $1340, has a U5MR of just 13.[218] Clearly, the contrasting wealth of these two countries does not reflect the relative health of their children.

Of course, GNPs per capita are misleading because they are a national average that tells us nothing about income distribution. For this reason the UNICEF report also includes income disparity indicators. We see that in countries with high child death rates, despite relatively high average income, income disparity is often extreme. Brazil and Botswana (the only two countries of the above six for which income distribution data are available) show the widest income disparity of all countries for which such data are listed. In Brazil—reputedly "among the most unequal and unjust nations in the world"[219]— the poorest 40% of the population earn only 7% of the national income, while the wealthiest 20% earn 68% of the income. Land distribution in Brazil is even more uneven than income: the richest 0.9% of landholders own 44% of the land while the poorest 53% hold just 2.7%.[220] From these and similar data, as shown on the chart in Figure 3–1, it appears that health levels of nations are strongly influenced by *distribution of wealth*, and in some cases more so than by the *average wealth* (GNP per capita) or *total wealth* (GNP) of nations.

Equity in terms of people's basic needs also appears to be of key importance. The extent to which a society meets all its members' basic needs may have a greater influence on the population's health and well–being than does the nation's aggregate wealth or economic growth. This would seem to hold true not only in poor countries, but also in rich ones. For example, Hong Kong and Singapore have GNPs per capita of US$13,340 and US$14,210 respectively, as compared with US$22,240 for the United States of America. However, Hong Kong and Singapore have U5MRs of 7 and 6 respectively, significantly lower than the US with a U5MR of 10. This is in part explained by greater commitment in Hong Kong and Singapore to meeting the entire population's basic needs. For example, in Singapore and Hong Kong the percentage of children fully immunized against polio and diphtheria, pertussis (whooping cough), tetanus and tuberculosis ranges from 80 to 99%. By contrast, in some poor inner city areas of the USA immunization coverage is as low as 10%.

The more equitable a society is — i.e. the more fairly its wealth, land, housing, access to health care and education, other basic resources and services are distributed — the healthier its people are likely to be. In short, there is a strong correlation between health and social equity. In this chapter, to understand the importance of equity in achieving a healthy population, we look at contrasting examples. First, to observe *poor health at high cost* we focus on one of the richest countries with the greatest inequities: the United States. Then, to examine *good health at low cost* we look at several poor countries which have striven to meet all people's basic needs and have achieved exceptionally high levels of health and low child mortality.

Poor Health at High Cost — The Socioeconomics of Health and Health Care in the United States

The United States of America may be the world's wealthiest nation, but it is certainly not the healthiest. For the growing number of American families living below the poverty line, the standard of living continues to deteriorate. According to UNICEF's 1994 *State of the World's Children Report*,

An increasing proportion of children in the world's richest nation are in trouble. While America's economy grew by approximately 20% in the 1980's some 4 million more American children fell into poverty. A total of one in five children now lives below the poverty line.[221]

The United States has the eighth highest GNP per capita in the world[222] ... and the highest *real gross domestic product (GDP) per capita,*[*] a better indicator of real wealth.[223] The nation also ranks first in the world in total spending on health care. (In 1990 the US alone consumed 41% of the global total spent on health care.)[224] Yet its health indices are worse than those of other rich nations and lag behind some countries with much lower GNPs. Of the 19 major industrial countries, the US has the highest mortality rate of children under age five (U5MR). In disease prevention the US also lags. Whereas in many underdeveloped countries at least 80% of young children currently receive complete immunization, in the US over 40% of 2-year-olds are not fully immunized and in some inner cities fewer than 10% of children are fully immunized. With an overall immunization rate of 58%, the U.S. immunization rate is lower than in Mexico, Thailand, India and Uganda.[225] Therefore, it is not surprising that in the 1990s the death rate from measles in the US has been rising.

The nutritional status of US children is equally disturbing. Although obesity is a growing health concern for middle-class children, undernutrition impedes children's physical as well as mental development in poor families. Of the 30 million Americans who regularly go hungry, over 12 million are children. These tend to be the same children who are not covered by any form of health insurance, and who often fall through the inadequate and increasingly under funded safety nets for high risk families. The United States ranks last among major industrial countries in percentage of population covered by health insurance.[226] And with the increasingly astronomical costs of services within the private, profit-hungry medical system, for those who lack health insurance, professional medical or dental care is ruinously costly. In the United States millions of citizens, undocumented immigrants, and growing numbers of the middle class suffer painful and chronic conditions without treatment because they simply cannot afford it.

The substandard health levels in the US compared to many other countries can be explained by growing inequality, not only in access to health care and essential services, but in education, employment opportunities, and fundamental human rights. Inequity, poverty, and hunger have worsened dramatically in the US during the last 15 years. Spiraling social deterioration has been largely a result of the regressive economic and social policies introduced by the Reagan and Bush Administrations, now being carried to greater extremes as the current conservative majority in Congress competes against President Clinton for the vote of big business. These market-friendly, poor-people-hostile policies parallel the Structural Adjustment Programs imposed on poor countries by the World Bank. They have drastically rolled back welfare benefits and social services, including health care, food subsidies, low-cost housing, and the Head Start program for poor inner city children. While taxation of the poor has increased, further tax benefits have been awarded to rich investors and corporations.[227]

> ### THE REALITY AND THE IDEAL
>
> *Big time Chief Executive Officers (CEOs) [in the US]... averaged $4.1 million in 1993... 149 times the earnings of average factory workers.*[228]
>
> —Business Week
>
> *No one in a community should earn more than five times the pay of the lowest paid worker.*
>
> — Plato said to Aristotle

By 1987, the income gap between rich and poor Americans was wider than at any time since the federal government began calculating it 40 years ago. Between 1977 and 1988, the inflation-adjusted income of the richest 5% of the population increased by 37%, while the income of the poorest 10% decreased by 10.5 percent.[229] Correspondingly, the number of Americans living below the poverty line has increased: from 24.7 million in 1977 to 32.4 million in 1986. Those with no health insurance rose over 30% from 1980 to 1992.[230] At the same time the rate of preventive health coverage for children, including immunization, has been falling, largely because parents are charged for such services.[231] It is estimated that in the USA at least 10,000 and possibly as many as 21,000 children die of poverty-related causes each year.[232]

---

[*]This is true because *real GDP per capita* takes into account the varying costs of items across countries—something GNP per capita does not do. Real GDP per capita compares how much it costs to buy the same bundle of goods in different countries. It shows that, while the US is eighth in average income, Americans can buy more with their money than citizens of other countries.

Wealth Class (% of population)	1962	1983	1989
Richest 0.5%	25.2	26.2	30.3
Next 0.5%	8.2	7.8	8.0
Next 4%	21.6	22.1	21.6
Next 5%	12.4	12.1	11.3
Next 10%	14.3	13.3	13.1
Richest Fifth (20%)	**81.7**	**81.5**	**84.3**
Fourth (20%)	12.9	12.5	13.0
Middle (20%)	5.2	5.2	2.7
Second (20%)	0.8	1.1	0.2
Lowest (20%)	–0.5	–0.3	–0.2
Poorest Four Fifths (80%)	**18.3**	**18.5**	**15.7**
Total	100	100	100

Fig. 3–16 Changes in Distribution of US Net Worth, 1962–1989. The poorest 20% of people owe more than they have, thus they have a negative net worth[233]

The Children's Defense Fund has the following to say about the new cutbacks on programs for high-risk children proposed by the conservative Congress' so-called Contract with America (a right-wing austerity plan to balance the national budget on the backs of the poor while increasing profits for the rich):

> Under the guise of welfare reform, House Republican leaders would permanently tear up the 60-year old federal safety net for poor, disabled, abused, and hungry children and replace it with a policy of national child neglect. If they succeed, millions more children will be left behind and denied a Healthy Start, a Head Start, a Fair Start, and a Safe Start in order to pay for tax breaks for rich corporations and individuals.[234]

Altogether, 67% of the massive budget cuts to finance tax breaks for the rich fall on children.[235] These cutbacks, which by default violate the basic rights of children, are sowing the seeds of future social breakdown and mounting violence. In the long run, initiatives like Head Start are probably among the most effective programs for violence prevention. Yet these protective programs are being ruthlessly gutted while expenditures on prisons and law enforcement are being increased. Every year the United States spends $25 billion on its prison services alone.[236]

With diminishing public assistance for poor urban communities, the sanitation infrastructure has been allowed to deteriorate, health education and preventive health mea-sures have been reduced, as has the access by poor Americans to health care. In the US today, it is estimated that one in four families does not have safe tap water. Deteriorating conditions have in turn set the stage for the rapid spread of tuberculosis and measles (two *diseases of poverty* that had been largely eradicated[237]), and AIDS.

Racism in the USA is another factor contributing to poor health. Of children living in poverty, a disproportionate number are African-American, Hispanic, or Native American. Members of these ethnic groups are systematically marginalized and discriminated against, and have fewer opportunities open to them. As a result of such inequality, life expectancy of African-Americans is five years less than that of whites.[238]

With such extreme and growing inequalities in the USA, between rich and poor, and between Caucasians and people of color, rates of crime and violence are bound to increase. According to the California Wellness Foundation:

> Murder has become an epidemic ravaging our youth. It is the leading cause of death among 20 to 24 year-olds... Most young people are neither victims nor violators. But they learn to live with violence in the schools and parks, on the streets, in their homes, in the movies and television programs they watch.[239]

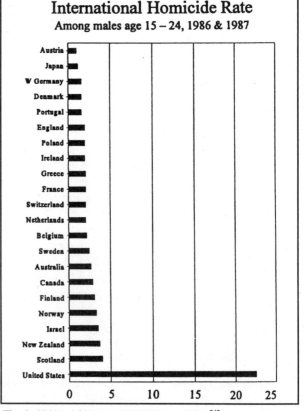

Fig. 3–17 Homicides per 100,000 population[240]

Startling Statistics on US Health, Race and Equity

- Number of Americans living in poverty:
  1977: 24.7 million
  1986: 32.4 million.[241]

- Percentage of children living in poverty:
  In 1980: 17%[242]
  In 1994: 25%.[243]

- Number of Americans who regularly go hungry: 30 million
  Children: over 12 million[244]

- Number of millionaires in US:
  In 1969: 121,000
  In 1989: 1.3 million[245]

- Between 1977 and 1988, the inflation-adjusted income of the richest 5% of the population increased by 37%, while the income of the poorest 10% decreased by 10.5 percent.[246]

- Of the nineteen major industrial countries, the country with the highest U5MR:
  United States.[247] (Higher than that of Singapore and Hong Kong.)

- Number of American children who die of poverty-related causes each year: At least 10,000.[248]

- Country which ranks last among major industrial countries in percentage of population covered by health insurance:
  United States[249]

- Number of Americans who have no health insurance: 40 million
  Children: 12 million
  (Another 20 million have inadequate coverage.)[250]

- Number of American children without health care:
  Approximately 8 million[251]

- Percentage of inner city children not fully vaccinated against childhood illnesses:
  Fewer than 10%[252]

- Infant mortality:
  White Americans:
  8 per 1000
  African-Americans:
  18 per 1000.[253]

- 35% of Hispanic children and 43% of African-American children live below the poverty line.[254]

- The rate of incarceration for African-American teenagers is nearly 44 times that for white teens.[255]

- African-American infants born in Chicago, Detroit, and Philadelphia are more likely to die before their first birthday than infants born in Shanghai, Jamaica, Costa Rica, or Chile.[256]

- Over half of all young children with AIDS in the US are African-American.[257]

- Number of teen-age girls in the US who become pregnant annually: 1 million.[258]

- Number of adolescents who contract sexually transmitted diseases: 2.5 million.[259]

- Number of prostitutes under the age of 18: 300,000.[260]

Inequality breeds violence

Murder rates in the US have been increasing 6 times faster than the population. Rape and other forms of violence have also escalated. A contributing cause, in addition to the widening gap between rich and poor, may be commercial television: *the drug with a plug*. For the sake of maximum profit, unscrupulous TV corporations bombard the public with a diet of murder and mayhem. Most American children spend more time watching TV than they do with their parents or in school. "By the age of 18 the average teenager has witnessed 15,000 murders and hundreds of thousands of other acts of violence on television. The primary goal of the television industry is not to develop children's character but to expand the market for fast food, toys, and other unnecessary goods."[261]

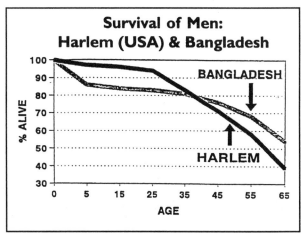

Fig. 3–18

The embers of racism and xenophobia in the US—never far below the surface—are currently being fanned into flames by the increasing polarization of opportunity and income. A wave of hate-crimes and terror has been spearheaded by self-seeking groups of the radical right (skin-heads, white-supremacists, neo-Nazis, Ku Klux Klan, and self-styled paramilitary "militia"). There is little doubt that some of these militia—or at least the doctrine of terrorism and cold-blooded violence that they espouse—are linked to the 1995 bombing of the Federal Building in Oklahoma City in which nearly 200 persons, including many children, were killed.

At the same time as hate crimes by the radical right have escalated, vindictive legislation has been promoted by the conservative right. As an example, the recent passage of Proposition 187 in California, if ruled constitutional, would deny education and health care to undocumented children. Mexicans and progressive North Americans have labeled this action racist and even fascist. Through such legislation, decades of social progress are being reversed. Health care and education cease to be basic human rights.

Blacks clearly, on the average, have fewer opportunities than whites; far more are unemployed or paid impover-ishing wages. An African-American man in Harlem is less likely to reach age 65 than a man in Bangladesh (see figure 3–18).[262] Such social violence against one sector of the population breeds violent repercussions. The budget cuts proposed through the "Contract with America" will inevitably cause greater hardship for Blacks, Latinos, and other minority groups.

As a reflection of the unhealthiness of our inequitable consumer society and the psychosocial strain which it imposes on young people, the rates of attempted suicide in the United States are shockingly high. Similarly, the use of alcohol and illicit drugs among older children and teenagers is disturbingly elevated. A study conducted by a 37-member commission including former Surgeon General C. Everett Koop and pollster George Gallup in 1990 reports that:

- Never before has one generation of American teen-agers been less healthy, less cared for, or less prepared for life than their parents were at the same age.

- Hundreds of thousands of adolescents [suffer from] excessive drug use, unplanned pregnancies, sexually transmitted diseases and social and emotional prob-lems that can lead to academic failure or suicide.

- The suicide rate for teens has doubled since 1968, and 10% of adolescent boys and 20% of girls have at-tempted suicide.

- Violence is part of many young people's daily lives … Every day 135,000 students bring guns to school, and homicide is the leading cause of death among 15 to 19-year old African-Americans.

- More than half of all high school seniors became drunk [at least] once a month, and alcohol-related accidents are the leading cause of death among teen-agers.

- 30% of tenth graders have experimented with drugs (as compared to 5% in the 1950s). Half a million 12- to 17-year olds have tried cocaine.

The study concluded that:

- Many of America's young people, both rich and poor, from all racial and ethnic backgrounds, have serious social, emotional, and health problems that have potentially disastrous consequences not only for the individual teen, but for society as a whole.

During its first years in the White House in the early 1990s the Clinton Administration called loudly for social reform. It talked of more jobs, benefits, and services for working people, especially the poor, and for a national health system to meet all people's needs. But actions speak louder than words. So far, Clinton—like his predecessors—has made many decisions in the interests of powerful lobbies (whose support he seeks for re-election) rather than the interests of the majority of the population. With the current shift to the conservative right in Congress—backed by the powerful lobbies of big business and the American Medical Association—the situation is likely to keep on deteriorating. Although Americans spend far more on medical care than any other nation, the American model based on private, exorbitant, inequitable services is definitely an example of *poor health at high cost.*

The United States and the Globalization of Poverty

The United States, as the only remaining superpower, continues to have an overarching influence on economic and social policies worldwide, both directly through economic and military strength, and indirectly through the international financial institutions (the World Bank, IMF, the World Trade Organization, etc.). Foreign aid, conditional loans, trade accords, and heavy-handed adjustment policies have tied most nations to a profit-before-people global market system largely structured and directed by the US. Those few countries bold enough to resist this greedy, myopic development para-digm, or that have pursued a path of more equitable social development, have been beleaguered by US-led embargoes, destabilization strategies, and either overt aggression or covert mercenary-conducted terrorism. The result has been growing disparity of wealth and health and the globalization of poverty.

The dominant development model based on unbridled economic growth for the rich has led to an intensification of inequality and underdevelopment worldwide. In a meager attempt to justify this state-sanctioned economic terrorism, the US Senate–House Joint Economic Committee flatly stated in a recent report that "all societies have unequal wealth and income dispersion, and there is no positive basis for criticizing any degree of market determined inequality."[263] The resulting unjust and unsustainable social order is held precariously in place by providing strategic economic and military aid to the *burgeoning low-intensity democracies* which are fiercely controlled by wealthy elites in alliance with the powerful monied interests in the North.

The parallels between the domestic policies pursued by the US government since the early 1980s and the development policies imposed on Third World countries are inescapable. Likewise, the Third World debt crisis parallels the US national debt: the largest in the world. In the United States, as in the Third World, the same powerful interest groups have both engendered and benefitted from the neoliberal policies that have deepened poverty,

undermined democratic process, and precipitated environmental demise.

Despite all its wealth and power, the US is surely not a healthy nation. Still less healthy are the inequitable policies it imposes on the rest of the world.

The Socioeconomics of Health in the Third World

In the Third World, generally speaking, national wealth (GNP per capita) tends to correlate with child mortality rates and other health indicators. Of the 35 countries that UNICEF lists as having "very high" under-five mortality rates (U5MRs) all but five have GNPs per capita of $500 or less.[264]

However, as mentioned earlier, how a country's wealth is distributed appears to be a more important determinant of health than is aggregate national wealth or average income. Let us compare Brazil with Costa Rica. Brazil has a relatively high GNP per capita of $2,770 and a U5MR of 63.[265] In comparison, Costa Rica has a GNP per capita of $1,960 and a U5MR of 16—one fourth that of Brazil.[266] Similarly, the maternal mortality rate in Brazil is 200 per 100,000 live births, in contrast to Costa Rica's 36.[267] And the average Brazilian dies at age 66, ten years younger than the average Costa Rican.[268]

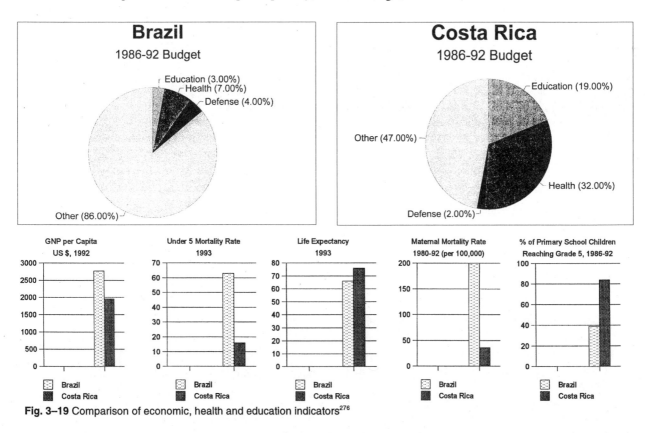

Fig. 3–19 Comparison of economic, health and education indicators[276]

Costa Rica's superior health indices may be due in part to its emphasis on health, and also may partly be explained by the fact that the gap between rich and poor is smaller there, while in Brazil it is enormous and continues to widen.[269] Today, one percent of Brazil's population owns 48% of the country's arable land.[270] The poorest 40% of Brazil's population receives only 7% of the country's total income[271] (as compared with 8% three years earlier).[272] In contrast, the poorest 20% of Costa Rica's population receives 13% of their country's total income.[273]

The inequity of Brazilian society is also reflected in the government's low spending on social services. Brazil spends 7% of its budget on health care and 3% on education.[274] Costa Rica, in contrast, spends 32% of its budget on health and 19% on education.[275] Correspondingly, only 39% of Brazilian children are in primary school, as compared with 84% of Costa Rican children.[276] (See figure 3–18.)

As we have already mentioned, there is a close correlation between women's education and child mortality. Thus, the fact that Brazil's primary school enrollment fell yet further during the 1980s does not bode well for the health of its children. (In 50 other Third World countries, school enrollment also fell during the 1980s, partly as a result of structural adjustment.)[277]

In the Third World as in the USA, income disparity among families correlates with disparities in child mortality. A recent study of 28 countries found that in lower income families neonatal mortality is 2 to 4 times as high as that of higher income families; post-neonatal mortality is 2 to 5 times as high; while child mortality is 4 to 30 times higher.[278] The effect that a wide disparity in wealth has on children's health is graphically expressed by a hospital official in El Salvador:

> It is a vicious cycle. We don't cure children, we simply revive them so that they can go out and starve once more. Sometimes they get sick from simple infections that become serious for children without any resistance, children who don't get enough to eat. Three-quarters of Salvadoran children under five suffer from some grade of malnutrition.
>
> There is food in the country but the poor cannot afford it. We have a twelve-year-old girl now, dying of malnutrition. Her father has a cow and chickens and grows beans and corn. He owes all of it to the man who owns his land, so his daughter and the rest of the family are starving. If he didn't hand over the milk, the eggs, and his crops,

someone would come and take them, so what could the man do? It is a social and economic problem, not a medical one. We just bandage the wound; we don't cure anybody here.[279]

Good Health at Low Cost

Despite the dismal and deteriorating living conditions and health situation in many poor countries, a few poor states have succeeded in making impressive strides in improving their people's health. In 1985 the Rockefeller Foundation sponsored a study titled *Good Health at Low Cost*.[280] Its purpose was to explore "the reasons why certain poor countries have achieved acceptable health statistics in spite of very low national incomes." Specifically, the study sought to "verify whether China, the state of Kerala in India, Sri Lanka, and Costa Rica did indeed attain life expectancies of 65–70 years with gross national products per capita of only $300–$1,300," and, if so, to discover why.*

On completing the study, its authors concluded that "the four states did achieve good health at low cost." Specifically, the states had dramatically reduced their infant and child mortality rates, and as a result increased their life expectancies to near-First World levels. The reductions in mortality attained by the four states were substantially greater than those registered by Third World countries that pursued conventional child survival strategies. Moreover, these reductions were accompanied by declines in malnutrition and, in some cases, the incidence of disease.

The authors of the study attributed these remarkable improvements in the health of entire populations to four key factors. These factors are:

1. Political and social commitment to equity (i.e. to meeting all people's basic needs).

2. Education for all with emphasis on the primary level.

3. Equitable distribution throughout the urban and rural populations of public health measures and primary health care.

4. Assurance of adequate caloric intake [enough food] at all levels of society in a manner that does not inhibit indigenous agricultural activity.[281]

---

*Ironically, the authors of this study—which provides a strong argument for Comprehensive Primary Health Care in the broadest sense—included Kenneth Warren and Julia Walsh, two of the earliest and strongest advocates of Selective Primary Health Care (see page 23).

The importance of a strong "political and social commit-ment to equity"—although pursued in different ways—cannot be over-emphasized. Henry Mosley, director of Johns Hopkins University's International Institute of Health and Population, points to the social and political factors underlying the improvements in health achieved in these four states:

> [To] guarantee access [to services] there must be an aggressive effort to break down the social and economic barriers that can exist between the disadvantaged subgroup and the medical services. This may be approached with a top-down strategy as illustrated by Costa Rica, or it may be gained through a bottom-up strategy where demand is generated by the organized poor as in Kerala . . . A passive approach of only making services available will not succeed in most situations unless the population has a heightened conscious-ness of their political rights.[282]

Mosley further notes that:

> The fundamental underpinnings of any mortality reduction effort involve the political commitment to equity as well as policies and strategies to provide essential services to all. Judging by the historical experiences of the case studies, this stage may be reached through a long history of egalitar-ian principles and democracy (Costa Rica), through agitation by disadvantaged political groups (Kerala), or through social revolution (China).[283]

Although in the Rockefeller investigation *mortality* and *life expectancy* were used as the primary indicators of relative health levels, a number of *quality of life* and *equity* factors were also considered. The *Gini coefficient* (GE) is an index that looks at relative equality in a population in terms of such factors as total income per household, land distribu-tion, and food consumption. Lower readings of the coeffi-cient indicate a greater degree of equality. All the countries in the *Good Health* study had relatively low (more equita-ble) GEs compared to neighboring states. However, among the four states studied some differences and trends were observed which may throw light on the probability of sustaining the health improvements achieved. In Sri Lanka, for example, there was a decline in the GE for total house-hold income (i.e. income disparities narrowed) from 0.46 in 1953 to 0.35 in 1973, but climbed again to 0.43 by 1981, reflecting the reversal of the egalitarian trend after 1977. (In response to an economic crisis in the late 1970s includ-ing an economic adjustment program in 1977, eligibility for food subsidies was greatly reduced.[284] In the late 1970s the caloric intake of the poorest 30% of Sri Lankans steadily declined, while that of the top 50% increased.)[285] Thus Sri

Lanka has experienced some reversals in its earlier social gains. Obviously, the ongoing civil war in the north of the country has not helped.

Of the 4 countries investigated, China proved by far the most ". . . exceptional in terms of equality. . . It has been reported that for some regions of China, the Gini coeffi-cient (GE) for the distribution of wealth (mostly land) declined from 0.80 [at the time of the Revolution] to as low as 0.22." Whereas decline in infant mortality rate (IMR) in the other three countries was largely accredited to remedial services (improved coverage of health care, immunization, water and sanitation, food subsidies, and education), China's improvements were rooted in fairer distribution of land use and food production. In other words, the popula-tion was encouraged to become more self-sufficient, rather than to become dependent on government assistance. The harvests of the cooperative production units [communes] were taxed by the government. This provided a reserve so that the government could assist communities at times of crisis and, where necessary, redistribute some of the surplus from more prosperous communities to those in difficulty.

How sustainable is "good health at low cost?" Trends since the Rockefeller study

In the years that have passed since the Rockefeller study, it is interesting to compare how the four states investigated have succeeded in sustaining their respective advances toward 'good health at low cost.' According to a number of indicators, China appears to come closest. By contrast, in Kerala, Sri Lanka, and Costa Rica, the gains in reducing malnutrition and disease have in the last few years been somewhat eroded, most notably (and predictably) in the case of Sri Lanka. In these 3 countries equity was less deep-rooted and institutionalized; also they have been hit hard by economic recession and by structural adjustment and, in the case of Sri Lanka, by civil war.

The trends in Costa Rica are especially revealing. Evidence suggests that its impressive decline in Under Fives Mortality Rate (from 112 in 1960 down to 29 in 1980, and 16 in 1992)[286] has mostly been due to reductions in diarrheal disease and respiratory infections. These are attributed mainly to health interventions: early treatment, expanded immunization coverage, water and sanitation, food supplements to young children and pregnant mothers, and later, wider access to hospitals (secondary care) and to family planning services.[287] In the Rockefeller study, "socioeconomic progress" was credited for only 25% of the total decline in infant mortality.[288]

However, with the growing debt crisis in Costa Rica in the early 1980s, as socioeconomic progress stagnated and began to reverse, the drop in infant mortality halted.[289] Rapid inflation and a fall in real wages "brought a deterioration in purchasing power and may have resulted in higher rates of malnutrition and mortality."[290] The percentage of the population who could not afford "the basic food basket" increased from 18% in 1980, to 37% in 1982. Nutritional levels, especially of children, began to decline; more than 1 in 3 children were not getting enough to eat. This situation improved somewhat in 1983 "because the inflationary process was slowed down and government increased the minimum wage."[291] Today health levels in Costa Rica remain fairly good. (For example, its percentage of low birth weight babies is lower than that in the United States.)[292] However, progress in most areas has come to a standstill, and in many ways quality of life for a large segment of the population is deteriorating.

Much of this deterioration appears to be related to structural adjustment policies imposed by the World Bank and the IMF, and they are generally implemented through USAID.[293] Rather than helping Costa Rica recover from its debt crisis, its debts have grown even bigger (through new loans tied to adjustment policies) and the earlier positive trends toward greater equality have been reversed.

Costa Rica's adjustment program calls for increasing export earnings to service foreign debt. It does this, in part, by "forcing farmers who have traditionally grown beans, rice, and corn [maize] to plant *nontraditional agricultural exports* (NTAEs) such as ornamental plants, flowers, melons, strawberries and red peppers." Incentives and tax/tariff breaks are given to larger growers for converting their farms by growing these NTAEs. According to Alicia Korten "Small farmers say that these policies are forcing them off the land and that the small farmer is disappearing as a productive social class."[294] Even the World Bank admitted in its 1988 *Costa Rica: Country Economic Memorandum* that "small holders unable to move into the new (nontraditional crop) activities might have to sell their land and become landless workers."[295]

As more people in Costa Rica become marginalized, to maintain stability the government relies increasingly on its civil police, whose numbers have increased dramatically since the early 1980s. The rise in police brutality, eviction at gunpoint, and mass burning of squatters' homes is a sad turn of events for a country that abolished its army in 1948 and has prided itself on a nonviolent tradition.[296] Even USAID official Arturo Villalobos agrees that the concentration of land into fewer hands and the creation of vast numbers of landless peasants "has been a terrible blow to Costa Rican democracy, social harmony and the environment." [297]

As Costa Rica has become more dependent on export crops and the fluctuation (mostly downward) of the international market, its economic difficulties have deepened. Money spent on the import of luxury goods for the rich outweighs the export income. The lifting of tariffs on basic grains from subsidized Northern agribusiness has undermined local production and driven even more farmers off the land. USAID economist Miguel Sagot suggests that "structural adjustment has increased the income gap in Costa Rica." He notes that "Social services ... have also been deteriorating in the last years. Many people believe that this is because the government has switched its budget priorities from social services toward export promotion."[298] In reality, the Costa Rican government has little choice. If it does not comply with the adjustment dictates of the World Bank and IMF it will be locked out of North American free trade agreements and will lose its access to further loans. As Alicia Korten concludes, "Costa Rica's leaders seem willing to sacrifice social equity, environmental sustainability and long-term economic stability for a place in the global market." By following such a course, it appears that they may also be on the road to sacrificing 'good health at low cost.'[299]

Kerala is one of the poorest states in India, but because its popular government for the past 30 years has given high priority to basic needs, this state far out-paces the rest of the country in terms of health and education. In Kerala over 90% of adults are literate compared to 52% for India as a whole. Kerala's infant mortality rate is about 10 per 1000 live births (one of the lowest rates in the Third World) compared to 81 for India as a whole. A vigorous program of land reform has benefitted millions of Kerala farmers, who no longer toil on feudal estates. Kerala also has some of the best transportation, electricity, and water supply systems in India.

Yet rising costs and unfavorable terms of trade in the late 1980s and 1990s have made it increasingly difficult for Kerala to maintain its welfare-state model. Unemployment has swelled and inflation is eroding living standards.[300] Like Sri Lanka and (to a lesser extent) Costa Rica, Kerala shows a divergence between its relatively low child mortality rates and quality-of-life indicators. Although child nutrition is better than in neighboring (wealthier) states, high rates of growth stunting and low birth-weight babies suggest that significant and widespread undernutrition persists in Kerala. (The Rockefeller study noted that rates of illness appear to have declined only in those causes related to immunization.)[301] Two local highly qualified researchers conclude: "The health status of Kerala presents an interesting picture of a low overall mortality coexisting with considerable morbidity, mostly caused by diseases linked to underdevelopment and poverty."[302]

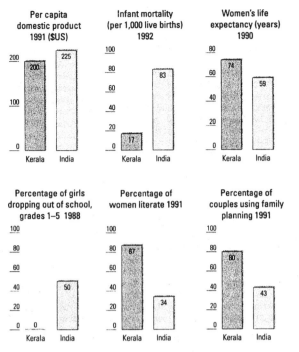

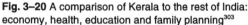

Fig. 3–20 A comparison of Kerala to the rest of India: economy, health, education and family planning[303]

This divergence between mortality and morbidity suggests that *health gains achieved through fundamental socio-economic change in the direction of overall equity, as was the case in China, are more secure against economic downturns than are health gains achieved through relatively superficial and more easily reversible welfare and health care policies, as in the other three examples.* In China, overall improvements in health—which included simultaneous mortality, malnutrition, and morbidity reductions—occurred as a result of improved socioeconomic conditions rather than of health care and public services alone. These improvements have therefore been more resilient.

However, in the present conservative global climate it remains to be seen whether even China's improvements will endure. With the country's steady shift toward a market economy, the barefoot doctors who were chosen by and accountable to their own communes are largely a thing of the past. With the introduction of private farms, the gap between rich and poor is again growing. As China falls more in line with the mainstream development model, its political commitment to equity appears to be slipping. Revealingly, during the early 1980s the number of underweight children in China rose by 10%; by 1990 one in five Chinese children was underweight.[304] Will it be possible for China—with one fifth of the world's population—to sustain its achievements of *good health at low cost?*

Lessons to be learned from the "good health at low cost" countries

Despite the difficulties encountered by the four countries studied in *Good Health at Low Cost*, they illustrate that even very poor countries can achieve profound improvements in the health of their populations. They did this by following development strategies that gave top priority to making sure the basic needs of all people were met. None of the countries—at least during the period of greatest improvements—followed the prevailing *growth-at-all-costs* development model which promotes unbridled expansion of private large scale industry, in the hope that some of the aggregate wealth will trickle down to the poor. Rather they followed a *basic needs* approach to development that focused on equitable forms of service and/or production aimed at involving as large a sector of the population as possible. In agriculture, in order to make sure that all people's (especially children's) food needs were met, these countries reinforced traditional, small scale farming methods to grow local, low-cost food staples. Production was mostly for local consumption, not export. Depending on the country, property ownership ranged from private (Costa Rica) to communal (China). But in all four countries a cooperative, community approach to resolving problems and meeting mutual needs was encouraged. A spirit of sharing and working together for the common good was an underlying motif. In their own ways, these four countries offer strong arguments for a comprehensive, equity-oriented approach to meeting national health needs.

The Health Achievements of Cuba

China, Sri Lanka, Kerala, and Costa Rica are, of course, not the only countries or states that have made progress toward good health at low cost. Cuba, with a per capita income (GNP) only two thirds that of Costa Rica, has a significantly lower U5MR (11 as compared to 16). Not only are Cuba's levels of health, education, and overall social welfare superior to any other 'Third World' country, but in many ways they are equal, if not superior, to many of the Northern 'developed' countries. For example, Cuba has an U5MR equal to that of Israel, whose GNP is 10 times as high. And Cuba has a much higher child immunization rate than the United States, whose GNP is 20 times as high. Indeed, for immunization of children against measles and of pregnant women against neonatal tetanus, Cuba has the highest coverage rates in the world (98%). Cuba has also placed strong emphasis on equal rights of women, and has a higher enrollment ratio of girls to boys in high school than does the United States. Even with its increasing economic difficulties due to loss of Soviet support and a stiffer US embargo under the Clinton Administration, Cuba

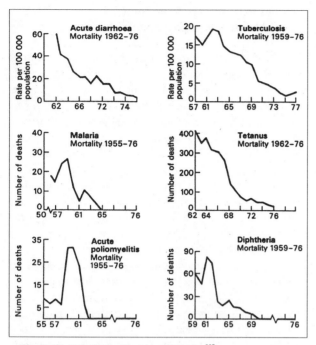

Fig. 3–21 Cuba's significant health gains[305]

has succeeded in making sure the basic needs of all people—and especially the nutritional needs of children—continue to be met.

However, Cuba was not included in the Rockefeller study. Nor are its spectacular child health achievements given any prominence in UNICEF's annual reports. The reason is clear: Cuba has followed a path of development radically outside that of the prevailing market system. By the United States it has been violently attacked, boycotted, refused development loans (until recently), and suffered repeated assassination attempts of its leadership. All this has been done in the name of US *national security*. But the most worrisome threat little Cuba poses to such a giant superpower is a development model that puts the needs of people before the profits of big business. Such a model—if permitted to succeed—could be dangerous to the *status quo*.

Cuba has managed, to date, to sustain the high levels of health of its children in spite of a 50 percent decline in its economy since the start of the 1990s. As with China, this may in part be because its comprehensive approach to health and well-being is rooted in revolutionary social change built on strong popular involvement.

Cuba has long used the slogan of "Power by the people!" (*¡Poder Popular!*). In some ways this citizen's power exists. But decision-making participation has been weakened, as in China, by a strongly centralized, authoritarian government. Unless Cuba and China succeed in making *poder popular* more of a practical reality, internal difficulties and outside pressures for free market modernization may undermine the enormous achievements of both these exceptional states.

Guyana's experiment with an equity-based alternative to structural adjustment[*]

Guyana, though rich in minerals and rainforests, is the poorest country in the Western Hemisphere. This small Caribbean country was once prosperous. But following independence from Britain in 1966 it was ravaged by a corrupt dictatorship that controlled most of the country's economic activity for its own benefit and that of the Northern powers that supported it.

In the 1980s Guyana became the most heavily indebted country in the world. Since 1988, 80% of government revenues have gone to service foreign debt. Under IMF-supervised adjustment policies, the value of the Guyanese dollar fell from 10 to one US dollar in 1988 to 144 Guyanese dollars to one US dollar in 1995. As part of adjustment, the country has subordinated the needs of the domestic economy to those of the international market place. Subsistence agriculture has largely been replaced by export crops. Forests have been cut and minerals mined for export to bring in short-term profit for servicing the debt. Budgets for health, education, and clean water have been slashed to pay for loans to finance the development of exports.

A few local elites benefit, but most of the people gain little and lose much. Throughout the 1980s and into the 1990s, malnutrition, child death rates, disease, unemployment, and overall poverty rose dramatically, as did crime, drug trafficking, street children, and prostitution.

An alternative path based on people's needs.

Then in 1992, in the first free election in 30 years, the people of Guyana elected Cheddi Jagan of the People's Progressive Party as their new president. Jagan had been overthrown 30 years earlier in a US-assisted coup.

At first, IMF policies kept Jagan from implementing social and economic reforms that could effectively combat poverty. But in August, 1993, the citizens of Guyana joined forces with the Bretton Woods Reform Organization (BWRO) to create the first concrete alternative to SAPs, called the Alternative Structural Adjustment

[*]This account of Guyana's alternative development strategy is adapted from "Guyana Takes on the IMF" by Susan Meeker-Lowry in the summer 1995 issue of *In Context*. Susan is the author of *Economics as if the Earth Really Mattered* (1988) and *Investing in the Common Good* (1995)—both published by New Society Publishers.

Program (ASAP). Heading the BWRO is Davison Budhoo who, after 12 years of working for the IMF designing SAPs, resigned in disgust. In his open letter of resignation, titled "Enough is Enough," he said that he hoped to "wash my hands of … the blood of millions of poor and starving people."[306] For two years Budhoo had been the IMF resident representative to Guyana, which is now the base for the BWRO.

Guyana's new alternative to structural adjustment goes far beyond UNICEF's rather cautious *Adjustment with a Human Face.* According to Budhoo it "involves democratically designing a comprehensive … economic policy to meet the basic needs of the entire population." The first step is to form a national committee which is responsible for getting input from all affected sectors and groups. Through a series of seminars and symposiums, a core group of people eager for an alternative development strategy brought together representatives from labor, women, educators, farmers, business people, and indigenous peoples. Together they discussed and formulated an economic development plan aimed at meeting the needs of the people of Guyana. According to Susan Meeker-Lowry,

> The result is an approach in marked contrast to that of the IMF and World Bank. It is based on

the principle that a healthy economy does not rely on exports for income and on imports for daily needs. Rather, a healthy economy provides for the needs of the people in a sustainable and egalitarian way that fosters self reliance.

Sustainable agriculture is a key component of the Guyana alternative. Exporting raw materials and importing processed products is no longer encouraged. Instead, domestic food production and domestic consumption receive priority. Crops are diversified, and nontraditional crops—which both lower the cost of food and increase employment—are encouraged.

This approach also promotes a broad economic base with priority given to small-scale, labor-intensive enterprises. Appropriate rural infrastructure is emphasized, including roads, communications, and affordable energy and technology. Friendly credit promotes local business development through Grameen-type banks, which make small loans at low or no interest, using a peer group lending process.

The Guyana [alternative] rejects the IMF freeze on social sector spending, asserting that 'increasing the standard of living of the majority must be the first and foremost objective.[307]

Deforestation has been a major issue; Guyana has one of the largest remaining rainforest areas in the world. However, most of it has been leased for exploitation by transnationals, which, under terms of the IMF's SAP, were offered a 10-year exemption from taxation. The resultant heavy timbering was rapidly destroying the environment of Guyana's indigenous forest dwellers.

As part of the new alternative to adjustment, an International Rainforest Tribunal was appointed to review the government's agreement with logging and mining TNCs. The tribunal will declassify and renegotiate the secret contracts between the government and the TNCs and facilitate the reformation of the currently nonfunctioning Guyanese Natural Resources Agency. It will also ensure the indigenous people that their land titles will be honored and that they will have a strong voice in all development affecting them.

In 1994, President Jagan declared the IMF program for Guyana "massively flawed and inappropriate" and agreed "to cancel the IMF SAP and renegotiate with that institution on the basis of the conclusions and recommendations of the people's ASAP." The Guyanese do not expect the IMF to agree easily to the alternative plan because of its emphasis on self-reliance rather than on serving the world market. But Budhoo and other social activists see this new approach as the beginning of a global movement for more people-friendly alternatives. A "big splash" is predicted when India and the Philippines stand up to the international financial institutions to push through their alternative, equity-oriented approaches to development. Already, in 1993 in India, half a million people, mostly farmers, protested against the IMF/World Bank agricultural policy and GATT (General Agreement on Tarriffs and Trade).[308]

Budhoo asserts that "Guyana is important because we need to show it can be done .... We are not speaking about technical problems in international finance, we're speaking about our role in shaping the destiny of humankind and about the legacy that we will leave to generation upon generation yet unborn."[309]

Equity as the Sustainable Solution to Population Growth and AIDS

In this chapter we look at two controversial subjects which relate to a sustainable future for the world's children: the growing global population, and the spread of the HIV virus/AIDS. Attempts have been made to stem the increase of both population and AIDS through technological measures which tend to blame poor and high-risk groups while seeking "behavioral change." In reality, however, it is the imbalance of wealth and power—the exploitation of the weak by the strong—which lies behind both rapid population growth and the rapid spread of AIDS. Only by combating the inequities of society, from the family to the international level, can we hope to achieve a sustainable equilibrium between humanity and the environment and to stem the spread of AIDS.

Is Population Control an Answer to Today's Global Crises?

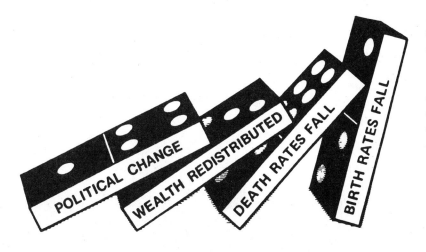

Take care of the people's problems, and the "population problem" will take care of itself.
— a popular slogan of the 1970s

Nearly all Northern countries that have achieved population stabilization have done so through promoting better quality of life rather than explicitly trying to reduce population growth.
— *Population Policies Reconsidered: Health, Empowerment and Rights,* Harvard School of Public Health, 1994[310]

The high rate of population growth in underdeveloped countries has been called "the most solemn problem in the world."[311] It was the theme of the International Conference on Population and Development (ICPD) held in September, 1994, in Cairo, Egypt. Arguments were put forth that the planet has reached—and in some areas exceeded—its "carrying capacity." Speakers equated the major crises of our times to the rapidly increasing population. These crises included world hunger, growing poverty, landlessness and urban drift, mushrooming squatter settlements, growing crime and violence, huge numbers of refugees, resurgence of cholera, inadequate coverage of health and education systems, and deterioration of the global environment.

Since most growth of the world's population takes place in the Third World, there was a tendency to define the core problem as "the poor have too many children." It was suggested that the ultimate solution to the population crisis, and thus many of the current crises facing human-

ity, might require reduction of poverty. But for more immediate action, there was a strong call to step-up family planning (i.e. fertility control) initiatives targeting poor countries and communities.

Rapid population growth is often blamed on the introduction of modern health services, which lower child death rates without a corresponding drop in fertility rates. Many high-level planners insist that *all health services in poor communities must have a strong family planning component.* (In some countries health care providers have been required to recruit monthly quotas of birth control *acceptors.* This has led to many abuses, including unsolicited sterilizations, and refusal to attend sick children until mothers agree to contraception or sterilization.) As pointed out by the progressive women's movement, this disproportionate emphasis on family planning can be counterproductive. For many socially disadvantaged families, having many children is an economic asset, providing the security that society does not deliver.[312] In both rural and urban areas children contribute to family income from an early age, and provide support and care in times of parental unemployment, sickness, and old age.

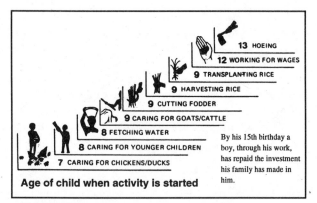

13 HOEING
12 WORKING FOR WAGES
9 TRANSPLANTING RICE
9 HARVESTING RICE
9 CUTTING FODDER
9 CARING FOR GOATS/CATTLE
8 FETCHING WATER
8 CARING FOR YOUNGER CHILDREN
7 CARING FOR CHICKENS/DUCKS

By his 15th birthday a boy, through his work, has repaid the investment his family has made in him.

Age of child when activity is started

Fig. 3–22

Should Children in an "Exploding Population" Be Allowed to Die?

Some prominent scientists even question the validity of promoting Child Survival interventions in poor, rapidly growing populations. For example, Dr. Maurice King, an early pioneer of Primary Health Care, agrees that when child mortality rates decline as part of an overall improvement in living standards (as has historically happened in the Northern countries), fertility rates also tend to decline. However, he asserts that when child mortality is provisionally reduced through selected vertical interventions such as ORT and Immunizations which leave poor living conditions unchanged, fertility rates remain high. The combination of lowered mortality and high fertility leads to rapid population growth, which in turn accelerates land scarcity, depletion of ecological reserves, unemployment, malnutrition, and further deterioration of living conditions. King calls this downward spiral the *Demographic Trap.* He warns that, "The life of a child in a trapped community may be preserved technologically in the short term, but only for a miserable and malnourished future and an early death."[313] King strongly criticizes UNICEF for its Child Survival strategy which, he asserts, focuses too much on life-saving interventions without adequately addressing family planning or quality of life.

Redefining the celebrated WHO definition of health, King suggests that "Health is a *sustainable* state of complete physical, mental, and social well-being, and not merely the absence of disease or infirmity." He asserts that in trapped communities, where "no adequately sustaining measures are possible, such de-sustaining measures as oral rehydration should not be introduced on a public scale, since they increase the man-years of human misery, ultimately from starvation." Needless to say, the implications of King's assertion—to let destitute children die for

the sake of the future common good—has led to protests by UNICEF and has triggered heated international debate. Some of Maurice King's observations are well-founded. Isolated efforts to lower child mortality through selected technological interventions—when promoted in ways that do nothing to improve children's quality of life—often do amount to merely postponing death and prolonging misery. As we pointed out in Chapter 6, a divergence between morbidity and mortality rates is being seen in a number of countries that have practiced selective child survival strategies. This predictably foreshadows slowdowns and reversals in reduction of child death rates (see p. 40). These patterns provide strong evidence that to achieve *a sustainable state of health* within a society, a comprehensive rather than a selective approach to health care is needed: one that gets at the social and economic roots of poor health, high mortality, and high fertility.

However, King's assertion that promotion of technologies such as ORT and immunization should be withheld from "demographically trapped" countries and communities is unconscionable. Every child—rich or poor, strong, weak, or disabled—has the same right to live, grow, be healthy, and realize her full potential. Potentially life-saving technologies such as ORT and immunization must be

Why bother immunizing children only to then starve them?

introduced in all communities in need. However, they should be introduced as part of a comprehensive approach which can help families and communities work decisively toward guaranteeing that the full range of all children's— and all people's—basic needs and rights are met.

In virtually all the impoverished communities King speaks of as *demographically trapped,* people are also trapped by powerlessness and oppression. Problems of squalor, landlessness, underemployment, and social deterioration which are often blamed on *overpopulation* frequently resolve themselves—as they did in Cuba— when land, resources, and services are more fairly distributed. Accordingly, when societies begin to make sure that the basic needs of the whole population are met, low income families can afford to have fewer children and see advantages in doing so. Hence population growth rates begin to decline. This decline is evident in many Northern industrialized countries. Those European countries that have adequate minimum wages, universal health care, and equitable social security have approached zero population growth.

By contrast, the United States, for all its enormous wealth, also has colossal inequities (see page 110). Not surprisingly, the USA has a higher birth rate than other Northern industrialized countries which are much more equitable in terms of meeting all of their citizens' basic needs. What is more, as inequity in the US grows, the total fertility rate has been climbing: from 1.8 in 1980 to 2.1 in 1992.[314]

Low population growth rates in some poor countries: examples

We saw that the four states in the *Good Health at Low Cost* study (see page 114) and also Cuba have dramatically reduced child mortality and greatly improved children's overall health and quality of life. They have done this by guaranteeing that all people's basic needs are met.

It is of interest to note that several studies which consider population trends point out that these same five countries with relatively low income inequality (especially China, Kerala, and Cuba) also have substantially reduced their birth rates.[315] Costa Rica's most rapid decline in child mortality coincided with its greatest decline in birth rate. After 1980 and structural adjustment, however, both mortality and fertility declines halted. Today Costa Rica has a total fertility rate of 3.2, higher than Colombia and Panama.[316]

Some of these countries with low income disparity have had strong family planning programs, while others have

not. China has forcefully pushed its "one family, one child" population policy (with frightening results in terms of human rights violations, including widespread killing of female fetuses and baby girls by parents who want a boy). However, Kerala, Sri Lanka, and Costa Rica all have relatively low fertility rates (compared to the average of Third World countries), in spite of less aggressive family planning campaigns.

For example, Kerala—despite being one of the poorest states in India—has not only achieved lower under-five mortality rates and longer life expectancy than other states in India, it also has achieved the country's lowest fertility rate.[317] (In 1986 Kerala had a birth rate of 22 per 1000 women of child-bearing age, compared to 32 for India as a whole, and 43 as the average for 37 "low income" countries. See figure 3–19.)[318] Population scientist John Ratcliffe concludes that:

> The Kerala experience . . . clearly supports the theoretical perspective that low levels of fertility result from public policies that effectively increase levels of social justice and economic equity throughout society.[319]

Cuba also provides an excellent example of how increased equity coincides with falling birth rates. During the Batista dictatorship, when the gap between rich and poor was enormous and people had few social guarantees, Cuba, like other Latin American countries, had a high fertility rate. As we discussed on page 112, after the overthrow of Batista the revolutionary government introduced one of the world's most equitable systems in terms of meeting all citizens' basic physical needs (if not always their political rights). Social guarantees included: universal, high quality health care and education, universal employment opportunities; adequate housing and sanitation for all; full care for the elderly, equal rights and opportunities for women, etc. Although the "New Cuba" made a variety of contraceptive methods available, for years it had no policy to promote family planning. Yet

Fig. 3–23[320]

during the first decade of the Revolution, the birth rate plummeted dramatically—far more than in those Latin American countries with strong family planning campaigns but few social guarantees for their impoverished masses.[321] Today Cuba, with a GNP per capita of only US $3 per day, not only has the best health status in the developing world, but also the lowest birth rate.[322] Significantly, it now has a lower fertility rate than the United States.[323]

Socioeconomic factors, not birth control, as the chief determinant of birth rates

Many nongovernment organizations (NGOs) and popular movements interpret the current international spotlight on population as an attempt by the privileged elite to forestall global disaster without upsetting the *status quo*. They protest that citing over-population as a cause of under-development is a strategy which blames growing poverty, hunger, and environmental demise on the poor and hungry, rather than on those who consume far more than their share.

However, the wealthy countries and individuals put far more strain on resources and the environment than do the poor. The average person in the US and Europe consumes about 50 times as much of the world's energy and other resources, and creates 50 times as much garbage and toxic waste, as does a poor person in the South.

Progressive women's groups—especially those in the Third World—see the basic issue as one of *Reproductive Rights*. In this view it is not the growing world population but rather today's unfair global economic policies that are the primary cause of the spiraling human and environmental crises on our planet. All women should have control over their own fertility. A wide range of birth-control methods should be available to everyone. But fertility control should be the free decision of each couple or individual, never an obligation.[324]

John Ratcliffe has done some interesting macro studies of population trends, comparing fluctuations in growth rates of different countries at different times and under varying socioeconomic and political systems. His studies confirm that fertility rates are determined much more by societal factors than by the presence or relative aggressiveness of family planning initiatives.[325]

Those who are genuinely concerned about population growth (as distinct from those who harp on "population" to avoid confronting social injustice as the root cause of our global crises) need to take the above observations very seriously. What they imply is that: Population growth cannot be substantially reduced through family planning programs alone. The only way to bring about substantial and sustainable reduction of fertility rates is through far-reaching social change. Such change entails more equitable systems, with policies to guarantee that the basic needs of all persons are met. Only under conditions of social justice can most people afford—much less experience the advantages of—having fewer children.

Aids in the Third World — A Disease of Poverty and Structural Injustice

Those at highest risk are those whose rights are least realized and whose dignity is least protected—from Blacks in the United States to Arabs in France to Koreans in Japan.
> —Jonathan M. Mann, first director of WHO's AIDS program

[Mann] is speaking about political issues. I have my hands full with the scientific issues.
> —William E. Paul, AIDS research director, US National Institute of Health

> — both quotes: *The Boston Globe*, August 10, 1994[326]

Any discussion of the impact of economic and political structures on children's well-being (or on the problem of children's diarrhea in the 1990s) would be incomplete without looking at the growing problem of AIDS. On August 9, 1994 at the Tenth International Conference on AIDS, Jonathan M. Mann, first director of WHO's AIDS program, stated that "It is now evident that [the current

global AIDS strategy is] manifestly insufficient to bring the pandemic under control." According to Mann, "Deep social problems—centering on sexual inequality, cultural barriers to open discussion of sexuality, and economic inequity—underlie the traffic in sex and drugs through which AIDS is often transmitted." Asserting that these underlying social problems must be addressed to contain the disease, Mann acknowledged that he was calling for an effort to "transform society in order to deal with AIDS."[327]

One study in Africa has concluded that the global recession and structural adjustment programs (SAPs) "further aggravate the transmission, spread and [inability to] control of HIV infection in Africa in two major ways: directly by increasing the population at risk through increased urban migration, poverty, women's powerlessness and prostitution, and indirectly through a decrease in health care provision."[328] AIDS has hit certain Third World countries particularly hard, especially areas where poverty and income disparity are extreme. In sub-Saharan Africa it is estimated that 1 in every 40 adults is infected with HIV, and in some cities the rate is 1 in 3.[329] In some African countries such as Zambia, up to 10% of the population is now thought to be HIV positive, including 20–25% of Zambian women aged 15 to 49.[330] In Zimbabwe, one in four adults in infected.[331] At its current rate of increase, AIDS is expected to lower life expectancy by 25 years in some African countries.[332] In Uganda, for example, life expectancy has already dropped from 52 to 42 years because of AIDS. (Similarly, in Thailand life expectancy is predicted to drop from 69 years in 1994 to 40 years by 2010.[333]) AIDS is projected to kill between 1.5 and 2.9 million African women of reproductive age by the year 2000,[334] having left more than 5 million African children motherless.[335]

AIDS is taking an especially heavy toll on Africa's children. Congenital transmission — i.e., from mother to fetus—is the second most common way the HIV virus is spread in Africa, after heterosexual contact. More and more children are being born with HIV. In some areas of Africa, 25% to 30% of pregnant women attending antenatal clinics are HIV positive.[336] By 1991, some 500,000 infants in sub-Saharan Africa had the HIV virus.[337] By the year 2000, that figure is expected to reach 11 million.[338] In Zimbabwe, AIDS has been the major cause of child deaths in urban hospitals since 1989.[339]

In large regions of Africa AIDS is contributing to the reversal of child survival gains. The following figures, cited in an article by Sanders and Sambo, make this clear:

> The United Nations projected that in 1990, the under-5 mortality rate (U5MR) in east and central Africa would have declined from 158 per 1,000 live births, to 132 by the year 1999 without the impact of AIDS. The U5MR, however, is already between 165 and 167 in 1990 as a result of the additional impact of AIDS and is predicted to rise to 189 by the year 2000.[340]

If present trends continue, AIDS will soon be the leading cause of child death in many other African countries. And although we have stressed the situation in Africa, in 1995 for the first time more people are believed to have contracted HIV in Asia than anywhere else.[341] Like diarrhea in its life-threatening form, AIDS is largely a disease of poverty and social injustice. (Indeed, in communities where diarrhea claims many children's lives, chronic diarrhea is often the first and most prevailing symptom of AIDS. Because of the severe wasting associated with chronic gastrointestinal distress, AIDS in Africa is referred to as *slim disease*.)

If we look at the "hot spots" of AIDS in the Third World—sub-Saharan Africa, Thailand, Brazil, Haiti, Honduras—we see that they tend to be in places where the gap between rich and poor is greatest, where the rights of women and children are most flagrantly violated, where social conditions are deteriorating, and where minimum wages have fallen so low that destitute people are forced into alternatives of income generation that they would not otherwise choose.

Poverty-driven migrant labor and the spread of AIDS

Some observers attribute the rapid spread of HIV in Africa at least in part to SAPs [Structural Adjustment Programs], which increased migration and urbanization, drove more people into poverty, forced women into prostitution, while at the same time depriving health ministries of enough money to provide health care and prevention.

—*The Lancet,* Vol 344, Nov. 19, 1994[342]

In those parts of Africa with the highest incidence of HIV infection, its rapid spread is linked to the high prevalence of poverty-driven migrant labor. This migrant labor pattern derives from a polarized class system dating back to colonial times. But during the last decade foreign debt, recession, and SAPs have made the plight of the poor more extreme. These factors have pushed down real wages, slashed public services for the poor, and required peasant farmers to grow cash crops for export at increasingly low prices. These desperate conditions have forced vast numbers of destitute peasants (especially men) to periodically migrate to distant mining towns and cities, where those fortunate enough to find work are packed into dismal dormitories and paid starvation wages for thankless, grueling work.

Having left their wives and girlfriends behind in the villages, these itinerant workers seek other sexual outlet, often with female sex workers (many of whom come from equally destitute situations and have only their bodies to sell). When the men occasionally return to their women and families in the villages, they take their STDs and HIV infections with them. The result is a rampant spread of these diseases.

Region	1970	1990	2025
		(percent)	
Africa	23	32	54
Asia (excl. Japan)	20	29	54
Latin America	57	72	84
Europe	67	73	85
North America	74	75	85
World	37	43	61

Fig. 3–24 Share of Population Living in Urban Areas, by Region, 1970 and 1990, with Projections to 2025.[343]

I SELL MY PERSUASIVE ABILITIES AND PROTECT BUSINESS

I SELL MY BRAIN POWER AND DEVELOP BUSINESS

I SELL MY MUSCLE AND DEFEND BUSINESS

I SELL MY LOOKS AND ADVERTISE BUSINESS

I SELL MY LABOR AND PROFIT BUSINESS

WHORE OUT OF THIS NEIGHBORHOOD!

I SELL MY BODY AND SUPPORT MY FAMILY

In Latin America, as in Africa, extreme inequity also appears to contribute to the proliferation of HIV and AIDS. Three countries with the highest incidence of HIV infection— Brazil, Mexico, and most recently Honduras—also have a widening gap between rich and poor, mushrooming squatter settlements, desperately low wages, and high rates of unemployment, crime, street children, and prostitution. A growing number of sex workers are destitute children, boys as well as girls, some of them as young as 8 or 10 years old.

In Honduras—similar to the Philippines and elsewhere—an increase in HIV infection has occurred in the areas surrounding foreign (US) army bases, for obvious reasons. (Likewise, it is reported that HIV infection has escalated where UN peace-keeping forces have been stationed in Cambodia and elsewhere.) Wherever some people have a lot of money and others are destitute, HIV and AIDS seem to flourish. Sexual tourism in Thailand is a prime example.

Until the recent crash of the peso, Mexico was lauded for its modest economic growth in recent years, as one of the few success stories of structural adjustment. But since the early 1980s unemployment has soared and the purchasing power of working people's daily wages has dropped by more than 50%. As in many countries subjected to liberalization and economic restructuring, the rapid spread of HIV in Mexico can be linked to a high rate of migrant labor that periodically separates men from their wives (see page 148). The North American Free Trade Agreement (NAFTA) has exacerbated the already dismal unemployment situation, compelling millions of *braceros* or "wetbacks" to illegally cross the border into the United States in search of work and decent wages. There they contract HIV and other STDs, and later take them back home to their wives and girlfriends. In this way, AIDS is likely to reach pandemic proportions in Mexico, just as it has in parts of Africa and elsewhere that harsh inequities cause massive migration of peasants into the mines and labor camps of the cities.[344]

What can be done to halt the spread of HIV/AIDS? In the pernicious social conditions where HIV is spreading fastest, educating high risk individuals to use condoms may be better than nothing. But it is not enough. Only by correcting the inequitable social structures that allow the affluent to exploit the destitute, that force long separations between husbands and wives, and that create such hopelessness that people throw precaution to the wind, can the rapid spread of HIV be contained. To get at the root cause of the Third World HIV/AIDS epidemic would require, for a start, cancellation of foreign debt and reversal of poverty-increasing structural adjustment policies. In rural areas it would require encouraging production of local foods for domestic consumption rather than for export, and public assistance to help poor farmers stay on their land and with their families. In urban areas it would require fairer wages, low cost family housing, and strengthening of independent labor unions permitting workers to demand their rights and hold both government and employers accountable. And it would also require the empowerment and greater equality of women. In the long run, social justice will do more to slow the spread of HIV than current attempts to promote safe sex. Both are necessary. Unfortunately, however, health planners and technocrats have once again tried to solve what is fundamentally a social problem with a technological fix.

CONCLUSION TO PART 3

In this third part we have seen that levels of health are determined more by social, political, and economic factors than by medical breakthroughs or technological fixes. In the North, improvements in health came only after workers began to organize and demand their rights. More recently, in the South, it has become clear that selected technological interventions—be they ORS packets to combat dehydration, condoms to prevent AIDS, or contraceptives to combat overpopulation—at best will give very limited results…unless they are integrated into a comprehensive, equity-oriented, and empowering approach.

We have seen several examples of countries that have approached *good health at low cost* by following a course of development that places the basic needs of all people before the tunnel-visioned pursuit of economic growth for a few. But as promising as they are, the equity-oriented paths of development—even in a country as large and independent as China—have proved difficult to sustain in an international climate that increasingly places the demands of the global marketplace (i.e. the unregulated accumulation of wealth by the already wealthy) before the needs of the entire population.

There are, however, many examples of people working together to achieve local, short-term needs within a broader context of building a healthier, more equitable society. In the final part of this book we will look at some of these alternative approaches, their strengths and weaknesses, and what we can learn from them to move forward during these difficult times.

PART 4

Solutions That Empower the Poor:
Examples of Equity-Oriented Initiatives

INTRODUCTION TO PART 4

In advocating Primary Health Care, the Alma Ata Declaration affirms that health is determined mainly by factors outside the domain of medical or public health services. In the five examples of countries that achieved *good health at low cost*—Sri Lanka, Kerala, China, Costa Rica, and Cuba—we saw that a key to widespread improvement in health is strong political commitment to equity in meeting all people's basic needs. The Alma Ata statement warns, however, that powerful interest groups both within and outside the health sector are inclined to steer health and development initiatives in directions contrary to the best interests of all, especially those of poor and vulnerable groups. To make sure that the design and implementation of Primary Health Care correspond to the concerns and abilities of local people, the Declaration called for active community participation. This was not to be the weak participation of compliance (as in many top-down programs) but rather strong participation of leadership and control, involving community members in analysis of needs and in the planning, evaluation and redesign of health actions according to popular demand. In short, Primary Health Care should be an emancipatory process. Unfortunately, there are too few examples of health initiatives that have put these Alma Ata ideals into effective, sustainable action. And most that have tried have confronted major obstacles.

The final part of this book begins, in Chapter 16, by exploring the process of confidence building, critical analysis, and enablement (or empowerment) necessary for people to stand up for their rights and take a decisive part in decisions that affect their health and their lives.

Chapters 17 to 20 look at four quite different community health initiatives which, to varying degrees, have been introduced in enabling or empowering ways. These range from a small nongovernmental initiative—as seen in Project Piaxtla in Mexico—to a nationwide mass mobilization for health, as part of Nicaragua's unending struggle for liberation. While one of these four examples—the community-run oral rehydration program in Mozambique—might be considered to be narrow-focused or *selective*, we will see that it actually responded to health-influencing factors far outside the health sector. It attempted to make schooling more relevant to children's daily lives by helping them to gain problem-solving skills for meeting health needs in their homes and communities. Through *participatory epidemiology* it helped prepare children as critical thinkers and advocates for health-promoting change. Likewise, the example from Zimbabwe, although essentially a government-sponsored program for supplementary feeding, helps to bring poor families together in defining a spectrum of health-related problems and taking cooperative action to solve them.

In all four of these initiatives, attempts were made to put into practice the democratic, participatory principles of Alma Ata. However, sooner or later, each of these programs ran into obstacles created by the existing power structure, not just locally or even nationally, but at an international level. Currently, global forces are dictating development and health policies. It is becoming harder for disadvantaged communities and countries to follow local alternatives that are empowering and democratic, equitable, and thereby sustainable. In view of these globalized obstacles to health, the closing chapter of this book explores the growing need for globally coordinated people-oriented solutions to help make the promise of Alma Ata—*health for all*— a real possibility.

CHAPTER 16

Health Care, Empowerment, and Social Change

As has been stressed throughout this book, far-reaching improvements in health depend more on social, economic, and political factors than on either medical breakthroughs or health care interventions per se. Countries with the most striking and durable improvements in health tend to be those with a commitment to equity that is broad-based and multisectoral. It has been argued that the health gains of poor countries that have pursued this sort of development model have seldom proved sustainable. However, it is important to recognize that the reasons for this have been largely external. Time and again, such countries have been attacked or destabilized by powerful, less egalitarian nations whose rulers fear that such people-centered endeavors may be contagious.

There have, of course, also been internal reasons for the difficulties in sustaining a need-based model of development. In some countries, following liberation from unjust regimes, there has been a reconcentration of power and a weakening of popular support. Commitment to equity has eroded as well, making health improvements hard to sustain. (In Chapter 21, we show how health improvements gained following national independence are being undermined by such reconcentration of power and wealth.)

The current stagnation and reversals of health and living standards in a growing number of countries demonstrate that the conventional, increasingly globalized development model is in many ways counterproductive: it makes the rich richer and the poor poorer. The pursuit of *growth without equity* (the neoliberal paradigm of development) has become the major obstacle to health for all. Even the World Bank now asserts that the alleviation of poverty is a precondition to a healthy society, and it calls for cost-efficient measures to meet all people's basic needs. Yet the Bank's reformed blueprint is still based on economic growth that benefits the rich and adjustment policies that further deprive the poor. Clearly, alternatives are needed.

Equity, Participation, and Empowerment

To achieve the equity essential for a healthy society, it appears that a strong, organized demand for accountability of government to the people may be a key prerequisite. Tacit recognition of this dynamic explains the Alma Ata Declaration's call for strong community participation. (It also explains why the ruling elites in the North and South joined forces to trivialize the Declaration, as we discussed in Part 1.)

To achieve and sustain the political will to meet all people's basic needs, a process of participatory democracy—or at least a well informed grassroots movement—is essential. And because the opposition to equity-oriented social development has become so pervasive, a coordinated global effort is urgently needed.

Recognizing the importance of such popular participation is a key to successful health care initiatives. This is illustrated by the impressive achievements of China's mass public health campaigns in the 1950s,[1] as it is by Nicaragua's mass immunization campaigns in the 1980s (see Chapter 20). Even at the provincial or district level the health benefits of popular involvement are excellent. The state of Kerala in India and the San Ramón district of Costa Rica are good examples. This latter initiative involved strong community participation in service provision as well as in planning. Guided not by health professionals but through large community gatherings, San Ramón District achieved the best health and child mortality statistics in all of Latin America, with the exception of Cuba.[2]

In countries where the political climate is not conducive to such popular participation or to equitable development (i.e. most countries), what approaches can be taken to meet the health needs of underprivileged groups? Should health activists work within the system, outside it, or both? Is it possible for community health work to become an arena for cultivating the political awareness and organization needed to introduce a more equity-oriented approach to health and development?

Two examples we cite in the next chapters (Mexico and Nicaragua) indicate that community health initiatives can be an entry point in organized pursuit of a healthier, more equitable society—although the difficulties and limitations may be great. Whether working under a repressive or progressive regime, health activists can facilitate a comprehensive empowering approach that helps people address their immediate ills while starting to tackle those problems' root causes. Examples from diverse situations show that *it is possible for health workers to function within an inequitable social order while working to transform it.*

Solutions that Empower the Poor

Health initiatives that are limited to technological interventions are, at best, limited in their impact. They perpetuate the misconception that health problems rooted in poverty and inequity can be solved by medical or health care alone, while leaving the causal inequities in place. As we have seen, UNICEF/WHO's strategy for promoting oral rehydration therapy (ORT) is at best a stop-gap solution. No matter how well designed and funded, it is unlikely to significantly decrease child deaths from diarrhea, for two reasons. First, as typically promoted, ORT campaigns seek merely to combat dehydration rather than to combat the socioeconomic conditions that make diarrhea deadly. Second, the emphasis on ORS packets fosters dependency, adds nutrition-depleting costs, and medicalizes what could be a simple solution. UNICEF/WHO's recent emphasis on the home management of diarrhea with "increased fluids and food" is a step in the right direction.

A more empowering approach is to help people improve their understanding of health problems and to build on their skills for dealing with them. This can help to break both the monopoly enjoyed by experts as well as people's dependency on needless commercial products. Encouragement of appropriate health technologies can help to reduce the indiscriminate adoption of sophisticated, extravagant, and mystifying ones.

As we discussed in Part 2, appropriate technologies for home use need to be implemented *at all levels* of the health care system, so that people will not consider them second best. With ORT, this means promoting the use of home drinks not only in homes but also in health centers and even in hospitals, as was done in Zimbabwe. Unfortunately, UNICEF and WHO recommend that health posts and clinics rely on packets, and reserve home fluids as first aid until "real" ORS can be obtained.

Diarrhea Management as a Process of Empowerment

For health interventions to have a significant and lasting impact, they must go beyond a merely curative or management focus to a truly preventive and promotive one. They need not only work to demystify and democratize health services, but also to help communities identify and address the root causes of their health problems.

As we saw in Chapter 1, the problem of child diarrhea provides an example of the chain of causes that can lead to a child's death. Successive levels of causal factors can be analyzed. The deeper we go (or the further back on the chain) to combat the problem, the more effective and lasting our efforts are likely to be. Consider the following example, adapted from a paper by David Werner (*Health Care and Human Dignity*):

> Each year millions of impoverished children die of diarrhea. We tend to agree that most of these deaths could be prevented. Yet diarrhea remains among the biggest killers of young children. Does this mean our so-called preventive measures are merely palliative? At what point in the chain of causes which makes death from diarrhea a global problem … are we coming to grips with the real underlying cause. Do we do it:
>
> - by preventing some deaths through treatment of diarrhea?
>
> - by trying to interrupt the infectious cycle through construction of latrines and water systems?
>
> - by reducing high risk from diarrhea through better nutrition?
>
> - [or] by curbing land tenure inequities through land reform?
>
> Land reform comes closest to the real problem. But the peasantry is oppressed by far more inequities than those of land tenure. The existing power structure both causes and perpetuates crushing inequities at the local, national, and multinational levels. It includes political, commercial, and religious power groups as well as the legal profession and the medical establishment. In short, it includes … ourselves …

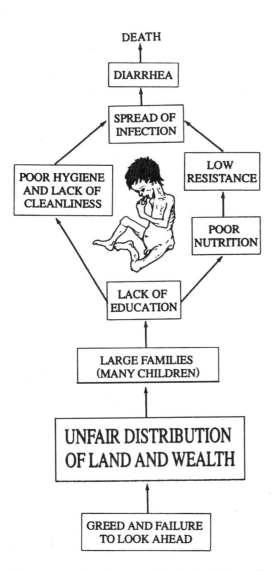

DEATH

DIARRHEA

SPREAD OF INFECTION

POOR HYGIENE AND LACK OF CLEANLINESS

LOW RESISTANCE

POOR NUTRITION

LACK OF EDUCATION

LARGE FAMILIES (MANY CHILDREN)

UNFAIR DISTRIBUTION OF LAND AND WEALTH

GREED AND FAILURE TO LOOK AHEAD

Where, then, should prevention begin? Beyond doubt, anything we can do to minimize the inequities perpetuated by the existing power structure will do far more to reduce high infant mortality than all our conventional preventive measures put together. We should, perhaps, carry on with our latrine-building rituals, nutrition centers and agricultural extension projects. But let's stop calling it prevention; we are still only treating symptoms. And unless we are very careful, we may even be making the underlying problem worse, through increasing dependency on outside aid, technology and control.

But this need not be the case. *If* the building of latrines brings people together and helps them look ahead, *if* a nutrition center is built and run by the community and fosters self-reliance, and *if* agricultural extension, rather than imposing outside technology encourages internal growth

of the people toward more effective understanding and use of their land, their potentials and their rights ... then, and only then, do latrines, nutrition centers and so-called extension work begin to deal with the real causes of preventable sickness and death.[3]

Thus, in evaluating any health or development strategy, we must constantly ask ourselves:

To what extent does the strategy promote the active, meaningful participation and the empowerment of those with the worst health (usually the poorest and most powerless members of society)? And do the methods used help or hinder the long-term process of correcting the underlying social, economic, and political causes of ill health?

By looking at the process of enablement or empowerment of marginalized people, we can learn something about the strategies and methods that seem to work. Then we can try to apply these at the local, national, and international levels.

The Empowerment Process

Empowerment is the process by which disadvantaged people work together to take control of the factors that determine their health and their lives. When high-level planners say that their programs or technologies will empower people, they therefore misuse the word. By definition, one cannot empower someone else: empowerment is something which people do for themselves. However, sometimes concerned health workers or facilitators can help open the way for poor people to empower themselves. Power cannot be given; it must be taken.

There is no formula for empowerment. It is a dynamic process that can happen in several ways. However, there are some constants. Empowerment is at once a personal and a group process. It is part of a process of building collective self-confidence. This is needed for people to shed the feelings of powerlessness and resignation which result, at least in part, from the lack of skills and confidence required to change their condition. Frequently this confidence is forged in a common struggle—whether it be against gender or ethnic oppression, economic exploitation, political repression, or foreign intervention.

The Methodology of Paulo Freire Applied to Health Care

In Part 1 we described briefly a methodology for helping people to empower themselves which the Brazilian educator Paulo Freire, in the 1960s, described as "education for liberation." The methodology was originally designed for an adult literacy program, but has since been adapted to community health. A small group, such as the residents of a shantytown neighborhood, is brought together in a dynamic problem-posing interchange in which everyone learns from each other. In this guided awareness-raising process, or *conscientization* the group moves from *discussion* of common problems, to *analysis* of the problems' underlying social causes, and then to *collective action* to remove these causes. (This typically involves a strategy for confronting the local, national, and/or international power structure). After a pause for *reflection* the sequence is repeated.

As the group's experience and confidence grows, it can begin to tackle more difficult problems, probe deeper in its analysis, and push for more basic changes. But the group needs to recognize the implications of this course. It must understand that as it progresses toward pursuing more fundamental changes, the risk of backlash increases. The logical conclusion of the empowerment process may be an attempt by disadvantaged people to redistribute wealth, land, other resources, rights, or power so that everyone has a fairer share. Such a step is likely to bring the group into confrontation with the privileged class and their guards, and thus expose its members to danger. Facilitators therefore have an obligation to make sure that all participants or trainees understand possible dangers from the outset. The group needs to weigh benefits against risks, and formulate strategies that maximize the former and minimize the latter.

> ### Paulo Freire:
> ### Educator, Author, Revolutionary
>
> Paulo Freire, the controversial Brazilian educator and author of *Pedagogy of the Oppressed*, designed an approach to adult literacy based on helping poor people learn to read and write through analyzing for themselves their problems of daily life, and then taking personal and collective action to "transform their world." Freire's approach was so successful in awakening people to their rights that he was exiled from Brazil after the military coup in 1964.
>
> Freire distinguished between two concepts of education: the "banking" approach and the "problem-posing" approach. In the banking approach, all-knowing teachers pour a predetermined body of information into "ignorant" learners, like water into an empty jug. Freire branded this form of teaching an "instrument of oppression." It permits society's rulers to shape the views and attitudes of the poor majority, thus keeping them in their place. In the problem-posing or "awareness-raising" approach, on the other hand, the facilitators relate to the learners as equals. They help them value and analyze their own experience and create their own plans of action to meet the needs which they themselves identify and prioritize. Freire considered this approach to learning to be an "instrument of liberation."

Groups or movements working for social change must be prepared to encounter repression on three successive levels: local, national, and international. At the local level, the first line of defense may consist of hired goons or the police. If these are unable to put a stop to the groundswell for change, the army may be called in. Or more powerful nations whose elites have an economic or political stake in the country in question may intervene to preserve the status quo.

In the struggle for equity-oriented change, mass mobilization is critical. To avoid being crushed by the ruling minority, marginalized groups need to unite with each other to form larger coalitions, and to recruit as many supporters as possible. If a substantial portion of the community is mobilized, the dominant forces may be more hesitant to crack down on the movement.

Community Based
Diarrhea Control
in Mozambique

CHAPTER 17

Commitment to *Health for All* Amidst War

Following liberation from the colonial rule of the Portuguese in 1975, the new popular government of Mozambique, headed by FRELIMO (the Front for the Liberation of Mozambique), began the process of social and economic restructuring to better meet the needs of all the country's people. Declaring health a basic right, the Health Ministry set out to build a network of health centers and health posts, and to train a legion of community health workers supported by paramedics, nurses and doctors to provide basic, but comprehensive primary health care to the entire population. The initiative focused on rural areas, where needs were greatest.

Combined with a strong emphasis on agriculture, nutrition, and education, this comprehensive initiative to improve health started to yield results. In spite of severe economic difficulties and a shortage of trained personnel, child mortality dropped and life expectancy increased dramatically. Unfortunately, this positive trend was interrupted by the escalation of terrorist attacks by the South Africa–sponsored paramilitary organization RENAMO (Mozambique National Resistance). But in spite of the relentless destabilization tactics by RENAMO and the staggering costs of fighting the brutal war, courageous efforts to help the people meet their health needs continued.

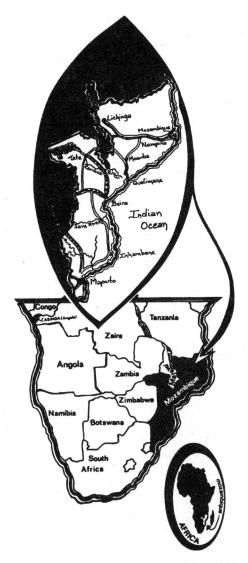

Problems with the Standard ORS Approach

In Mozambique, as in other poor countries, diarrhea has been a major killer of children. Soon after liberation Mozambique launched a comprehensive, multi-sectoral campaign against diarrheal disease. Components included:

- promotion of Oral Rehydration Therapy (ORT);

- promotion of *breastfeeding,* with legislated restrictions on the availability of baby bottles and artificial milk;

- *vaccination* campaigns against infectious diseases that cause diarrhea and weaken children's resistance to diarrheal disease (such as measles);

- *growth monitoring* of children under five, with counseling to parents. And, in critical cases, *food supplements* to underweight children;

- *health and sanitation education* through a variety of media, including radio, public loudspeakers, and the rural newspaper called *O Campo;*

- measures to improve *sanitation* and introduce the use of latrines;

- improvements in *water supply.*

While all these activities helped, it was recognized that reducing the incidence and severity of diarrhea is a difficult long-term process that depends, above all else, on improving the economy and living conditions of the entire population. Given the logistical and economic constraints, the Ministry of Health decided that the best stop-gap option was to focus diarrhea control efforts on oral rehydration therapy.

In doing this, the ministry loosely followed the WHO and UNICEF guidelines emphasizing the production and use of ORS packets, working with the United Nations Industrial Development Organization to construct a factory to produce ORS packets in the city of Beira. The factory began production in March 1983, with a target of two million packets a year—an output that, to the best of our knowledge, was never reached.

Evaluations in 1985, two years after the Beira factory had opened, showed that the introduction of ORS packets had not significantly reduced child mortality from diarrhea. The under-five mortality rate (U5MR) for Mozambique as a whole was between 252 and 375 per 1,000, one of the highest rates in the world.[4] In Beira itself, the death rate from diarrhea among children under five remained very high, with diarrhea taking the lives of 14.7 percent of all children under five, or about 40% of all child deaths.[5]

A subsequent analysis gave the following reasons for the failure of Mozambique's initial ORT strategy:

- terrorism that obstructed factory production of packets, destroyed avenues and means of transportation, burned down health posts, and often targeted health workers;

- inadequate packet supply and difficulty in supplying outlying areas;

- medicalization of ORS—including people's belief that ORS is a medicine that stops or slows down the diarrhea (which it does not), or that it can be taken like other anti-diarrheal drugs for children: 1 spoonful 4 times a day (far too little to do any good);

- the common practice of giving only one packet per episode of diarrhea;

- inadequate and inappropriate education, with a continuation of authoritarian colonial teaching methods;

- insufficient consideration of people's beliefs, traditions, and home remedies;

- inadequate health infrastructure, especially in remote parts of the country.[6]

Seeking the Advice of Village Women

Realizing that the standard WHO/UNICEF approach was not working adequately in their country, the Mozambique Ministry of Health decided to explore alternatives that might better respond to the special needs of their situation. A look at hospital mortality data from different parts of the country revealed that the death rate of children from diarrhea in the vicinity of Inhambane on the southern coast was lower than in most other parts of Mozambique. An investigation of health center records and interviews with mothers confirmed this observation.

A team from the Ministry of Health decided to learn from the mothers of Inhambane what they were doing that might explain the exceptionally low child mortality rate from diarrhea in the area. The team met with a group of 40 mothers from a poor, semi-rural *barrio* of the city. The health officials opened the meeting by informing the women that they had come to them to ask for their help. They explained that Mozambique's diarrhea control program, based on the recommendations of foreign experts, was failing—except in the Inhambane area. The mothers confirmed that few of their babies had died from diarrhea: of the 40 mothers present, only one said she had lost a child to diarrhea. However, they admitted that their babies fell ill with diarrhea quite often.

Initially, the mothers were reluctant to speak openly, and told officials what they thought they wanted to hear—that they were all using ORS packets, just as

they had been taught. Later, once assured they could speak honestly, they admitted that they had tried ORS but were no longer using it because the health center was far away, and often it had run out of packets. If the center did have packets, it would only give a mother one at a time—just enough to begin treatment. In any case, the ORS medicine tasted bad; often their child refused it. And if they could get the child to drink it, it did not even slow down the diarrhea! So why bother?

The health officials continued their questions: if the mothers of Inhambane were not using ORS, then what were they giving to treat their children's diarrhea? The mothers said they had gone back to their traditional remedies. They were giving their babies drinks which they made with ground-up maize, or rice flour, or certain native tubers, or they made drinks from cooked or roasted wheat flour donated to the area for famine relief. They would put about one tablespoonful of the finely mashed cereal in a glass of water. These drinks obviously worked better than the ORS packets, the mothers explained, because they quickly slowed down the diarrhea. And the children liked them better. In addition, the home drinks cost almost nothing—much less than the bus fare to the health center.

The health officials recognized that this successful traditional method of treating diarrhea practiced by the

School children in Mozambique are involved in participatory epidemiology of diarrheal disease.

Inhambane mothers was strikingly similar to cereal-based ORT. After a long debate, the Mozambique Health Ministry decided to try a pilot program with the possibility of revising its national diarrheal disease control program—in line with the experience and advice of local village women.

The pilot program in Nampula

The pilot community and school-based diarrhea control program was initiated on a small scale in the rural area outside Nampula, in the north of Mozambique. Although the program was selective in that it focused on the problem of child diarrhea, from another perspective it was unusually comprehensive. Rather than being restricted to the health sector, it involved close collaboration between the ministries of health and education. The educational component of the pilot program was in some ways revolutionary (in keeping with the goals for a new, more egalitarian society in Mozambique). By introducing participatory, problem-solving learning methods into primary schools, and by involving both teachers and schoolchildren in practical action related to community needs, the pilot program addressed one of the major barriers to social progress in Third World countries: that of an archaic, authoritarian school system.

Mozambique's attempt to transform its public schools was quite a challenge. In most Third World countries the educational system, like the health system, has failed to meet the most pressing needs of ordinary people, and for similar reasons. It is a relic from colonial times, based more on the needs of the colonizers than of the colonized. To colonial rulers, education of the "natives" meant stern discipline, good work habits, and obedient, unquestioning respect for authority. It did not help students learn to think for themselves, develop problem-solving skills, or to analyze and take organized action to meet their most pressing needs. From the colonial perspective (or the perspective of any elitist, nonrepresentative government) education—and especially literacy—is a double-edged sword. On the one hand, it can inculcate standardized behavior and instruct people in the new skills needed for a productive and compliant work force. But on the other hand, it can open avenues of communication and empowerment that could be dangerous in the hands and minds of a subjugated people. In this sense, education is potentially subversive. Not surprisingly, therefore, the colonial school system was based on rote learning, parrot-like repetition of facts, and unquestioning, subservient submission to rules, norms, codes, limits, schedules, timetables, restrictions, and other forms of psychosocial incarceration designed to teach children and other second-class citizens their designated stations in an unfair and hierarchical society. What is more, much of the subject matter taught in colonial schools was based on the life and times of the European colonizers, and was largely irrelevant to the needs and lives of poor rural people in the South.

After independence, the new Mozambique government aimed to make educational content and methodology more relevant to the daily reality and needs of the children, their families, and communities. To achieve this, the government encouraged close intersectoral collaboration between the Ministry of Health and the Ministry of Education. So, in the early planning phase of the pilot project, a meeting of high officials of the two ministries was held.

The goal was to teach information that would be of immediate value to the children and their families. The idea of involving the school children in a pioneering venture to save the lives of their baby brothers and sisters as part of their basic schooling was perfectly suited to this objective. The pilot program was therefore launched as a joint project of both ministries. The enthusiasm on both sides and at all levels—from planners to facilitators to teachers to children—was impressive.

Perhaps the most revolutionary component of this pilot project was what might be called *participatory epidemiology:* involving teachers and children in collecting, recording, and analyzing health information in their communities, in conjunction with research by the Ministry of Health. In this way schoolchildren not only began to learn about such things as math, functional human biology, and practical record-keeping, but they actually contributed to epidemiological research at the national level. Such an approach has the potential not only for making a country's diarrhea control program more participatory, but also more tuned-in to the real situation, the obstacles, and potentials which exist locally. There is much rhetoric about community participation in the planning, implementation, and evaluation of health care interventions at national and international levels, but few examples of it actually happening. This pilot program in Mozambique—however circumscribed and short-lived it proved to be— is one example.

The program was designed to function as follows. Within each village there are five groups of primary actors in the diarrhea control program: volunteer home visitors, school teachers, schoolchildren, mothers, and community health workers. The home visitors—mostly women who belong to the local women's political organization—were women who had had special training in the home management of diarrhea. (In the Nampula pilot program the home visitors were trained by a group of "monitors"—in this case midwives—who, in preparation for their role as "multipliers," had been trained both in diarrheal manage-

ment and in nonformal discovery-based teaching methods.) Each primary school teacher in the village was also trained by the visiting monitor to teach the schoolchildren what to do about diarrhea.

The teacher asked all the children to check to see whether of their baby brothers or sisters had diarrhea before they came to school each morning. Then, the first thing each morning, the teacher would ask the children if any of their little brothers or sisters had diarrhea that day. Any child who answered "yes" was asked to go at once to the volunteer home visitor who lived nearest their home, to tell her about the child with diarrhea, and to have her accompany them to the child's home.

The volunteer home visitor then guided the sick child's mother and the school child through the steps of home management: increasing fluids and foods, and seeing a health worker if certain signs of danger occur. She then would help them prepare a special home-made drink— either a cereal drink or a sugar and salt drink, depending on what seemed easiest, and most appropriate.

Back at school, the teacher would ask the pupil to help each day in caring for the sick child during the entire episode of diarrhea. Each day, the school child was asked to report to the class on the sick child's progress. The class discussed the problem and asked how the diarrhea was being managed. In this way, each time a child in the community had diarrhea, the basic lessons of home care were reinforced.

The teacher, with the help of the pupils, kept a record on a wall chart supplied by the Ministry of Health of all the children reported to have diarrhea and how they were managed. The teacher also recorded which rehydration liquids were used, how long the diarrhea lasted, how many children were referred to the health center, and other epidemiological information.

The district health officer periodically collected these records from the teachers and sent the results to the Diarrheal Disease Control research team in the capital city. There the information was used to evaluate the community action approach as well as to augment studies of diarrhea for the country. In addition to this home management program, each village had a community health brigade which met periodically with the head of the local health post to review progress, to provide additional teaching of home visitors and, where possible, to expand the program to include diarrhea prevention (latrines, clean water, improvements in nutrition, etc.) and other aspects of primary health care.

⌘

The response to this new approach to community/school/home-based diarrhea management was very positive. Although both the methods and approach were new to school teachers, they became excited about working with an activity that brought schooling closer to the lives and needs of the children and their families. Through the participatory, learning-by-doing methods, they could see the children's self-confidence and problem-solving abilities begin to grow.

Another innovative aspect of this pilot program was that it introduced methods of oral rehydration based on the recommendations of Mozambican mothers, with a strong emphasis on home cereal and food-based drinks. This process-oriented approach to health education—rather than a product-oriented approach to the delivery of health services —was not only empowering, but in terms of long-term cost-effectiveness and sustainability, has the potential to be self-perpetuating. People tend to remember what they actively learn.

Although there are initial costs associated with teaching and reinforcing new ideas and practices, these diminish in time. By contrast, investment in nonreusable products such as ORS packets is never-ending. As a product-oriented program is expanded, costs continue to mount, making sustainability increasingly difficult. Conversely, as a process-oriented approach evolves, at some point the new knowledge reaches a critical number of people. Discovering the effectiveness of their new knowledge, people share it with others, and the health messages gather their own momentum and become self-spreading. Except for occasional updates, refreshers, and monitoring, little new financial input is needed.

In summary, the initial trials of the pilot program for diarrhea control in Mozambique showed great promise. Both the health and education ministries were involved from central to local levels. Although the program was initiated by government ministries, it was based on the advice of successful village mothers and implemented by schoolchildren and their teachers, who also took part in relevant epidemiological research. Many participants felt that this pilot program held promise for extension (with local adaptation) throughout the country. It not only had potential for meeting pressing short-term needs in a highly effective way, but also for advancing the long-term national goal of a participatory development process through which government would listen and respond more closely to people's needs.

Unfortunately, this progressive approach to diarrhea control in Mozambique—despite initial enthusiasm and success—was nipped in the bud. Instead of being expanded nationwide, as had originally been the plan, it was canceled after only a year and a half. The program's demise was reportedly caused by a lack of funding as well as pressure from WHO officials, who were apparently upset that the program was advocating home ORT drinks over ORS packets, and were concerned that other Third World countries might follow Mozambique's example in this regard.[7]

Like so many initiatives that are designed with and for the people in greatest need, this small pilot project ran into opposition from high level policy-makers. But although it came to an untimely end, the project remains an important example of how a government initiated program can take a genuinely participatory approach which links urgent short-term interventions with long-term transformative goals. For a government to facilitate such an approach is exceptional. We are in touch with dozens of community health initiatives throughout the Third World which, like the Mozambique initiative, try to meet people's immediate needs in ways that also help lay the groundwork for long-term social change. But most of these forward-looking, empowering initiatives are initiated by small nongovernmental organizations. What makes this Mozambique example noteworthy is the fact that it was an intersectoral initiative in which a national government listened to and worked closely with the people. That it ran into high-level opposition from international policy-makers gives little cause for surprise.

Zimbabwe's National Children's Supplementary Feeding Program

The struggle for health in Zimbabwe has been a long uphill battle, with many achievements and disappointments.[8] The country achieved independence from Britain in 1980 after a protracted and bitter liberation war fought by the black majority against white minority rule. In Zimbabwe inequitable distribution of land has been a key cause of undernutrition and poor health. Before independence, 45 million acres of prime agricultural land was allocated to about 5,000 white settler farmers and a few agro-industries owned by multinational corporations. Meanwhile, some 750,000 peasant families were crowded into a similar number of acres in "Tribal Trust Lands" which were much inferior in soil type and rainfall.

Economic and social conditions declined during the liberation war, largely due to externally-imposed economic sanctions, increased military spending and social disruption. While chronic food problems from historical inequities in land tenure and income distribution had already existed for many years, they worsened dramatically during and after the war due to the destruction of agricultural resources by the old regime and the return of refugees.

Economic Adjustment

Although the first two years after liberation brought a number of improvements to the general population, since then they have been steadily eroded. National minimum wages were introduced by the government in July 1980. Real wages (what people can buy with what they earn), on the average, rose significantly until early 1982 and were substantially greater than pre-independence levels. But the early gains following independence were undermined by a wage freeze between January 1982 and September 1983, and by the 1982 devaluation and subsequent depreciation of the Zimbabwean dollar.

These measures were associated with an economic "stabilization" package imposed by the government in 1982 as part of an International Monetary Fund (IMF) stand-by credit scheme. (Although the IMF agreement was suspended in 1991, the government retained most of its elements, and in 1991 a new structural adjustment program [SAP] was adopted, adding further stringent measures to reduce government spending and to "liberalize trade.")

As part of the IMF stabilization package, the government removed subsidies on basic foods in 1982 and 1983, and prices of the basic staples of the poor rose dramatically: by some 100 percent for maize meal, 69–95 percent for beef, 50 percent for milk, 25–30 percent for bread, and 25 percent for edible oils. Further price increases have occurred regularly since then, especially following the introduction of the 1991 SAP.

Preparing for Crisis

Surveys by OXFAM shortly after independence in 1980 revealed that 30% of children aged under 5 years were underweight. A more extensive Health Ministry survey confirmed a high prevalence of severe undernutrition in children which correlated directly with the availability of food in the areas where they lived. An estimated 150,000 children were at risk.

To forestall an impending hunger crisis in the 1980–1981 planting season, a nutrition intervention program was set up by the Ministry of Health and concerned nongovernmental organizations. This focused on high risk areas where provincial committees were set up to address the issue. These committees consisted of health workers, school teachers, community development workers and women's advisors. The program's had three important objectives: (1) immediate short-term relief, (2) long term nutritional education, and (3) influencing agricultural practices towards production of more nutritious foods.

In approaching all of these objectives, emphasis was placed on extensive community involvement. This involvement was key to the evolution and sustainability of the programs, even after government and outside input was severely cut.

Immediate, short-term relief

Understanding the unfolding relationship between the state and popular organizations is central to understanding the process of the population's involvement in all areas of social development, including health. It is in situations where the old order and power structures are being contested or have recently been overthrown by a unified popular struggle that comprehensive primary health care often has the best chance of succeeding. This was the case in Zimbabwe in 1980, as it was in revolutionary China, Cuba, and Sandinista Nicaragua (which we will discuss in Chapter 20). It is under such conditions that popular participation in decision-making, and collective—rather than individual—self-reliance, grow and flourish.[9]

In Zimbabwe, this situation was most evident in the semi-liberated communal areas, where ZANU, the leading party in the national liberation movement, had long been active. In these areas the party had created popular organizations, initially responsible for supporting the liberation effort but later structured to perform essential social and economic tasks, as an alternative to the Rhodesian state's rudimentary district administration. Grassroots village committees dealt with the day-to-day problem of feeding and clothing the ZANU guerrillas and of providing basic services to the community. Matters involving larger outlays of money were passed to higher-level committees.

The existing community-based administrative infrastructure that had developed during the war permitted a more rapid and better-organized implementation of the nutrition program than would otherwise have been possible. Mothers evaluated the children's nutritional status by measuring and recording their upper arm circumferences. Those with mid-upper-arm-circumferences less than 13 cms were included in the program. The reasons for this cut-off point were explained to all parents, both those of children admitted to the program, as well as those considered not at risk. Then they established locations for supplementary feedings (which the mothers preferred to be located close to their homes and fields), and themselves cooked the food and fed the underweight children.

To understand the rationale for the foods that were chosen for the nutrition program, it is important to realize that the primary cause of undernutrition is *energy deficiency,* not shortage of protein. This is because children are typically fed a watery porridge of unrefined cereal or root staple. Their stomachs fill before they get enough calories to meet their needs. Usually, such diets have a crude energy density of 1 kcal g^{-1} (4.2kJg^{-1}). This means that a 1-year-old child would have to eat a kilogram of food each day simply to meet her energy needs, which is between two and three times the amount that an English child of the same age has to eat. These bulky, low-energy foods, coupled with infrequent feedings, result in an insufficient energy-intake by children. This then leads to secondary protein deficiency, as the child burns up the protein she eats for lack of other adequate sources of energy.

Taking this into account, the program emphasized supplements prepared with high-energy, commonly used local foods. It offered a daily meal—based on maize, beans, groundnuts and oil—that provided about one half of the daily energy requirement of one-to-three-year-olds, and about one third of the daily energy needs of three-to-five-year-olds. The rest of the child's nutritional needs were provided by their parents or the community.

The first feeding point opened in January 1981 and during the next three months feeding points were established all over the country. The number of children registered rose from 5,824 in January to 56,200 in March. It peaked at 95,988 in May with over 2000 feeding points and fell gradually to 57,556 in August. Screening and remeasuring of children registered by the mothers at feeding points was performed regularly, ensuring turnover.

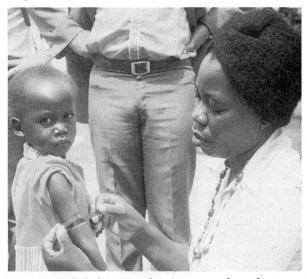

The Shakir Strip for measuring upper arm circumference

Long-Term Nutritional Education

An informative poster in the local languages (and in English) was displayed and discussed at the feeding points as well as in health facilities. The poster, which read, "With Sadza have groundnuts, beans and oil," helped to reinforce the message that *high-energy foods that could be grown locally would provide a nutritious meal for young children if added to the staple maize meal porridge.* (Sadza is a porridge made by cooking maize meal with water.) Thus the relief effort prompted greater self-reliance by affirming the value of locally cultivable foods.

The discussions about the poster helped to influence people's thinking about nutrition. It replaced the old "3 food groups" approach with a much more useful and relevant message, that of providing a more energy-rich diet. This new, more appropriate information proved to have a far-reaching impact on the nutritional health of the children, even after the decline of the program.

The Children's Supplementary Feeding Program was evaluated in 1981. Children in the program were weighed and compared to children of a similar age range who lived in the same area, who had not been in the program. On average, children attending the program put on weight at twice the rate of the other children. Children who had attended 30 or more meals gained weight at three times the rate of the better nourished children who had not particpated in the program.[10] Many of the children graduated out of the program when their arm circumferences improved significantly and their families had sufficient food at home.

During the evaluation most mothers reported improvement in their children's health, and were therefore enthusiastic about the educational messages. However, home production and use of foods varied widely. Although some families were producing considerable amounts of crops, others had very little. Significantly, the percentage of parents who stated their desire to grow groundnuts in the following agricultural season increased from 48 to 80 percent.[11] In fact, many said that they wanted to participate in expanding the program into a food production phase (a possibility that had been considered at the outset, when the relief foods were chosen).

Local production of supplementary food

The intention of the supplementary food production phase of the program was to move from relief and education to local production. Through community discussions, it was agreed that communal farming plots should be established. The harvest from these plots would go to preschool centers which, if not already in existence, would be constructed adjacent to the plots. It was calculated that roughly one half hectare of land could yield enough

groundnuts to provide 70 children with 30 grams of groundnuts each day (providing about 280 calories), leaving ten percent for seed for the following season. The land selected for this use, taken from communal grazing lands, was allocated by the local government authorities. The national feeding program committee provided the initial seed and fertilizer. Such community decisions were possible because the popular mobilization during that period of Zimbabwe's history was significant in influencing both national and local development thinking and programs.

It should be emphasized that the food grown for the preschool centers was not intended to meet the full dietary needs of the children. Rather it was intended as a supplement for those children whose nutritional needs were not being otherwise met. The rest of the child's food was provided by either the parents or through a self-imposed levy by the community members. This functioned as a sort of community determined progressive taxation to assure that these children had proper meals.

Through this communal farming enterprise, the weaker people in the community were helped by the better off members who farmed with them, and by technical support given by government agricultural extension workers. While almost all of the groups grew groundnuts, some opted for more diversity, including crops of maize and beans.

In some areas, the pre-school centers adjacent to communal plots became community focal points for various child care activities. In time, many of these centers developed into comprehensive child health centers, and formed part of the infrastructure used later for immunization programs.

By 1983–84 there were 292 supplementary food production units in 31 districts. Unfortunately, because of a severe and recurrent drought, most of these failed. However, the existing infrastructure facilitated the rapid remounting of relief efforts. (Again in 1991 and 1992, when the worst drought in recorded history hit Southern Africa, it was remarkable to see how this infrastructure for supplementary feeding, which had been created 10 years before, was revitalized within a few weeks. This occurred even though outside support for the program had largely been withdrawn in the late 1980s.)

By the late 1980s, there were between two and three thousand supplementary food plots distributed throughout all eight provinces of Zimbabwe. In some districts this scheme has been highly successful, with all of the young child population in large areas being served. Perhaps the best example is in the Musami area of the Murehwa District, some 80 kilometers from Harare, where there were over 50 food production plots and associated pre-school centers. Maize, groundnuts and beans were produced, and in several centers a surplus existed even after the allocation for all pre-school children and retention for seed had taken place.

In Musami these centers served not only as activity and day care centers for all pre-school children, but also as outreach points for health services. Each month immunization, health education and growth monitoring were performed. The registers kept at Musami's Mission Hospital indicated that the prevalence of child undernutrition in the program areas declined markedly from the early 1980s, and was considerably lower than the national average.

Impact on children's health

Looking at studies of Zimbabwe as a whole, trends in child mortality and under-nutrition during the 1980s show a revealing discrepancy. From 1980 to 1988 the infant mortality rate was cut in half (from 110 to 53 per 1000), an astonishing accomplishment. Likewise, the percentage of wasted (severely underweight) young children fell impressively (from 17.7 to 1.3%). However, the percentage of stunted (under-height, chronically undernourished) young children remained disproportionately high (having dropped only from 35.6% in 1982 to 29% in 1988).

Zimbabwe's data, though sketchy, suggest a marked divergence between mortality indicators on the one hand, and long-term nutrition indicators (stunting) on the other.

Emergency feeding, with emphasis on the use of local foods, evolved into a long term nutrition program.

The fall in mortality probably resulted from the energetic expansion and reorganization of health care, and especially the greatly improved coverage of immunization, ORT, and later, the treatment of malaria and pneumonia. Likewise, the relief child feeding programs which grew into a broad health care and food production initiative helped to partially offset the adverse effects of droughts, recession and stabilization policies. However, as the recession and economic stabilization reduced real incomes for large numbers of households, even relatively comprehensive health services and feeding programs could not offset the effects of growing poverty and difficulty in obtaining enough food.

Conclusion

The Children's Supplementary Feeding Program in Zimbabwe is an example of the ways in which a relatively progressive government can help to initiate an empowering, community-based program providing preferential benefits to those in greatest need. Strong community decisions were possible because the popular mobilization during that period was successful in significantly influencing both national and local development thinking.

In evaluating the overall effect of the Program, many factors need to be considered. As a relief effort, it certainly had its benefits. But more importantly, as a broader, community-based approach, there have been long-term benefits which have endured beyond the original inputs to the system. The education and production aspects of the program continue to promote better nutrition and health for the participants in these communities.

As important as these gains are, however, they still have not addressed the larger question of social inequity (including persisting land maldistribution) and increasing economic hardship which put the children of these families at risk. The Structural Adjustment Programs of the 1990s, and the enforcement of user fees for many health services, have only added to the burden of poor families and have partially reversed earlier improvements in child health and nutrition.

From Village Health Care to the Struggle for Land and Social Justice:
An Example from Mexico

CHAPTER 19

Project Piaxtla

Project Piaxtla in western Mexico is a rural primary health care program run entirely by local villagers. Named after a nearby river and located in the foothills of the Sierra Madre mountain range, Piaxtla was started 30 years ago to serve a large, rugged, sparsely populated region in the state of Sinaloa. Until recently the area was traversed only by mule trails and footpaths. The program is based in Ajoya, the largest village (population 1,000) in Piaxtla's area of coverage. David Werner has been involved with this program as an advisor and facilitator since its inception.

When the program started in 1965, the "diseases of poverty" dominated the health scene. One in three children died before reaching the age of five, primarily of diarrhea and infectious disease combined with chronic undernutrition. Seven in ten women were anemic, and one in ten died during or after childbirth.

This adverse situation stemmed in large part from an inequitable distribution of land, wealth, and power. Most campesino or poor rural families owned little or no land, and what land they did own was of inferior quality. In contrast, a handful of rich local families held large tracts of fertile, river valley land, owned large herds of cattle, and were quite wealthy. These few wealthy families completely controlled Ajoya's community council. They repeatedly blocked all attempts by poor farmers to organize or demand their constitutional land rights, resorting to violence when they felt it was necessary in order to maintain their dominant position.

Land distribution has long been a critical issue. The 1910 Mexican Revolution was largely triggered by the feudal land policies of the president-turned-dictator, Porfirio Diaz, who had given huge tracts of land to wealthy cronies. As the best farmland had become concentrated in giant plantations, or latifundio, the landless peasants had few options. Either they worked for the powerful landholders as serfs or sharecroppers, or they retreated into the hills to grow scanty crops on steep slopes using slash-and-burn farming. Either way, survival was difficult.

In the Mexican Revolution—with the war cry: "¡Tierra y Libertad!" (Land and Liberty!)—landless campesinos throughout the countryside united behind popular leaders such as Pancho Villa and Emiliano Zapata. At last, the Diaz dictatorship was overthrown and a new revolutionary Constitution was drawn up.

At the heart of this Mexican Constitution was, until recently, its agrarian reform legislation, which included the famous ejido system. According to this system, a group of villages could join to form an ejido or communal land holding. The local farmland was divided equitably among all families. Each family would receive provisional title to their parcel, and they could farm it and benefit from the produce as they chose. But ultimate ownership stayed with the ejido. The family could not sell its parcel nor have it seized for unpaid debt. This protected small farmers from losing their land. To further prevent the return of huge plantations, legal limits were placed on the size of property holdings.

Some social analysts say the ejido system contains the best of the political Right and the Left, encouraging the personal incentive and high production of private ownership, while guaranteeing the equity of land use intended by socialism. However, the ejido system has worked better in theory than in fact. Since the Mexican Revolution, the biggest problem has been institutionalized corruption. Although the Constitution calls for a democratic multi-party system, for 60 years a single political party—the Institutional Revolutionary Party (PRI) backed by brutal military and police force—has remained in power. In spite of growing inequities and hardships for the poor, it has clung to power by resorting to vote fraud, intimidation, torture, and strategic assassination of human rights leaders. The killing of outspoken journalists has been wryly dubbed "the ultimate form of censorship."

Under such a corrupt regime, both the ejido system and the laws limiting the size of land holdings have often failed to protect small farmers' land rights. The rich and powerful routinely pay off government officials to break the rules and to silence those who protest. Nevertheless, the land reform statutes of the Mexican Constitution have, until recently, provided a legal and moral base whereby poor farmers could organize to defend their revolutionary rights to Land and Liberty.

Piaxtla's Evolution: from Curative Care to Social Action

In this setting, Project Piaxtla's strategies to improve health evolved through three phases. In its earliest phase it had no political agenda, but focused on *curative care,* the immediate need of the people. Village health promoters were trained using participatory, learning-by-doing methods, and became relatively competent in the treatment of common illnesses and injuries. But as time went on, the health team and the villagers it served became aware that the same illnesses and injuries kept recurring. In response, they gradually shifted the program's focus to *preventive and promotive measures* such as immunizations, latrines, and water systems. As a result, during this second phase of the program, certain illnesses became less common and health improved noticeably. Fewer children died of tetanus and whooping cough, and fewer were left disabled by polio and complications from measles. Nevertheless, many children and women were still malnourished and sick, particularly in years when harvests were not good. The Under-Five Mortality Rate remained high, especially among children of the poorest families, who were landless, underpaid, underserved, and in many ways taken advantage of by a small minority with land, wealth, and power. So the program's main focus changed again: this time to *organized action* to defend people's basic needs and rights. In this way, the village health program evolved from *curative care* to *preventive and promotive measures* to *sociopolitical action.*

The shift in the program's focus from more conventional health measures to organized action was partly the result of a learner-centered, discovery-based, problem solving approach to health education. Workshops led by health promoters with farmers, mothers, or schoolchildren would start off with a "situational analysis" or "community diagnosis" in which participants identify and discuss health-related problems in their community and how these problems interrelate. Rather than looking at the death of a child as having a single cause (such as diarrhea), they would learn to explore the chain of causes that leads to that child's death. The links would be identified as biological, physical, cultural, economic, and political, or (in simpler terms) having to do with worms and germs, things, customs and beliefs, money, and power.

In the early phases of the program when the focus was mainly curative and preventive, the links people identified in the chain of causes tended to be mostly biological, physical, and cultural. The chain traced back from a child's death from diarrhea might have included death, dehydration, diarrhea, gut infection, germs carried from feces to mouth, and lack of latrines, hygiene and sufficient water. But as people began to explore more deeply, the chains of causes they discovered tended to include more economic and political links. For death from diarrhea, the chain might now include: *death, frequent bouts of diarrhea, undernutrition, not enough food, no money, father works as a sharecropper, good farmland held by a few rich men, land reform laws not applied, payoffs to government officials, institutionalized corruption, lack of participatory democracy, insufficient organization and action by the people.* After common problems and the root causes were defined, the group would explore possible solutions. Sometimes this was done through story-telling or role plays, or—to involve a wider audience—by publicly staged *"campesino* theater." Finally, when the group agreed that the circumstances and timing were right, a strategy for action might be developed.[*]

Actions to defend the health and rights of the least advantaged

As the health promoters and community looked deeper into the underlying causes of poor health, they began to look for ways in which, through collective action, they might break some of the links in the chain of events leading to sickness and death. They started with some of the links which they thought might be easier to do something about at the local level, and which carried less risk of violent response from the power structure. However, they soon discovered that any attempt by the poor to correct inequities of the status quo can precipitate a heavy-handed response from those in positions of privilege.

Early actions organized through the Piaxtla health program mostly related to the ways in which poor *campesinos* were systematically cheated, mistreated, or exploited. Some of the activities initiated to address these issues included:

- Demanding the owner of the local bus route to lower fares to the legal rates;

- Starting a farmworkers-run maize bank;

- Initiating a cooperative fencing program;

- Organizing, led by village women, to shut down the public bar in order to reduce drunkenness and violence; and

- Organizing a protest to take control of the village water supply away from a wealthy man and to introduce a public water system controlled by the community.

We will briefly describe a few of these initiatives.

------

[*]The problem-posing methodology used by the Piaxtla health team—including situational analysis, awareness raising, and action-oriented learning—is presented in the book *Helping Health Workers Learn,* by David Werner and Bill Bower.

The farmworkers-run maize bank

One of the first, most entrenched forms of exploitation which the small farmers decided to tackle was the landowners' usurious system for loaning maize. By the start of the planting season (the summer monsoons) poor families had often exhausted their stores of maize and were forced to borrow some from their wealthy neighbors. At harvest time, six months later, the poor farmers were required to repay three sacks of maize for every one borrowed. After payment, many families had almost no grain left. If they were unable to repay the debt, their creditors would seize their possessions, often pushing poor families into complete destitution. Many were forced to give up farming and migrate to urban slums in search of work. (This sort of exodus from the rural areas by land-deprived peasants has caused a whole new dimension of urban health problems which further jeopardize child well-being and survival, see page 77.)

To combat this exploitative loan system, the Piaxtla team helped the poor farmers set up a cooperative maize bank. This bank charged much lower interest than the rich farmers, and the interest collected was used to increase the bank's lending capacity. This community-controlled loan program eventually spread to five villages. It helped to improve the economic position of the poorer families, and with it their nutrition and health. It also fostered greater cooperation and accountability among the small farmers, helping them to develop organizational, management, and even accounting skills. Most importantly, people began to gain confidence in their ability to improve their own situations. In the course of establishing the cooperative maize banks, the subsistence farmers were learning to fight for their rights. Within a few years, in Ajoya and the surrounding communities, the poor farmers' organization became so large and strong that it began to break the control that the few wealthy families had over the community council.

Farmworkers' theater skit demonstrates how rich landholders usuriously lend maize to poor campesinos.

The cooperative fencing program

The next problem the poor farmers took on to improve their economic base was to find a cost-effective way to keep the rich farmers' cattle from entering their mountainside maize fields and from eating their crops. Among the poorest farmers are those who plant the steep hillsides by the slash-and-burn method. Each year they would timber a new patch of land, and fence it to keep the rich farmers' cattle from eating their crops. To buy fencing wire, they had to borrow from the rich cattle owners. In return, they were forced to grant the rich families grazing rights on the land they had cleared, fenced and harvested. Thus the cattle owners got new grazing areas timbered, fenced, and planted with fodder, all for only the cost of the wire.

After discussing and analyzing the implications of this situation to people's well-being, the Piaxtla health team, together with members of the small farmers' organization, began to explore possible solutions. They organized poor farmers to join together to cooperatively fence in a whole hillside. Within this large enclosure, all could plant their small plots of land. To buy the large quantity of barbed wire needed, the health team obtained start-up money from a nongovernmental organization. Once the fencing project was completed, by charging the wealthy cattle owners for grazing rights, the poor farmers' were able to pay back the loan for the fencing wire within two years. From then on, grazing fees produced an income which could be used for the food and health needs of their families.

When the first group of poor farmers succeeded in paying off their loan, the same money was lent to a new group. Through this revolving fund, a growing number of poor farmers became more self-sufficient. The gap in wealth and power between rich and poor narrowed somewhat, and the health of some of the poorest children began to improve.

Through these and other organized actions, people began to gain confidence and experience strength through unity. This empowering process proved contagious and soon neighboring communities began to join the informal but cohesive organization of poor farm workers. As the numbers and solidarity of the peasant farmers grew, they and their health team began to combat bigger, potentially more dangerous issues.

Women Unite against Men's Drunkenness

The women of Ajoya and the surrounding area also began to discover and exercise their power. One way they did this was to take collective action to address the problem of male alcohol abuse. This has long been a major cause of interpersonal and domestic violence in the region, with women and children often on the receiving end. Apart from direct physical violence, the drinking habits of men also indirectly damage the nutrition and health of women and children, because men often buy alcohol with money needed to feed their families.

In previous times there had been several bars in Ajoya, but many years ago they had been officially closed because of alcohol-related violence. For some twenty years the village was free of bars, although some illegal sales of alcohol continued. In 1982 the son of the municipal president announced that he was going to open a *cantina*, or bar, in Ajoya as a private business venture.

With help from Piaxtla's health workers, the women organized to fight this move. They put on a public farmworkers' theater skit dramatizing how the drinking habits of men bring harm to women and children. All parts were played by women and children, with women bedecked in pants and mustaches to act the roles of men. The skit showed how, if they worked together, women could do something about this "men's problem."

Village women in a theater skit to oppose the drinking patterns of men.

In response to the skit and other awareness-raising activities, the village women of Ajoya took united action to protest against the opening of the bar. As a result, several health workers who had helped organize the

women were jailed. But the women held a protest rally at the jail until the last health worker was released. Next, they persuaded several newspapers to publish editorials criticizing the municipal president's use of public office to advance private business interests. The women were ultimately successful in blocking the bar's opening, and soon women's groups throughout the state were making similar protests and closing down local bars.

Theater skit: "Women unite to overcome drunkenness"

The invasion and redistribution of large land holdings

After gaining greater confidence, organizational skills, and unity through combating other problems, finally the poor farmers were ready to tackle the most basic problem contributing to hunger and poor health: the inequitable distribution of the fertile, river valley farmland. They began to systematically invade and cultivate some of the large holdings of rich families—land to which they knew they had a constitutional right. They divided up the land fairly and then demanded *ejidal* land titles from the government. When the authorities at the state level ignored their demands, the poor farmers sent a committee to the Ministry of Agrarian Reform in Mexico City. The villagers persisted until the officials finally relented, and ordered the state authority to grant title to the poor farmers' land claims.

To date, the peasant farmers have reclaimed, won legal title to, and parceled out nearly half of the local riverside farmland. To increase food production, they purchased water pumps and began to irrigate the land during the dry season. This enabled them to harvest two crops a year instead of one. As a result, their families were able to eat better, to earn income by selling some of their produce, and to save some money for medical emergencies and other needs.

⌘

The impact of these various actions toward greater fairness—between rich and poor and between men and women—has had a significant impact on health, especially that of children. When the villager-run health program began in 1965, the Under Five Mortality Rate for this remote mountainous area was around 340 per thousand. Today it is down to between 50 to 70 per thousand. Equally important, there are now far fewer malnourished, sickly, and stunted children. More youngsters are healthy, growing well, and bursting with energy and life.

Undoubtedly a number of factors have contributed to the impressive drop in child death rate. Most families agree that the Piaxtla health program has played a key role in reducing child death and improving health. But if you ask "What actions brought the biggest improvements?" few people will say curative or preventive medicine. Many will mention organized action to reclaim their rights and their land. Most families realize that the main reason why so many of their children used to get sick and die is that often they didn't get enough to eat. With their collective efforts to set up a peasant-controlled maize bank and cooperative fencing program, to combat excessive use of alcohol, and above all, to more fairly distribute the best farmland, the families of the village have been able to increase their economic base and to put more food on the table. All in all, they have gained more control over their health and their lives through cooperative action.

Since the early years of the health program, there has been a visible shift in power at the local level. In the first years, village council meetings had been strongly controlled by a few forceful land barons and cattle owners, but as the poor gained strength and unity, the few wealthy men who previously dominated decisions were so disempowered that they seldom attended *ejido* meetings. Outnumbered, they could no longer swing votes by threatening to evict sharecroppers or refuse them loans. In this way, the local *struggle for health,* which had turned into a *struggle for land and liberty,* also led to a more democratic and equitable community with greater accountability of leaders.

However, the process remained local and incomplete. The *campesinos* realized that if improvements in health were to be sustained, more good riverside land needed to be invaded and redistributed: not only in the Piaxtla valley but throughout the country.

Of course, this struggle for land, liberty, and health in the Sierra Madre was not an isolated event. In many parts of Mexico, grassroots groups were beginning to organize and demand their rights. As these groups gained in numbers and strength, high level attempts to silence them became more frequent and repressive. On occasion, Piaxtla health workers were jailed. And in a program which the Piaxtla team had helped to start in the neighboring state of Durango, two health workers were killed by the state police for organizing local residents to stand up for their timber rights. (An American plywood company was paying the corrupt leaders of the local *ejido* for the timber they removed. When the health workers organized their local *ejido* to demand fair disbursement of this money among all the families, the lead health workers were assassinated by the State Police.)

In response to this and other misfortunes, grassroots groups felt the need to unite in mutual self defense. To stabilize their tenuous gains, the health team joined with other grassroots programs to organize educational interchanges. This eventually led to both a national and a regional network of community-based health programs, covering Mexico and Central America. These grassroots networks share the conviction that the struggle for health is a struggle for liberation from hunger, poverty and unfair social structures.[12]

New Threats to the Peasants' Gains: Free Trade and the Global Economy

During the 1990s a new and bigger obstacle has threatened to reverse the gains in land and health achieved over the years through the Piaxtla initiative. This new threat stems not so much from the local or state levels as from international and global forces. It is a consequence of the post-Cold War *New World Order* with its pervasive push for liberalization of national economies (see Chapter 11). In the 1980s this liberalization process was to a large extent implemented in Mexico through structural adjustment policies dictated by the World Bank and International Monetary Fund (IMF). In the 1990s this *neo-liberal* agenda has been further expanded through the North American Free Trade Agreement (NAFTA), an accord between Canada, the United States, and Mexico.

In preparation for NAFTA, the United States pressured the Mexican government to eliminate the progressive land reform statutes from Mexico's Constitution. It argued that these statutes—primarily the size limit for private landholdings and the *ejido* system that safe-guards small farmers from losing their land through sale or debt—are *barriers to free trade.* Since these constitutional clauses were preventing US agribusiness from buying up huge tracts of Mexico's land to grow winter vegetables for export into the US, the White House insisted that the

Mexican Constitution be changed. As it turned out, then President Salinas de Gotari was quite willing to disembowel the Mexican Constitution of its progressive land policies. The ruling party (PRI) was (and still is) controlled by a powerful club of bureaucrats, businessmen and big land owners who for decades have sought ways to sidestep the equity-enforcing statutes of the country's Constitution. The US pressure for free trade provided a perfect excuse to dismantle the revolutionary statutes that protected the needy from the greedy. So, even before NAFTA was passed, President Salinas and his Congress gutted the Mexican Constitution of its progressive land statutes. The *ejido* system was dismantled and laws limiting the size of land holdings were repealed. In effect, these regressive changes in the Constitution catapulted Mexico back to the pre-revolutionary feudal system with its *latifundia* or giant plantations.

To convince poor farmers to accept the spaying of their Constitution, which could cause millions of small farmers to lose their land, the Mexican government launched a massive disinformation campaign telling farmers that, with the end of the *ejido* system, at last they could become full owners of their own land, to do with it as they chose. This official media blitz—broadcast day and night on radio and TV—for a time caused a split within poor farmworkers' organizations throughout Mexico. Even within the Piaxtla program a division arose. Some farmers swallowed the government line and said, "For the first time the land is completely our own!" But those who were more astute understood that, with the loss of the *ejido* system, small land owners would soon begin to lose their land, either selling it in hard times or forfeiting it for debt.

Nevertheless, the constitutional changes instigated by NAFTA have effectively terminated the legal reclamation and redistribution of large land holdings. Before NAFTA, the *campesinos* in the Sierra Madre had proudly invaded large holdings as citizens defending their constitutional rights. Now, under the modified Constitution, if they invaded large holdings they would be common criminals, and treated as such.

Free trade in poverty, racial violence, repression and AIDS

The changes in the Mexican Constitution in preparation for NAFTA were officially hailed as a progressive step toward national economic growth and prosperity. But many social analysts correctly predicted that these measures would have devastating human and environmental costs.[13] Indeed, thousands of small farms are being bought up by big land holders or confiscated for debt. The concentration of farmland into fewer hands, together with the flood of tariff-free US farm products into Mexico as result of NAFTA, have caused the mass exodus of more than 2 million landless peasants to the mushrooming city slums, where they have swelled the ranks of unemployed persons competing for jobs. Mexico's courtship with foreign speculative investment contributed to the crash of the peso at the end of 1994. In the first six months of 1995, the unemployment rate more than doubled; more than 1.4 million Mexican workers lost their jobs.[14] Independent unions estimate unemployment and under-employment to be around 50 percent.[15] The inflation rate reached 39.91 percent in July, 1994,[16] while the sales of basic food stuffs decreased by 25%, a harbinger of widespread malnutrition.[17]

With such a huge surplus of hungry people ready to work under any conditions, wage levels have dropped and the already minimal bargaining power of organized labor has been further weakened. The combination of falling wages and rising unemployment inevitably takes a high toll on people's health, especially that of children.

Along the US/Mexico border, many poor Mexican workers toil in the *maquiladoras* (manufacturing plants), which now number over 2,700. These sweat shops employ over 605,000 workers who have fled to the *colonias* (unincorporated areas) on both sides of the border in search of a better life. Including worker's families, more than 1.5 million men, women and children live in these slums in which "there is a pressing need for basic sanitation ... [and which] have no potable drinking water, sewer systems, garbage collection or adequate medical facilities. In many *colonias*, garbage is left in open dumps or scattered in urban streets, attracting and proliferating vermin and contributing to surface and groundwater pollution."[18]

As landlessness, poverty, disease and unemployment in Mexico increase as a result of NAFTA and structural adjustment, more and more *braceros* illegally cross the US border in search of work. With increased job competition and unemployment in the United States, more people will resort to prostitution, drug peddling, and drug use. At the same time, fewer illegal immigrants will get

Summary of the Impact on Mexico of NAFTA and the Structural Adjustment/ Austerity Measures Intensified after the December, 1994 Crash of the Peso[19]

- Between 1994 and 1995 sales of major wholesalers dropped by 75%.

- Food production fell by 80%.

- Basic food prices rose faster than overall prices (by 43% in the first 7 months of 1995).

- While cutting back on services and subsidies for the poor and taxing them more, the government increased subsidies for the rich. In 1995 it spent 13 billion (5% of the GDP) to bail out commercial banks, and 2 billion to assist private road-building contractors (who put tolls so high that few can afford to use the highways they built).

- Over 60% of all Mexican businesses reduced their workers, and 1/3 of businesses have closed down.

- In the first 9 months of 1995, over 2 million people fell into extreme poverty. Today over 40% of population lives in poverty.

- Mexico's foreign debt has swollen to suffocating size. Interest payments in the first half of 1996 were almost $18 billion, nearly double that in the first half of 1994.

- Since December, 1994 the average wage lost 54% of its purchasing power.

- During 1995, between 1½ and 2 million more workers became unemployed, raising total unemployment to 10 million (26% of the active workforce).

- In 1996, the President's "secret budget item" (a discretionary fund for which he does not have to account) was raised to US$85 million — 30% higher than the year before.

- In response to growing poverty, crime has escalated. In response, Congress legalized gun ownership by private citizens. Gun-related violence, already extremely high, is predicted to increase.

the health care they need, since new legislation is threatening to reduce the opportunities for undocumented workers to receive public health services. If, as predicted, the US army is recruited to assist the Border Patrol, expulsion rates back to Mexico will increase along with the numbers of illegal workers. Thousands who have acquired sexually transmitted diseases, HIV and/or drug habits will carry their new afflictions home with them. The incidence of AIDS in Mexico is beginning to skyrocket as it has in Africa (see Chapter 15). For the poor of Mexico, however, concern about combating AIDS is at present eclipsed by the more immediate need to combat landlessness, joblessness, and hunger.

In the United States, NAFTA's effects are precipitating an upsurge of racism and human rights violations. As more US industries move factories south of the border to take advantage of low Mexican wages and weak enforcement of workers rights and safety, thousands of US workers have lost their jobs. According to an article by journalist Patrick Buchanan, "In the first eight months of … [1994], 224 US factories—a factory every single day—laid off workers or shifted production overseas as result of NAFTA…. NAFTA has put American workers into competition with 80 million Mexicans … labor there is only 15% of the cost of US labor."[20] Correspondingly, in the US the real wages of workers has continued to fall.

Because US workers are poorly informed about the root causes of their loss of jobs and falling wages, they tend to put the blame for their economic hardships on the influx of Latinos. This appears to be sparking racial violence.

Anti-immigrant cartoon from a prominant U.S. hate group.

Within eight months of the passing of NAFTA, the Southern Poverty Law Center reported that, "Hostility towards immigrants and efforts by white supremacists to exploit fears about immigration are at their highest levels in 70 years, causing a rash of violent bias crimes against anyone who is perceived as 'foreign.'"[21] This anti-immigrant paranoia is so severe that in November of 1994 the voters of California—a state which has a large immigrant population—passed the so-called "Save Our State" initiative (Proposition 187). This draconian initiative, if implemented (its constitutionality is being questioned in the courts), would prohibit undocumented children from utilizing public education and health services (except in cases of emergency). This is in blatant violation of the International Declaration of Children's Rights.

The Chiapas uprising to the rescue

The ratification of NAFTA was a devastating blow to Project Piaxtla and the farmworkers organization. With it came the imminent danger of losing the land and the health gains for which they had struggled during the last 20 years. Throughout Mexico, *campesino* groups staged protests against the dissolution of the *ejido* system and the signing of NAFTA. But as usual, the PRI and President Salinas turned a deaf ear.

However, at the beginning of 1994 an unprecedented turn of events was triggered by the uprising of the Zapatista National Liberation Army (EZLN) in Chiapas, Mexico's poorest and most southern state. The uprising was symbolically launched on January 1, 1994, the day that NAFTA went into effect. Described as "one of the most unexpected, brilliantly staged peasant uprisings in living memory," the mini-revolution has forced Mexico's ruling party to respond seriously to popular demand for social justice.[22]

It is too early to know the long-term results of this mini-war waged by Mexico's poorest, most exploited indigenous people. But as things look now, the uprising may have done more to defend the rights and health of the country's people than any event since the Mexican Revolution 80 years ago. For one, the Chiapas insurrection has helped the Piaxtla health team and farmworkers in far off Sinaloa to retain the gains of their 20 year struggle for land and health.

At the start of the Zapatista uprising, the Mexican Army responded with brutal collective punishment, attacking, bombing, and destroying entire Indian villages. But throughout the nation, the majority of citizens (70% of the population according to polls) and much of the national press sided with the rebels. The EZLN's clear demands for land rights and social justice, voiced eloquently by the mysterious *sub-comandante* Marcos, struck a sympathetic chord with millions of *campesinos*. Fearing a possible national revolt (or possible overturn of the PRI in forthcoming national elections), the Mexican government was forced to call off the army—and eventually to capitulate to some of the Zapatista's demands.

The Zapatistas' demands called on the government to uphold the statutes of the original 1917 Mexican Constitution, especially those that protect the rights of the common citizen. This included both restoration and honest implementation of the agrarian reform program which, due to institutionalized corruption, had never effectively reached the indigenous peoples of Chiapas. They called for reinstatement of the *ejido* system to protect the land rights of small farmers. They demanded fair, genuinely democratic elections and an end to discrimination against indigenous people and the poor. And they called for a minimum wage high enough for poor people to adequately feed their children and for an end to institutionalized corruption and graft. The EZLN made it clear they did not want to take over and run the government. They simply wanted it cleaned up, to make it more representative of and accountable to the people.

At the bargaining table, President Salinas offered to pardon the Zapatistas if they gave up their weapons and called off the insurrection. However, *sub-comandante* Marcos—his face, as ever, masked in a ski-cap—publicly replied:

> Why do we have to be pardoned? What are we going to be pardoned for? For not dying of hunger? For not being silent in our misery? For not humbly accepting our historic role of being the despised and outcast? ... For carrying guns into battle rather than bows and arrows? For being Mexicans? For being primarily indigenous peoples? For having called on the people of Mexico to struggle, in all possible ways, for that which belongs to them? For having fought for liberty, democracy, and justice? ... For not giving up? For not selling out? ...
>
> Who must ask for pardon and who must grant it?
>
> Those who for years and years have satisfied themselves at full tables, while death sat beside us so regularly that we finally stopped being afraid of it?
>
> Or should we ask pardon from the dead, our dead, those who died 'natural' deaths from 'natural' causes like measles, whooping cough, dengue, cholera, typhoid, tetanus, pneumonia,

malaria and other lovely gastrointestinal and lung diseases? Our dead—the majority dead, the democratically dead—dying from sorrow because nobody did anything, because the dead, our dead, went just like that, without anyone even counting them, without anyone saying "ENOUGH ALREADY," which would at least have given some meaning to their deaths, a meaning that no one ever sought for them, the forever dead, who are now dying again, but this time in order to live?

Among the various concessions that Salinas made to the EZLN, at least two may have a substantial impact on the people's health:

First, Salinas agreed to a fairer, more open election process with greater accountability to the public. Although the PRI won the national elections again in August, 1994, the electoral process is now under more critical public scrutiny, and the possibility of a more accountable and representative government in the future is somewhat increased. Already opposition parties have won elections in some municipalities and states.

Second, Salinas agreed to partly reinstate the land reform and *ejido* system which he had dismantled in preparation for NAFTA. He signed a presidential decree whereby the members of previously existing *ejidos* could decide by vote to keep or dissolve their ejidal structure. The government, of course, continues its propaganda to induce *campesinos* to dissolve their *ejidos*.* But through out Mexico, many small farmers—inspired by the clear thinking and just demands of the EZLN in Chiapas—are electing to keep their *ejidos*.

Among these, in the Sierra Madre of Sinaloa, the community of Ajoya and many surrounding communities have voted strongly to keep the *ejido*. Roberto Fajardo, health activist of Project Piaxtla and leader of the farm workers' organization, is delighted. He and others had feared that the villagers' 20 year struggle for land and health had been irrevocably lost. Roberto is first to acknowledge that the "barefoot revolutionaries" in Chiapas have given a new lease on life and possibilities for a healthier future to the children of Sinaloa's Sierra Madre.

---

*Officials from *PROCEDE,* the federal agency for the privatization of lands, visit villages and tell people that if they don't dissolve their *ejidos* and privately register their ejidal land now, they may soon be required to do so at high cost. They also promise them that as soon as they register their private holdings, they are entitled to big loans. Of course, they fail to mention that this is the first step toward losing their land for unpaid debt.

The 1994 Zapatista uprising in Chiapas has brought new inspiration to *campesinos* struggling for their rights in Sinaloa and throughout Mexico.

Village and Global Health Are Now Inseparable

Roberto and his fellow *campesinos* are relieved that in their corner of Mexico the people's land rights have, at least for the present, been partially preserved. They know that their right to land is crucial to freedom from hunger which is key to health. Yet Roberto and the Piaxtla health team also realize that their gains are tenuous. Like many community workers, he has learned that the biggest threats to health are now on a global scale. The small farmers of Mexico's Sierra Madre may for the moment have partially recovered their land rights. But the inequities of the world economic order persist. NAFTA remains in place, legally binding Mexico to the corporate interests of the United States. Already many small farmers in Mexico are being forced off their land. With the tariffs lifted by NAFTA, the United States is now exporting tons of surplus maize into Mexico. Subsidized by the US government, the selling price of this maize is half that of Mexican maize (although the buying price for families has not dropped). Unable to compete, countless *campesinos* who are giving up farming and moving in desperation to the growing slums of the cities, are finding that, as a result of the competitive market forces of free trade, the prices of food staples rise faster than wages.

Many health workers, including Roberto, are already suffering from NAFTA. During 20 years and at considerable sacrifice, Roberto had gradually built up a small herd of eight cattle. The cattle were an investment, the proceeds from which with which he planned to send his oldest son to college and then medical school (in the hopes his son would become one of those rare doctors who return to serve the villagers). But now with NAFTA, the US beef industry is shipping hybrid cattle into Mexico at wholesale prices, thus undercutting the value of local cattle. Almost overnight the selling price of Roberto's cattle has dropped to half of what it was. Thus, NAFTA has slashed Roberto's life savings and his son's dream of medical school.

Yet things could be worse. Whatever his losses, Roberto knows he is relatively lucky. His family still has a plot of land to plant. His children for the time being do not go hungry. He knows that millions of families in Mexico and throughout the world are much worse off.

Roberto gives veterinary care to a calf

While many critics predicted grim outcomes from NAFTA, few foresaw the plummeting of the peso, starting in December, 1994, which has suddenly converted Mexico from the success story of trade liberalization into a global economic basket case. To keep the wolf from the door (and foreign investors from losing vast sums) Mexico has already borrowed billions of dollars from the US government, the World Bank, and the IMF, and has a line of credit for billions more. Even if the peso can be kept from slipping further—and so far there is no certainty of this—the burden of repaying the debt, along with the hardships of the devaluation itself, have fallen largely on the backs of the poor, whose real wages continue to plunge.[23]

To keep servicing its increasing debt, Mexico has had to escalate the austerity measures already demanded by the World Bank's structural adjustment programs (see Chapter 11). Already, the Mexican people have suffered further reductions in public services, further declines in real wages, increased taxation, and more user fees for health, education and other social services. By mid–1995 the price of oil had risen 35% and a federal sales tax on most goods had been raised from 10% to 15%.

Mexico provides a stark example of the global trend we examined in Part 3 of this book. With NAFTA and other free market strategies designed to favor the privileged, the plight of the poor is worsening in both poor countries and rich. In 1991 Mexico had only 2 billionaires. Today it has 28. Reportedly, one of these billionaires, Carlos Slim, controls as much wealth as 17 million of his poor compatriots.

Internationally there has been much high-level discussion about Universal Human Rights: the Rights of Children, the Rights of Women, the Rights of Indigenous Peoples, etc. But the New World Order—spearheaded by the international financial institutions (the World Bank and the IMF)—has denied humanity the most fundamental rights of all: the right to have enough to eat and, ultimately, the right to live.

Conclusion

It is hard to evaluate the success of a small, grassroots program like Project Piaxtla—especially when it comes to gauging its contribution to long-term social change, which is the ultimate determinant of health. Piaxtla and the organization of poor farmers that grew out of it have sparked a process of empowerment which has had a limited but significant impact locally. Child mortality has declined to 20% of what it was when the program began. Despite a drop in real wages in Mexico as a whole, extreme poverty in the program's area of coverage is less common than it used to be. The gap between rich and poor in the distribution of land, wealth, and power has narrowed substantially. And the people's election to conserve their *ejido* status for the time being helps make their gains in land and health more sustainable.

But the Piaxtla team knows it is playing with fire. The government has made several attempts to shut down the villager-run program. Members of the Piaxtla team and of the organization of poor farmers have been jailed and threatened. The government has also tried to put Piaxtla out of business by starting its own rival health services in the area (instead of turning its attention to the many areas of Mexico which are still without health services). Paradoxically, however, while the government clinic has seriously weakened Piaxtla's actual health service (which is currently in disarray) it has also freed the program's most motivated health workers to focus on addressing the more basic social, economic, and political causes of poor health. In the final analysis, the Piaxtla team's work in these areas has done far more to reduce child mortality and improve people's health—and overall quality of life—than a narrow medical approach alone could have accomplished.

Now in the 1990s, the villagers recognize that the future is less certain than ever. They foresee that the improvements in health won through years of community organizing and struggle may be lost tomorrow due to greed-driven global policies. They have seen the constitution that their forefathers fought for violated by foreign powers in conspiracy with their own self-seeking leaders. For them, the "free trade" agreement is not free; it has cost them their land, their health, their most basic human rights, and the dignity of self-determination. The plight of poor farming and working people in Mexico is not an isolated situation. Similar hardships are being wrought on disadvantaged peoples in every corner of today's endangered planet. The global power structure—comprised of big government, big business, and the international financial institutions—has imposed its New World Order worldwide. It has tied most areas of production and development to the global market in a way that benefits powerful interests and weakens the bargaining power of the poor. Today no nation—and, indeed, virtually no village—has the liberty of self-determination.

Health Care in the Context of Social Revolution:
The Example of Nicaragua

In Nicaragua, the people's quest for health has been inseparable from their struggle against unjust social and political forces, both internal and external. During the last two decades this small Central American country has seen three very different forms of government: the Somoza dictatorship up to 1979, the Sandinista regime from 1979 to 1990, and the United Nicaraguan Opposition/Chamorro coalition government from 1990 to the present. The first and last of these governments were controlled by elites who put the interests of big business, both domestic and foreign, before the needs and rights of the population. In marked contrast, the Sandinistas gave high priority to social justice, to popular participation, and to trying to meet the basic needs of the poor majority.

The health situation has varied accordingly. Consistent with the Rockefeller study, which found that "social and political commitment to equity" was a key determinant of "good health at low cost," the Sandinista period brought remarkable improvements in health. By contrast, the country's health status under the highly inequitable, repressive Somoza regime was abysmal (among the worst in Latin America, alongside Honduras and Bolivia).[24] And in post-Sandinista Nicaragua both living conditions and the health status of the poor majority are again rapidly deteriorating. By comparing these three periods in Nicaragua's recent history, much can be learned about the determinants of a population's well-being.

The Somoza Regime: 1936–1979

In 1934 the first Anastasio Somoza, who had been installed by Washington as the head of the US-created National Guard, had Nicaraguan national hero Augusto Cesar Sandino assassinated. Two years later Somoza assumed the presidency and installed himself as dictator. For the next 43 years the Somoza family ruled Nicaragua as its personal fiefdom, taking direct control over 20% of the country's farmland and many of its big industries. Wages were kept insupportably low, people's rights were methodically violated, and attempts at labor and community organizing were violently repressed. Health services were mostly curative, doctor/hospital based, private, and oriented toward serving the country's tiny elite class. In the 1970s it was estimated that 90% of the health resources were consumed by just 10% of the population.[25] The main causes of child death were diarrhea, tetanus, measles, and whooping cough. More than one in ten children died before reaching age one[26] and more than half of the Nicaraguan children were undernourished.[27]

Under Somoza—as in many countries where human rights are systematically denied—community-based health initiatives began to spring up. Many of these initiatives were assisted by foreign nongovernmental organizations and by religious groups that initially had no political motives other than to help those in need. But the desperate situation of the disadvantaged was so clearly a product of an unfair social order that those concerned with people's well-being inevitably became more socially and politically aware. Community health workers facilitated organized action at the local level in order to alleviate some of the underlying man-made causes of poor health. Thus they gradually became agents of change—and were soon branded as subversives.

By the late 1970s, an extensive network of nongovernmental community health programs extended throughout Nicaragua, especially in rural areas and poverty-stricken urban *barrios*. When one of the authors (David Werner) visited the country in 1977, these grassroots health initiatives had begun to play a key role in mobilizing people in defense of their well-being and rights. And the health programs were encountering repression. In an attempt to co-opt these popular initiatives or make them redundant, Somoza's Health Ministry—with the help of the United States Agency for International Development (USAID)—launched an ambitious project to train government-managed *health promoters*. But despite millions of dollars of US funding, the government's program received limited community support. Meanwhile the network of community-based programs continued to expand. In response, Somoza's much feared National Guard increasingly targeted grassroots health workers—along with union leaders and other community organizers—for harassment, detention and execution.

The grassroots network of community-run health initiatives played a key role in the broad-based popular awakening and mobilization that eventually led to the overthrow of the oppressive Somoza dynasty. In the last years of Somoza's rule, the persecution of community health workers—as well as doctors, nurses, and medical students—led many health workers to go underground and join the growing Sandinista resistance. When the govern ment cut off water, food, and other basic supplies, the communities that supported the Sandinistas set up Civil Defense Committees which acted as provisional local governments. These communities not only distributed food, water, and other basic supplies, but also trained and coordinated health volunteers, known as *brigadistas de salud* (health brigadiers). Thus it was the National Guard's collective punishment of liberated areas that forced the Sandinistas to launch a new health system based on volun teers. This experience provided the groundwork for strong community participation in national health campaigns after the Sandinistas took control of the government in July, 1979.[28]

The Sandinista Period: 1979 – 1990

As a part of its approach to equity-based development, the revolutionary government gave high priority to health, thereby fulfilling a pledge the FSLN (Sandinista Front for National Liberation) had made in its "Historic Program" of 1969. One of its first actions was to create scores of health centers and posts, extending from the most remote rural areas to the poorest urban slums. To achieve this, the Sandinistas drew on one of their strongest resources: enthusiastic community support and the Peo-

ple's Health Councils. These People's Health Councils were umbrella organizations set up in 1980 which brought together organizations of workers, farmers, women, youth, etc. that had been set up during the resistance. The Health Ministry relied greatly on the mobilizing capacity of these organizations, which, since liberation, had evolved into neighborhood associations that performed administrative, political, and some disciplinary functions.

By 1982, half of the new health posts had been set up by the communities themselves. One community converted a notorious prison into a health center; the community did the same with a brothel owned by Somoza's colonels.[29] Health care was seen as part of a comprehensive, multi-sectoral approach to improve the well-being and quality of life of all citizens through mass participation.

The Sandinistas recognized the importance of literacy to health. Soon after they came to power the National Literacy Campaign recruited nearly 100,000 volunteers—mostly high school and college students—to go into the countryside and teach 400,000 adults how to read and write. The new Health Ministry (MINSA) trained 15,000 of these literacy *brigadistas* in first aid, sanitation, and control of malaria and diarrhea. The level of participation attained is demonstrated by the fact that by 1983 the nationwide health campaigns "were being planned and implemented by the People's Health Councils with only technical assistance from the Ministry of Health."[30]

Community health workers, or *brigadistas,* were trained using the "multiplier" approach the Sandinistas had developed during the resistance. After their training, all *brigadistas* were expected to share what they had learned with several other community members, and the most capable teachers were graduated to the role of *multiplicadores,* or trainers of other *brigadistas.*

The People's Health Councils also organized *Jornadas Populares de Salud* (People's Health Days): massive popular mobilizations against specific health problems. In 1980 an estimated 30,000 volunteers carried out a series of *Jornadas* to combat polio and measles (through mass immunization of children), dengue (by eliminating mosquito-breeding sites near homes), and various other diseases (by sanitation work and garbage disposal). All this was accompanied by public education campaigns, and home visits to immunize children whose families did not take them to the neighborhood posts during the Health Days.[31]

In 1981 malaria was added to the list of health problems addressed by the *Jornadas.* In a single nationwide effort involving 200,000 volunteer workers, three daily doses of anti-malarial drugs were given to over 80% of the population. Within the next three years the incidence of malaria fell by 62% (with almost no use of pesticides).[32]

Overall, during the first three to four years of the Sandinista government the health status of the population improved dramatically. Infant mortality declined from the official figure of 92 (probably much higher due to unrecorded births and deaths) to 80.2, while life expectancy climbed from 53 to 59 years. Thanks to enormous popular involvement in the immunization *Jornadas,* the incidence of communicable diseases of childhood greatly declined. Nicaragua became the second Latin American country to eliminate polio. (Cuba was the first.) Between 1980 and 1984, diarrhea fell from the first to the sixth most common cause of infant and child hospital mortality, although it remained the leading cause of death among infants nationally. (It is worth noting that the

Health Ministry chose to emphasize ORS packets over home fluids, even though the latter would have been more in keeping with the Sandinista ideals of popular participation and self-reliance. Even progressive decision makers can succumb to the lure of quick-fix technologies—and the advice of foreign experts.)

In both its successes and limitations, the Sandinista experience with immunization campaigns, and with health care in general, demonstrates the far-reaching impact that mass mobilizations for health can have when they are based on meaningful popular participation and input.

Internal disputes and contradictions

Although the FSLN's strong commitment to equity led to impressive health gains in the early years (before the escalation of the Contra war), internal contradictions within the revolutionary government undercut this progress. There was dissension within the Health Ministry regarding what was the best course of action to take. Three factions proposed three sharply different national health care strategies. The first faction wanted to emphasize training more *brigadistas*, expand the network of community health posts, and encourage more popular involvement in health. The second faction advocated a Cuban-style health care model, with complete nationalization of the health care system and a primary health care movement led by government-employed doctors. In complete contrast, the third faction, composed mainly of conservative doctors, sought more openings for private medical practice. Both of these two latter factions wanted an emphasis on training more doctors and nurses and expanding curative services, rather than on a greater investment at the community level.

Eventually a compromise was reached and large numbers of doctors and *brigadistas* were trained. However, the skills taught to the *brigadistas* were rather restricted, reflecting the medical establishment's fear of relinquishing their monopoly on medical skills. In a move aimed to bridge the divide between the two more conservative, medically-oriented factions, the membership of People's Health Councils was expanded to include doctors. However, many community activists felt that this allowed doctors to dominate the Councils, and diminished the autonomy of the local committees. Indeed, attendance at Council meetings fell and more *brigadistas* became inactive. In the words of Richard Garfield, on whose work we have drawn extensively for this account of the Nicaraguan health care system:

> The constant see-saw between centralized
> socialist policies and decentralized community

control and initiative, between professional health care pushed more into the periphery and paramedical ... services arising among community groups, made the development of health care erratic.[33]

Power to the people?

Some analysts feel that a major weakness in the Sandinista's leadership was its failure to allow popular participation to realize its full potential. These critics claim that, although the revolutionary government mobilized widespread grassroots involvement, this involvement remained somewhat superficial. They point out that *"¡Poder Popular!"* (Power to the People!) was a favorite rallying cry throughout the 1980s, an equally common slogan was *"¡Dirección Nacional: ordene!"* ("National Directorate: we await your command!"). In other words, popular participation, including participation in health initiatives, sometimes seemed to be directed more at eliciting compliance than at fostering true local control of decisionmaking. Some analysts believe that this limited approach to participation contributed to the FSLN's defeat in the 1990 national elections.

Even the former Director of the Division of Preventive Medicine, Leonel Arguello, felt that people's participation in the "People's Health Days," while important, was not enough. With reference to the popular *jornadas*, he observed:

> ... concentrating efforts on one day can help. But what about next month or next year? We need to pay less attention to slogans and put more emphasis on reaching a basic understanding. Only then will the people be in a position to take initiative, rather than just respond to MINSA requests.[34]

Sometimes the Sandinista leadership did exhibit a tendency toward paternalism and centralization. However, the picture is mixed. In a number of instances, high-level Sandinista government leaders appeared to listen to the people and respond to their wishes. One of the authors (David Werner) had a chance to observe this process. He accompanied a team of village health workers from Project Piaxtla in Mexico who had been invited to Nicaragua to share some of their discovery-based, problem-solving teaching methods in a training workshop for *brigadistas, multiplicadores*, and health educators. The workshop had been organized by the local health committee of Ciudad Sandino, a sprawling, very poor settlement on the outskirts of Managua. The workshop

got off to a good start. Enthusiasm was high. Role plays, puppet shows, and creative involvement of mothers, schoolteachers, and children helped bring learning to life. Everyone was eager to continue.

However, after the first few days, a message arrived from the Health Ministry ordering the committee to terminate the workshop immediately so that the *brigadistas* could take part in a national *jornada* to immunize children against measles, which was to take place the following weekend. On receiving this order, the workshop participants were disappointed and upset. They felt that they were learning methods that would enable them to conduct more effective community health work, and did not want to end the workshop prematurely.

The workshop participants held an emergency meeting with the town's health committee and community leaders. The participants reached a consensus that the workshop should continue. The community group drafted a response to the Health Ministry reminding it that *the Ministry's role was to advise and support the brigadistas and community health committees, not to tell them what to do.* The *brigadistas* pointed out that they were accountable to and took their directives from their community. The community had decided that the workshop was important and should continue. However, since everyone agreed that the national measles campaign was also important, the *brigadistas* would use the workshop to educate residents about the upcoming measles *jornada* and encourage their participation.

The visiting facilitators from Piaxtla were astounded by the audacity of the *brigadistas* and the local health committee in challenging the authority of the Health Ministry. Perhaps their daring was rooted in the fact that many were seasoned Sandinistas who had first become health activists during the uprising against Somoza. This may have given them the courage and solidarity to stand up to abuses of authority. Or maybe they simply took the revolutionary government at face value, and felt confident that it would respond to their letter with dialogue, not repression.

The visitors were even more surprised when the health committee received a reply from the Health Ministry later that afternoon. The Health Ministry apologized for having given such paternalistic and high-handed orders, and praised the community for helping keep the Ministry in line. It endorsed the *brigadistas'* plan to continue the workshop, while using it to prepare people for the measles campaign. This confrontation between the Ministry of Health and the people of Ciudad Sandino did much to convince the visitors that the Nicaraguan revolutionary process was dedicated to meeting people's needs.[35]

POPULAR PARTICIPATION IN ACTION: THE MEASLES MONSTER

One of the biggest successes of the Ciudad Sandino workshop was a participatory street theater production titled "The Measles Monster." In this skit the monster—an actor with a sweeping red cloak, a huge devil's mask, and giant clawed hands—chases after children in the street trying to catch those who have not been immunized against measles. After a wild chase, the monster catches a child (one of the actors) wearing a white, happy-faced mask. The monster envelops the child in its cloak, and when the child reappears he is wearing another mask, covered with the red spots of measles. The boy becomes very sick and nearly dies. His distraught parents vow to never miss an immunization date for their children in the future.

At the end of the skit an actor calls out to the audience, "Why did the little boy get measles?" The question is repeated until everyone present shouts back, "Because he wasn't immunized!" Then the actor asks, "And how can the community finally defeat the Measles Monster?" The audience shouts back, "Immunize all our children!" "Then what are you going to do this Saturday?" challenges the actor. And the audience trumpets back, "IMMUNIZE EVERY CHILD!"

This skit, developed by the workshop participants in Ciudad Sandino, has since been reenacted hundreds of times in poor communities throughout Nicaragua, Latin America, and many parts of the world. Descriptions of the skit, complete with photos, have been included in the Spanish and Portuguese editions of *Helping Health Workers Learn* and English editions of *Disabled Village Children* (books by David Werner). Many groups have recreated the skit as the Diarrhea Monster, the Cholera Monster, etc. It is anybody's guess how many children's lives this simple skit has helped to save. The Nicaraguan Health Ministry did well to follow the wishes of the community.

The impact of the US destabilization campaign on health care and health

The differences of opinion within the revolutionary government's Health Ministry and the Sandinistas' failure to mobilize more substantive popular participation may well have been moot points. Whatever negative impact these internal contradictions may have had on the Sandinistas' health policies was dwarfed by the devastation inflicted on the Nicaraguan health care system by the US government's all-out destabilization program. This campaign—which included sponsorship of counter-revolutionary armies (the Contras), CIA covert military and political operations, a trade embargo, an international credit boycott, a strident internal and external propaganda

campaign, and a diplomatic drive to isolate the Sandinista government—took a heavy toll on the Nicaraguan economy. This economic damage, in turn, led to more poverty and deteriorating living conditions, and thus to poorer health.

Washington's destabilization campaign also forced the revolutionary government to divert to defense funds that were desperately needed to respond to the population's health needs and to the growing popular demand for universal access to health services. And within the health sector, the Contra war forced the Health Ministry to shift resources to the treatment of casualties. Between 1983 and 1986, nearly one in ten persons admitted to a hospital was suffering from a war-related injury.[36] The trade embargo and credit boycott further undermined the Sandinistas' health initiatives and the entire national health care system by causing shortages of vaccines, essential medications, and other medical supplies.

In addition to these indirect effects, the Contras also directly targeted the country's health system. They did so deliberately, because they knew that the revolutionary government's health achievements were one of the major reasons for its popularity. By December, 1987, the Contras had killed 48 health workers, wounded 26, and kidnapped 32.[37] By the end of the war in 1990, Contra attacks had forced the closure of 128 of the country's 600 health facilities.[38] The threat of Contra ambushes prevented health workers from carrying out immunization campaigns and other health initiatives in some regions. In these areas malaria made a comeback. To add insult to injury, the CIA launched a disinformation campaign that blamed the Sandinista government for the health, social, and economic problems caused by Washington's destabilization campaign. All this was in keeping with the objective of low-intensity conflict: to wear people down and make their lives so miserable that they abandon their dreams and turn against their government as the only way out.

More generally, the Contra war and the US destabilization campaign led the revolutionary government to institute an unpopular military draft, and to create an atmosphere of distrust where dissent could easily be viewed as treason. Government crackdowns on political opposition forces, although less severe than in El Salvador, Guatemala or Honduras, became common. These developments significantly undercut popular support for the revolution, thereby reducing participation in the Sandinistas' health and other social campaigns.

The gradual escalation of the Contra war, together with the related economic crisis, prevented the revolutionary government from building on its early rapid progress in improving the Nicaraguan people's health. But the fact that the Sandinistas were at least able to keep most major health indicators from declining during the later years of the revolution in the face of adverse circumstances is proof that they remained true to their commitment to equity and health to the end.

The Chamorro Government: 1990 to the Present

Before the 1990 national elections in Nicaragua the US government poured millions of dollars into further undermining the Sandinistas and into backing the newly formed United Nicaraguan Opposition (UNO) party, a coalition of virtually every non-Sandinista political group from the

extreme right to the extreme left. The US backed Contras also stepped up their indiscriminate terrorist attacks on civilians just a few days before the election in an effort to gain votes for UNO. Nicaraguans got the message loud and clear. If they voted for the Sandinistas, the US sponsored terrorism and embargo would continue. Deprivation, hardship, and deterioration of the economy would become more extreme. Young people would continue to be conscripted and to die. And all to what end? The enemy was the most powerful nation in the world, backed by the world's most powerful economic force: multinational big business. The Nicaraguan people were exhausted and demoralized, worn down by the relentless war. So at the polls a small majority of voters, many reluctantly, chose to end the bloodletting and the bullying; they voted for Violeta Chamorro of UNO.

But since the elections, as the Nicaraguan people have discovered to their dismay, the nature of the bullying has changed, but has not ended. With the UNO coalition in power, the health system has suffered a series of setbacks. USAID, the World Bank and the International Monetary Fund pressured the new government to institute structural adjustment policies. This entailed massive privatization of government services and enterprises, resulting in layoffs of many thousands of workers, including in the health sector. By 1995, unemployment soared to over 75 percent. Prices skyrocketed while real wages plummeted. Poverty became increasingly widespread and acute. The numbers of homeless people and street children rose sharply. The number of prostitutes in Managua more than doubled in the year following the change in government, as mothers and older girls desperately sought the means to feed their hungry families. Orphanages overflowed with babies abandoned by destitute mothers. Crime, including drug trafficking and abuse, escalated.

The Health Ministry—which still had some Sandinistas within its ranks—initially tried to resist the drive to privatize health services. But with the acute cutbacks in staffing and medicines, especially in rural areas, it was often faced with the choice of closing community health centers or turning them over to private practice.

More US Aid, Less Health

When the U.S.-orchestrated embargo lifted, more money became available for health-related services than during the Sandinista regime. But most of this money has been tied to the political agendas of the donors. USAID gave $14 million for health services to the Contras returning from Honduras, and several million dollars more through conservative US organizations. The World Bank has poured money into modernizing public hospitals by adding plush private wings where those who can afford "business class" medical care can now pay for it on a fee-for-service (cost recovery) basis. The idea is that by charging wealthier clients, the hospitals will become self-sufficient and the profits can help cover service costs for the poor. But, according to health activist Maria Zuniga, in reality "the poor, when they go there, may have to sit for three days or die, while [the hospital staff] attend to the people who have money to pay."[39]

Meanwhile, urgently needed medicines have also been priced out of reach of the poor. Due to Northern pressure for trade liberalization, the Essential Drugs Policy initiated by the Sandinistas has been largely dismantled. Consequently, an increasing portion of people's shrinking income is being wasted on useless, overpriced, and sometimes dangerous medicines. When the Chamorro administration abruptly withdrew subsidies for all medication, the price for essential drugs shot up fivefold. And since community Oral Rehydration Centers have begun to charge for ORS packets, use of these packets has reportedly declined.[40]

With the growing polarization between rich and poor and the decentralization (or, more accurately, disintegration) of the health system, popular participation in government health initiatives has noticeably eroded. In the national health campaigns of 1991, only about half as many people took part as in earlier years. Immunization coverage also fell, and a large outbreak of measles occurred in 1991.

By 1993, eroding health and living conditions in poor communities began to reverse the progress the Sandinistas had made in reducing Nicaragua's infant mortality rate. Nearly 20 percent more infants died in the first 8 months of 1993 than in the whole of 1992.[41] Many of the additional deaths were attributed to diarrheal disease including cholera, which now appears to have become endemic due to deteriorating sanitation. Similarly, maternal mortality, which had dropped sharply during the Sandinista years, rose by 50% from 1991 to 1993.[42] Witness for Peace, a support group for nonviolence and human rights in Latin America, sums up the current situation as follows:

> Today in Nicaragua, hundreds of children are in the streets—sniffing glue to forget their hunger or selling bubble gum and cigarettes– rather than in school. More than 60% of their parents are unemployed. The health care and social services that once reached every citizen are now vanishing due to the deep spending cuts required by the international lending agencies in order for Nicaragua to have access to credit. *The United States determines the policies* of these international banks.[43]

Why Did the United States Consider Sandinista Nicaragua a Threat to its National Security?

Why was the US government so determined to overthrow the Sandinistas that it was willing to blatantly violate international law, make secret arms deals with Iran, lie to Congress and the public, and traffic cocaine into the US to finance illegal weapons shipments to the Contras? How could the world's most powerful nation regard a small, impoverished, struggling nation like Nicaragua as a threat?

According to the nongovernmental organization OXFAM, Nicaragua posed "the threat of a good example." OXFAM, which has worked in 76 underdeveloped countries, observed that during the period the Sandinistas were in power, "Nicaragua was... exceptional in the strength of that government's commitment ... to improving the condition of the people and encouraging their active participation in the development process."[44] In the words of José Figueres, the father of Costa Rican democracy, "for the first time, Nicaragua [had] a government that cares for its people."[45] Even the World Bank in the early 1980s (before the Reagan Administration pressured it to cut all credit to the Sandinistas) called the Sandinista's social programs "extraordinarily successful ... in some sectors, better than anywhere else in the world."

The threat that Nicaragua posed to the Washington-based global economic power structure was indeed "the threat of a good example"—the example it gave to other progressive Third World governments and political movements of an alternative approach to development that puts the needs of the poor first. Were such an example to succeed it could become infectious. This explains why US officials were quoted in the *Boston Globe* as saying that, even if the US destabilization campaign failed to achieve a complete military victory, they would be "content to see the Contras debilitate the Sandinistas by forcing them to divert scarce resources toward the war and away from social programs." After all, the Sandinistas' social programs were at the heart of their good example.[46]

For all its imperfections, Nicaragua under the Sandinistas served as a living prototype of health and development strategies based on need rather than greed. The US government did not try to crush the Sandinista government because it was *undemocratic,* but because it was *too democratic.* It was much more responsive to the needs of its ordinary citizens—and in particular the needs of the poor—than the Third World regimes the US supports (or for that matter, than the US itself). As a result, it posed a threat to the regional and global status quo.

Noam Chomsky, in discussing the US assault on the Sandinistas and other popular movements in Central America, concludes:

US achievements in Central America in the past 15 years are a major tragedy, not just because of the appalling human cost, but because a decade ago there were prospects towards meaningful democracy and meeting human needs, with early successes in El Salvador, Guatemala and Nicaragua.

These efforts might have worked and might have taught useful lessons to others plagued with similar problems—which was, of course, exactly what US planners feared. The threat has been successfully aborted, perhaps forever.[47]

Yet, despite the daunting odds they face, the of Nicaraguan people have not given up their struggle for health. Confronted with the failure of the present government to answer to their needs, they are again beginning to take health care into their own hands. Rather than work as closely with the government as they used to, they protest against its neglect. Women's self-help groups have begun to organize. With the assistance of a few remaining progressive voluntary agencies, some communities have once again begun to train nongovernment *brigadistas* much as they did in the days of Somoza.

It is clear that Arnoldo Alemán's election to the presidency in October, 1996 will ensure both the entrenchment of neo-liberal economic policy and, at the same time, the intensification of people's resistance and their struggles for basic needs and justice. The revolution, in its own way, continues in Nicaragua, as it does among marginalized and disadvantaged peoples around the world. But the powers they must fight are now global.

CHAPTER 21

Health for No One or Health for All:
The Need for a Unified Effort from the Bottom Up

History is the long and tragic story of the fact that privileged groups do not give up their privileges voluntarily.

—Martin Luther King, Jr., letter from Birmingham City Jail

The Evolution of Social Responsibility— and Recent Reversals

In the last part of this book we have looked at four initiatives, large and small, which have tried to address the health needs of disadvantaged people in fair and participatory ways. None was without flaws and contradictions. But each represented an alternative, equity-oriented strategy that sought to empower people to address their immediate health problems while simultaneously sowing the seeds for the ultimate emergence of fairer, healthier social structures.

However, each of these initiatives encountered obstacles which can be traced back to the global power structure. Today that structure is so pervasive that it is difficult for any village or nation to chart its own autonomous course toward health and development. We have seen how the deteriorating economic situation of many Third World countries, exacerbated by staggering foreign debt and structural adjustment policies, has further depressed the living standards of poor families and their children. At the same time that real wages are falling, government spending on social services is being ruthlessly cut.

This grim situation threatens to reverse the hard-won social progress that has occurred during the modern era. During the last two centuries the seeds of social responsibility have gradually taken root, along with an emerging ethic of fairness, equity, and well-being to which all people are entitled. Slavery has largely been abolished and racism has lost its legal underpinnings and is less socially acceptable.

Most importantly, during the last century an ethos of collective responsibility gradually emerged whereby those with more than their share of wealth were expected to contribute to the common good and to the welfare of those who have less. In this spirit, progressive taxation was institutionalized to assure that all citizens' basic needs could be met. The communal sense of the extended family—which had shrunk to the nuclear family in the course of Western civilization—reappeared in the form of civic responsibility. As the interconnectedness of all life and events on the planet has become more apparent, there has been growing awareness of the need for an interactive and mutually supportive global community. Today's eco-crises (both economic and ecologic) make the building of a balanced and sustainable global community more urgent than ever.

A major milestone in the evolution of this social consciousness, was the 1945 founding of the United Nations, with its various agencies and its charters to protect vulnerable groups (children, women, refugees, poor people, etc.). In recent decades we have witnessed a gradual shift toward a basic-needs approach to development. In 1978, the Alma Ata Declaration proclaimed that health was a basic human right. The world's nations endorsed Primary Health Care as a strategy to reach the utopian goal of *Health for All.*

However, as the year 2000 approaches, the goal of Health for All grows more distant despite all the high level campaigns to achieve it. It is increasingly evident that the greatest obstacle to achieving satisfactory levels of health is the inequitable global economic order, dominated by the transnational corporations.[48] Because they fail to address this central fact, the health and development strategies promoted by the ruling class are mere bandages on the wounds of social injustice.

As the power structures of the North, in alliance with the elite of the South, have joined in a global united front, progressive alternative health and development initiatives have found it increasingly difficult to survive. Until recently, it was still possible for people in a small community or country to implement alternative health and development strategies that could achieve impressive improvements in citizens'—and children's—well-being. Today such self-determined autonomy has become virtually impossible.

Toward a Healthier Society

There are no easy answers to the question of how to meet the needs of poor and disadvantaged children. It is much easier to analyze the causes of high child mortality than to find workable solutions. Many social analysts agree that to correct the root causes of high child mortality will require nothing short of sweeping transformation of the present social order, both within countries and at the global level.

The underlying thesis in this book is that health for all can only be attained through a more equitable distribution of wealth, resources, opportunity, and ultimately, power. If this is so, how can the sweeping social changes necessary to realize this goal be brought about? Disadvantaged and concerned people around the world are seeking ways to forge an alternative path of development, leading toward a healthier, more compassionate and more sustainable global community. Although there is no road map, let us briefly examine some existing attempts to find a way forward.

History and common sense tell us that people and groups with entrenched interests rarely surrender their privileged positions without a fight. The changes that are needed can only be achieved through an organized popular movement for social change. But given the globalized front of the prevailing economic order, this movement cannot hope to prevail unless it too becomes global in scope. Paradoxically, in order to ensure accountability to its disadvantaged constituency, this movement must remain diverse, decentralized, and locally supported. The slogan, "think globally and act locally," has never been more timely.

In order to be effective, any effort to reduce the mortality and improve the quality of life of the world's most vulnerable groups, including children, will have to be comprehensive and holistic. Citizens will need to address the issues at all levels, from the local to the international,

and extending well beyond the boundaries of the formal health sector. The following suggestions for action are drawn from the experiences of various activists, advocates, and community organizers from around the world.

Laying the Groundwork for Change: A Strategy for Health Improvement

- Ensure that measures intended to improve the situation of disadvantaged people encourage their active participation and foster self-determination.

- Take care that such interventions are implemented in ways that facilitate equity, power sharing, and group problem solving.

- Beware of recommendations, technologies, or funding sources that increase dependency, subservience, or unquestioning compliance.

As we have seen, even a stopgap intervention like oral rehydration therapy can be introduced in ways that encourage self-reliance and help people to collectively analyze and solve their problems. The pilot diarrhea control project in Mozambique, involving participatory research by schoolchildren, is a good example. The greater the number of community members—especially those who are most marginalized—who participate in a project's planning, implementation, and evaluation, the more likely it is that they will be able to foster healthful change.

When assessing any initiative, consider not only its short-term impact on health but also its long-term implications for social change. Try to answer the following questions:

- Does this initiative help people to gain greater control of their health and their lives?

- Does it help them to develop the confidence and collective ability to solve their own problems and to stand up for their rights?

- Does it help to equip the most disadvantaged people with analytical, organizing, communication, and other skills that will be needed to defend their rights?

- Does it strengthen the economic base or increase the political leverage of the weakest members of the community relative to the strongest members?

- Does it facilitate or impede the long-term structural changes that are needed to achieve meaningful, lasting health gains?

One of the authors, David Sanders, has outlined a strategy that progressive health workers can follow to lay the groundwork for the transformation of the health sector and of society as a whole:

HOW HEALTH WORKERS CAN LAY THE GROUNDWORK FOR CHANGE

The present model for medical and health services in the South—as it is in the North from which it comes—is determined and dominated by the combined influences of the medical profession, business interests, and the state. Health-care consumers are relegated to the role of passive recipients (objects) rather than active participants (subjects) in decisionmaking related to health.

Clearly, ways need to be devised for changing this relationship of forces. To improve overall levels of health, especially the health status of the least advantaged members of society, community health initiatives need to be part of a wider process aimed at stimulating progressive social change. Granted, the essential character of health care will only be changed when the present economic and political system is transformed. But introducing changes in the balance of power within the health sector—through certain basic reforms—can help to create popular pressure for thorough-going social transformation. Increasing the power of nonprofessionals within the health sector is a necessary part of a struggle for popular control of all areas of society.

Possible approaches to improving and democratizing the health sectors in both developed and underdeveloped countries include:

- *fighting for democratic control over health care by representatives of the majority of the people rather than by appointees of the state; and*

- *weakening the monopoly of the medical profession on medical knowledge, which allows it to maintain control over health care;*

- *limiting the excesses of medical business interests by exposing their operations to the scrutiny of the public.*[49]

---

1. Suggestions for Those Who Are Involved in Community Health Work, or Who Have Any Way of Influencing It:

Community health workers (CHWs) can play a key role in carrying out the strategy outlined above. Health workers are in an excellent position to act as agents of change, especially if they are trained to take an enabling approach, and are given the power to facilitate autonomous decisionmaking in their communities.

A health initiative is more likely to be empowering if CHWs are selected democratically and are sustained or remunerated by the community in which they work. There are two reasons for this. First, the CHW is more likely to feel accountable to the people rather than the medical profession or the state. Second, it is easier for CHWs to demystify and disseminate their skills if community members view them as being "one of us." The local CHW can also help people to analyze their situation and to realize that many of their health problems are rooted in their living and working conditions and other social factors. This empowers community members by enabling them to recognize the sources of ill health.[50]

It is true that the most important role of the community health worker is preventive, but this work should be preventive in the fullest sense of the word. Ultimately, the health worker should help put an end to oppressive inequities, and help her people—as individuals and as a community—liberate themselves, not only from outside exploitation and oppression, but also from their own short-sightedness, greed, and futility. To quote a slogan of the Health Workers Association of South Africa (an independent coalition which helped lead the battle against apartheid), *"The struggle for health is a struggle for liberation."*

2. Suggestions for Teachers, Writers, and Communicators (And We All Are Communicators in One Form or Another):

Become as well informed as you can about the major problems facing humanity, especially those that compromise the health and well-being of children and other vulnerable groups. Try to see how these problems are related, why the current global social order has failed to resolve them, and what prevents the people who suffer from the inequities of the status quo from openly revolting against it.

You can become better informed about these issues by reading and by conversing with reliable sources. But remember, the mass media will feed you a lot of disinformation. Even where the press is officially free, as in the US, economic realities dictate otherwise. Most of us, for instance, cannot afford to buy access to television, radio or newspapers. The individuals and corporations that own media outlets (which are becoming concentrated into ever fewer hands) are part of the global power structure. Governments and wealthy interests count on the mainstream media to paint a distorted, incomplete picture of reality. (In fact, this is one of the most effective tools of social control that the ruling elite has at its disposal.) Therefore, you may have to rely primarily on the alternative press.

But whatever the source, chew before you swallow. Critically analyze all you read or are told. Consider the source, the author's biases, and whether the information squares with your own experiences and observations, and whether it makes sense.

As you become better informed, share what you are learning with others. Help people begin to ask probing questions such as: "Why do prevailing health and development policies bring neither health nor development for growing numbers of destitute people?" "Why does the gap between the haves and the have-nots keep growing wider?" "In what ways are these trends rooted in the present economic order and development paradigm?" Only when enough people start thinking critically about their current situation can an effective movement for a more equitable, accountable, and democratic system be launched.

At the end of this book, you will find a short annotated reading list on "The Politics of Health." Some of the topics covered range well beyond child survival, primary health care, or even development issues. Yet the social, economic, and political factors addressed in these publications have a far greater impact on child survival and well-being than all of our more narrowly focused health care interventions combined. (For those interested, a more extensive *Annotated Reading List on the Politics of Health,* updated yearly, is available from HealthWrights and the International People's Health Council.)

3. If You Are an Activist, a Community Organizer, a Member of a Group of Disadvantaged People, or a Concerned Citizen Working for Change:

Encourage your neighbors and coworkers to think globally and act locally. Collectively analyze the causes of current hardships and poor health, reflect on root causes and possibilities for change, and explore ways to take collective action. But be prepared for forceful opposition.

Remember, when disadvantaged people—or even members of the middle class—stand up for their rights, they run the risk of triggering a repressive backlash by the local, national or global power structure. After all, the elite are not likely to share or yield decisionmaking control without a battle. Initiating confrontation without sufficient preparation can be disastrous. It is generally wiser to gradually build the group's confidence and skills through an incremental series of nonconfrontational activities *before* directly challenging the local power structure. Remember that strength lies in numbers. This is especially true for groups who traditionally have been relatively powerless.

Forge alliances with other groups struggling for their rights.

As we have seen, the world's elite have already joined forces to form a global front: a New World Order dedicated to preserving the inequities of the status quo.

They are pursuing a divide-and-conquer strategy designed to pit marginalized groups against each other. It is therefore essential for people from different socio-economic backgrounds, creeds, ethnic communities, national origins, and areas of interest to set aside their biases and stereotypes, end their feuding, and find common ground. We must learn to respect our differences and work together to realize our shared goal of a healthier social order. All of us who are working for change—progressive health workers, human rights advocates, social reformers, labor organizers, feminists, liberation theologians, environmentalists, and activists working on issues ranging from development to disarmament, from corporate accountability to breastfeeding to rational use of medicines—are fighting the same war on different fronts. This idea is eloquently captured in a quote from Samora Machel, the late president of Mozambique:

> Solidarity is not an act of charity. It is an act of unity between allies fighting on different terrains toward the same objectives.[51]

The Need for a Grassroots United Front for World Health

> *Our historic challenge is to add, sift, stir, spice, knead, and otherwise blend ourselves together, over time, into a genuine people's political power.*[52]
> —James Hightower

Given the united front of the global power structure, it is imperative that progressive regional, national, and global coalitions and networks mobilize a broad-based demand for a more equitable, health-promoting world order. Both South-South and South-North coalitions are important.

A number of South-South networks have already formed around issues of health, development, consumer protection, and trade. South-North coalitions are equally essential. Collectives of unemployed, underpaid, homeless, and otherwise disadvantaged groups in the North need to form bonds with oppressed groups in the South, in recognition that their struggles are essentially one and the same. After all, the gap between rich and poor is widening in the developed as well as in the underdeveloped countries. The global trend is staggering. In 1960 the average income ratio of the richest 20% to the poorest 20% of the world's people was 30 to 1. By 1991 the ratio was 61 to 1.[53] Similar forces of exploitation and social control are at work both in the Third World and the First, though they sometimes express themselves in different ways. Therefore disadvantaged and concerned people from all societies need to work together for a common cause.

Al Senturias of the Asia-Pacific Task Force on Human Rights argues that as long as the international financial institutions dictate—and self-seeking government officials implement—policies that cause massive unemployment, unjust low wages, and loss by peasants of their control over land and resources, there will never be improvements in the rights or health of our peoples. As the Piaxtla health team and many others have done, Senturias notes the global forces that increasingly violate or obstruct local self-determination. And he stresses the need for a united struggle for healthier social structures, from the bottom up:

> We have seen that as soon as people organize themselves, as soon as they get together, as soon as they demonstrate and march together, they also get the iron hand of the government, again following the dictates of these unjust economic and political structures that are dictated and abetted by the IMF and World Bank.
>
> You cannot talk about human rights [or health rights] for all, as long as the neo-colonial hold on the economic and political structures in the Third World remains untouched.
>
> In order to guarantee that human rights are respected, we have to collectively mobilize the strengths of entire peoples, not through a coup d'état or some political party coming to power in one country or other. It means the education and mobilization of the entire population in order to transform society so that the society will truly be in the hands of the people. Only in this way will the people themselves be able to decide their own future and come to enjoy the rights that are due them, to have dignity as human beings.[54]

In many parts of the world—especially in the South—activists, members of popular health movements, and grassroots organizers are likewise concluding that, "We have to collectively mobilize the strengths of the popular majority." In order to change the course of development so that it responds to the needs of all people, more people need to strongly participate. This means that today's dangerously undemocratic global power structure must be replaced by a truly participatory democratic process.

African Social Scientists Unite in Favor of an Equity-Oriented Alternative

On no other continent is the mounting crisis in health and development more severe than it is in Africa. In a paper titled "From Development to Sustained Crisis: Structural Adjustment, Equity and Health," the authors, who are social scientists and health workers, argue that:

> The economic crisis in sub-Saharan Africa cannot be understood outside the context of the legacy of colonialism and class formation. Structural adjustment programmes serve to exacerbate inequalities and threaten to reverse the social gains of the majority achieved through the struggle for independence. Under such circumstances social scientists have a social responsibility to take a stand against the current policies that have led to an unprecedented decline of the health status of the poor; their skills must be put at the disposal of the oppressed with a view to giving voice to the experiences and needs of the majority.[55]

In keeping with the above commitment, at the first Regional Conference of Social Science and Medicine, social scientists and health workers from various African countries formulated what has become known as the Ukunda Declaration.[56] The Declaration covers, in brief, much of the analysis we have included in this book, and ends with a call for sweeping structural change. Because it presents such an excellent summary of much of what we have tried to say, and because it is such an important early step by concerned professionals to take a united stand in favor of an alternative development strategy based on social justice and human needs, we include the Ukunda Declaration in its entirety:

THE UKUNDA DECLARATION ON ECONOMIC POLICY AND HEALTH
13th September 1990

1. Africa's recent colonial history, experience of capitalist underdevelopment, and more recently recession, debt and the impact of structural adjustment policies (SAPs) have severely affected the health status and survival chances of the overwhelming majority of the population. There is accumulating evidence that the current economic crisis and attendant responses (including SAPs) have severely hampered the ability of Africa's people, especially "vulnerable groups," to maintain their already inadequate living standards and minimal access to effective health and social services. In addition, the gains of independence have already been largely eroded.

2. It is well recognized that health (and disease) experience is the outcome of social, economic, political and cultural influences. Much historical evidence exists to show that without sustained improvements in socioeconomic conditions and consequent standards of living, advances in health are unlikely to be achieved and maintained.

3. Both as a result of the economic crisis and as a consequence of the SAPs, there are growing sections of the population who have become marginalized, disempowered, and are increasingly unable to meet their basic needs. These are primarily low paid workers in the formal and informal sectors, a growing stratum of rural producers. Within these groups, it is women and their dependents who have been most adversely affected. In short, the greatest burden of these economic policies is being borne by those least capable of shouldering it.

4. In response to this crisis, there has been increasingly widespread popular opposition in the form of food riots, strikes, and other forms of protest. Advocacy initiatives such as UNICEF's *Adjustment with a Human Face* and the World Bank's *Social Dimensions of Adjustment*, have manifestly failed to address the underlying structural causes and have not even succeeded in their objective of mitigating the effects of SAPs. Worse still, these initiatives may have contributed to obscuring the fundamental bases of this crisis, and thus further disempowered the most vulnerable.

5. The core of these "recovery" programmes posits export-led growth as a strategy not only for resolving the short term economic crisis but also for creating the basis for future sustained development. The experiences of the

last decades demonstrate—even during the long post war boom—the hollowness of this model. Indeed the pursuance of this approach even in the rich countries, is leading to increasing stratification and the impoverishment of significant strata within societies. Moreover, the unprecedented accumulated debt, particularly of the USA, underscores the bankruptcy of this approach and furthermore, cynically shifts the real burden of this debt to the underdeveloped world through the agency of the IMF and the World Bank, to maintain the value of the dollar and the high standard of living of the American middle class.

6.   These policies have been implemented through the (sometimes unwilling) agency of African governments. While these policies have had disastrous effects on the majority of Africans, a few have benefitted inter-alia, from trade liberalization, currency devaluation, and reduction in the value of real wages. Moreover, these groups have been relatively unaffected by sharp reductions in social sector spending because of the existence of alternatives—e.g., private sector health, education and welfare services.

7.   Within the health sector itself, important and promising initiatives such as primary health care (PHC) have not escaped the influence of "adjustment" to the present reality. Programmes such as the child survival initiative have been interpreted in a narrow and overly technical way, and in many countries have been reduced to limited, vertical and often externally funded immunization and rehydration programmes. Even such limited interventions have been hampered in their implementation by the effects of the economic crisis—lack of transport, spare parts, equipment, vaccines, drugs and now even salaries. This situation has led to the devising and promotion of such initiatives as "cost sharing" and the "Bamako Initiative" which putatively seek to generate income to "improve the quality of services" and foster "community participation" in PHC. It is already becoming apparent that such programmes are further aggravating inequity, particularly since the distinction between willingness and ability to pay has not been addressed in policy formulation. Although the implementation of such programmes will save costs in the public sector, it is clear that the economic crisis and SAPs have resulted in the rapid expansion of the private sector where foreign exchange consumption for often irrational importations (unnecessary, expensive patent drugs for the least needy) dwarfs the income generated through cost sharing initiatives in the public sector.

8.   These limited technocratic and piecemeal approaches in the context of the crisis have led to unprecedented and disturbing demographic changes. While reductions in infant mortality (probably temporary) have been achieved in some countries, morbidity and malnutrition rates have increased in most sub-Saharan African countries and in some where the recession has been most severe, even mortality rates have started to rise. Additionally, the crucial social mobilizing content of the PHC initiative which holds the solution to some of these problems, appears to have been lost.

9.   Clearly the long term solution to this crisis will require fundamental structural changes at national and international levels. It is suggested that inter-alia, the following policy options be seriously considered:

● diversification of the productive base away from the legacy of the colonial past

● development of indigenous technologies

● emphasis on regional self-sufficiency in food

● expenditure switching towards agriculture and social sectors

● environmental protection

● establishment of a debtor's club that could in a united way argue from a position of relative strength for debt repudiation

The adoption of the above policies will require political will on the part of African governments. The best guarantee of such bold initiatives is the sustained pressure from the majority who have been so adversely affected in this crisis. For this process to be initiated and maintained, fundamental democratization of the political and social structures is a prerequisite.

10. A minimum responsibility of health and social scientists is to facilitate the above enterprise. While there are a number of areas where research is necessary, it is our firm belief that for any research to have any operational or political outcome, the objects of research must become the subjects. Thus the definition of the research agenda and its implementation and utilization must result from a democratic dialogue between researchers and those most affected by the current crisis. Research areas should include a focus on the evolving impact of the economic crisis and SAPs on:

- living conditions of those most affected.

- the development of cost recovery programmes and their effects on equity in health service access, utilization and quality.

- social stratification, integrity and social violence.

- social organizations and community responses in health and development related areas.

Among other actions, progressive groups must endeavor to restructure, realign, and then empower the United Nations—including WHO, UNICEF, UNDP, and the World Court—to speak out against the global obstacles to health and well-being. It is urgent that such bodies as the United Nations and nongovernmental organizations take a united, nonaligned stand for the rights of all people—even if this means defying Washington and big business and thereby suffering drastic cutbacks in their present budgets.

With the goal of working toward a healthier global community, a wide range of international groups and networks have been forming. Their activities focus on concerns as diverse as human rights, women's and children's rights, minority and indigenous rights, disability rights, poor people's rights, workers' rights, civil rights, immigrant and refugee rights, gay rights, and legislative and penal reform, as well as concerns related to health, development, education, communications, environmental protection, alternative economics, fair trade, arms control, and watchdogging of the various multinational industries, UN organizations, and the international financial institutions. Organized action around each of these concerns is important for building a healthier, more equitable social order. But since all these concerns are interrelated—and strength comes through unity that respects differences—alliances and solidarity need to be formed between these various networks and movements.

Two broad-based networks with which the authors are most familiar are the *Third World Network* based in Malaysia, and the *International People's Health Council (IPHC)* based in Nicaragua. The idea for the IPHC grew out of a meeting on "Health Care in Societies in Transition" in Managua, Nicaragua in December, 1991. The founders are health rights activists and leaders of progressive community health programs from Africa,

South East Asia, the Far East, and Latin America. The IPHC has close links with the Third World Network (TWN) and a sub-group of the TWN called the People's Health Network. The primary authors of this book, David Werner and David Sanders, are the IPHC regional coordinators for Africa and North America, respectively.

Time to Transform the World Bank and the IMF

THE INTERNATIONAL PEOPLE'S HEALTH COUNCIL

What is it? The International People's Health Council is a worldwide coalition of people's health initiatives and socially progressive groups and movements committed to working for the health and rights of disadvantaged people … and ultimately of all people. The vision of the IPHC is to advance toward health for all—viewing health in the broad sense of physical, mental, social, economic, and environmental well-being. We believe that:

- Health for All can only be achieved through PARTICIPATORY DEMOCRACY (decision-making power by the people), EQUITY (in terms of equal rights and everyone's basic needs), and ACCOUNTABILITY of government and industry, with strong input by ordinary people in the decisions that effect their lives.

- The policies of today's dominant power structures—tied as they are to powerful economic interests—have done much to precipitate and worsen humanity's present social, economic, environmental, and health crises. Those who prosper from unfair social structures are resistant to change. They also have vast power and global reach. So today, changes leading toward a healthier world order must be spearheaded through a worldwide grassroots movement that is strong and well-coordinated enough so it can force the dominant power structures to listen and finally to yield.

The IPHC intends to facilitate sharing of information, experiences, methods, and resources among a wide range of persons and coalitions involved in community health work who are oriented toward empowerment and self-determination. Its goal is to contribute toward a broad base of collective grassroots power which can have leverage in changing unfair and unhealthy social structures at local, national, and international levels.

Who can participate? The IPHC has no formal membership. It is an informal coalition of persons and groups who identify with its objective and wish to participate. Although most of the founding members of the IPHC are from the South, we feel the IPHC should be a South-North network, including grassroots struggles for health and rights of the growing numbers of poor and disadvantaged people in both underdeveloped and overdeveloped countries.

If you want to learn more about the IPHC, its plan of action, future meetings, publications, or if you want to join the network or help out either on projects or with donations, please contact:

Overall Coordinator
Maria Hamlin Zuniga
CISAS
Apartado # 3267
Managua
Nicaragua

Europe, Australia, etc.
Pam Zinkin
Institute of Child Health
30 Guilford Street
London WC1N 1EH
UK

North America
David Werner
HealthWrights
964 Hamilton Avenue
Palo Alto, CA 94301
USA

Africa
David Sanders
UWC Public Health Programme
P. Bag X17
Bellville
Capetown 7535
South Africa

Far East
Mira Shiva
A – 60 Hauz Khas
New Delhi, 110016
India

Latin America and the Caribbean
Ricardo Loewe
PRODUSSEP
Kramer 71
Col. Atlántida
Coyoacán, Mexico D.F.
Mexico

Near East
Mustafa Barghouthi
P.O. Box 51483
Jerusalem, Israel

Conclusion: The need for a "Child Quality-of-Life Revolution"

As we have discussed, the Child Survival Revolution has failed to reduce child mortality to acceptable levels. It has accomplished even less in terms of improving impoverished children's quality of life, which continues to deteriorate. Millions of children live in deplorable circumstances, lacking access to adequate food, water, health care, and other basic necessities. Even as the wealthy are suffering from the diseases of excess, poor children are ravaged by chronic undernutrition that stunts their bodies and their minds. Meanwhile, the gap between global haves and have-nots continues to grow, as does overconsumption of world resources and environmental destruction. (Between 1987 and 1993, the number of billionaires in the world more than doubled, from 98 to 233. The richest 101 individuals and families now control wealth valued at $452 billion. This is more than the total yearly income of the entire population of India, Pakistan, Bangladesh, Nigeria, and Indonesia combined, comprising more than one fourth of the world's population.)[57]

What can be done to guarantee that all the world's children not only survive, but are healthy in the fullest sense of sustainable physical, mental, emotional, and social well-being? What the world's children desperately need and deserve is a *Child Quality-of-Life Revolution.* Such a revolution must go beyond Selective Primary Health Care and quick-fix technologies. It requires a comprehensive strategy that extends beyond the health sector and combats the structural causes of poverty, malnutrition and poor health. It must promote a model of development that gives higher priority to meeting the basic needs of the poor than to fueling economic growth that benefits only the rich. Such a model must assure that all families have an adequate livelihood (either land to work or jobs with fair wages and safe working conditions). The health sector must work closely with other social and economic sectors, to assure that the needs and rights of women, children and other vulnerable groups are put first, not last.

To promote sustainable health, all children—and especially girls—must be encouraged (and enabled) to attend school. The full cost of their education should be funded through progressive taxation (not through user fees, which penalize the children of the poor). Also, schooling needs to become more relevant and more empowering. It should help children learn basic survival and coping skills, as well as the more sophisticated problem-solving and organizational skills needed to collectively analyze and act upon the conditions that shape their lives.

In short, a health strategy that seriously seeks to improve children's quality of life must be acutely and astutely political. The structural changes needed for a health-promoting society are only likely to be realized through sustained demand from an informed and organized populace. Hence health education must be comprehensive in an ethical, political, and organizational context. Awareness-raising educational materials, adapted to be accessible and exciting to persons with little schooling, need to be developed and made widely available. These materials can nurture problem-solving skills to enable communities to meet short-term health-related needs. But they can also provide analytic tools for seeking solutions to more fundamental long-term needs. They can help people analyze for themselves the local and global causes of poor health.

Above all, a comprehensive approach to health and development will encourage disempowered people the world over to unify and take a stand, demanding accountability of governments, of the UN (including WHO and UNICEF), and of the international financial institutions. Only when global decision-makers and planners are accountable for their actions through a process of participatory democracy can we realistically hope that the basic needs of the world's children will be met.

Achieving an equitable social order conducive to health will require nothing less than a worldwide uprising—a global nonviolent revolution. We can work toward such global solidarity through a two-step process. The first step is to act at the local level, where we can help to increase people's awareness of the causes of their day-to-day hardships and help them formulate strategies to improve their immediate situation and defend their rights. The second step is to link these local initiatives to broad national and international coalitions. To stand a chance of success, this "people's health movement" must be as global as the system it seeks to transform.

The struggle that lies ahead will be an uphill battle against daunting odds. But, win or lose, the struggle itself—with the friendships, shared experiences, insights, and personal growth it brings us—is worth the effort. We must not give up. The accountability of tomorrow's leaders and the well-being of today's children depend on our united efforts.

APPENDIX

The Role of UNICEF and WHO

The 20th Century will be chiefly remembered in future centuries not as an age of political conflicts or technical inventions, but as an age in which human society dared to think of the welfare of the whole human race as a practical objective.

—Arnold Toynbee, quoted in UNICEF's 1995 *The State of the World's Children* report (p. 54)

On reviewing an early draft of this book, several readers expressed uncertainty about the authors' perception of UNICEF and the World Health Organization (WHO). They asked us whether we believe these United Nations agencies play a positive or negative role in terms of working toward the structural changes that are a prerequisite for meaningful and lasting improvements in health. And how important do we consider these agencies' role to be? In answer to such queries, we would like to clarify where our view.

Although we are sometimes critical of UNICEF and WHO, we recognize that both agencies have made important contributions to world health, especially for those in greatest need. Both agencies have many dedicated, highly qualified, and caring people on their staffs. The initiatives they have spearheaded have saved millions of lives, at least temporarily.

Perhaps the most valuable contribution made by WHO and UNICEF has been to help win acceptance of the relatively new perception that *health is a basic human right* and to promote the idealistic goal of *Health for All.* The conceptualization of *Primary Health Care*—as a comprehensive approach for meeting the health needs of all people through participatory, equity-building action—was a great step forward. Persuading the world's governments to endorse such a potentially revolutionary approach, at least on paper (in the Alma Ata Declaration), was an extraordinary achievement.

Had they received more support from progressives, however, and less interference from conservatives, and had they listened more to grassroots organizations and popular movements for social change, UNICEF and WHO could perhaps have done much better. It is unfortunate that they have not stood up more firmly to pressure from governments, wealthy elites, and multinational corporations.

As we have discussed in this book, UNICEF and WHO have not realized many of the goals they have set.

Indeed, the earlier, more ambitious goals now appear more distant than ever. Especially in the poorest nations and communities, *many of the gains achieved through narrowly focused health technologies have been offset by regressive social trends,* cutbacks in public services, and a widening income disparity between rich and poor.

The globalized growth-oriented free-market development paradigm of the last decades has posed formidable obstacles to the progressive social changes some UNICEF and WHO policymakers have sought to promote. One high UNICEF official acknowledges that his agency is "bound and gagged."[1] There are several reasons for this.

First, most UNICEF and WHO funding comes from rich countries in the North. It is hardly surprising that the agencies more inclined to lick than bite the hand that feeds them. The United States government—which provides roughly one quarter of UNICEF's and WHO's operational budgets—has repeatedly threatened to slash the its contribution if the agencies *become too political:* that is, if they defend the interests of the poor when they conflict with those of big business, or if they call too emphatically for the macro-economic changes needed to reduce poverty and thus achieve lasting health gains.[2] The executives of the UN organizations know such threats are real. They remember what happened to UNESCO (from which the US completely withdrew its funding in 1984).

Both UNICEF and WHO have been repeatedly warned, and occasionally disciplined through reduced or delayed funding, for not toeing the line dictated by the United States.[3] In Part 3, we saw how the US government used threats of funding cuts and other sanctions to obstruct efforts by UNICEF and WHO to regulate and curtail the health-threatening marketing practices of transnational corporations. The examples we cited involve breast milk substitutes and irrational drugs. But, as many UN policymakers have discovered, the US government is quick to attack any national or international initiative that attempts to restrict or even question the freedom of the global market to place profit before people.

To some extent, the actions of UNICEF and WHO are further constrained by Third World governments. The agencies fear that if they are overly critical of a host country's policies, that government will retaliate by shutting down their local field offices.[4]

Transnational corporations also exert indirect pressure on UN agencies by lobbying government officials. More directly, some corporations that are notorious for unscrupulous marketing practices have made substantial donations to relevant UN programs (see pages 96–98). Although the parties concerned strongly deny it, at times such "collaboration" may influence the formulation and implementation of health strategies in ways that favor big business at the expense of children's well-being.

On a more basic level, UNICEF and WHO, like other UN agencies, represent different nations' governments, not their people (at least not directly). Unfortunately, most governments—including those in most Third World countries—are in large part controlled by a privileged elite class of people. These governments tend to resist health and development initiatives that work seriously toward a fairer distribution of resources and decisionmaking power.

On the most fundamental level of all, UNICEF and WHO are constrained in their advocacy for the poor by the fact that they themselves are part of the dominant power structure. One indication of this is the fact that many top officials in these organizations previously held high-level posts either in governments of dominant First World countries or in giant corporations. The current Directors General of both WHO and UNICEF represent two of the world's most wealthy and powerful nations, Japan and the United States. Both officials were appointed following pressure campaigns by their respective governments, in spite of angry protests by less powerful states and non-government organizations in both the North and South.

For a combination of reasons, as mentioned above, UNICEF and WHO have often followed the path of least resistance. Unable to effectively implement their muted call for a more equitable social and economic world order, they tend to embrace stopgap technological interventions as a way to limit the harm done by the present unjust world order—without radically changing that order or offending its dominant interests.

During the 1980s, UNICEF painstakingly (though cautiously) documented the deadly toll that economic recession, the debt crisis, structural adjustment, and resultant deepening poverty were taking on the health and lives of Third World children. But instead of vigorously protesting against this situation and calling for sweeping changes in the unfair global economic system, UNICEF tacitly accepted the "adverse economic climate" as an unalterable fact of life. Accordingly, it called for "adjustment with a human face."[5] This strategy, which in essence amounts to damage control to ameliorate unfair policies, has been partially adopted by the International Monetary Fund and the World Bank. It seeks to provide safety nets to protect vulnerable groups from the most devastating effects of structural adjustment.

In keeping with this compromise, as we saw in Chapter 4, UNICEF also "adjusted" its own strategy for reducing child death rates. Sidestepping the politically progressive challenge of comprehensive primary health care, it narrowed its focus to a few "cost-effective" interventions that debtor countries could afford within the harsh constraints of economic transition and structural adjustment. This strategy, although politically expedient within the context of the conservative socio-political climate of the last decade, failed to effectively address the root causes of poor health. As the distribution of wealth and resources worldwide became less equitably distributed than ever, child mortality and morbidity rates among the growing underclass, especially in the Third World, remained unacceptably high… and in some cases actually rose.

We can criticize UNICEF and WHO for having compromised their goal of "Health for All through Comprehensive Primary Health Care." But we should not write these agencies off as hopelessly co-opted. The constraints they operate under, while formidable, are not insurmountable. This is demonstrated by the important, sometimes courageous stands that both agencies have on occasion taken in defense of the disadvantaged.

For example, in its 1989 report on *The State of the World's Children,* as in many of its reports and analyses since then, UNICEF acknowledged that the technological interventions of the Child Survival Revolution are inadequate to offset the devastating impact of the debt crisis, structural adjustment, and the widening gap between rich and poor.[6] UNICEF has repeatedly called for effective debt relief.[7] It has urged policymakers to discard today's counterproductive, top-down development policies in favor of more egalitarian, ecologically viable strategies that it calls "real development."[8]

However, throughout the 1980s and the early 1990s, UNICEF failed to follow through on its call for *real development* (which it now calls "sustainable development") by rethinking its own strategy for reducing child mortality. Although it acknowledges the social determinants of ill-health, it has been slow in returning to the more comprehensive, more liberating, and more socially equalizing approach embraced in the Alma Ata Declaration. In practice, both UNICEF and WHO have usually been hesitant to challenge the status quo. This is hardly surprising, given the monumental constraints they face.

Encouragingly, UNICEF's 1995 *The State of the World's Children* report in some ways appears to be taking a more outspoken stand against the dominant development model and in favor of fairer, more equitable and participatory social structures.[9] The report cites numerous stark examples of growing inequity and social injustice, and traces these trends' devastating impact on children's health. These examples include the following:

- In Latin America today, fewer than 10% of landowners own almost 90% of the land.... In Africa, it is increasingly the case that most productive lands are devoted to export agriculture while the lands of the poor majority are of lesser quality, receive less investment, and are rapidly becoming degraded and depleted. (p. 43)

- In much of Asia, 50% of government educational spending is devoted to the best educated 10% (p. 45)

- Most countries could go a long way towards the meeting of basic needs by a fairer allocation of existing social expenditures. In Indonesia, for example, government spending on the richest 10% amounts to 3 times more than on the poorest 10%. (p. 45)

- Only about 25% of today's aid goes to the countries where the world's poorest billion people now live. (p. 46)

- For two decades, military spending in the developing world has grown more than twice as fast as per capita incomes... (p. 46)

- In the wars of the last decade far more children than soldiers have been killed and disabled. Over that period, approximately 2 million children have died in wars, between 4 and 5 million have been physically disabled, more than 5 million have been forced into refugee camps, and more than 12 million have been left homeless. (p. 2)

- In the last 10 years ... falling commodity prices, rising military expenditures, poor returns on investment, the debt crisis, and structural adjustment programs have reduced the real incomes of approximately 800 million people in some 40 developing countries.... At the same time, cuts in essential social services have meant health centres without drugs and doctors, schools without books and teachers, family planning services without staff and supplies. (p. 2)

- Internationally, inequality has now reached monstrous proportions. Overall, the richest fifth of the world now has about 85% of the world's GNP. (p. 44) Meanwhile, the poorest 40 or 50 countries have seen their share of the world income decline to the point where a fifth of the world's people now share less than 1.5% of world income. (p. 3)

- This tendency is not confined to the developing world ... During the decade of the 1980s, for example, 4 million more American children fell below the official poverty line even as average incomes rose... by 25%. (p. 3)

- The United States spends $25 billion a year on its prison services alone. (p. 59)

- The total cost of providing basic social services in the developing countries, including health, education, family planning, clean water... would be an additional $30 billion to $40 billion a year... The world spends more than this on playing golf. (p. 59)

- The poor remain poor principally because they are under-represented in political and economic decisions. (p. 47)

In addition to critiquing the regressive thrust of the dominant free market approach to development, UNICEF's 1995 report also calls for regulatory measures to contain the damage it is doing to the health of Third World communities (although the report carefully avoids using the term *regulation,* which is currently in disfavor among elites in the US and elsewhere). For instance, the report notes that:

- In recent commitment to free market economic policies, insufficient account has been taken of the effects on the poor, on the vulnerable, or on the environment. (p. 40)

- In too many countries economic policy is acting as a kind of reverse shock absorber, ensuring that the poor suffer first and most in bad times and gain last and least in good times. Economic development of this kind ... screws the poor even more tightly to their poverty. (p. 44)

- The problem of the economic marginalization of the poorest nations, and of the poorest people within nations, must be confronted. No social progress can be sustained ... if social and economic exclusion continues to be the chief characteristic of national and global economic systems. (p. 43)

- Free market economic policies have shown that they are successful in short term creation of wealth.

Governments now have the responsibility to harness that power to the cause of sustainable development. In particular, they have a responsibility to counterbalance the inbuilt tendency of free-market economic systems to favour the already advantaged. (p. 43)

In the report, UNICEF argues that "fundamental change is necessary" for sustainable development, and that "the problems of discrimination, landlessness, and unemployment must be addressed by land reform, restructuring of government expenditures in favour of the poor, reduction of military expenditures, and considerable increases in the resources available for environmentally sustainable development." (p. 43) However, the report acknowledges that "the way forward is obstructed by political and economic vested interests." (p. 43)

UNICEF's 1995 report strongly emphasizes the importance of "people's involvement in the struggle for change" (p. 56) and notes that social progress "is brought about less by governments than by people's movements, by a people-led sea change in public perceptions of what is and is not acceptable in human affairs—and by a corresponding change in the perception of democratic political leaders as to what constitutes good politics" (p. 56). The report goes on to state that: "It is, above all, the power of concerned and committed people, and their organizations, that can bring what needs to be done within the bounds of what can be done" (p. 56). "No longer are people willing to accept that societies should be so organized that progress, knowledge, and rights should remain the monopoly of the few." (p. 57)

Despite this progressive rhetoric, however, it would be premature to conclude that UNICEF is out from under the thumb of the global power structure. Although in one breath the report criticizes the inequities of the free market system, in the next it speaks enthusiastically of the "development consensus" reached at the 1995 World Summit on Social Development (Social Summit) in Copenhagen. There is a broad consensus, it says, that "the way forward lies along the path of democratic politics and *market-friendly economics*; of meeting human needs and investing in human capital." (Italics added.)(p. 5)

UNICEF's view-point and language are disturbingly similar to those of the World Bank, whose monetarist global perspective permeated the official Social Summit. There may have been more or less of a consensus on the "way forward" among the high-level officials behind the closed doors of the official summit. However, the official "Declaration and Plan of Action" was strongly criticized by the grassroots delegates attending the separate NGO Forum at the Social Summit, which accused the official assembly of "addressing the symptoms of [humanity's major] problems without challenging the policies that have helped create them,"[10] and of subscribing to "a declaration that—despite progressive rhetoric—promises only a continuation of the neoliberal policies that many of us have come to see as the core of the problem."[11] A group of over 600 nongovernmental organizations (NGOs), grassroots coalitions, and popular movements represented at the NGO Forum drafted and signed an "Alternative Copenhagen Declaration" which attacks the current world economic order as untenable and demands a dramatic change of course. The following passages are abstracted from the Alternative Declaration:

> We expected that the Social Summit would address the structural causes of poverty, unemployment and social disintegration, as well as environmental degradation, and would place people at the center of the development process.... While some progress was achieved in placing critical issues on the table during the Summit, we believe that the economic framework adopted in the [official declaration] is in basic contradiction with the objectives of equitable and sustainable social development. The over-reliance that the document places on unaccountable "open, free-market forces" as a basis for organizing national and international economies aggravates, rather than alleviates, the current global social crises....

> This system has resulted in an even greater concentration of power and control over food and other critical resources in the hands of relatively few transnational corporations and financial institutions. It creates incentives for capital to externalize social and environmental costs. It generates jobless growth, derogates the rights of workers, and . . . leads to an unequal distribution of resources between and within countries. . . .

> **We, representatives of civil society, call upon governments and political leaders to recognize that the existing system has opened the most dangerous chasm in human history between an affluent, over-consuming minority and an impoverished majority of humankind in the South and also, increasingly, in the North.**

> In rejecting the prevailing global economic model, we do not suggest the imposition of another universal model. Rather, it is a question of innovating and devising local answers to community needs, promoting the skills and energy of women in full equality with men, and benefitting from valuable traditions, as well as new technologies.[12]

As these excerpts from the Alternative Copenhagen Declaration make clear, the so-called "development consensus" arrived at in the official Declaration was a "consensus" that excluded input from disadvantaged people and their spokespersons.

The World Bank—which played a key role in the Social Summit—has perfected the art of doublespeak. With a tone of moral authority, it speaks convincingly of giving "top priority to elimination of poverty," while further entrenching policies that widen the gap between rich and poor. The 1995 UNICEF report is similar. While it describes in heart-rending detail the marginalization and poverty caused by the free market system, in apparent sincerity it quotes the World Bank's misleading refrain that "health conditions across the world have improved more in the past 40 years than in all of previous human history."[13]

At no point in its social analysis does UNICEF's 1995 Report point to the lethal contradictions in the World Bank's global plan for *Investing in Health* (see p. 103). Nor does it even mention that the Bank—whose health strategies it appears to endorse—is the driving force behind the structural adjustment programs, the deregulation of the free market, and the global "monopoly of the few," all of which UNICEF correctly identifies as obstacles to achieving health gains.

UNICEF's 1995 Report merits careful analysis. On the one hand, its celebration of "the people" rather than governments as the main actors in sustainable development sounds empowering and progressive. But, on the other hand, its downplaying of the importance of government in the development process carries an odor of the current World Bank dogma. It fits comfortably into the neo-liberal design to down-scale government and strengthen the private sector. The language is, of course, somewhat different from that of the Bank. Whereas UNICEF speaks of "the people" as the impetus for sustainable development, mainstream economists now glorify and distort the term "civil society"—by which they mean nongovernmental groups and organizations, including (predominantly, one soon discovers) private industry and transnational corporations. Once again, we discover the wolf in sheep's clothing: the rhetoric of "power to the people" cloaking the bid to give profit-hungry big business yet more of an upper hand.

By no means do we mean to imply that UNICEF is as disingenuous or firmly in the corner of the privileged as the World Bank. Far from it! UNICEF's commitment to defend the health and rights of disadvantaged people is, no doubt, sincere. However, UNICEF's bold talk of leadership by the people rather than government is

tolerated because, paradoxically, such an assertion reinforces the dominant laissez-faire view of the global lords. This is the view that government spending and control should be drastically reduced (including public services, proportionate taxation, and regulation of private enterprise) and that "civil society" (i.e. primarily big business) should take over the helm of national and global development. By similar reasoning, when the World Bank speaks of "encouraging self reliance at the family level," what it really means is *cutting back on government spending for the needy* and *cost sharing* (making the poor pay for health care, education, and other services that used to be significantly contributed to, through progressive taxation, by the rich).

Today's problems are complex. At present (1996) the conservative Republican-controlled Congress in Washington is determined to roll back the socially progressive legislation of the last half century. It is also strongly critical of the United Nations in general, claiming that it is bureaucratic and inefficient. (In short, it fears the UN as a threat to the unbridled globalization of the free market.) Proposals to cut back on US funding for several UN agencies are being seriously considered.

Paradoxically, an effort by the conservative US Congress to sabotage the UN by withdrawing its funding might prove to be a blessing in disguise. The budget short-fall, of course, would be worrisome to many United Nations personnel, whose high salaries depend on the US dollar. But in the long run, the distancing of the United States from the UN might be a god-send for the world's disadvantaged people. For if the US withdraws its predominant financial support of UN organizations, it will also—we must hope— lose some of its disproportionate control. For this reason and others, we must encourage UNICEF and WHO to courageously stand up to the crushing inequities of today's neo-colonial development model, which is jeopardizing the well-being both of the Earth and its people.

UNICEF is, of course, correct in asserting that momentum for progress toward a more democratic, equitable world must come from the bottom up. More than ever, it is vitally important that *all of us who are concerned about the health of the world's children actively support and maintain constant, friendly pressure upon UNICEF and WHO.* We must strongly support and defend these agencies when they take a stand on behalf of the disadvantaged, when they dare to call attention to and attack the structural injustice that underlies poverty, underdevelopment and poor health. And we must offer firm but constructive criticism when UNICEF and WHO retreat from their ideals under the browbeating of the powerful.

At the same time, we must be realistic. UNICEF, WHO, and other bodies of the United Nations have a valuable role to play as allies of grassroots movements in the struggle to achieve "health for all." However, because of their inherent structural limitations and ties to the global power structure, we clearly cannot count on these or other UN agencies to be decisive leaders in the struggle for equitable social change. As UNICEF itself points out, only grassroots organizations and popular movements can realistically be expected to play that leading role.

Ultimately, each of us who has a deep concern for the well being of others has a role to play. Stressing this point, UNICEF'S 1995 *State of the World's Children* report quotes Martin Luther King Jr.:

> *Human progress is neither automatic nor inevitable. Even a superficial look at history reveals that no social advance rolls in on the wheels of inevitability. Every step toward the goals of justice requires sacrifice, suffering, and the tireless exertions of dedicated individuals.*

Key Readings Relevant to The Politics of Health

Compiled by the International People's Health Council, and HealthWrights

Note: This is a short list, mainly of books and magazines, most of which are accessibly written and should be fairly easy to find. Many such articles pertinent to the themes in this book are listed in the endnotes located at the end of the book. We recognize that this list is very incomplete, but have tried to limit it to key writings, mainly for the concerned student or lay reader. Some of the writings are published recently, others are older, but still represent some of the best, most relevant writings in their field. The International People's Health Council is continuing to develop more complete lists, and would appreciate suggestions of new and important materials. So as you come across such works, please keep us informed.

PRIMARY HEALTH CARE and DETERMINANTS OF HEALTH:

Macdonald, John. *Primary Health Care: Medicine In Its Place.* University of Bristol, UK. 1993. Available through Kumarian Press, 630 Oakwood Ave., Suite 119, West Hartford, CT 06110–1529, USA. Traces the development of Primary Health Care since its inception at Alma Ata in 1978 to the present, providing strong arguments for the rationale of PHC. Emphasizes the need for equity and strong community participation.

Navarro, V. "A Critique of the Ideological and Political Position of the Brandt Report and the Alma Ata Declaration." *International Journal of Health Services.* Vol. 14, No. 2 (1984): pp 159–172.

Social Science and Medicine. "The Debate on Selective or Comprehensive Primary Health Care." Vol 26, No 9 (1988): pp 877–878. Introduction to and historical background of the debate. Editors question whether there is really a fundamental conceptual conflict between SPHC and CPHC. They assert that donors should support nations to develop national health systems based on primary health care. Several good papers by key critics.

Werner, David and Bower, Bill. *Helping Health Workers Learn.* A people-centered guide to teaching community health workers. Intended for those who feel that their first allegiance lies with working and poor people. Discusses (and simplifies) the awareness-raising methodologies developed by Paulo Freire.

Halstead, SB, Walsh, Julia A, and Warren, Kenneth S, eds. *Good Health at Low Cost.* New York: The Rockefeller Foundation. 1985. An important study investigating why certain countries—China, Kerala state in India, Sri Lanka and Costa Rica—have attained widespread good health despite low GNP per capita.

Daly, Herman. *For the Common Good: Redirecting the Economy toward Community, the Environment, and a Sustainable Future.* Boston: Beacon Press, 1989. Daly, a former World Bank economist who left in disgust, argues for an *eco-economic* model of development based on equilibrium, not growth, with *full cost pricing* that builds in human and environmental costs.

UNICEF *The State of the World's Children.* Oxford, England: Oxford University Press. Annually updated progress ln Child Survival. Has useful statistics and graphs on health, education and economic indicators in most of the world's countries with year by year comparisons. Clearly presented.

McKeown, Thomas. *The Role of Medicine: Dream, Mirage or Nemesis?* Oxford, UK. Basil Blackwell Publisher. 1979. A superb review of how medical interventions had relatively little to do with public health improvements in Europe and the US between 1800 and 1950. Challenges myths about the contribution of biomedicine.

Sanders, David. *The Struggle for Health.* Hampshire, UK: Macmillan Education. 1985. A perceptive overview of the causes of widespread poor health and early death in situations of underdevelopment. It demonstrates clearly that far-reaching improvements in health depend more on social factors than on biomedical advances.

Ehrenreich, J. ed. *The Cultural Crisis in Modern Medicine.* Monthly Review Press. 1978. This book is a collection of writings by 14 authors divided into 3 parts: The Social Functions of Medicine, The Historical and contemporary Roots and Devastating Impact of Medical Sexism, and the Use of the Art of Healing in Promoting and Maintaining Imperialism.

Kent, George. *The Politics of Children's Survival.* New York. Praeger. 1991. This book provides a clear, trenchant analysis of how "structural violence" impacts the lives and mortality of children in the Third World. Kent makes a strong case for equity-oriented development and strategies that empower the poor.

Werner, David. *The Life and Death of Primary Health Care, or, The McDonaldization of Alma Ata.* 1993. Available from HealthWrights, 964 Hamilton Ave, Palo Alto, CA 94301, USA. Talk given to Medical Aid for the Third World. Reprinted in *Third World Resurgence* (see below). Gives a cogent history of the 3 major attacks on PHC since Alma Ata: Selective Primary Health Care, User Financing and Cost-Recovery Schemes, and the World Bank's *Investing In Health* report.

DEVELOPMENT and SOCIAL CHANGE: ISSUES THAT AFFECT HEALTH

Isbister, John. *Promises Not Kept: The Betrayal of Social Change in the Third World.* West Hartford, Connecticut: Kumarian Press 1991. Reveals how world leaders rose to power on promises for social progress and how they blatantly broke those promises. Packed with hard-hitting facts, the book gives a chronology on how poverty evolved.

UNDP *Human Development Index.* Provides important, useful data on distribution of wealth and resources within and between countries, along with social indicators (rather than merely economic ones) of a population's progress and well-being. Presents a more honest (people friendly) description and analysis of global trends than does the World Bank's *World Development Report.*

Watkins, Kevin. *The Oxfam Poverty Report.* Oxfam Publishing, BEBC Distribution, PO Box 1496, Parkstone, Poole, Dorst BH123YD, UK. 1995. A comprehensive analysis of the state of poverty in the world today, this well documented book identifies the structural forces that deny people their basic economic and social rights. It outlines some of the wider policy and institutional reforms needed to create an enabling environment in which people can take self-determined action to reduce poverty.

Magazines (monthly):

Third World Resurgence. Published by Third World Network, 228 Macalister Road, 10400 Penang, Malaysia. Perhaps the best periodical critique and analysis from the Third World on development, environmental, and health issues. Aims at "fair distribution of world resources and forms of development which are ecologically sustainable and fulfill human needs." If you subscribe to just one Third World periodical, consider this one.

The New Internationalist. Subscriptions: PO Box 79, Hertford, SG14 1AQ, UK. "Exists to report on issues of world poverty and inequality; to focus attention on the unjust relationship between the powerful and the powerless in both rich and poor nations ..." Each issue focuses on a different theme relevant to development and basic needs. Quality varies, but many issues carry important debate on "the radical changes needed within and between nations if the basic ... needs of all are to be met."

GLOBAL POWER STRUCTURES, FINANCIAL INSTITUTIONS and TRANSNATIONAL CORPORATIONS THAT IMPACT HEALTH

World Bank. *World Development Report, 1993. Investing in Health.* Oxford, UK. Oxford U. Press. 1993. This is the position paper for the World Bank's take-over of Third World health policy planning. It calls for more equitable and efficient health systems. But stripped of its Good Samaritan face lift, it is a rehash of the conservative strategies that have derailed Comprehensive Primary Health Care, but with the added shackles of structural adjustment, including privatization of public services and user-financed cost-recovery. A masterpiece of disinformation, this market-friendly version Selective Primary Health Care has ominous implications. By tying its new policy to loans, the Bank can impose it on countries that can least afford it. In sum, the Report promotes the same top-down development paradigm that has perpetuated poverty, foreign debt, and the devastating impact of structural adjustment policies.

Critical Reactions to the World Bank's *World Development Report 1993: Investing in Health:*

• Various papers assembled in 1993 by Health Action International—Europe. Address: Jacob van Lennepkade 334T, 1053 NJ Amsterdam, The Netherlands. This is a packet of extremely important analysis and criticism, including responses from Save the Children Fund (UK), Tony Klouda on behalf of the PHC-NGO group (IPPF, UK) and an article by Dorothy Logie and Jessica Woodroffe from the British Medical Journal, July 3, 1993.

• Legge, David. "Investing in the Shaping of World Health Policy," Prepared for the AIDAB, NCEPH and PHA workshop (Canberra, Australia, Aug. 31, 1993). Long, in depth review of *Investing in Health.* (Available from HealthWrights)

• Epprecht, Marc. "The World Bank, Health, and Africa," *Z Magazine,* Nov. 1993, p. 31–38. Lengthy in-depth review of harm caused by World Bank health plan in Africa.

Danaher, Kevin, editor. *Fifty Years is Enough: the case against the World Bank and International Monetary Fund.* South End Press, Boston MA, USA, 1994. A revealing collection of essays, country studies, and statements by marginalized groups of the reversals in social progress and deepening of poverty caused by structural adjustment and other lop-sided development policies pushed by these powerful financial institutions.

Meeker–Lowry, Susan, *Investing in the Common Good.*1995. New Society Publishers, PO Box 734, Montpelier, VT 05601, USA. Alternative development strategy which calls strongly for equity and participatory democratic process. Critical of the top-down, status-quo preserving strategy of the World Bank's *Investing in Health* report.

Tan, Michael. *Dying for Drugs: Pill Power and Politics in the Philippines.* Published by Health Action Information Network (HAIN), 1156 PO Box 1665, Central Post Office, Quezon City, Philippines. 1988. One of the best books from the Third World exposing the exploits and abuses and double standards of the multinational drug companies. HAIN also puts out an excellent bulletin, *Health Alert*, which looks at many health related issues, Philippine and international, from a pro-people perspective.

Chetley, Andrew and Allain, Annelies. *Protecting Infant Health: A health worker's guide to the International code of Marketing of Breastmilk Substitutes.* Published by International Baby Food Action Network (IBFAN) PO Box 19, 10700 Penang, Malaysia. 1993 (revised). An excellent well-illustrated booklet for awareness raising in community groups.

Korten, David. *When Corporations Rule the World.* Kumarian Press, 630 Oakwood Ave. Suite 119, West Hartford, CT 06110–1592, USA. 1995. "A searing indictment of an unjust international world order" together with a very rational alternative strategy for "People Centered Development" (the title of his first major book). Korten is the founder of the People-Centered Development Forum, based in New York City.

Magazine (monthly):

Multinational Monitor. Subscriptions: PO Box 19405, Washington DC 20036, USA. Excellent, balanced, well documented articles that expose the unscrupulous actions of transnational corporations, their influence on national and global politics, and their violations of international codes. Some articles are directly related to health concerns; almost all are at least indirectly related.

1   Abram S. Benenson, ed., *Control of Communicable Diseases in Man* (Washington, D.C.: American Public Health Association, 1990), p. 90.

2   Except where otherwise noted, the information in the following two paragraphs is drawn from: Tony Dajer, "Cholera: The Deadliest Wake-Up Call," *Links Health and Development Report,* Vol. 9, No. 2 (Spring 1992), p. 7.

3   "Cholera in 1991," *Weekly Epidemiological Record* (a publication of the World Health Organization), Vol. 67, No. 34 (August 21, 1992), p. 253.

4   "Update: Cholera—Western Hemisphere, 1992," *Morbidity and Mortality Weekly Report,* Vol. 42, No. 5, February 12, 1993, p. 1.

5   Andrew Downie, "Killer Cholera Returns to Mexico with a Vengeance," *Houston Chronicle,* May 26, 1995, p. 26A.; Cited in *Mexico NewsPak,* Vol. 3, No. 9, May 22–June 4, 1995, p. 8.

6   "Cholera in 1991," *Weekly Epidemiological Record* (a publication of the World Health Organization), Vol. 67, No. 34 (August 21, 1992), p. 257.

7   Ibid., p. 256.

8   Tony Dajer, "Cholera: The Deadliest Wake-Up Call," *Links Health and Development Report,* Vol. 9, No. 2 (Spring 1992), p. 25; Anne Platt, "Environmental Intelligence," *World Watch,* November/December 1995, p. 6.

9   UNICEF, *State of the World's Children, 1994.*

10 Ibid.

11 David Sanders and Adbulrahman Sambo, "AIDS in Africa: The Implications of Economic Recession and Structural Adjustment," *Health Policy and Planning,* Vol. 6 (1991), No. 2.

12 UNICEF, *State of the World's Children, 1994.*

13 UNICEF, *State of the World's Children, 1996,* p. 10.

14 UNICEF, *State of the World's Children,* 1987, p. 5; 1991, p. 5; 1996, p. 10.

15 Victor W. Sidel, *Perspectives: The Impact of Arms Spending on Health and Health Care in Industrialized and Developing Countries* (paper), p. 5.

16 UNICEF, *State of the World's Children, 1994,* p. 20.

17 "World Still Plagued by Poverty and Hunger," *Health Alert,* No. 135 (November 1992), p. 356.

18 *UNICEF, State of the World's Children, 1994,* p. 16.

19 Katrina Galway, Brent Wolff, and Richard Sturgis, *Child Survival: Risks and the Road to Health* (Columbia, Md.: Institute for Resource Development/Westinghouse/USAID, 1987), p. 34. Cited in George Kent, *The Politics of Children's Survival* (New York: Praeger, 1991), p. 60.

20 UNICEF, *State of the World's Children, 1994* p. 3.

21 "Zaire battles epidemic of polio, its worst ever" *New York Times International,* June 21 1995.

22 UNICEF, *State of the World's Children, 1995,* p. 20 (graph).

23 UNICEF, *State of the World's Children, 1995,* p. 27.

24 UNICEF, *State of the World's Children, 1994,* p. 6.

25 UNICEF, *State of the World's Children, 1994,* p. 9.

26 UNICEF, *State of the World's Children, 1993,* p. 22

27 "Cholera in 1991," *Weekly Epidemiological Record* (a publication of the World Health Organization), Vol. 67, No. 34 (August 21, 1992), p. 253.

28 Tony Dajer, "Cholera: The Deadliest Wake-Up Call," *Links Health and Development Report,* Vol. 9, No. 2 (Spring 1992), p. 25, p. 7.

29 Vincente M. Witt and Fred M. Reiff, "Environmental Health Conditions and Cholera Vulnerability in Latin America and the Caribbean," *Journal of Public Health Policy,* 12(4) (Winter 1991), p. 453.

30 Tony Dajer, "Cholera: The Deadliest Wake-Up Call," *Links Health and Development Report,* Vol. 9, No. 2 (Spring 1992), p. 25, p. 7.

31 World Bank, *Investing in Health,* 1993, p. 93.

32 "Poverty Linked to Cholera Epidemic, Says WHO," *Third World Resurgence,* No. 10 (June 1991), p. 7.

33 Michael Toole, et al, Goma Epidemiology Group, "Public Health Impact of Rwandan Refugee Crisis: What Happened in Goma, Zaire, in July, 1994?," *The Lancet,* p. 339, Feb 11, 1995.

34 Perlez, Jane. "A New and More Vicious Killer: Dysentery." *New York Times.* August 5, 1994, p. A6.

35 Bonner, Raymond "Cholera's Spread Raised Fear of Toll of 40,000 Rwandans." *New York Times.* July 24, 1994, pp. 1 and 10. *Division of Diarrhoeal and Acute Respiratory Disease Control—Interim Report 1994,* World Health Organization, 1995, pp. 27–28.

36 Boston Globe, July 24, 1994.

37 "Saving Lives Takes More Than Charity," *Child Health Foundation News,* Issue 1, 1995, p. 5.

38 "Cholera Aid in Rwanda" *Child Health Foundation News,* #3, 1994, p. 6.

39 Personal correspondence by William Greenough with David Werner, January 31, 1995.

40 UNICEF, *State of the World's Children, 1995,* p. 25.

41 Hal Kane, "Life Expectancy Lengthens," The Worldwatch Institute, *Vital Signs 1994,* p. 135.

42 Rakiya Omaar and Alex de Waal, "U.S. Complicity by Silence, Genocide in Rwanda," *CovertAction Quarterly,* Spring 1995, pp. 7–9.

43 Hal Kane, *The Hour of Departure: Forces that Create Refugees and Migrants,* Worldwatch Institute, June 1995, pp. 14–15.

44 Hal Kane, *The Hour of Departure: Forces that Create Refugees and Migrants,* Worldwatch Paper #125, Worldwatch Institute, June 1995, p. 19.

45 Rakiya Omaar and Alex de Waal, "U.S. Complicity by Silence, Genocide in Rwanda," *CovertAction Quarterly,* Spring 1995, pp. 7–9.

ENDNOTES: PART 1

1   Sheila Zurbrigg, *Rakku's Story: Structures of Ill-Health and the Source of Change,* Madras, India: George Joseph/Sidma Offset Press, 1984.

2   Carl E. Taylor and William B. Greenough, III, "Control of Diarrheal Diseases," *Annual Review of Public Health,* Vol. 10, 1989, p. 221.

3   David Sanders, *The Struggle for Health: Medicine and the Politics of Underdevelopment,* London: Macmillan, 1985, pp. 85–87.

4   Ibid., p. 87.

5   From personal correspondence with Michael Tan of Health Action Information Network, The Philippines, August, 1995.

6   Gish, "The Political Economy of Primary Care and Health by the People: an Historical Exploration," *Social Science and Medicine,* Vol. 136, pp. 203–211, 1979.

7   David Morley, *See How They Grow: Monitoring Child Growth for Appropriate Health Care in Developing Countries,* (1979 Macmillan Press), p. 20.

8   David Werner and Bill Bower, *Helping Health Workers Learn,* Hesperian Foundation, 1982, p. **26**–12 — **26**–19

9   *The Declaration of Alma Ata,* September 12, 1978. International Conference on Primary Health Care jointly sponsored by WHO and UNICEF, paragraph 10.

10   *The Declaration of Alma Ata,* September 12, 1978. International Conference on Primary Health Care jointly sponsored by WHO and UNICEF, Paragraph 1.

11   Scott B. Halstead, Julia A. Walsh and Kenneth S. Warren, eds. *Good Health at Low Cost,* Rockefeller Foundation, New York, 1985, pp. 42–43.

12   Ibid., pp. 44–45.

13   Ibid., p. 50.

14   From the proceedings of the *International Conference on Primary Health Care,* Alma Ata, Kazakhstan, 1978.

15   David Werner, "The Village Health Worker—Lackey or Liberator," pp. 5–10, and "Health Care and Human Dignity: A Subjective Look at Community-based Rural Health Programs in Latin America," pp. 8–15. (HealthWrights papers).

16   See for example Robert Chambers, *Rural Development: Putting the Last First* (New York: John Wiley and Sons, 1983).

17   From personal observation by David Werner in Project Piaxtla, Mexico, and also reported to him by leaders of other community-based programs in other parts of Mexico and Latin America.

18   See for example Ben Wisner, *Power and Need in Africa* (Trenton, New Jersey: Africa World Press, 1989), pp. 53–86. Also, David Werner, "The Life and Death of Primary Health Care or The McDonaldization of Alma Ata," (HealthWrights paper).

19   Anthony Zwi, Joanna Macrae, and Antonio Ugalde, "Children and War," *The Kangaroo: Bibliographic Archives for Maternal and Child Health in Developing Countries,* Vol. 1, No. 1 (December 1992), pp. 47–48.

20   Claudio Schuftan, "The Child Survival Revolution: A Critique," *Family Practice,* Vol. 7, No. 4, 1990, p. 329.

21   UNICEF, *State of the World's Children, 1989,* p. 2.

22   Ibid., p. 1.

23   Ibid., p. 18.

24   Ibid., p. 1.

25   Medea Benjamin and Kevin Danaher, "Latin America's Struggle for Democratic Development," *Global Exchanges* (newsletter of Global Exchange), Issue #11 (Summer 1992), p. 1.

26   UNICEF, *State of the World's Children, 1989,* p. 1.

27   UNICEF, *State of the World's Children, 1987,* p. 2.

28   Ibid.

29   James P. Grant, "A Child Survival and Development Revolution," *Assignment Children: A Journal Concerned with Children, Women and Youth in Development,* 61/62, 1983, p. 23.

30   Ibid., p. 30.

31   Ben Wisner, "GOBI Versus PHC? Some Dangers of Selective Primary Health Care," *Social Science and Medicine,* Vol. 26, No 9, p. 963, 1988.

32   W. Farrant, "Health Promotion and Community Health Movement: Experiences from the UK" (paper presented at the International Symposium on Community Participation and Empowerment Strategies in Health Promotion, Biefeld University, Germany, June 1989), p. 8. Cited in John J. Macdonald, *Primary Health Care: Medicine in its Place* (West Hartford, Connecticut: Kumarian Press, 1993), p. 84.

33   George Kent, *The Politics of Children's Survival* (New York: Praeger, 1991), p. 162.

34   Claudio Schuftan, "The Child Survival Revolution: A Critique," *Family Practice,* Vol. 7, No. 4, 1990, p. 329.

35   Zafrullah Chowdhury, "Basic Service Delivery in Underdeveloping Countries; A View from Gonoshasthaya Kendra," a working paper prepared for UNICEF for the Special Meeting on the Situation of Children in Asia with Emphasis on Basic Services, E/ICEF/ASIA/9, May 4, 1977, pp. 18–19.

36   Giorgio Solimano and Clara Haignere, *Free-Market Politics and Nutrition in Chile: A Grim Future after a Short-Lived Success* (Center for Population and Family Health, Faculty of Medicine, Columbia University, Working Paper #7, May 1984); C.A. Monteiro, H.P. Pino Zuniga, M.H.A. Benicio, and C.G. Victora, "Better Prospects for Child Survival," *World Health Forum,* Vol. 10 (1989), pp. 222–227; Rob Davies and David Sanders, "Economic Strategies, Structural Adjustment and Health Policy: Issues in Sub-Saharan Africa for the 1990s," Transformation 21, 1993, pp. 78-93; Giovanni Andrea Cornia, Richard Jolly, and Frances Stewart, eds., *Adjustment with a Human Face: Protecting the Vulnerable and Promoting Growth* (Oxford: Clarendon Press, 1987), pp. 109, 111, 118; R.F. Florentino and R.A. Pedro, "Nutrition and Socio-Economic Development in Southeast Asia," *Proceedings of the Nutrition Society,* May 1992, pp. 95–101.

37   Rob Davies and David Sanders, "Economic Strategies, Structural Adjustment and Health Policy: Issues in Sub-Saharan Africa for the 1990s," Transformation 21, 1993, pp. 78-93; Giovanni Andrea Cornia, Richard Jolly, and Frances Stewart, eds., *Adjustment with a Human Face: Protecting the Vulnerable and Promoting Growth* (Oxford: Clarendon Press, 1987), p. 112.

38   George Kent, *The Politics of Children's Survival* (New York: Praeger, 1991), p. 158.

39   *Facts for Life,* UNICEF/WHO/UNESCO, 1989, front cover.

40   George Kent, *The Politics of Children's Survival* (New York: Praeger, 1991), p. 27.

41   Ibid., pp. 28–29.

42   Ibid., p. 164.

43   James Grant, "Marketing Child Survival," *Assignment Children,* Vol. 65/68, 1984, p. 3.

44   UNICEF, *State of the World's Children, 1995,* p. 25.

1 Ruxin, Joshua N, "Magic bullet: The history of oral rehydration," *Medical History 1994; 38: 363–397.*

2 Interview with Dr. Fernando Silva, former director of La Mascota Children's Hospital in Managua, Nicaragua, *Barricada Internacional,* September 8, 1988, p. 4.

3 UNICEF, *State of the World's Children, 1993,* p. 7, p. 22.

4 UNICEF, *State of the World's Children, 1994,* p. 1.

5 I.W. Booth and J. T. Harries, "Oral Rehydration Therapy: An Issue of Growing Controversy," *Journal of Tropical Pediatrics,* Vol. 28 (June 1982), p. 116.

6 M.A. Rub, "Oral Rehydration Therapy (ORT)," *In Touch,* September/October 1983, p. 3.

7 M. Santosham and W. Greenough, "Oral Rehydration Therapy: A Global Perspective," *Journal of Pediatrics,* April 1991, 118(4) Pt. 2:S44–S51, discussion S52.

8 Hirschhorn, Norbert. "The treatment of acute diarrhea in children. An historical and physiological perspective." *American Journal of Clinical Nutrition,* 1980;33:637–663.

9 Jay Siwek, "Diarrhea in Children," *International Child Health Foundation Newsletter,* Issue 13 (Spring 1993), p. 4; Stina Almroth, Michael Latham, "Rational home management of diarrhoeas," *The Lancet,* Vol. 345, March 18, 1995, p. 709–711.

10 From personal correspondence with Norbert Hirschhorn, recalling his experience at the Boston city hospital in the 1960s.

11 "Cholera Review Meeting: 26–27 April 1993, Zimbabwe" Proceedings. Ministry of Health and Child Welfare, and WHO.

12 Quoted in USAID, *Oral Rehydration Therapy: A Revolution in Child Survival.* Oelgeschlager, Gunn & Hain, Weston MA, 1988. p. 19.

13 Carl E. Taylor and William B. Greenough, III, "Control of Diarrheal Diseases," *Annual Review of Public Health,* Vol. 10 (1989), p. 227.

14 Carl E. Taylor and Xu Zhao Yu, "Oral Rehydration in China," *American Journal of Public Health,* Vol. 76, No. 2 (February 1986), pp. 187–188.

15 See for example Carl E. Taylor and Xu Zhao Yu, "Oral Rehydration in China," *American Journal of Public Health,* Vol. 76, No. 2 (1986), pp. 187–188.

16 R.A. Cash, D. R. Nalin, R. Rochat, L.B. Rellar, Z.A. Haque, A.S. Rahman, "A Clinical Trial of Oral Therapy in a rural cholera-treatment Center," *American Journal Trop Med Hygiene* 19:653, 1970.

17 Ruxin, Joshua N, "Magic bullet: The history of oral rehydration," *Medical History 1994; 38: 363–397.*

18 D. Mahalanabis, A.B. Chowdhury, N.G. Bagchi, et al., "Oral Fluid Therapy of Cholera among Bangladesh Refugees," *Johns Hopkins Medical Journal,* Vol. 132 (1973), pp. 197–205; Norbert Hirschhorn and William B. Greenough III, "Progress In Oral Rehydration Therapy, *Scientific American,* Vol. 264, No. 5 (May 1991), p. 53; Roger I. Glass, Mariam Claeson, Paul A. Blake, Ronald J. Waldman, and Nathaniel F. Pierce, "Cholera in Africa: Lessons on Transmission and Control for Latin America," *The Lancet,* Vol. 338, No. 8770 (September 28, 1991), pp. 793–794.

19 "Water with Sugar and Salt" (editorial), *Lancet,* 1978, 2, pp. 300–301.

20 Glen Williams, *A Simple Solution: How Oral Rehydration is Averting Child Death from Diarrhoeal Dehydration* (a UNICEF special report).

21 Grisanti KA, Jaffe DM. "Dehydration syndromes. Oral rehydration and fluid replacement." *Pediatric Emergencies. Emergency Medical Clinics of North America* 1991; 9: 565–588.

22 Snyder, John, "Global training needs: U.S. perspective." *Journal of Diarrhoeal Disease Research* 1987; 4:297–282.

23 George Kent, *The Politics of Children's Survival* (New York: Praeger, 1991), p. 43.

24 Kent, p. 43.

25 UNICEF, *State of the World's Children, 1986,* p. 20.

26 USAID. *Oral Rehydration Therapy, A Revolution in Child Survival,* Oelgeschlager, Gunn & Hain. Weston MA, USA. 1988. p. 1.

27 UNICEF, *State of the World's Children,* reports, 1993, p. 22; 1995, p. 27.

28 UNICEF, *State of the World's Children, 1993,* p. 22.

29 Anne Gadomski, Robert Black and W. Henry Mosley, "Constraints to the Potential Impact of Child Survival in Developing Countries," *Health Policy and Planning,* 5(3) (1990), pp. 235–236.

30 Tulloch J, Burton F. "Global access to oral rehydration salts and use of oral rehydration therapy. *World Health Stats. Quarterly. 1987; 40: 110–115.*

31 Jay Siwek, "Diarrhea in Children," *International Child Health Foundation Newsletter,* Issue 13 (Spring 1993), p. 4; Stina Almroth, Michael Latham, "Rational home management of diarrhoeas," *The Lancet,* Vol. 345, March 18, 1995, p. 709–711.

32 *WHO Programme for Control of Diarrhoeal Diseases. Ninth Programme Report.* 1992–1993. ; WHO *Division of Control of Diarrhoeal and Acute Respiratory Disease Control, Interim Report 1994.* 1995, p. 40.

33 WHO *Division of Control of Diarrhoeal and Acute Respiratory Disease Control, Interim Report 1994.* 1995, p. 40.

34 UNICEF, *State of the World's Children, 1995,* p. 25.

35 "Global ORT Use Rates 1994," graph sent to the authors by UNICEF in May, 1995.

36 *WHO Programme for Control of Diarrhoeal Diseases. Ninth Programme Report.* 1992–1993, p. 79.

37 Ibid.

38 WHO, *Weekly Epidemiological Record.* 6 September 1991.

39 WHO Programme for Control of Diarrhoeal Diseases, *Interim Programme Report 1990,* pp. 14, 17.

40 UNICEF, *State of the World's Children, 1994,* p. 6.

41 Ruxin, Joshua N, "Magic Bullet: The History of Oral Rehydration," *Medical History* 1994; 38: 363–397. Page 363.

42 From personal communication with Norbert Hirschhorn. Also see: Riyad S, El Mougi M, Wahsh AA, and Hirschhorn N "After Rehydration: What Happens to the Child?" *Journal of Tropical Pediatrics 1991; 37:1–3.*

43 Programme for the Control of Diarrhoeal Disease: Ninth Programme Report 1992–1993 World Health Organization, 1994 p. 23.

44 WHO Programme for Control of Diarrhoeal Diseases: Seventh Programme Report, 1988–1989.

45 Barros FC, Victoria CG, Forsberg B, et al. "Management of childhood diarrhoea at the household level: a population based survey in north-east Brazil. *Bull World Health Organ* 1991; 57: 21–24.

46   Oyoo AO, Burstrom B, Forsberb B, Makhulo J. "Rapie feedback household surveys in PHC planning: an example from Kenya. *Health Policy Planing* 1991; 6: 380–83.

47   Programme for the Control of Diarrhoeal Disease: Ninth Programme Report 1992–1993 World Health Organization, 1994 p. 36.

48   **In Bangladesh:** Hoyle B, Yunus M, Chen LC "Breastfeeding and food intake among children with acute diarrheal disease. *Am J Clin Nit* 1980; 33:2365–71; **in Saudi Arabia:** Rasheed P. Perception of diarrhoeal diseases among mothers and mothers-to-be: implications for health education in Saudi Arabia. *Soc Sci Med* 1993; 36: 373–77; **in India:** Bentley ME. The household management of childhood diarrhea in rural North India." *Soc Sci Med* 1988; 27: 75–85. Also Viswanathan and Rohde, *Diarrhoea in Rural India,* p. 11; **in Peru:** Huffman SI, Lopez de Romana G, Madrid S, Brown KH, Bentley M, Black RE. "Do child feeding practices change due to diarrhoea in the Central Peruvian Highlands?" J Diarrhoeal Dis Res 1991; 9: 295–3300. Also: Bentley ME, Pelto GH, Straus WI, et al. "Rapid ethnographic assessment: application in a diarrhea management program." *Soc Sci Med* 1988; 27: 107–16; **in Mexico:** Martinez H, Saucedo G. "Mothers' perception about childhood diarrhea in rural Mexico." *J Diarrhoeal Dis Res* 1991; 9: 235–43; **in Kenya:** Oyoo AO, Burstrom B, Forsberg B, Makhulo J. "Rapid feedback from household surveys in PHC planning: an example from Kenya. *Health Policy Plan* 1991; 6: 380–83; **in Swaziland:** Green EC, "Traditional healers, mothers, and childhood diarrheal disease in Swaziland: the interface of anthropology and health education. *Soc Sci Med* 1985; 20: 277–85; **in Lesotho:** Stina Almroth, Michael Latham, "Rational home management of diarrhoeas," *The Lancet,* Vol. 345, March 18, 1995, pp. 709–711.

49   Mathuram Santosham, "Nutritional Aspects of ORT" in *Symposium Proceedings, Cereal-Based Oral Rehydration Therapy: Theory and Practice (proceedings of a symposium sponsored by the* International Child Health Foundation and the National Council for International Health), Washington, D.C., February 17, 1987, p. 24.

50   Ibid., pp. 24–25.

51   USAID. *Oral Rehydration Therapy, A Revolution in Child Survival,* Oelgeschlager, Gunn & Hain. Weston MA, USA. 1988. P. 10.

52   Moy, Robert, letter to the authors, January, 1995.

53   Carl E. Taylor and William B. Greenough, III, "Control of Diarrheal Diseases," *Annual Review of Public Health,* Vol. 10 (1989), p. 223.

54   Anne Gadomski, Robert Black and W. Henry Mosley, "Constraints to the Potential Impact of Child Survival in Developing Countries," *Health Policy and Planning,* 5(3) (1990), p. 236, p. 241; Robert Halpern, "A Child Survival and Development Revolution?," *International Journal of Early Childhood,* Vol. 18, No. 1 (1986), p. 45; Carl E. Taylor and William B. Greenough, III, "Control of Diarrheal Diseases," *Annual Review of Public Health,* Vol. 10 (1989), p. 223.

55   Henry Fitzroy, André Briend, and Vincent Fauveau, "Child Survival: Should the Strategy Be Redesigned? Experience from Bangladesh," *Health Policy and Planning,* 5(3) (1990), p. 229; Anne Gadomski, Robert Black and W. Henry Mosley, "Constraints to the Potential Impact of Child Survival in Developing Countries," *Health Policy and Planning,* 5(3) (1990).

56   Vincent Fauveau, M. Yunus, M. Shafiqul Islam, André Briend, and Michael L. Bennish, "Does ORT Reduce Diarrhoeal Mortality?," *Health Policy and Planning,* Vol. 7 (1992), No. 3, pp. 243–250.

57   Ibid.

58   Woodall, Nicholas, *Appropriate Technology in the Developing World: Oral Rehydration Therapy in Bangladesh.* Dissertation for the Wellcome Unit for the History of Medicine, Oxford, UK (1992).

59   Hirschhorn N, Stienglass R. "Are we ignoring different levels of mortality in the primary health care debate?" *Health Policy and Planning* 1989, vol 4.

60   *Programme for the Control of Diarrhoeal Diseases: Ninth Programme Report 1992–1993* World Health Organization, 1994 p. 19.

61   Ibid.

62   Cash R, Keusch G.T., and Lamstein, J. *Child Health and Survival: The UNICEF GOBI–FFF Program,* Croom Helms 1987 p.35.

63   Ibid.

64   Glen Williams, *A Simple Solution* (a UNICEF special report), p. 9.

65   *Programme for the Control of Diarrhoeal Disease: Ninth Programme Report 1992–1993,* World Health Organization, 1994 p. 16.

66   David Werner, *Where There Is No Doctor, A Village Health Care Handbook,* p. 152.

67   "Diarrhoea and Potassium," *Dialogue on Diarrhoea,* No. 41 (June 1990), p. 7.

68   Gore, Fontaine, Pierce, BMJ 1992, 304: 287–91. Also: *25 Years of ORS: Joint WHO/ICDDR,B Consultative Meeting on ORS Formulation.* WHO, 1995. p. 3.

69   From a letter commenting upon an early draft of this book, by a friend writing "not in an official capacity."

70   *Dialogue on Diarrhoea,* No. 41 (June 1990), p. 2.

71   WHO, *The Management and Prevention of Diarrhoea, Practical Guidelines,* Third Edition, 1993, p. 38.

72   From personal correspondence with Norbert Hirschhorn, March, 1995.

73   WHO, "The Selection of Fluids and Food for Home Therapy to Prevent Dehydration from Diarrhoea: Guidelines for Developing a National Policy," 1993, p. 2.

74   C. MacCormack and A. Draper, *Cultural Meanings of Oral Rehydration Salts in Jamaica, 1988,* p. 258, from *The Context of Medicines in Developing Countries: Studies in Pharmaceutical Anthropology, 1988,* Edited by Sjaak Van Der Geest and Susan Reynolds Whyte.

75   Stina Almroth, Michael Latham, "Rational home management of diarrhoeas," *The Lancet,* Vol. 345, March 18, 1995, p. 709 – 711.

76   Personal conversation by David Werner with participants at ICORT–2.

77   Hema Viswanathan and Jon Eliot Rohde, *Diarrhoea in Rural India: A Nationwide Study of Mothers and Practitioners,* New Delhi: UNICEF/Vision Books, 1990.

78   Ibid., p. 14.

79   Ibid.

80   UNICEF, *State of the World's Children, 1994,* pp. 6 and 15.

81   "AID's Unpublicized Failure," *Links Health and Development Report,* Vol. 7, No. 3/4 (fall/winter 1990), p. 7.

82   UNICEF and Honduran Ministry of Public Health, *Evaluation of the Distribution System of Oral Rehydration Salts in Honduras,* pp. ii–iii.

83 K. Siener, *Wheat based ORS for Afghans* (1989), International Rescue Committee, Peshawar, Pakistan. Cited in *Dialogue on Diarrhoea,* No. 41 (June 1990), p. 5.

84 Study by Rahaman and colleagues published in 1982 in the *American Journal of Public Health,* cited in *Links Health and Development Report,* Vol. 7, No. 3/4 (fall/winter 1990), p. 11.

85 Brady, Niel. Forward to *Oral Rehydration Therapy: A Revolution in Child Survival,* USAID. Oelgeschlager, Gunn & Hain; Weston MA, USA, 1988. P. x.

86 C. MacCormack and A. Draper, *Cultural Meanings of Oral Rehydration Salts in Jamaica, 1988,* p. 286, from *The Context of Medicines in Developing Countries: Studies in Pharmaceutical Anthropology, 1988,* Edited by Sjaak Van Der Geest and Susan Reynolds Whyte.

87 Programme for the Control of Diarrhoeal Disease: Ninth Programme Report 1992–1993 World Health Organization, 1994 p. 15.

88 Carl E. Taylor and William B. Greenough, III, "Control of Diarrheal Diseases," *Annual Review of Public Health,* Vol. 10 (1989), p. 228.

89 Izzedin I. Imam, "Peasant Perceptions: Famine," *People-Centered Development,* David C. Korten, Rudi Klauss, ed. (Kumarian Press 1984), p. 122.

90 E. Green, "Diarrhea and the Social Marketing of Oral Rehydration Salts in Bangladesh," *Social Science and Medicine,* Vol. 23, No. 4 (1986), pp. 357–366. Cited in PRITECH's *Technical Literature Update,* Vol. II, No. 9 (December 1987), p. 3.

91 Information in letters received from Third World respondents in response to inquiries. Also, David Sanders and David Werner conducted an informal survey of costs of packets relative to poor peoples' earnings among participants from a number of Third World countries at the International Symposium on Food-Based Oral Rehydration Therapy (a conference sponsored by the International Child Health Foundation and Aga Khan University that was held in Karachi, Pakistan in November 1989).

92 Alan Myers, Benjamin Siegel, and Robert Vinci, "Economic Barriers to the Use of Oral Rehydration Therapy: A Case Report," the *Journal of the American Medical Association,* Vol. 265 (April 3, 1991), pp. 1724–1725.

93 M.A. Rub, "Oral Rehydration Therapy (ORT)," *In Touch,* September/October 1983, p. 3.

94 Norbert Hirschhorn, "Appropriate Health Technology in Egypt," *Middle East Report,* No. 161 (November–December 1989), p. 26; Fitzroy Henry, André Briend, and Vincent Fauveau, "Child Survival: Should the Strategy Be Redesigned? Experience from Bangladesh," *Health Policy and Planning,* 5(3) (1990), p. 228; Williams, Baumslag, and Jelliffe, *Mother and Child Health: Delivering the Services* (Oxford: Oxford University Press, 1985), p. 84.

95 Norbert Hirschhorn, "Appropriate Health Technology in Egypt," *Middle East Report,* No. 161 (November–December 1989), p. 26.

96 Pan American Health Organization, Pan American Sanitary Bureau, Regional Office of the World Health Organization, 1990, *Health Conditions in the Americas,* 1990 Edition, Volume II, (Washington, D.C.) p. 49.

97 Black, Robert E., Brown, H.H., Becker, S., "Effects of Diarrhea Associated with Specific Enteropathogens on the Growth of Children in Rural Bangladesh," *Pediatrics,* 73:799 (1984). Cited in Mathuram Santosham, "Nutritional Aspects of ORT," in *Symposium Proceedings, Cereal-Based Oral Rehydration Therapy: Theory and Practice* (proceedings of a symposium sponsored by

the International Child Health Foundation and the National Council for International Health, Washington, D.C., February 17, 1987), p. 24.

98 M.R. Islam et al., "Lobon-gur (Common Salt and Brown Sugar) Oral Rehydration Solution in the Treatment of Diarrhoea in Adults," *Journal of Tropical Medicine and Hygiene,* No. 83 (1980), p. 44.

99 M. El-Rafie, W.A. Hassouna, N. Hirschhorn, S. Loza, P. Miller, A. Nagaty, S. Nasser, and S. Riyad, "Effect of Diarrhoeal Disease Control on Infant and Childhood Mortality in Egypt," *Lancet,* Vol. 335, No. 8685 (February 10, 1990), pp. 334–338.

100 Ibid., p. 336.

101 Peter Miller and Norbert Hirschhorn, "The Effect of a National Control of Diarrheal Diseases Program on Mortality: the case of Egypt." Social Science and Medicine, 1995. pp. S1–S30.

102 Ray Langsten, Kenneth Hill, "Diarrhoeal disease, oral rehydration, and Childhood Mortality in Egypt." *Journal of Tropical Pediatrics* Vol. 40. Oct. 1994, p. 272.

103 Norbert Hirschhorn, "Appropriate Health Technology in Egypt," *Middle East Report,* No. 161 (November–December 1989), p. 27.

104 David Werner, "Egypt: Another Approaching Storm on the Desert," *Newsletter from the Sierra Madre,* #24 June, 1991, p. 6. (HealthWrights papers).

105 UNICEF, State of the World's Children, 1994, p. 6

106 Cited in WHO, *Division of Diarrhoeal and Acute Respiratory Disease Control, Interim Report 1994,* 1995, p. 35.; In August, 1994 the National Control of Diarrhoeal Disease Programme (NCDDP) and the National Acute Respiratory Infections Programme (NARIP) of the Ministry of Health of Egypt carried out a combined CDD/ARI household case management survey in collaboration with WHO and UNICEF.

107 Peter Miller and Norbert Hirschhorn, "The Effect of a National Control of Diarrheal Diseases Program on Mortality: the case of Egypt." Social Science and Medicine, 1995. p. S1–S30.

108 Hada Rashad, *The impact on infant and child mortality, reappraisal of the evidence,* 1991, report delivered at a conference sponsored by the World Bank and USAID.

109 Hada Rashad, "The Mortality Impact of Oral Rehydration Therapy in Egypt: Re-appraisal of Evidence," in Kenneth Hill, ed., *Child Health Priorities for the 1990s* (report of a seminar sponsored by USAID and the World Bank and held at Johns Hopkins University School of Hygiene and Public Health, Baltimore, Maryland, June 20–22, 1991, published by the Johns Hopkins University School of Hygiene and Public Health Institute for International Programs, Baltimore, Maryland, 1992), pp. 154–155.

110 Peter Miller and Norbert Hirschhorn, "The Effect of a National Control of Diarrheal Diseases Program on Mortality: the case of Egypt." *Social Science and Medicine,* 40 (10), May, 1995, p. S21.

111 David Werner and Bill Bower, *Helping Health Workers Learn,* pp. 7–4 to 7–5, 18–1 to 18–8.

112 *Oral Rehydration Therapy: An Annotated Bibliography,* Pan American Health Organization, Washington, D.C., 1980.

113 "Roundtable: The Politics of the Solution," *Links Health and Development Report,* Vol. 7 No. 3/4 (fall/winter 1990), p. 12 (the suggestion is drawn from comments by Ronald Wilson); Carl E. Taylor and William B. Greenough, III, "Control of Diarrheal Diseases," *Annual Review of Public Health,* Vol. 10 (1989), p. 241.

114 Vincent Fauveau, M. Yunus, M. Shafiqul Islam, André Briend, and Michael L. Bennish, "Does ORT Reduce Diarrhoeal Mortality?," *Health Policy and Planning,* Vol. 7 (1992), No. 3, pp. 243–250.

115 Riyad S, El Mougi AA, and Hirschhorn N. "After Rehydration, What Happens to the Child? J. Trop. Pediatr. 1991;37; 1–3.

116 "WHO Guidelines: Selection of Home Fluids," *Dialogue on Diarrhoea,* No. 41 (June 1990), p. 2; David Werner, *Trip Report: Consultation by David Werner for the Mozambique Ministry of Health and UNICEF, September 1 to September 27, 1987, Maputo and Nampula, Mozambique,* p. 17; F. Cutts, J. Cliff, R. Reiss, and J. Stuckey, "Evaluating the Management of Diarrhoea in Health Centres in Mozambique," *Journal of Tropical Medicine and Hygiene,* Vol. 91 (1988), pp. 61–66.

117 Hema Viswanathan and Jon Eliot Rohde, *Diarrhoea in Rural India: A Nationwide Study of Mothers and Practitioners* (New Delhi: UNICEF/Vision Books, 1990).

118 Ibid., p. 13.

119 The information in this paragraph is based on the first-hand experience of David Sanders.

120 World Health Organization, *Case Management for the Control of Diarrhoeal Diseases in Zimbabwe* (1992), p. 3.

121 Ibid.

122 From letter to the authors from Dr. Robert Moy, Zimbabwe.

123 R. Bradley Sack, "Global View of ORT," in *Symposium Proceedings, Cereal-Based Oral Rehydration Therapy: Theory and Practice* (proceedings of a symposium sponsored by the International Child Health Foundation and the National Council for International Health, Washington, D.C., February 17, 1987, p. 18; Mathuram Santosham, "Nutritional Aspects of ORT," in ibid., pp. 24–25.

124 Ruxin, Joshua N, "Magic Bullet: The History of Oral Rehydration Therapy" Medical History. 1994. 38: 363–397, page 396.

125 See David Werner and Bill Bower, *Helping Health Workers Learn,* pp. 27–17 to 27–18.

126 Milton Silverman, Philip R. Lee, and Mia Lydecker, *Prescriptions for Death: The Drugging of the Third World,* pp. 40–59; J.A. Walker-Smith, "Underutilisation of Oral Rehydration in the Treatment of Gastroenteritis," *Drugs,* Vol. 36, Supplement 4 (1988) (Seminar-in-Print on "Advances in Oral Rehydration"), p. 63; Logan Brenzel and Norbert Hirschhorn, *Executive Summary of the UNICEF Macro and Micro Studies* (a report prepared by John Snow, Inc.), p. 1; Michael Tan, "Who Killed Rosario," *The New Internationalist,* No. 165 (November 1986), p. 8; David Gilbert, "Too Much of a Good Thing," *The New Internationalist,* No. 165 (November 1986), p. 18; Norbert Hirschhorn, "Appropriate Health Technology in Egypt," *Middle East Report,* No. 161 (November–December 1989), p. 27; WHO, *"Division of Diarrhoeal and Acute Respiratory Disease Control, Interim report 1994,"* 1995, p. 35.

127 Health Action International, "No Justification for Continued Production and Sale of Antidiarrhoeals for Children, States New WHO Report" (press release, February 15, 1991).

128 *The Prescriber,* Nov. 1992, #4 p.1.

129 UNICEF, *State of the World's Children, 1994,* p. 6.

130 David Werner, *Where There Is No Doctor: A Village Health Care Handbook,* p. 156, p. 369; Carl E. Taylor and William B. Greenough, III, "Control of Diarrheal Diseases," *Annual Review of Public Health,* Vol. 10 (1989), p. 231; Dianna Melrose, *Bitter Pills,* OXFAM, 1982, p. 99.

131 WHO, *The Rational Use of Drugs in the Management of Acute Diarrhoea in Children* (Geneva: WHO, 1990).

132 WHO Programme for Control of Diarrhoeal Diseases, *Interim Programme Report 1990,* pp. 7–8; WHO Diarrhoeal Disease Control Programme, *Report of the Twelfth Meeting of the Technical Advisory Group* (Geneva, March 18–22, 1991), pp. 15–16.

133 WHO Programme for Control of Diarrhoeal Diseases, *Interim Programme Report 1990,* p. 8.

134 WHO, *The Rational Use of Drugs in the Management of Acute Diarrhoea in Children,* p. 1.

135 UNICEF, *State of the World's Children, 1994,* p. 15.

136 Andrew Chetley, "Dumped on Third World: Harmful, Useless Drugs for Diarrhoea," *Third World Resurgence,* No. 10 (June 1991), p. 5; Hilbrand Haak, "Withdrawal of Antidearrhoeal Drugs: Still Some Way to Go!," HAI News, Health Action International, October, 1996, p. 1.

137 D. Mahalanabis, "Development of an Improved Formulation of Oral Rehydration Salts (ORS) with Antidiarrhoeal and Nutritional Properties: a 'Super ORS'" (paper issued by the Diarrhoeal Diseases Control Programme of the World Health Organization), p. 2.

138 Logan Brenzel and Norbert Hirschhorn, *Executive Summary of the UNICEF Macro and Micro Studies* (a report prepared by John Snow, Inc.), p. 3.

139 Glen Williams, *A Simple Solution* (a UNICEF special report), pp. 5–7.

140 David A. Sack, "Use of Oral Rehydration Therapy in Acute Watery Diarrhoea: A Practical Guide," *Drugs* 41(4) 566–573; Parveen Rasheed, "Perceptions of Diarrhoeal Diseases among Mothers and Mothers-to-Be: Implications for Health Education in Saudi Arabia," *Social Science and Medicine,* Vol. 36 No. 3, 1993, pp. 373–377.

141 James Grant, "Marketing Child Survival," *Assignment Children: A Journal Concerned with Children, Women and Youth in Development* (A UNICEF publication), 65/68, 1984, p. 3.

142 C. MacCormack and A. Draper, *Cultural Meanings of Oral Rehydration Salts in Jamaica, 1988,* pp. 286, 287, from *The Context of Medicines in Developing Countries: Studies in Pharmaceutical Anthropology, 1988,* Edited by Sjaak Van Der Geest and Susan Reynolds Whyte.

143 Viswanathan and Rohde, *Diarrhoea in Rural India,* pp. 12–13.

144 See David Werner and Bill Bower, *Helping Health Workers Learn,* pp. 1–26 to 1–28, 15–10 to 15–18, 24–17 to 24–22, 24–28 to 24–29.

145 David Werner, *Trip Report: Consultation by David Werner for the Mozambique Ministry of Health and UNICEF, September 1 to September 27, 1987, Maputo and Nampula, Mozambique,* p. 17.

146 "WHO Guidelines: Selection of Home Fluids," *Dialogue on Diarrhoea,* No. 41, June 1990, p. 2; David Werner, *Trip Report: Consultation by David Werner for the Mozambique Ministry of Health and UNICEF, September 1 to September 27, 1987, Maputo and Nampula, Mozambique,* p. 17; F. Cutts, J. Cliff, R. Reiss, and J. Stuckey, "Evaluating the Management of Diarrhoea in Health Centres in Mozambique," *Journal of Tropical Medicine and Hygiene,* Vol. 91, 1988, pp. 61–66.

147 C. MacCormack and A. Draper, *Cultural Meanings of Oral Rehydration Salts in Jamaica, 1988,* pp. 286, 287, from *The Context of Medicines in Developing Countries: Studies in Pharmaceutical Anthropology, 1988,* Edited by Sjaak Van Der Geest and Susan Reynolds Whyte.

148 Richard Feachem, "Oral Rehydration with Dirty Water?," *Diarrhoea Dialogue,* No. 4, February 1981, p. 14; David Werner and Bill Bower, *Helping Health Workers Learn,* p. 15–4.

149 Enteric Disease Control Program, Communicable Diseases Control, Division of Disease Prevention and Control, Pan American Health Organization, *Epidemiological Bulletin* (a publication of the Pan American Health Organization), Vol. 3, No. 4, 1982, p. 14.

150 *The Prescriber.* November, 1992; # 4, UNICEF in cooperation with The United States Pharmacopoeial Convention, Inc. P. 2.

151 Ibid, p. 6.

152 Anne E. Platt, *Infecting Ourselves: How Environmental and Social Disruptions Trigger Disease*, Worldwatch Institute paper 129, April 1996, pp. 43, 60.

153 Iftikhar A. Malik, Seema Azim, Mary Jo Good, Muhammad Iqbal, Muhammad Nawaz, Lubna Ashraf, and Noreen Bukhtiari, "Feeding Practices for Young Pakistani Children: Usual Diet and Diet During Diarrhoea," J Diarrhoeal Dis Res, Sept. 1991, 213–218.

154 WHO *Division of Diarrhoea and Acute Respiratory Disease Control, Interim Report 1994*, 1995, p. 72.

155 Joshua Ruxin, *Magic Bullet: The History of Oral Rehydration Therapy*, Medical History, 1994, **38:** 363–397, pp. 376– 377.

156 "Roundtable: The Politics of the Solution," *Links Health and Development Report,* Vol. 7, No. 3/4 (fall/winter 1990), p. 15 (statement by Norbert Hirschhorn); Bradley Sack, "Global View of ORT," in *Symposium Proceedings, Cereal-Based Oral Rehydration Therapy: Theory and Practice* (proceedings of a symposium sponsored by the International Child Health Foundation and the National Council for International Health, Washington, D.C., February 17, 1987, p. 16.

157 Daniel Pizarro, Bernardita Catillo, Gloria Posada, et al., "Efficacy Comparison of Oral Rehydration Solutions Containing Either 90 or 75 millimoles of Sodium per Liter, *Pediatrics,* Vol. 79, No. 2 (February 1987), cited in PRITECH's *Technical Literature Update,* Volume II, No. 4 (July 1987), pp. 4–5; Mac Otten, "Manual for Teaching Women Cereal, Flour, Salt ORT (Save the Children Federation Health Unit, November 1986), p. 17.

158 World Health Organization, "Oral Rehydration Therapy for Treatment of Diarrhoea in the Home" (working paper, 1986); "Household Management of Diarrhea and Acute Respiratory Infections" (Occasional Paper #12, "Report of a Scientific Meeting at the Johns Hopkins School of Hygiene and Public Health in Collaboration with the United Nations Children's Fund and the Diarrhoeal Diseases and Acute Respiratory Infections Control Programmes of the World Health Organization," November 1990), p. 5.

159 Bonita F. Stanton, Michael G.M. Rowland, John D. Clemens, "Oral Rehydration Solution—Too Little or Too Much," the *Lancet,* January 1987, pp. 33–34. Cited in PRITECH's *Technical Literature Update,* Vol. II, No. 4 (July 1987), pp. 2–3; World Health Organization, "Oral Rehydration Therapy for Treatment of Diarrhoea. in the Home" (working paper, 1986); "Household Management of Diarrhea and Acute Respiratory Infections" (Occasional Paper #12, "Report of a Scientific Meeting at the Johns Hopkins School of Hygiene and Public Health in Collaboration with the United Nations Children's Fund and the Diarrhoeal Diseases and Acute Respiratory Infections Control Programmes of the World Health Organization," November 1990), p. 2.

160 David Werner, *Where There Is No Doctor: A Village Health Care Handbook,* p. 152, p. 368.

161 L.O. Nwoye, P.E. Uwagboe, and G.U. Madubuko, "Evaluation of Home-Made Salt-Sugar Oral Rehydration Solution in a Rural Nigerian Population," *Journal of Tropical Medicine and Hygiene,* 91(1) (February 1988), pp. 23–27; WHO *Division of Diarrhoea and Acute Respiratory Disease Control, Interim Report 1994,* 1995, p. 67.

162 *Programme for the Control of Diarrhoeal Disease: Ninth Programme Report 1992–1993,* World Health Organization, 1994 p. 51.; *Division of Diarrhoeal and Acute Respiratory Disease Control, Interim Report 1994*, World Health Organization, 1995 p. 67.

163 "25 Years of ORS: Joint WHO/ICDDR, Consultative Meeting on ORS Formulation" 1994 p. 5. In WHO's, "Division of Diarrhoeal and Acute Respiratory Disease Control, Interim report 1994," 1995, p. 70, a total osmolarity range of 225–260 mmol/l is given, with glucose 75–90 mmol/l and sodium 60–75 mmol/l.

164 World Health Organization, "Summary of Guidelines for Early Home Therapy to Prevent Dehydration," Annex 1, pp. 1–2.

165 Personal correspondence by William Greenough with David Werner, January, 1995.

166 M.K. Bhan, N.K. Arora, et al., "Major Factors in Diarrhoea Related Mortality among Rural Children," *Indian Journal of Medical Research,* Vol. 83 (January 1986), pp. 9–12 (cited in PRITECH's *Technical Literature Update,* Vol. 1, No. 5 (July 1986), pp. 1–2; Bonita Stanton, John Clemens, Tajkera Khair, et al., "Follow-up of Children Discharged from Hospital after Treatment for Diarrhoea in Urban Bangladesh," *Tropical and Geographical Medicine,* 1986, pp. 113–118.

167 Kent, pp. 64–65.

168 Iftikhar A. Malik, Seema Azim, Mary Jo Good, Muhammad Iqbal, Muhammad Nawaz, Lubna Ashraf, and Noreen Bukhtiari, "Feeding Practices for Young Pakistani Children: Usual Diet and Diet During Diarrhoea," J Diarrhoeal Dis Res, Sept. 1991, 213–218.

169 E. Isolauri, T. Vesikari, P. Saha, et al., "Milk versus No Milk in Rapid Refeeding after Acute Gastroenteritis," *Journal of Pediatric Gastroenterology and Nutrition,* Vol. 5, No. 2 (1986), pp. 254–261 (cited in PRITECH's *Technical Literature Update,* Vol. 1, No. 7 (September 1986), pp. 2–3 (see "Editorial Comment" as well); "Editorial Comment," PRITECH's *Technical Literature Update,* Vol. II, No. 3 (March 1987), p. 3; Mathuram Santosham, "Nutritional Aspects of ORT," in *Symposium Proceedings, Cereal-Based Oral Rehydration Therapy: Theory and Practice* (proceedings of a symposium sponsored by the International Child Health Foundation and the National Council for International Health, Washington, D.C., February 17, 1987), pp. 24–27; Bradley Sack, "Global View of ORT," ibid., p. 18.

170 Anne Gadomski, Robert Black and W. Henry Mosley, "Constraints to the Potential Impact of Child Survival in Developing Countries," *Health Policy and Planning,* 5(3) (1990), p. 236, p. 241; Robert Halpern, "A Child Survival and Development Revolution?," *International Journal of Early Childhood,* Vol. 18, No. 1 (1986), p. 45.

171 Anne Gadomski, Robert Black and W. Henry Mosley, "Constraints to the Potential Impact of Child Survival in Developing Countries," *Health Policy and Planning,* 5(3) (1990), p. 236, p. 241; Robert Halpern, "A Child Survival and Development Revolution?," *International Journal of Early Childhood,* Vol. 18, No. 1 (1986), p. 45.

172 Carl E. Taylor and William B. Greenough, III, "Control of Diarrheal Diseases," *Annual Review of Public Health,* Vol. 10 (1989), p. 221.

173 UNICEF, *State of the World's Children, 1988*, p. 3.

174 UNICEF, *State of the World's Children, 1992*, p. 11.

175 UNICEF, *State of the World's Children, 1993*, p. 22.

176 André Briend, "Is Diarrhoea a Major Cause of Malnutrition among the Under-fives in Developing Countries? A Review of Available Evidence," *European Journal of Clinical Nutrition,* 44 (1990), pp. 611–628; André Briend, Kh. Zahid Hasan, K.M.A. Aziz, and Bilais A. Hoque, "Are Diarrhea Control Programmes Likely to Reduce Childhood Malnutrition? Observations from Rural Bangladesh," *Lancet,* August 5, 1989, pp. 319–322; Fitzroy Henry, André Briend, and Vincent Fauveau, "Child Survival: Should the Strategy be Redesigned? Experience from Bangladesh," *Health Policy and Planning,* Vol. 5 (1990), No. 3, pp. 226–234; R.J.D. Moy, et al, "Is diarrhea a major cause of malnutrition in developing countries? Analysis of data from rural Zimbabwe." Institute of Child Health, University of Birmingham, UK.

177 R.J.D. Moy, et al, "Is diarrhea a major cause of malnutrition in developing countries? Analysis of data from rural Zimbabwe." Eur J Clin Nutr 1994; 48:810–821.

178 Becker Stan, Black Robert E., Brown, Kenneth H. "Relative effects of diarrhea, fever, and dietary energy intake on weight gain in rural Bangladeshi children. *American Journal of Clinical Nutrition,* June, 1991; 53: pp. 1499–1503.

179 Becker Stan, Black Robert E., Brown, Kenneth H. "Relative effects of diarrhea, fever, and dietary energy intake on weight gain in rural Bangladeshi children. *American Journal of Clinical Nutrition,* June, 1991; 53: pp. 1499–1503.

180 Carl E. Taylor and Xu Zhao Yu, "Oral Rehydration in China," *American Journal of Public Health,* Vol. 76, No. 2 (1986), p. 187.

181 Fitzroy Henry, André Briend, and Vincent Fauveau, "Child Survival: Should the Strategy be Redesigned? Experience from Bangladesh," *Health Policy and Planning,* Vol. 5 (1990), No. 3, p. 230.

182 Norbert Hirschhorn and William Greenough III, "Progress in Oral Rehydration Therapy," *Scientific American,* Vol. 264, No. 5 (May 1991), p. 56; "Household Behavior and the Role of Community Participation in ORT Efforts" (ICORT III Panel Issue Paper), pp. 9–10; Jon E. Rohde, "Therapeutic Interventions in Diarrhoea," *Food and Nutrition Bulletin,* Vol. 3, No. 4, p. 35; Mohamed I. Hegazy, Osman M. Galal, Mahmoud T. El-Mougy, Sue Wallace-Cabin, and Gail G. Harrison, "Composition of Egyptian Home Remedies for Diarrhea," *Ecology of Food and Nutrition,* Vol. 19 (1987), p. 248; Jaime L. Palacios Treviño and Gabriel Manjarrez, "Nuevos aspectos de la rehidratación por vía oral en niños: un método sencillo de tratamiento," *Revista Mexicana de Pediatría,* February 1982, p. 70; Soeprapto, Yati Soenarto, Nelwan, P.A. Moenginah, and Ismangoen, "Feeding Children with Diarrhea" (Department of Child Health, Faculty of Medicine, Gadjah Mada University, Yogyakarta, Indonesia); M.A. Rub, "Oral Rehydration Therapy (ORT)," *In Touch,* September/October 1983, p. 3; E. Isolauri, T. Vesikari, P. Saha, et al., "Milk versus No Milk in Rapid Refeeding after Acute Gastroenteritis," *Journal of Pediatric Gastroenterology and Nutrition,* Vol. 5, No. 2 (1986), pp. 254–261 (cited in PRITECH's *Technical Literature Update,* Vol. 1, No. 7 (September 1986), pp. 2–3 (see "Editorial Comment" as well); "Editorial Comment," PRITECH's *Technical Literature Update,* Vol. II, No. 3 (March 1987), p. 3; Daniel Pizarro, Bernardita Catillo, Gloria Posada, et al., "Efficacy Comparison of Oral Rehydration Solutions Containing either 90 or 75 Millimoles of Sodium per Liter," *Pediatrics,* Vol. 79, No. 2 (February 1987), pp. 190–195 (cited in PRITECH's *Technical Literature Update,* Vol. II, No. 4 (July 1987), p. 5—see "Editorial Comment"); Richard A. Cash, "A History of the Development of Oral Rehydration Therapy (ORT)," in *Symposium Proceedings, Cereal-Based Oral Rehydration Therapy: Theory and Practice* (proceedings of a symposium sponsored by the International Child Health Foundation and the National Council for International Health, Washington,

D.C., February 17, 1987), p. 10; Bradley Sack, "Global View of ORT," in ibid., pp. 17–18; "Household Management of Diarrhea and Acute Respiratory Infections" (Occasional Paper #12, "Report of a Scientific Meeting at the Johns Hopkins School of Hygiene and Public Health in Collaboration with the United Nations Children's Fund and the Diarrhoeal Diseases and Acute Respiratory Infections Control Programmes of the World Health Organization," November 1990), p. 2; Carl E. Taylor and William B. Greenough, III, "Control of Diarrheal Diseases," *Annual Review of Public Health,* Vol. 10 (1989), p. 225, p. 241; World Health Organization, "Summary of Guidelines for Early Home Therapy to Prevent Dehydration," Annex 1, pp. 1–2.

183 E. Isolauri, T. Vesikari, P. Saha, et al., "Milk versus No Milk in Rapid Refeeding after Acute Gastroenteritis," *Journal of Pediatric Gastroenterology and Nutrition,* Vol. 5, No. 2 (1986), pp. 254–261 (cited in PRITECH's *Technical Literature Update,* Vol. 1, No. 7 (September 1986), pp. 2–3 (see "Editorial Comment" as well); "Editorial Comment," PRITECH's *Technical Literature Update,* Vol. II, No. 3 (March 1987), p. 3; Mathuram Santosham, "Nutritional Aspects of ORT," in *Symposium Proceedings, Cereal-Based Oral Rehydration Therapy: Theory and Practice* (proceedings of a symposium sponsored by the International Child Health Foundation and the National Council for International Health, Washington, D.C., February 17, 1987), p. 27; Bradley Sack, "Global View of ORT," ibid., pp. 17–18.

184 Norbert Hirschhorn and William B. Greenough III, "Progress in Oral Rehydration Therapy," *Scientific American,* Vol. 264, No. 5 (May 1991), pp. 55–56; Mathuram Santosham, "Nutritional Aspects of ORT," in *Symposium Proceedings, Cereal-Based Oral Rehydration Therapy: Theory and Practice* (proceedings of a symposium sponsored by the International Child Health Foundation and the National Council for International Health, Washington, D.C., February 17, 1987), pp. 24–27.

185 Personal correspondence with Norbert Hirschhorn, which is supported in his article: "The Effect of a National Control of Diarrheal Diseases Program on Mortality, the case of Egypt," *Social Science and Medicine,* March, 1995.

186 Carl E. Taylor and William B. Greenough, III, "Control of Diarrheal Diseases," *Annual Review of Public Health,* Vol. 10 (1989), p. 225; Iftikhar A. Malik, Seema Azim, Mary Jo Good, Muhammad Iqbal, Muhammad Nawaz, Lubna Ashraf, and Noreen Bukhtiari, "Feeding Practices for Young Pakistani Children: Usual Diet and Diet During Diarrhoea," J Diarrhoeal Dis Res, Sept. 1991, 213–218.

187 Beaton, G., Martorell, R., L'Abbe, K., Edmonston, B., McCabe, G., Ross, A. & Harvey, B., *Effectiveness of Vitamin A Supplementation in the Control of Young Child Morbidity and Mortality in Developing Countries,* Final Report to CIDA, University of Toronto, 1992.

188 "Controlling Vitamin A Deficiency," ACC/SCN State-of-the-Art Series, Nutrition Policy Discussion Paper No. 14, WHO., Geneva, 1994.

189 Peter Miller and Norbert Hirschhorn, "The Effect of a National Control of Diarrheal Diseases Program on Mortality: the case of Egypt." *Social Science and Medicine,* 40 (10), May, 1995, p. S1–S30.

190 Felicity Savage King and Ann Burgess, *Nutrition for Developing Countries,* 2nd edition, 1992, p. 93; "Reducing Infection," *Dialogue on Diarrhoea,* No. 46 (September 1991), p. 5.

191 Sandra L. Huffman and Adwoa Steel, *Do Child Survival Interventions Reduce Malnutrition: The Dark Side of Child Survival* (paper prepared published by Nurture/Center to Prevent Childhood Malnutrition, 1992), pp. I–ii.

192 Carl E. Taylor and William B. Greenough, III, "Control of Diarrheal Diseases," *Annual Review of Public Health,* Vol. 10 (1989), p. 235.

193 John D. Clemens, et al., "Breast Feeding and the Risk of Severe Cholera in Rural Bangladeshi Children," *American Journal of Epidemiology,* Vol. 131, No. 3 (1990), pp. 400–411; C.G. Victora, et al., "Evidence for Protection by Breast-Feeding Against Infant Deaths from Infectious Diseases in Brazil," *Lancet,* 1987, No. 2, pp. 319–321. Cited in Fitzroy Henry, Andre Briend, and Vincent Fauveau, "Child Survival: Should the Strategy Be Redesigned? Experience from Bangladesh," *Health Policy and Planning,* Vol. 5, No. 3 (1990), p. 231; UNICEF/WHO/UNESCO, *Facts for Life,* 1989, p. 20.

194 Margaret E. Bentley, "Sociocultural Factors Involved in an Intervention to Improve Weaning Practices in Kwara State, Nigeria" (a paper presented at the Workshop on Improving Infant Feeding Practices to Prevent Diarrhea or Reduce its Severity: Research Issues, sponsored by WHO's Diarrhoeal Disease Control Programme and the Johns Hopkins University School of Hygiene and Public Health, Baltimore, Maryland, April 25–28, 1988); Kenneth H. Brown, "Nutritional Status during Weaning and its Relation to Diarrheal Morbidity" (a paper presented at the same workshop cited above).

195 W. Henry Mosley and Lincoln C. Chen, "An Analytic Framework for the Study of Child Survival in Developing Countries," in W. Henry Mosley and Lincoln C. Chen, eds., *Child Survival* (Cambridge: Cambridge University Press, 1984), pp. 25–45. Cited by Kent, p. 66.

196 W. Henry Mosley and Lincoln C. Chen, "An Analytic Framework for the Study of Child Survival in Developing Countries," in W. Henry Mosley and Lincoln C. Chen, eds., *Child Survival* (Cambridge: Cambridge University Press, 1984), pp. 25–45. Cited in Kent, p. 66.

197 Quoted in USAID, *Oral Rehydration Therapy: A Revolution in Child Survival.* Oelgeschlager, Gunn & Hain, Weston MA, 1988. p. 16.

198 A.M. Molla, et al., "Rice-powder Electrolyte Solution as Oral Therapy in Diarrhoea due to Vibrio Cholera and Escherichia Coli," the *Lancet,* June 12, 1982, pp. 1317–1319; J.W. Kleevens, "Rice Water for Infant Gastroenteritis," the *Lancet,* August 8, 1981; T.F. Ho, William C.L. Yip, John S.H. Tay, and K. Vellayappan, "Rice Water and Milk: Effect on Ileal Fluid Osmolality and Volume," *Lancet,* January 16, 1982, p. 169; F.C. Patra, et al., "Is Oral Rice Electrolyte Solution Superior to Glucose Electrolyte Solution in Infantile Diarrhoea?," *Arch. Dis. Child,* 57 (1982), pp. 910–912; William B. Greenough, III, "Status of Cereal-Based Oral Rehydration Therapy," in *Symposium Proceedings, Cereal-Based Oral Rehydration Therapy: Theory and Practice* (proceedings of a symposium sponsored by the International Child Health Foundation and the National Council for International Health, Washington, D.C., February 17, 1987), pp. 30–31; Bradley Sack, "Global View of ORT," ibid., p. 17; M.K. Bhan et al., "Comparison of Acceptability and Use of Different Home Made Solutions for Early Treatment of Diarrhoea in Rural Children," (paper prepared for Department of Pediatrics, All India Institute of Medical Sciences); M.K. Bhan et al., "Efficacy of 'Mung' Bean (Lentil) and Pop Rice Based Rehydration Solutions in Comparison with the Standard Glucose Electrolyte Solution" (paper prepared for Department of Pediatrics of All India Institute of Medical Sciences); Daniel Pizarro, et al., "Rice-Based Oral Electrolyte Solutions for the Management of Infantile Diarrhea," *The New England Journal of Medicine,* February 21, 1991, pp. 517–521; P.R. Kenya, et al., "Cereal-Based Oral Rehydration Solutions," *Archives of Diseases in Childhood,* Vol. 64 (1989), pp. 1032–1035; "Recent Advances

in the Development of Improved ORS" (a report issued by the World Health Organization's Diarrhoeal Disease Control Programme), p. 9.

199 T.F. Ho, William C.L. Yip, John S.H. Tay, and K. Vellayappan, "Rice Water and Milk: Effect on Ileal Fluid Osmolality and Volume," the *Lancet,* January 16, 1982, p. 169; J.W.L. Kleevens, "Rice Water for Infant Gastroenteritis," the *Lancet,* August 8, 1981, p. 306.

200 A.M. Molla et al., "Rice-Powder Electrolyte Solution as Oral Therapy in Diarrhoea due to Vibrio Cholera and Escherichia Coli," the *Lancet,* Vol. 1, No. 8285 (June 12, 1982), p. 1319.

201 World Health Organization, "Oral Rehydration Therapy for Treatment of Diarrhoea in the Home" (working paper, 1986).

202 Carl E. Taylor and Xu Zhao Yu, "Oral Rehydration in China," *American Journal of Public Health,* Vol. 76, No. 2 (February 1986), pp. 187–189 (cited in PRITECH's *Technical Literature Update,* Vol. 1, No. 6 (August 1986), p. 4); J.W.L. Kleevens, "Rice Water for Infant Gastroenteritis," the *Lancet,* August 8, 1981, p. 306.

203 George Davey Smith, "Beliefs and Action," *Links Health and Development Report,* Vol. 7, No. 3/4 (fall/winter 1990), p. 13.

204 World Health Organization, "Oral Rehydration Therapy for Treatment of Diarrhoea in the Home" (working paper, 1986).

205 A.M. Molla et al., "Rice-Powder Electrolyte Solution as Oral Therapy in Diarrhoea due to Vibrio Cholera and Escherichia Coli," *Lancet,* Vol. 1, No. 8285 (June 12, 1982), pp. 1317–1319; W.B. Greenough, III and A.M. Molla, "Cereal-based Oral Rehydration Solutions," *Lancet,* Vol. 2, No. 8302 (October 9, 1982), p. 823. Also see F.C. Patra, D. Mahalanabis, K.N. Jalan, A. Sen, and P. Banerjee, "Is Oral Rice Electrolyte Solution Superior to Glucose Electrolyte Solution in Infantile Diarrhoea?," *Arch Dis Child,* No. 57 (1982), pp. 910–912; D. Mahalanabis, M.H. Merson, D. Barua, "Oral Rehydration Therapy—Recent Advances," *World Health Forum,* Vol. 2, No. 2 (1981), pp. 245–249; William B. Greenough, III, "Status of Cereal-Based Oral Rehydration Therapy," in *Symposium Proceedings, Cereal-Based Oral Rehydration Therapy: Theory and Practice* (proceedings of a symposium sponsored by the International Child Health Foundation and the National Council for International Health, Washington, D.C., February 17, 1987), pp. 30–31; AN Alam, SA Sarker, AM Molla, MM Rahaman, and WB Greenough, "Hydrolysed Wheat Based Oral Rehydration Solution for Acute Diarrhoea," *Archives of Disease in Childhood,* Vol. 62, p. 440–444, 1987.

206 F.C. Patra, et al., "Is Oral Rice Electrolyte Solution Superior to Glucose Electrolyte Solution in Infantile Diarrhoea?," Arch. Dis. Child, No. 57 (1982), pp. 910–912; D. Mahalanabis, "Development of an Improved Formulation of Oral Rehydration Salts (ORS) with Antidiarrhoeal and Nutritional Properties: a 'Super ORS'" (paper issued by the Diarrhoeal Diseases Control Programme of the World Health Organization), p. 9; "ORT Today and Tomorrow," *Dialogue on Diarrhoea,* No. 41 (June 1990), p. 1; P. Lepage, et al., "Food based Oral Rehydration Salt Solution for Acute Childhood Diarrhoea," cited in *Dialogue on Diarrhoea,* No. 41 (June 1990), p. 4; A. Bari, et al., "Community Study of Rice Based ORS in Rural Bangladesh, International Centre for Diarrhoeal Diseases Research, Bangladesh, cited in *Dialogue on Diarrhoea,* No. 41 (June 1990), p. 5; "Roundtable: The Politics of the Solution," *Links Health and Development Report,* Vol. 7, No. 3/4 (fall/winter 1990), p. 12 (comment by Norbert Hirschhorn); William B. Greenough, III, "Status of Cereal-Based Oral Rehydration Therapy," in *Symposium Proceedings, Cereal-Based Oral Rehydration Therapy: Theory and Practice* (proceedings of a symposium sponsored by the International Child Health Foundation and the National Council

for International Health, Washington, D.C., February 17, 1987), pp. 30–31; UNICEF, *State of the World's Children, 1987*, p. 39; M.K. Bhan et al., "Comparison of Acceptability and Use of Different Home Made Solutions for Early Treatment of Diarrhoea in Rural Children," (paper prepared for Department of Pediatrics, All India Institute of Medical Sciences); M.K. Bhan et al., "Efficacy of 'Mung' Bean (Lentil) and Pop Rice Based Rehydration Solutions in Comparison with the Standard Glucose Electrolyte Solution" (paper prepared for the Department of Pediatrics of the All India Institute of Medical Sciences); "Household Management of Diarrhea and Acute Respiratory Infections" (Occasional Paper #12, "Report of a Scientific Meeting at the Johns Hopkins School of Hygiene and Public Health in Collaboration with the United Nations Children's Fund and the Diarrhoeal Diseases and Acute Respiratory Infections Control Programmes of the World Health Organization," November 1990), p. 6; "More on Rice-Based ORS for Children with Diarrhoea," *Essential Drugs Monitor* (a publication of the WHO Action Programme on Essential Drugs and Vaccines), No. 11 (1991), p. 14; "Rice-Based ORS," *Update* (a publication of the World Health Organization's Programme for the Control of Diarrhoeal Diseases, No. 7 (August 1990), p. 3; "Recent Advances in the Development of Improved ORS" (a report issued by the World Health Organization's Diarrhoeal Disease Control Programme), pp. 7–9; "Notes on the Composition and Presentation of Products for Oral Rehydration" (a report issued by the World Health Organization's Programme for the Control of Diarrhoeal Diseases), p. 2; D. Pizarro, G. Posada, L. Sandi, and J.R. Moran, "Rice-based Oral Electrolyte Solutions for the Management of Infantile Diarrhea," *New England Journal of Medicine*, 324 (1991), pp. 517–521.

207   "25 Years of ORS: Joint WHO/ICDDR,B Consultative Meeting on ORS Formulation" WHO, 1994. P. 3.

208   Norbert Hirschhorn and William B. Greenough III, "Progress in Oral Rehydration Therapy," Scientific American, Vol. 264, No. 5 (May 1991), p. 54; D. Mahalanabis, "Development of an Improved Formulation of Oral Rehydration Salts (ORS) with Antidiarrhoeal and Nutritional Properties: a 'Super ORS'" (paper issued by the Diarrhoeal Diseases Control Programme of the World Health Organization), p. 2; Bradley Sack, "Global View of ORT," in *Symposium Proceedings, Cereal-Based Oral Rehydration Therapy: Theory and Practice* (proceedings of a symposium sponsored by the International Child Health Foundation and the National Council for International Health, Washington, D.C., February 17, 1987, p. 16; UNICEF, *State of the World's Children, 1987*, p. 39; Robert Halpern, "A Child Survival and Development Revolution?," *International Journal of Early Childhood*, Vol. 18, No. 1 (1986), pp. 48–49.

209   M.K. Bhan et al., "Efficacy of 'Mung' Bean (Lentil) and Pop Rice Based Rehydration Solutions in Comparison with the Standard Glucose Electrolyte Solution" (paper prepared for the Department of Pediatrics of the All India Institute of Medical Sciences), p. 8–9, 11.

210   *Division of Diarrhoeal and Acute Respiratory Disease Control, Interim Report 1994*, WHO, p. 69, 1995.

211   *25 Years of ORS*, Joint WHO/ICDDR,B Consultive Meeting on ORS Formulation, Dhaka, Bangladesh, 10–12 December, 1994, p. 1.

212   *25 Years of ORS*, Joint WHO/ICDDR,B Consultive Meeting on ORS Formulation, Dhaka, Bangladesh, 10–12 December, 1994, p. 3.

213   WHO Diarrhoeal Disease Control Programme, *Report of the Twelfth Meeting of the Technical Advisory Group* (Geneva, March 18–22, 1991), p. 13.

214   From letters and personal communications with leaders of the International Child Health Foundation, Columbia, Maryland.

215   William B. Greenough, III, "Status of Cereal-Based Oral Rehydration Therapy," in *Symposium Proceedings, Cereal-Based Oral Rehydration Therapy: Theory and Practice* (proceedings of a symposium sponsored by the International Child Health Foundation and the National Council for International Health, Washington, D.C., February 17, 1987), pp. 30–31; Bradley Sack, "Global View of ORT," ibid., p. 17.

216   See for example K. Siener, "Wheat based ORS for Afghans," International Rescue Committee, Peshawar, Pakistan (cited in *Dialogue on Diarrhoea*, No. 41 (June 1990), pp. 4–5), for wheat; and P. Lepage, et al., "Food based Oral Rehydration Salt Solution for Acute Childhood Diarrhoea" (cited in *Dialogue on Diarrhoea*, No. 41 (June 1990), p. 4), for sorghum; Bradley Sack, "Global View of ORT," in *Symposium Proceedings, Cereal-Based Oral Rehydration Therapy: Theory and Practice* (proceedings of a symposium sponsored by the International Child Health Foundation and the National Council for International Health, Washington, D.C., February 17, 1987), p. 17, for maize.

217   William B. Greenough, III, "Status of Cereal-Based Oral Rehydration Therapy," in *Symposium Proceedings, Cereal-Based Oral Rehydration Therapy: Theory and Practice* (proceedings of a symposium sponsored by the International Child Health Foundation and the National Council for International Health, Washington, D.C., February 17, 1987), pp. 30–31; P. Howard, et al., "Proposed Use of Sweet Potato Water as a Fluid for Oral Rehydration Therapy for Diarrhoea," Papua New Guinea Institute of Medical Research, Goroka, Papua New Guinea (cited in *Dialogue on Diarrhoea*, No. 41 (June 1990), p. 4); Bradley Sack, "Global View of ORT," in *Symposium Proceedings, Cereal-Based Oral Rehydration Therapy: Theory and Practice* (proceedings of a symposium sponsored by the International Child Health Foundation and the National Council for International Health, Washington, D.C., February 17, 1987), p. 17, for gram.

218   S.S. Buccimazza, I.D. Hill, M.A. Kibel, and M.D. Bowie, "The Composition of Home-made Sugar/Electrolyte Solutions for Treating Gastro-enteritis," *South Africa Medical Journal*, Vol. 70 (December 6, 1986), p. 730.

219   Molla, A.M, Ahmed, S.M., and Greenough III, W.B. "Rice-based Oral Rehydration Solution Decreases Stool Volume in Acute Diarrhoea." *Bulletin of the WHO, 63:4, 1985, pp 751–56.* F.C. Patra, et al., "Is Oral Rice Electrolyte Solution Superior to Glucose Electrolyte Solution in Infantile Diarrhoea?," Arch. Dis. Child, 57 (1982), pp. 910–912; D. Mahalanabis, "Development of an Improved Formulation of Oral Rehydration Salts (ORS) with Antidiarrhoeal and Nutritional Properties: a 'Super ORS'" (paper issued by the Diarrhoeal Diseases Control Programme of the World Health Organization), p. 9; "ORT Today and Tomorrow," *Dialogue on Diarrhoea*, No. 41 (June 1990), p. 1; P. Lepage, et al., "Food based Oral Rehydration Salt Solution for Acute Childhood Diarrhoea," cited in *Dialogue on Diarrhoea*, No. 41 (June 1990), p. 4; A. Bari, et al., "Community Study of Rice Based ORS in Rural Bangladesh," International Centre for Diarrhoeal Diseases Research, Bangladesh, cited in *Dialogue on Diarrhoea*, No. 41 (June 1990), p. 5; "Roundtable: The Politics of the Solution," *Links Health and Development Report*, Vol. 7, No. 3/4 (fall/winter 1990), p. 12 (comment by Norbert Hirschhorn).

220   *Oral Rehydration Therapy: A Revolution in Child Survival.* Oelgeschlager, Gunn & Hain, Weston MA, 1988. p. 25. Also Molla, A.M, Ahmed, S.M., and Greenough III, W.B. "Rice-based Oral Rehydration Solution Decreases Stool Volume in Acute Diarrhoea." *Bulletin of the WHO*, 63:4, 1985, pp. 751–56.

221 J.C. Waterlow and P.R. Payne, "The Protein Gap," *Nature*, Vol 258, Nov. 13, 1976, p. 117.; David Morley and Margaret Woodland, *See How They Grow, Monitoring Child Growth for Appropriate Health Care in Developing Countries*, Macmillan Press, 1979, p. 80.

222 Vincent Fauveau, M. Yunus, M. Shafiqul Islam, André Briend, and Michael L. Bennish, "Does ORT Reduce Diarrhoeal Mortality?," *Health Policy and Planning,* Vol. 7 (1992), No. 3, pp. 243–250; Juliana Yartey, Francis Nkrumah, Hiroki Hori, Kofi Harrison and Doris Armar, "Clinical Trial of Fermented Maize-based Oral Rehydration Solution in the Management of Acute Diarrhoea in Children," *Annals of Tropical Paediatrics,* (1995), 15, 61–68.

223 Carol P. MacCormack, "Health and the Social Power of Women," *Social Science and Medicine,* 26 no. 7 (1988), p. 677. Cited in Kent, p. 115.

224 Raj. K. Sachar et al., "Home-Based Education of Mothers in Treatment of Diarrhoea with Oral Rehydration Solution," *Journal of Diarrhoeal Disease Research,* Vol. 3, No. 1 (March 1985), p. 30; Vincent Fauveau, M. Yunus, M. Shafiqul Islam, André Briend, and Michael L. Bennish, "Does ORT Reduce Diarrhoeal Mortality?," *Health Policy and Planning,* Vol. 7 (1992), No. 3, pp. 243–250.

225 Norbert Hirschhorn and William B. Greenough III, "Progress in Oral Rehydration Therapy," *Scientific American,* Vol. 264, No. 5 (May 1991), p. 54; "Roundtable: The Politics of the Solution," *Links Health and Development Report,* Vol. 7, No. 3/4 (fall/winter 1990), p. 12 (comment by Norbert Hirschhorn).

226 C. MacCormack and A. Draper, *Cultural Meanings of Oral Rehydration Salts in Jamaica, 1988,* p. 285, from *The Context of Medicines in Developing Countries: Studies in Pharmaceutical Anthropology, 1988,* Edited by Sjaak Van Der Geest and Susan Reynolds Whyte.

227 David Werner and Bill Bower, *Helping Health Workers Learn,* 1982, pp. **24**–17—**24**–22.

228 *Dialogue on Diarrhoea,* No. 41 (June 1990), p. 1.

229 Juliana Yartey, Francis Nkrumah, Hiroki Hori, Kofi Harrison and Doris Armar, "Clinical Trial of Fermented Maize-based Oral Rehydration Solution in the Management of Acute Diarrhoea in Children," *Annals of Tropical Paediatrics,* (1995) 15, pp. 61, 67.

230 WHO Programme for Control of Diarrhoeal Diseases, *Interim Programme Report 1990,* p. 23.

231 Unpublished study by Helen Murphy, Mojid Molla, Abdul Bari, and Norbert Hirschhorn, conducted with Afghan refugee families. (This study was submitted to the Journal of Tropical Paediatrics, whose referees said cereal based ORT is already proven, why another report!?)

232 D. Mahalanabis, "Development of an Improved Formulation of Oral Rehydration Salts (ORS) with Antidiarrhoeal and Nutritional Properties: A 'Super ORS'" (paper issued by the Diarrhoeal Diseases Control Programme of the World Health Organization), p. 9; Roger M. Goodall, "Editorial Perspective," *Journal of Diarrhoeal Disease Research,* 3 (4) (December 1985), pp. 197–198.

233 WHO Diarrhoeal Disease Control Programme, *Report of the Twelfth Meeting of the Technical Advisory Group* (Geneva, March 18–22, 1991), p. 13.

234 A workshop on "Improving Young Child Feeding in Eastern and Southern Africa" sponsored by UNICEF, SIDA (the Swedish International Development Authority), and IDRC (the Canadian International Development Research Committee) and held in Nairobi, Kenya in October 1987 provided substantial documentation of the benefits of fermented porridges and germinated flour as weaning foods. See A. Tomkins, D. Alnwick, and P. Haggerty, "Fermented Foods for Improving Child Feeding in Eastern and Southern Africa: A Review," in D. Alnwick, S. Moses, and O.G. Schmidt (eds.), *Improving Young Child Feeding in Eastern and Southern Africa: Household-Level Food Technology—Proceedings of a Workshop Held in Nairobi, Kenya,* 12–16 October 1987, p. 136.

235 Juliana Yartey, Francis Nkrumah, Hiroki Hori, Kofi Harrison and Doris Armar, "Clinical Trial of Fermented Maize-based Oral Rehydration Solution in the Management of Acute Diarrhoea in Children," *Annals of Tropical Paediatrics,* (1995) 15, pp. 61– 68; Mensah PPA, Tomkins AM, Drasar BS, Harrison TJ, "Effect of Fermentation of Ghanaian Maize Dough on the Survival and Proliferation of Four Strains of Shigella Flexneri," *Transactions of the Royal Society of Tropical Medicine and Hygiene,* (1988) **82**, pp. 635–636; Mensah et al, "Fermentation of Cereals for Reduction of Bacterial Contamination of Weaning Foods in Ghana," *Lancet* (1990), **336**: pp. 140–143; Nout MJR, Rombouts FM, Hautvast GJ, "Accelerated Natural Lactic Acid Fermentation of Infant Food Formulations," *International Journal of Food Microbiology,* (1989) Jul. 8(4) pp. 351–361 (Cited in Yartey).

236 David Werner, "Egypt: Another Approaching Storm in the Desert," *Newsletter from the Sierra Madre,* June, 1991, p. 1–11. (HealthWrights papers)

237 A. Tomkins, D. Alnwick, and P. Haggerty, "Fermented Foods for Improving Child Feeding in Eastern and Southern Africa: A Review," in D. Alnwick, S. Moses, and O.G. Schmidt (eds.), *Improving Young Child Feeding in Eastern and Southern Africa: Household-Level Food Technology—Proceedings of a Workshop Held in Nairobi, Kenya, 12–16 October 1987,* p. 138; Patience P.A. Mensah, Andrew Tomkins, and Bohumil Drasar, "Fermented Food: Reducing Contamination," *Dialogue on Diarrhoea,* No. 40 (March 1990), p. 3.

238 Ibid., A Tomkins et al., p. 138.

239 Ibid., p. 157.

240 Ibid., "Executive Summary," p. xv.

241 Ibid., p. 138.

242 K.H. Brown, K.L. Dickin, M.E. Bentley, G.A. Oni, V.T. Obasaju, S.A. Esrey, S. Mebrahtu, I. Alade, and R.Y. Stallings, "Consumption of Weaning Foods from Fermented Cereals in Kwara State, Nigeria," in D. Alnwick, S. Moses, and O.G. Schmidt (eds.), Improving Young Child Feeding in Eastern and Southern Africa: Household-Level Food Technology—Proceedings of a Workshop Held in Nairobi, Kenya, 12–16 October 1987, p. 138, pp. 186–187; "Solving the Weanling's Dilemma: Power-Flour to Fuel the Gruel?," *Lancet,* Vol. 338, September 7, 1991, pp. 604–605.

243 K.H. Brown, K.L. Dickin, M.E. Bentley, G.A. Oni, V.T. Obasaju, S.A. Esrey, S. Mebrahtu, I. Alade, and R.Y. Stallings, "Consumption of Weaning Foods from Fermented Cereals in Kwara State, Nigeria," in D. Alnwick, S. Moses, and O.G. Schmidt (eds.), Improving Young Child Feeding in Eastern and Southern Africa: Household-Level Food Technology—Proceedings of a Workshop Held in Nairobi, Kenya, 12–16 October 1987, p. 138; Stephanie Gallat, "Improved Weaning Foods: Germinated Flours," *Dialogue on Diarrhoea,* No. 40 (March 1990), p. 4.

244 Stephanie Gallat, "Improved Weaning Foods: Germinated Flours," *Dialogue on Diarrhoea,* No. 40 (March 1990), p. 4.

245 Tara Gopaldas, Pallavi Mehta, Asha Patil, and Hemangini Gandhi, "Studies on Reduction in Viscosity of Thick Rice Gruels with Small Quantities of an Amylase-Rich Cereal Malt," *Food and Nutrition Bulletin,* Vol. 8, No. 4, pp. 42–47.

ENDNOTES: PART 3

1   Thomas McKeown and C.R. Lowe, *An Introduction to Social Medicine,* Blackwell, Oxford, 1974, p. 237.

2   *Weekly Reports of the Department of Health, New York City,* vol. ZZI, no. 50, December 17, 1932, p 396, cited in Walsh McDermott, Modern medicine and the demographic-disease pattern of overly traditional societies: a technological misfit, also cited in *Assignment Children 61/62,* UNICEF, 1983.

3   Edgar Mohs, "Changing Health Paradigms in Costa Rica," in *Reaching Health for All,* eds. Jon Rohde, Meera Chatterjee and David Morley, Oxford University Press, 1993, p. 391.

4   Thomas McKeown, *The Role of Medicine: Dream, Mirage or Nemesis?* (Princeton, New Jersey: Princeton University Press, 1979), pp. 50–55.

5   Thomas McKeown, *The Role of Medicine: Dream Mirage or Nemesis?,* Nuffield Provincial Hospitals Trust, 1976, p. 40.

6   The information in this section is drawn from David Sanders with Richard Carver, *The Struggle for Health: Medicine and the Politics of Underdevelopment* (London: Macmillan, 1985), pp. 25–37.

7   Alastair Gray, ed., *World Health and Disease* (Buckingham, England: Open University Press, 1993), p. 58.

8   Ibid.

9   Ibid.

10 David Sanders, *The Struggle for Health: Medicine and the Politics of Underdevelopment* (London: Macmillan, 1985), p. 31; David Alnwick, "The Weight, Length, and Mid Upper Arm Circumference of Kenyan Children in Nairobi Nursery Schools," *Unicef Social Statistics Bulletin,* Vol. 3, No. 1, 1980.

11 Alastair Gray, ed., *World Health and Disease* (Buckingham, England: Open University Press, 1993), p. 61.

12 UNICEF, *State of the World's Children, 1993,* p. 26.

13 David Sanders, *The Struggle for Health,* Macmillan, 1985, p. 49.

14 From a speech Douglass made in New York in 1857. James MacGregor Burns and Stewart Burns, *A People's Charter: The Pursuit of Rights in America* (New York: Alfred A. Knopf, 1991), frontispiece.

15 "Multinationals—The Facts," *New Internationalist,* August 1993, p. 18.

16 Frances Moore Lappé and Rachel Schurman, *The Missing Piece in the Population Puzzle,* Food First Development Report no. 4 (San Francisco: Institute for Food and Development Policy, 1988), p. 20. Cited in Kent, p. 127.

17 Hal Kane, *The Hour of Departure: Forces that Create Refugees and Migrants,* Worldwatch Institute, June 1995, p. 15.

18 Anne E. Platt, *Infecting Ourselves: How Environmental and Social Disruptions Trigger Disease,* Worldwatch Institute, April 1996, p. 26.

19 David Sanders, *The Struggle for Health,* Macmillan, 1985, p. 68.

20 Martin Brockerhoff, "Child Survival in Big Cities: The Disadvantages of Migrants," Social Science and Medicine, Vol. 40, No. 10, May 1995, pp. 1371–1383.

21 Giovanni Andrea Cornia, Richard Jolly and Frances Stewart, eds., *Adjustment with a Human Face, Volume 1, Protecting the Vulnerable and Promoting Growth,* (Clarendon Press, Oxford, 1987, p. 6.

22 Kent, p. 69.

23 Ibid, pp. 164–165.

24 Ibid, p. 165.

25 Hilary F. French, "Forging a New Partnership," *State of the World 1995,* Worldwatch Institute, 1995, p. 176.

26 UNICEF, *State of the World's Children, 1989,* p. 15.

27 The US banks involved included Banker's Trust, Bank of America, Chase Manhattan, Chemical, Citicorp, Continental, Illinois, First Chicago, Manufacturers Hanover, and Morgan Guaranty. Source: "A Review of Bank Performance, 1986," *New Internationalist,* November 1988, p. 16.

28 Periodistas del Tercer Mundo, *Third World Guide, 1986–87* (New York: Grove Press, 1987), p. 548.

29 Quoted by Ned Daly, "Empty promises at the Social Summit," *Multinational Monitor,* April 1995, p. 6–7.

30 Chakravarthi Raghavan, "World's Poor Got Poorer in 1980s," *Third World Resurgence,* No. 10 (June 1991), p. 10.

31 UNICEF, *State of the World's Children, 1989,* p. 15.

32 Gary Gardner, "Third World Debt Still Growing," *Vital Signs 1995,* Worldwatch Institute, 1995, p. 73.

33 UNICEF, *State of the World's Children, 1989,* p. 15.

34 Ibid., p. 15.

35 Medea Benjamin and Kevin Danaher, "Latin America's Struggle for Democratic Development," *Global Exchanges* (newsletter of Global Exchange), Issue #11 (Summer 1992), p. 6.

36 Chakravarthi Raghavan, "World's Poor Got Poorer in 1980s," *Third World Resurgence,* No. 10 (June 1991), p. 10.

37 Grant, p. 85.

38 UNICEF, *State of the World's Children, 1992,* p. 16.

39 Gary Gardner, "Third World Debt Still Growing," *Vital Signs 1995, The Trends That Are Shaping Our Future,* Worldwatch Institute, 1995, p. 72.

40 Hal Kane, "Third World Debt Still Rising," *Vital Signs 1994,* Worldwatch Institute, 1994, p. 75.

41 Medea Benjamin and Kevin Danaher, "Latin America's Struggle for Democratic Development," *Global Exchanges* (newsletter of Global Exchange), Issue #11 (Summer 1992), p. 1.

42 Gary Gardner, "Third World Debt Still Growing," *Vital Signs 1995, The Trends That Are Shaping Our Future,* Worldwatch Institute, 1995, p. 72.; John Darton, "In Poor, Decolonialized Africa, Bankers are Overlords," *New York Times,* June 20, 1994.

43 Medea Benjamin and Kevin Danaher, "Latin America's Struggle for Democratic Development," *Global Exchanges* (newsletter of Global Exchange), Issue #11 (Summer 1992), p. 6.

44 Jesse Jackson, to eleven African heads of state, Libreville, Gabon, May 27, 1993.

45 "Reining in the IMF" (editorial), *Multinational Monitor,* June 1991, p. 5.

46 Jonathan Cahn, "Challenging the New Imperial Authority: The World Bank and the Democratization of Development," *Harvard Human Rights Journal* 6 (1993): 160, Cited in David Korten, "When Corporations Rule the World," (Kumarian Press, West Hartford, Connecticut, 1995), p. 165.

47 Samir Amin, "Don't Adjust — Delink!," *Toward Freedom,* April/May 1993, p. 2.

48 Imogen Evans, "SAPping Maternal Health," *The Lancet,* Vol. 346, p. 1046, Oct 21 1995.

49 UNICEF, *Problems and Priorities Regarding Recurrent Costs* (1988), p.12.

50 Medea Benjamin and Kevin Danaher, "Latin America's Struggle for Democratic Development," *Global Exchanges* (newsletter of Global Exchange), Issue #11 (Summer 1992), p. 6.

51 Andrea Bárcena, "De 80 a 90% de Mexicanos Fue Desnutrido Infantil y Perdió Capacidad Física y Mental," *Proceso,* June 1, 1987, p. 6.

52 David Werner and Jason Weston, "The Hidden Costs of Free Trade: Mexico Bites the Bullet," *Newsletter from the Sierra Madre,* #31, (HealthWrights) May 1995, p. 5.

53 "Update, Human Rights," *New Internationalist,* April 1996, p. 6.

54 UNICEF, *State of the World's Children, 1989,* p. 2.

55 Davies, R. and D. Sanders, "Economic Strategies, Structural Adjustment and Health Policy: Issues in Sub-Saharan Africa for the 1990s," *Transformation 21,* 1993, pp. 78–93; David Sanders and Adbulrahman Sambo, "AIDS in Africa: The Implications of Economic Recession and Structural Adjustment," *Health Policy and Planning,* Vol. 6 (1991), No. 2, p. 160.

56 See, for example, Robert Weissman, "The IMF and Labor Repression in Central America," *Multinational Monitor,* June 1991, pp. 25–27.

57 UNICEF, *State of the World's Children, 1989,* pp. 30–31. Cited in Kent, p. 88.

58 Kent, p. 88.

59 Samir Amin, "Don't Adjust — Delink!," *Toward Freedom,* April/May 1993, p. 2.

60 *New Internationalist,* Nov. 1988, pp. 16–17.

61 Gary Gardner, "Third World Debt Still Growing," *Vital Signs 1995, The Trends That Are Shaping Our Future,* Worldwatch Institute, 1995, p. 72.; Rafael Soifer, "Stealth Lending: The Quiet Return of LDC Debt," *Banking Outlook* (Brown Brothers Harriman & Co.), September 29, 1994.

62 David Korten, "When Corporations Rule the World," (Kumarian Press, West Hartford, Connecticut, 1995), p. 171.

63 Both quotes cited in Ned Daly "Empty promises at UN summit" *Multinational Monitor* April 1995.

64 Dinyar Godrej, "Hunger in a world of plenty" *New Internationalist,* May 1995, p 7–10.

65 Lester Brown, Nicholas Lenssen, Hal Kane, *Vital Statistics 1995,* Worldwatch Institute, p. 146.

66 UNDP, 29/6/94, quoted in *The Social Summit Seen From the South.* Page 31. Norwegian Summit for Environment and Development, 1995.

67 Speth, J.G., UNDP, 29/6/94, quoted in *The Social Summit Seen From the South.* Page 31. Norwegian Summit for Environment and Development, 1995.

68 Dinyar Godrej, "Hunger in a world of plenty" *New Internationalist,* May 1995, p 7–10; David Korten, "When Corporations Rule the World," (Kumarian Press, West Hartford, Connecticut, 1995), p. 83.

69 Dinyar Godrej, "Hunger in a world of plenty" *New Internationalist,* May 1995, p 7–10.

70 Ibid.

71 David Korten, "When Corporations Rule the World," (Kumarian Press, West Hartford, Connecticut, 1995), p. 157.

72 William Greider, *Who Will Tell the People? The Betrayal of American Society,* (New York: Simon and Schuster, 1992), p. 331.

73 Baby Milk Action, *Profits Before Health, An Analysis of Nestlé's Baby Food Marketing Policy,* May 1995, p. 3.

74 Russell Mokhiber, "Infant Formula: Hawking Disaster in the Third World," *Multinational Monitor,* Vol. 8, No. 4 (April 1987), p. 22; Marsha Walker, "A Fresh Look at the Risks of Artificial Infant Feeding," *Journal of Human Lactation,* 9(2) 1993, pp.97–98.

75 UNICEF, *State of the World's Children, 1995,* p. 20.

76 UNICEF, *State of the World's Children, 1993,* p. 44.

77 Ibid.

78 Ibid.

79 IBFAN, *Protecting Infant Health, A Health Worker's Guide to the International Code of Marketing of Breastmilk Substitutes,* 7th edition, June 1993, p. 8.

80 Ibid., p. 9.

81 John D. Clemens, et al., "Breast Feeding and the Risk of Severe Cholera in Rural Bangladeshi Children," *American Journal of Epidemiology,* Vol. 131, No. 3 (1990), pp. 400–411.

82 C.G. Victora, et al., "Evidence for Protection by Breast-Feeding Against Infant Deaths from Infectious Diseases in Brazil," *Lancet,* 1987, No. 2, pp. 319–321. Cited in Fitzroy Henry, Andre Briend, and Vincent Fauveau, "Child Survival: Should the Strategy Be Redesigned? Experience from Bangladesh," *Health Policy and Planning,* Vol. 5, No. 3 (1990), p. 231.

83 R. Hogan and J. Martinez, "Breastfeeding as an Intervention within Diarrheal Diseases Control Programs: WHO/CDD Activities," *International Journal of Gynecology and Obstetrics,* Vol. 31, Supplement 1 (1990), pp. 115–119.

84 UNICEF (in collaboration with WHO and UNESCO), *Facts for Life,* 1989, p. 20.

85 BUNSO, "Breastmilk. Wasted Natural Resource," in Health Action Information Network (HAIN), *Health Alert,* Vol. VII, No. 122 (October 1991), p. 289.

86 Leonard A. Sagan, *The Health of Nations: True Causes of Sickness and Well-Being.* Cited in Kent, p. 61.

87 UNICEF, "Breast-feeding and Health," Assignment Children, 55/56, 1981.

88 Patti Rundall, "Nestle Boycott Success," *Child* (the magazine of the International Child Health Group), April 1993, p. 10., International Baby Food Action Network (IBFAN), *Breaking the Rules, 1994, A Worldwide Report on Violations of the WHO/UNICEF International Code of Marketing of Breastmilk Substitutes,* p. 27.

89 Logan Brenzel and Norbert Hirschhorn, *Executive Summary of the UNICEF Macro and Micro Studies* (a report prepared by John Snow, Inc.), p. 4. The five countries are Bolivia, Colombia, Indonesia, Kenya, and Senegal.

90 C. Marmet, "Summary of Institutional Actions Affecting Breastfeeding," *Journal of Human Lactation,* 9(2), 1993, p. 110.

91 Felicity Savage King and Ann Burgess, *Nutrition for Developing Countries,* 2nd edition, 1992, Oxford University Press, p. 107.

92 Ibid., IBFAN, p. 12.

93 Medea Benjamin and Andrea Freedman, *Bridging the Global Gap: A Handbook to Linking Citizens of the First and Third Worlds,* (Washington, D.C.: Seven Locks Press, 1989), p. 142.

94 IBFAN, *Protecting Infant Health, A Health Worker's Guide to the International Code of Marketing of Breastmilk Substitutes,* 7th edition, June 1993, p. 11. Medea Benjamin and Andrea Freedman, *Bridging the Global Gap: A Handbook to Linking Citizens of the First and Third Worlds* (Washington, D.C.: Seven Locks Press, 1989), p. 142.

95 Patti Rundall, "Nestle Boycott Success," *Child* (the magazine of the International Child Health Group), April 1993, p. 10.

96   Ibid.

97   Medea Benjamin and Andrea Freedman, *Bridging the Global Gap: A Handbook to Linking Citizens of the First and Third Worlds* (Washington, D.C.: Seven Locks Press, 1989), p. 143; "Nestle's Again," *World Development Forum*, Vol. 6, No. 18 (October 15, 1988), p. 4.

98   Patti Rundall, "Nestle Boycott Success," *Child* (the magazine of the International Child Health Group), April 1993, p. 10.

99   IBFAN, *Breaking the Rules, 1994, Worldwide Report on Violations of the WHO/UNICEF International Code of Marketing of Breastmilk Substitutes,* July, 1994, pp. 27–29.

100   Baby Milk Action, *Profits Before Health, An Analysis of Nestlé's Baby Food Marketing Policy,* May 1995, p. 4.

101   Patti Rundall, "Nestle Boycott Success," *Child*, April 1993, p. 10.

102   John W. Egan, Harlow N. Higinbotham and J. Fred Weston, *Economics of the Pharmaceutical Industry*, (Praeger Publishers) 1982, p. 4; *Standard and Poor's Industry Surveys*, April, 1995, p. H19; Meri Koivusalo, Eeva Ollila, *International Organizations and Health Policies*, (Stakes/Hedec) Helsinki, 1996, p. 175.

103   "Golden Pills," *The Economist*, March 20, 1993, p. 74. This estimate, like all the information in this article, is drawn from a study by the Office of Technology Assessment. The study defines excess profits as profits over and above the profit incentive required to stimulate investment in research and development.

104   Peretz, S.M. "Pharmaceuticals in the Third World: the problem from the suppliers point of view," *World Development*, 1983:11:(259–64), cited in Meri Koivusalo, Eeva Ollila, *International Organizations and Health Policies*, (Stakes/Hedec) Helsinki, 1996, p. 175.

105   Andrew Chetley, *Problem Drugs,* Zed Books, 1995, p. 9.

106   Askin, "Pills, Potions and Placebos," *Environmental Action*, Vol. 17, No. 5 (March/April 1986), p. 25.

107   WHO, *The Management of Diarrhea, Practical Guidelines*, Third Edition, 1993, p. 24.

108   Iris Rosendahl, "Antacids/Antidiarrheals Churn up Sales Gains," *Drug Topics*, Vol. 135, No. 14, July 22, 1991, p. 55.

109   Askin, "Pills, Potions and Placebos," *Environmental Action*, Vol. 17, No. 5 (March/April 1986), p. 23.

110   Christopher Scanlan, "Unsafe Drugs Find Buyers Abroad," *Detroit Free Press,* May 20, 1991, p. 4A.

111   Christopher Scanlan, "Unsafe Drugs Find Buyers Abroad," *Detroit Free Press,* May 20, 1991, p. 1.

112   Ibid.

113   Dianna Melrose, *Bitter Pills: Medicines and the Third World Poor* (Oxford: OXFAM, 1982), p. 113. Many similar examples are given in *Bitter Pills,* Milton Silverman, *The Drugging of the Americas* (Berkeley: University of California Press, 1976), and Michael Tan, *Dying for Drugs: Pill Power and Politics in the Philippines* (Quezon City, Philippines: Health Action Information Network, 1988).

114   Christopher Scanlan, "Unsafe Drugs Find Buyers Abroad," *Detroit Free Press,* May 20, 1991, p. 4A.

115   Steve Askin. "Pills, Potions and Placebos," *Environmental Action*, Vol. 17, No. 5 (March/April 1986), p. 23.

116   "Disadvantages of the Irrational Use of Drugs for Diarrhoea," *Essential Drugs Monitor* (a publication of the WHO Action Programme on Essential Drugs and Vaccines), No. 11 (1991), p. 11.

117   David Sanders, *The Struggle for Health: Medicine and the Politics of Underdevelopment* (London: Macmillan, 1985), p. 136.

118   Milton Silverman, *The Drugging of the Americas,* University of California Press, 1976, p. 119–120; Dr. K Balasubramaniam, "Retail Drug Prices in the Asia-Pacific Region," *HAInews*, Consumers International for Health Action International, Penang, Malaysia, Number 86, December 1995.

119   David Werner, "Dying for Doctors," the *New Internationalist,* No. 182 (April 1988), p. 9; David Werner and Bill Bower, *Helping Health Workers Learn,* p. 18–7.

120   Joel Lexchin, "Pharmaceutical Promotion in the Third World," *Journal of Drug Issues*, 22(2), Spring 1992, p. 420.

121   Ibid.

122   Ibid., p. 421.

123   "Drug Prices," *Health Letter* (the newsletter of the Public Citizen's Health Research Group), p. 11.

124   David Sanders, *The Struggle for Health: Medicine and the Politics of Underdevelopment* (London: Macmillan, 1985), p. 137; "Drug Prices," *Health Letter* (the newsletter of the Public Citizen's Health Research Group), p. 11.

125   Milton Silverman, Philip R. Lee and Mia Lydecker, *Prescriptions for Death: The Drugging of the Third World,* University of California Press, 1982, p. 124.

126   UNICEF, *State of the World's Children, 1993,* p. 52.

127   Milton Silverman, Mia Lydecker, Philip R. Lee, *Bad Medicine,* Stanford University Press, 1992, pp. 129–136.

128   Ibid., pp. 140–141.

129   See for example "Baker Urges Cutting Off of Funds if UN Agencies Upgrade PLO," *New York Times,* May 2, 1989, p. A6.

130   Askin, "Pills, Potions and Placebos," *Environmental Action*, Vol. 17, No. 5 (March/April 1986), p. 26.

131   Andrew Chetley and Wilbert Bannenberg, "Skirmishes in the Pill Jungle," *South,* February 1986, p. 64.

132   Ibid.

133   Ibid.

134   Ibid.

135   AnitaHarden, Health Action International, as reported in Koivusalo, Meri, and Ollila, Eeva, *International Health Policies with Special Reference to the WHO, World Bank and UNICEF,* 1995, unpublished independent evaluation. Pages 48–49

136   Koivusalo, Meri, and Ollila, Eeva, *International Health Policies with Special Reference to the WHO, World Bank and UNICEF,* 1995, unpublished independent evaluation. Page 49.

137   Orr, "Rexall for Profits," *Dollars and Sense,* No. 128 (July/August 1987), p. 21.

138   WHO, *The Rational Use of Drugs in the Treatment of Acute Diarrhoea in Children* 1990.

139   Olle Hansson, *Inside Ciba-Geigy* (The Hague: International Organization of Consumer Unions, 1989), pp. 21–22.

140   Olle Hansson, *Inside Ciba-Geigy* (The Hague: International Organization of Consumer Unions, 1989), pp. 14–24; Milton Silverman, Philip R. Lee, and Mia Lydecker, *Prescriptions for Death: The Drugging of the Third World* (Berkeley: University of California Press, 1982), pp. 48–49.

141   Olle Hansson, *Inside Ciba-Geigy* (The Hague: International Organization of Consumer Unions, 1989).

142   Ibid., pp. 14–15.

143 Ibid., p. 15.

144 Ibid., pp. 25–28, pp. 59–62; Milton Silverman, Philip R. Lee, and Mia Lydecker, *Prescriptions for Death: The Drugging of the Third World* (Berkeley: University of California Press, 1982), pp. 47–48.

145 Ibid., Hansson, pp. 8–11.

146 Ibid., p. 13. This was the number of victims that was eventually recognized officially; the real figure may be as high as 20,000 to 30,000. Ibid.., p. 12.

147 This was the total as of mid–1985. Ibid., p. 211.

148 Ibid., p. 10; Milton Silverman, Philip R. Lee, and Mia Lydecker, *Prescriptions for Death: The Drugging of the Third World* (Berkeley: University of California Press, 1982), p. 49.

149 Ibid., Silverman, p. 49, pp. 52–58.

150 Olle Hansson, *Inside Ciba-Geigy* (The Hague: International Organization of Consumer Unions, 1989), p. 14, p. 204.

151 "Antidiarrhoeals in Latin America," *HAI News,* No. 58 (April 1991), p. 5.

152 *Programme for the Control of Diarrhoeal Disease: Interim Programme Report 1992,* World Health Organization, 1993 p. 54.

153 *Programme for the Control of Diarrhoeal Disease: Ninth Programme Report 1992–1993* World Health Organization, 1994 p. 103.

154 Both David Werner and David Sanders attended this conference.

155 "Comment," *The Kangaroo: Bibliographic Archives for Maternal and Child Health in Developing Countries,* Vol. 1, No. 1 (December 1992), p. 23.

156 This list of sponsors was on the printed Program of the International Symposium on Food-Based Oral Rehydration Therapy, November 12–14, 1989, the Aga Khan University, Karachi, Pakistan.

157 These observations were made by the authors, talking with the meeting participants.

158 Milton Silverman, Philip R. Lee, and Mia Lydecker, Prescriptions for Death: The Drugging of the Third World, pp. 119–130; Milton Silverman, Mia Lydecker, Philip R. Lee, *Bad Medicine,* Stanford University Press, 1992, pp. 238–240; Dianna Melrose, *Bitter Pills: Medicines and the Third World poor,* OXFAM, 1982, pp. 83–85.

159 Michael Renner, *Budgeting for Disarmament: The Costs of War and Peace,* Worldwatch paper 122, Nov 1994, p. 5.

160 United Nations Development Program, *Human Development Report 1994* (New York and Oxford, Oxford University Press, 1994). Cited in Michael Renner, *Budgeting for Disarmament: The Costs of War and Peace,* Worldwatch paper 122, Nov 1994, p. 10.

161 UNICEF, *State of the World's Children 1996,* p. 13.

162 Randall Forsberg, "Force Without Reason," *Boston Review* vol XX no. 3.

163 Marek Thee, "The Third Special Session of the UN General Assembly Devoted to Disarmament: between Armaments and Disarmament," *Transnational Perspectives,* Vol. 14, No. 3 (1988), pp. 6–11.

164 UNICEF, *State of the World's Children, 1996,* p. 25.

165 "We Arm the World: US is Number One Weapons Dealer," *The Defense Monitor,* Vol. XX, No. 4 (1991), p. 3.

166 UNICEF, *State of the World's Children, 1987,* p. 17. Cited in Kent, pp. 98–99.

167 UNICEF, *State of the World's Children, 1986,* p. 72.

168 Ibid., p. 72.

169 UNICEF, *State of the World's Children, 1990,* p. 1.

170 Oscar Arias Sanchez, "Demilitarisation the Key to Development," *Third World Resurgence,* No. 11 (July 1991), p. 9.

171 Kent, p. 117.

172 Kent, pp. 111–112. Kent cites Ruth Leger Sivard, *World Military and Social Expenditures 1986* (Washington, D.C.: World Priorities, 1986), pp. 24, 36–41.

173 Ibid., pp. 117–118.

174 Ibid., p. 112.

175 Ibid, p. 112.

176 Sivard, *World Military and Social Expenditures, 1987–88,* p. 5.

177 Susan George, *A Fate Worse than Debt,* p. 22; Oscar Arias Sanchez, "Demilitarisation the Key to Development," *Third World Resurgence,* No. 11 (July 1991), p. 9.

178 Lappé and Collins, *World Hunger: Twelve Myths,* p. 118.

179 Frances Moore Lappé, Rachel Schurman, and Kevin Danaher, Betraying the National Interest (Grove Press, 1987), p. 11.

180 Lappé, Schurman, and Danaher, *Betraying the National Interest,* p. 31.

181 Michael Renner, *Budgeting for Disarmament: The Costs of War and Peace,* Worldwatch paper 122, Nov 1994, p. 6.

182 "Protecting Children from the Scourge of War," *The Coordinators' Notebook: An International Resource for Early Childhood Development* (a publication of The Consultative Group on Early Childhood Care and Development), No. 10 (October 1991), p. 2.

183 Neil Boothby, "Children and War," *Cultural Survival Quarterly,* 10, no. 4 (1986), pp. 28–30. Cited in Kent, p. 95.

184 Kent, p. 95.

185 "Protecting Children from the Scourge of War," *The Coordinators' Notebook: An International Resource for Early Childhood Development* (a publication of The Consultative Group on Early Childhood Care and Development), No. 10 (October 1991), p. 5.

186 "Protecting Children from the Scourge of War," *The Coordinators' Notebook: An International Resource for Early Childhood Development* (a publication of The Consultative Group on Early Childhood Care and Development), No. 10 (October 1991), p. 5.

187 Philip Shenon, "Clinton to Act on Banning Many Types of War Mines," *New York Times,* May 16 1996, p. A7.

188 Michael Renner, *Budgeting for Disarmament: The Costs of War and Peace,* Worldwatch paper 122, Nov 1994, p. 20.

189 Philip Shenon, "Clinton to Act on Banning Many Types of War Mines," *New York Times,* May 16 1996, p. A7.

190 "Health and Welfare in Iraq: Excerpts from the Report of the International Study Team," *War Watch,* Issue #11–12 (November–December 1991), p. 5. This is a summary of the Report of the International Study Team on the Gulf Crisis, a follow-up to the original report of the Harvard Study Team.

191 Associated Press, "Iraqi Civilian Deaths in War's Aftermath Estimated at 70,000: Precise Allied Bombing Crippled the Nation," *San Francisco Chronicle,* January 9, 1992, p. A8.

192 *Evaluation of Food and Nutrition Situation in Iraq,* United Nations Food and Agriculture Organization report, 1995; cited in *The Children are Dying,* Ramsey Clark, FAO Report et al. (World View Forum, Inc., 1996).

193 Associated Press, "Iraqi Civilian Deaths in War's Aftermath Estimated at 70,000: Precise Allied Bombing Crippled the Nation," *San Francisco Chronicle,* January 9, 1992, p. A8.

194   Former Attorney General Ramsey Clark in an interview by Granma, March 12, 1995. From the Institute of Global Communications.

195   Kent, p. 55.

196   Reported to David Werner by members of the Ministry of Health during his visit to Mozambique, September, 1987; Gill Walt and Julie Cliff, "The Dynamics of Health Policies in Mozambique 1975–85," *Health Policy and Planning,* 1(2): 148–158, 1986.

197   UNICEF, *Adjustment with a Human Face.*

198   A. Creese, "User Charges for Health Care: A Review of Recent Experience," *Health Policy and Planning,* 6(4) (1991), pp. 309–319; S. Moses, F. Manji, J.E. Bradley, N.J. Nagelkerke, M.A. Malisa, and F.A. Plummer, "Impact of User Fees on Attendance at a Referral Centre for Sexually Transmitted Diseases in Kenya," *Lancet,* 1992, No. 340, pp. 463–466; C.J. Waddington and K.A. Enyimayew, "A Price to Pay: The Impact of User Charges in Ashanti-Akim District, Ghana," *International Journal of Health Planning and Management,* Vol. 4 (1989), pp. 17–47.

199   Slim Haddam and Pierre Fournier, "Quality, Cost and Utilization of Health Services in Developing Countries. A Longitudinal Study in Zaïre," *Social Science and Medicine,* Vol. 40, No. 6, March 1995, pp. 743–753.

200   Moses S, Manji F, Bradley JE, Nagelkerke NJ, Malisa MA, Plummer FA. "Impact of user fees on attendance at a referral centre for sexually transmitted diseases in Kenya." *Lancet* 1992; 340:463–6.

201   Editorial "Structural adjustment too painful" *Lancet,* Vol 344, Nov. 19, 1994, p 1377. The reference for this statement is Sanders D, Sambo A. "AIDS in Africa: the implication of economic recession and structural adjustment." *Health Policy Planning 1991; 6: 157–65.*

202   Editorial "Structural adjustment too painful" *Lancet.* Vol 344, Nov. 19 1994, p.1377–1378. (Also see *Lancet* Nov 12, p 1356.)

203   Alderman, H. "Downturn and Economic Recovery in Ghana: Impacts on the Poor," 1991 Cornell Food and Nutrition Policy Program Monograph 10.

204   "World Bank's Cure for Donor Fatigue," *Lancet.* Vol. 342, Number 8863, July 1993, p. 63.

205   Enyimayew *Cost and Financing of Drugs Supplied in Ghana—The Ashanti-Akim Experience,* (Paper presented at WHO conference, 1988, cited in *Beyond Adjustment: Responding to the Health Crisis in Africa,* Inter-Church Coalition on Africa (ICCAF), 1993.

206   David Werner, *The Life and Death of Primary Health Care or The McDonaldization of Alma Ata,* HealthWrights paper, 1994, p. 6.

207   World Bank, World Development Report, *Investing in Health,* 1993, p. 157.

208   Ibid., p. 2.

209   David Legge, "Applying the Leech," (A critique of *Investing in Health,* 1993, the World Bank's 16th World Development Report. Talk given to PHAA Annual Conference, Adelaide, Australia, Sept 26, 1994. Data extracted from *Investing in Health,* Table A5, p. 203.

210   World Bank, World Development Report, *Investing in Health,* 1993, p. 62.

211   Legge D, "Investing in the Shaping of World Health Policy," Prepared for the AIDAB, NCEPH and PHA workshop (Canberra, Australia, Aug. 31, 1993) to discuss the World Bank's 16th World Development Report, *Investing in Health.*

212   Werner D, "Health for No One by the Year 2000," *Third World Resurgence, No. 21, 1992.*

213   Ruck N, Stefanini A, "World Development Report 1993 – 'Investing in Health'—Old Wine in New Bottles?" *The Kangaroo,* December, 1993.

214   Legge D, "Investing in the Shaping of World Health Policy," Prepared for the AIDAB, NCEPH and PHA workshop (Canberra, Australia, Aug. 31, 1993) to discuss the World Bank's 16th World Development Report, *Investing in Health.*

215   "World Bank's Cure for Donor Fatigue," *Lancet.* Vol. 342, Number 8863, July 1993, p. 63.

216   Quoted in Harry Qasserman, *America Born and Reborn,* (New York: Collier Books, 1983), pp. 89–90.

217   UNICEF, *State of the World's Children Report, 1995,* pp. 66,67.

218   Ibid.

219   "Brazil: the persistence of inequality" *NACLA, Vol XXVII, No 6,May/June 1995,p. 16.*

220   Ibid.

221   UNICEF, *State of the World's Children Report, 1994,* p. 46.

222   UNICEF, *State of the World's Children, 1993,* p. 69.

223   Andrew L. Shapiro, *We're Number One!: Where America Stands — and Falls — in the New World Order* (New York: Vintage Books, 1992), p. 189.

224   World Bank, *World Development Report 1993, Investing in Health,* p. 4.

225   Associated Press, "U.S. Trails Poor Nations in Early Innoculation," *Washington Post,* June 6, 1993; Associated Press, "Million Toddlers Said to Need Vaccinations," *Washington Post,* May 5, 1995. Both cited in Anne E. Platt, *Infecting Ourselves: How Environmental and Social Disruptions Trigger Disease,* Worldwatch Paper 129, April 1996, p. 58.

226   Andrew L. Shapiro, *We're Number One!: Where America Stands—and Falls—in the New World Order* (New York: Vintage Books, 1992), pp. 8–9.

227   Thomas J. Lueck, "Tax Breaks for Companies Flow Despite Budget Cuts in New York," and Eric Schmitt, "Military Budget Would See Gains Under G.O.P. Plan, Pentagon Asks for Less," *New York Times,* July 5, 1995.

228   Business Week, quoted in "Life Imitates Shlock Art: Money Can't Buy You Love," *Too Much,* Council on International and Public Affairs, p. 4.

229   Figures from the Congressional Budget Office, as reported in *Time,* October 10, 1988, p. 29. Cited in George Kent, *The Politics of Children's Survival* (New York: Praeger, 1991), p. 83.

230   Victor W. Sidel, "Health Care in the United States: A Thousand Points of Blight," *Arthritis Care and Research,* Vol. 5, No. 2 (June 1992), p. 64.

231   Shapiro, pp. 20–21.

232   The estimate of 10,000 child deaths from poverty and hunger related causes comes from Sally Reed and R. Craig Sautter, "Children of Poverty," *Kappan Special Report,* June 1990, p. 3. Cited in Clarence Lusane, *Pipe Dream Blues: Racism and the War on Drugs* (Boston: South End Press, 1991), p 12. The estimate of 21,000 is calculated from UNICEF's *State of the World's Children 1995,* page 67, by comparing the Under 5 Mortality Rate of children in the US (10 per 1000) to that of Finland (U5MR of 5 per 1000), and thereby estimating that if living conditions for all children in the US were as good as in Finland, half of the 42,000 annual deaths in children under five could have been prevented.

233 Economic Policy Institute, Washington, D.C., Cited in Walden Bello, *Dark Victory: The United States, Structural Adjustment and Global Poverty,* Pluto Press, 1994, p. 137.

234 "House Block Grants = Permanent & Immoral National Child Neglect" Children's Defense Fund, Washington, D.C., March 28, 1995, p. 1.

235 Ibid. p. 1.

236 UNICEF, *State of the World's Children, 1995.* p. 59.

237 Brynn Craffey, "A Killer Returns," *Image* (the Sunday magazine of the *San Francisco Examiner*), June 14, 1992, pp. 6–13; Andrew L. Shapiro, *We're Number One!: Where America Stands — and Falls — in the New World Order* (New York: Vintage Books, 1992), p. 20.

238 Shapiro, p. 4.

239 "Who says there are no more heros?" *New York Times,* May 1, 1995. p. 9. In an ad by the California Wellness Foundation.

240 Fingerhut LA, Kleinman JC, "International and Interstate Comparison of Homicide Among Young Males," *JAMA*, 1990, 263:24; pp. 3293–3295.

241 Ibid., p. 270.

242 UNICEF, *State of the World's Children, 1992,* p. 22.

243 UNICEF, *State of the World's Children, 1994,* p. 46.

244 Tufts University study cited in "U.S. Children Going Hungry, Study Says," *San Francisco Chronicle,* June 15, 1993, p. A9.

245 "The State of Greed," *US News and World Report,* June 17, 1996, p. 62–63. 1989 is the most recent year analyzed by the internal revenue service.

246 Figures from the Congressional Budget Office, as reported in *Time,* October 10, 1988, p. 29. Cited in George Kent, *The Politics of Children's Survival* (New York: Praeger, 1991), p. 83.

247 Shapiro, p. 16; UNICEF, *State of the World's Children, 1993,* p. 69.

248 Sally Reed and R. Craig Sautter, "Children of Poverty," *Kappan Special Report,* June 1990, p. 3. Cited in Clarence Lusane, *Pipe Dream Blues: Racism and the War on Drugs* (Boston: South End Press, 1991), p 12.

249 Shapiro, pp. 8–9.

250 Victor W. Sidel, "Health Care in the United States: A Thousand Points of Blight," *Arthritis Care and Research,* Vol. 5, No. 2 (June 1992), p. 64.

251 UNICEF, *State of the World's Children, 1994,* p. 46.

252 UNICEF, *State of the World's Children, 1994,* p. 46.

253 "Health Index," *Links,* Vol. 9 #4, Fall, 1992, p. 13.

254 Shapiro, p. 73.

255 Clarence Lusane, *Pipe Dream Blues: Racism and the War on Drugs* (Boston: South End Press, 1991), p. 23.

256 Shapiro, p. 17.

257 "Forgotten Americans" (editorial), *American Health,* November 1990, pp. 41–42.

258 1990 study conducted by a 37-member commission including former Surgeon general C. Everett Koop and pollster George Gallup.

259 Ibid.

260 UNICEF, *The Progress of Nations,* p. 34, 1995.

261 Tom Peck and Christine Vida, "Media violence and its relationship to violent crime." Copyright 1993. Unpublished paper.

262 Shapiro, p. 4.

263 Affirmative Action is Under Election Year Attack," *The Washington Spectator,* July 1, 1995, p. 3.

264 UNICEF, *State of the World's Children, 1995,* p. 66.

265 Ibid.

266 Ibid.

267 Ibid, pp. 78,79.

268 Ibid, pp. 66, 67, 72–79.

269 UNICEF, *State of the World's Children, 1993, 1994,* a comparative analysis.

270 Graham Hancock, *Lords of Poverty: The Power, Prestige, and Corruption of the International Aid Business,* p. 131.

271 UNICEF *State of the World's Children* 1995, p. 66.

272 UNICEF, *State of the World's Children, 1993, 1994,* a comparative analysis.

273 UNICEF, *State of the World's Children, 1995,* p. 67.

274 UNICEF, *State of the World's Children, 1995,* p. 76.

275 UNICEF, *State of the World's Children, 1995,* p. 77.

276 UNICEF, *State of the World's Children, 1995,* pp. 72, 73.

277 UNICEF, *State of the World's Children, 1989,* p. 1.

278 J.N. Hobcraft, J.W. McDonald, and S.O. Rutstein, "Socio-Economic Factors in Infant and Child Mortality: A Cross-national Comparison," *Population Studies,* 36 (1984), pp. 193–223. Cited in Kent, p. 112.

279 Alison Acker, *Children of the Volcano* (Westport, Connecticut: Lawrence Hill, 1986), p. 81. Cited in Kent, pp. 157–158.

280 Scott B. Halstead, Julia A. Walsh, and Kenneth S. Warren, eds., "Good Health at Low Cost" (Rockefeller Foundation, New York, 1985). Also see Kenneth Warren, "Tropical Medicine vs. Tropical Health," *Review of Infectious Diseases,* Vol. 12, No. 1. It is the latter study, which refers back to the earlier Rockefeller report, that quotes and facts have been drawn from.

281 Scott B. Halstead, Julia A. Walsh, and Kenneth S. Warren, eds., *Good Health at Low Cost* (a conference report) (New York: The Rockefeller Foundation, 1985), p. 246; Kenneth Warren, "Tropical Medicine vs. Tropical Health," *Review of Infectious Diseases,* Vol. 12, No. 1.

282 Halstead, Walsh, and Warren, eds., *Good Health at Low Cost,* p. 243.

283 Ibid., p. 242.

284 UNICEF, *Adjustment with a Human Face,* Vol. 1, p. 202.

285 UNICEF, *Adjustment with a Human Face,* Vol. 1, p. 122.

286 UNICEF, *State of the World's Children Report, 1994,* p. 81

287 Halstead, Walsh, and Warren, eds., *Good Health at Low Cost,* p. 129, p. 137.

288 Ibid., p. 136.

289 Ibid., p. 129.

290 UNICEF, *Adjustment with a Human Face,* Vol. 1, p. 122.

291 Ibid., p. 204.

292 UNICEF, *State of the World's Children Report, 1994.* Page 67

293 Alicia Korten, "Structural Adjustment and Costa Rican Agriculture;" in Kevin Danaher, *50 Years is Enough: the case against the World Bank and the International Monetary Fund.* Global Exchange. South End Press, Boston. 1994. pp. 56–61.

294 Ibid., p. 58.

295   Ibid.

296   Ibid, p. 59.

297   Ibid, p. 58.

298   Ibid, p. 61.

299   Ibid, p. 61.

300   Prakash Chandra, "What accounts for Kerala's success?" *Toward Freedom* Feb. 1992, Vol 41, # 1, p. 9–10.

301   Halstead, Walsh, and Warren, eds., *Good Health at Low Cost*, p. 42.

302   Ibid., p. 43.

303   UNICEF, *State of the World's Children, 1995*, p. 49.

304   Lester Brown, Nicholas Lenssen and Hal Kane. *Vital Signs 1995*. Worldwatch Institute, 1995, p. 146, 147.

305   David Morley, Jon Rohde & Glen Williams, *Practising Health for All*, Oxford University Press, 1983, p. 19.

306   Susan Meeker-Lowry "Guyana Takes on the IMF," *In Context*, #41, summer 1995, p. 34.

307   Ibid., p. 33–35.

308   Ibid., p. 35.

309   Ibid. p. 35.

310   Gita Sen, Adrienne Germain, Lincoln Chen, eds. *Population Policies Reconsidered: Health, Empowerment and Rights*, Harvard University Press, 1994, p. 11.

311   Hill AV. Presidential address to the British Association for the Advancement of Science, 1952. Quoted in Maurice King, "Health is a sustainable state." *Lancet*, Sept 15, 1990.

312   "Why the poor need children: a study from Java." *Population and Development Review*. Sept. 1977. Readapted in David Werner and Bill Bower, *Helping Health Workers Learn*. Hesperian Foundation, 1982. p. 23–2.

313   Maurice King, "An anomaly in the paradigm: the demographic trap, UNICEF's dilemma and its opportunities." *News on Health Care in Developing Countries*, Upsala University, January 1991. This is the lead article in this issue of the journal, devoted to the "Debate: Population Growth and Child Mortality." The issue also includes a copy of Maurice King's original controversial article "Health is a sustainable state," published in *The Lancet*, Sept. 15, 1990.

314   UNICEF, *State of the World's Children Report, 1994*, p. 81.

315   Toward Wiser Population Policies. *Contact*, No 135, Feb. 1994. Geneva. The Christian Medical Commission. Page 4.

316   UNICEF, *State of the World's Children Report, 1994*, p. 81.

317   John Ratcliffe, "Social justice and the demographic transition: lessons from India's Kerala State." in D. Morley, J. Rohde, and G. Williams (eds.) *Practising Health for All. Oxford. Oxford University Press, 1983.*

318   Richard Franke, Barbara Chasin, *Kerala, Radical Reform as Development in an Indian State*. The Institute for Food and Development Policy. San Francisco, CA, 1989.

319   John Ratcliffe, "Toward a Social Justice Theory of Demographic Transition: Lessons from India's Kerala State." *JANASAMKHYA*, Vol. 1, June,1983.

320   Government of Cuba, Junta Central de Planificacion. *Publicacion 5*, Direccion de Demografia, Sept. 1977. World Bank, World Development Report 1981; Cited in David Morley, Jon Rohde and Glen Williams, *Practising Health for All*, Oxford University Press, 1983, p. 21; Also: UNICEF, *State of the World's Children* reports,

1986, 1991, 1996.

321   David Werner. *Health Care in Cuba Today: A model system or a means of social control*. October, 1978. (Available through HealthWrights.)

322   UNICEF, *State of the World's Children Report, 1994*, p. 73.

323   Ibid.,p. 81.

324   See *Declaration of People's Perspectives on "Population" Symposium*, Comilla, Bangladesh, Dec 12–13, 1993. Available through UBINIG, 5/3 Barobo Mahanpur, Ring Road, Shaymoli, Dhaka, Bangladesh.

325   John W. Ratcliffe, "China's One Child Family Policy: Solving the Wrong Problem." ("Les Politiques Chinoises de la Poblacion essai pour 'Resourdre un Faux Problem'," *Politiques de Population, Vol. 3, No 4, Mars 1989, pp. 5–58.*

326   Charles A. Radin, "AIDS fight portrayed as a failure," *Boston Globe*, August 10, 1994, p. 1, p. 10.

327   Charles A. Radin, "AIDS fight portrayed as a failure." *Boston Globe*, August 10, 1994, p. 1, p. 10.

328   David Sanders and Adbulrahman Sambo, "AIDS in Africa: The Implications of Economic Recession and Structural Adjustment," *Health Policy and Planning*, Vol. 6 (1991), No. 2, p. 161.

329   UNICEF, *State of the World's Children, 1994*, p. 44.

330   Lester Brown, Nicholas Lenssen, Hal Kane, *Vital Signs 1995*, Worldwatch Institute, p. 18.

331   Anne E. Platt, *Infecting Ourselves: How Environmental and Social Disruptions Trigger Diseases*, Worldwatch Paper 129, Worldwatch Institute, April 1996, p. 30.

332   Lester Brown, Nicholas Lenssen, Hal Kane, Vital Signs 1995, Worldwatch Institute, p. 18.

333   Anne E. Platt, *Infecting Ourselves: How Environmental and Social Disruptions Trigger Diseases*, Worldwatch Paper 129, Worldwatch Institute, April 1996, p. 29.

334   David Sanders and Adbulrahman Sambo, "AIDS in Africa: The Implications of Economic Recession and Structural Adjustment," *Health Policy and Planning*, Vol. 6 (1991), No. 2, p. 162.

335   Anne E. Platt, *Infecting Ourselves: How Environmental and Social Disruptions Trigger Diseases*, Worldwatch Paper 129, Worldwatch Institute, April 1996, p. 30.

336   UNICEF, *State of the World's Children Report, 1995*, p. 22.

337   David Rogers, "An African AIDS Diary: Presidential Mission to Africa, January 4–19, 1991," *The Club of Kos for Health Care Newsletter*, Vol. 14, No. 3 (May 16, 1991), p. 8.

338   Ibid.

339   Ibid.

340   Ibid.

341   Anne E. Platt, *Infecting Ourselves: How Environmental and Social Disruptions Trigger Diseases*, Worldwatch Paper 129, Worldwatch Institute, April 1996, p. 21.

342   Editorial "Structural adjustment too painful" *The Lancet*, Vol 344, Nov. 19, 1994, p 1377. The reference for this statement is Sanders D, Sambo A. "AIDS in Africa: the implication of economic recession and structural adjustment." *Health Policy Planning 1991; 6: 157–65.*

343   United Nations, *World Urbanization Prospects, 1992 Revision* (New York), 1993; Cited in Hal Kane, *The Hour of Departure*, Worldwatch Paper 125, June 1995, p. 38.

344   Anne E. Platt, *Infecting Ourselves*, p. 30.

1   Carl E. Taylor, Robert L. Parker, and Steven Jarrett, "The Evolving Chinese Rural Health Care System," *Research in Human Capital Development*, Vol. 5, p. 222.

2   Personal visit to San Ramón by David Werner, 1980.

3   David Werner, "The Village Health Worker—Lackey or Liberator?," (Available through HealthWrights) p. 8.

4   Reports vary widely on Mozambique's U5MR in 1985. UNICEF puts the number at 252 (*The State of the World's Children, 1987,* p. 128.), Mozambique's Ministry of Health estimates between 325–375 (*The Impact on Health in Mozambique of South African Destabilization*, Ministry of Health, People's Republic of Mozambique, March 1987, p. 4.), while Dr. Ana Novoa reports the number in the city of Beira at 364 (Dr. Ana Novoa et al., *Morbilidade e Mortalidade por Diarreia em Criancas Menores de 5 Años de Idade, na Cidade da Beira* [Direccao Provincial de Saude de Sofala, Faculdade de Medicina de UEM, Mozambique, July 1985], p. 1.).

5   Dr. Ana Novoa et al., *Morbilidade e Mortalidade por Diarreia em Criancas Menores de 5 Años de Idade, na Cidade da Beira* (Direccao Provincial de Saude de Sofala, Faculdade de Medicina de UEM, Mozambique, July 1985), p. 1.

6   *The Impact on Health in Mozambique of South African Destabilization*, Ministry of Health, People's Republic of Mozambique, March 1987, p. 1.

7   WHO's role is borne out by the authors' correspondence and conversations with several close observers of the program.

8   This section based on D. Sanders, "The Potential and Limits of Health Sector Reforms in Zimbabwe," in *Reaching Health for All*, Rohde, H., Chatterjee, M and Morley, D. (eds.), Oxford University Press 1993, pp. 239–266.

9   International People's Health Council, *Health Care in Societies in Transition, A Report on a Small International Meeting Held in Managua, Nicaragua, December 4–9, 1991,*1992, p. 64.; N.H. Antia, "Alternative Policy for Health for All," *The Concept of Health Under National Democratic Struggle*, International People's Health Council, 1995, p. 52–56.

10 Working Group, *The Children's Supplementary Feeding Program in Zimbabwe*. Report presented to the Ministry of Health, Harare, 1982.

11 Ibid.

12 International People's Health Council, *Health Care in Societies in Transition, A Report on a Small International Meeting Held in Managua, Nicaragua, December 4–9, 1991,*1992, p. 110.

13 David Werner. "¡Viva Zapata! How the Uprising in Chiapas Revitalized the Struggle for Health in Sinaloa," *Newsletter from the Sierra Madre*, #29, June 1994, pp. 7–9.

14 "Is the Worst Yet to Come in Mexico?," *Bankcheck Quarterly*, No. 12, September 1995, p. 3.

15 Ibid.

16 Ibid.

17 Dennis Dunleavy, "Mexico's Hard Times Get Harder," *Juntos por la Salud News*, June 1995, p. 3.

18 Lynda Taylor, "Cleaning Up the Border, Will sustainability be a priority?," *The Workbook*, Southwest Research and Information Center, Summer 1995, p. 51.

19 Data in this list extracted from: Mary Purcell, "Mexico: One year later, the crisis continues." *Third World Resurgence* No. 67, March, 1996, reprinted from *The Other Side of Mexico, January–February 1996*.

20 Patrick J. Buchanan, "NAFTA is working wonders—for Mexican jobs" *San Jose Mercury,* September 19, 1994.

21 "Anti-immigrant violence rages nationwide," *Intelligence Report,* August 1994, #74. The Southern Poverty Law Center, Montgomery, AL, USA.

22 Luis Hernandez, *The Nation*, March 28, 1994

23 David Werner and Jason Weston, "The Hidden Costs of Free Trade: Mexico Bites the Bullet," *Newsletter from the Sierra Madre #31* May 1995, pp. 4–6.

24 Richard Garfield, "Nicaragua: Health under Three Regimes," in Jon Rohde, Meera Chatterjee, David Morley, *Reaching Health for All*, 1993. Oxford University Press. p. 268.

25 Ibid., p. 270.

26 Tony Dajer, "Why Nicaraguan Children Survive, *Links Health and Development Report,* Spring 1991, p 12.

27 Richard Garfield, "Nicaragua: Health under Three Regimes," in Jon Rohde, Meera Chatterjee, David Morley, *Reaching Health for All*, 1993. Oxford University Press, p. 268.

28 Ibid., p. 271–172.

29 Ibid., p. 274–275.

30 Richard Garfield, E. Prado, J. R. Gates, and S. H. Vermund, "Malaria in Nicaragua: Community-based Control Efforts and the Impact of War," *International Journal of Epidemiology,* 18(2) (1989).

31 Richard Garfield, "Nicaragua: Health under Three Regimes," in Jon Rohde, Meera Chatterjee, David Morley, *Reaching Health for All*, 1993. Oxford University Press. p. 276–277.

32 Ibid., p. 277.

33 Ibid., p. 278.

34 Garfield and Williams, pp. 200–201, citing B. Smith, *Health Situation analysis, Nicaragua, 1990* (Managua: Mimeo, 1990), p. 39.

35 David Werner, from the foreword of Richard Garfield's *Health Care in Nicaragua, Primary Care Under Changing Regimes*, Oxford University Press, 1992, pp. ix–x.

36 Richard Garfield, *Health Care in Nicaragua, Primary Care Under Changing Regimes*, Oxford University Press, 1992, p. 70.; MINSA, *Plan de Salud 1987*, Managua, MINSA, 1986.

37 Richard Garfield, *Health Care in Nicaragua, Primary Care Under Changing Regimes*, Oxford University Press, 1992, p. 68.

38 Ibid.

39 From personal communication with Maria Zuniga, formerly with the Sandinista Health Ministry.

40 Richard Garfield, "Nicaragua: Health under Three Regimes," in Jon Rohde, Meera Chatterjee, David Morley, *Reaching Health for All*, 1993. Oxford University Press, p. 284–285.

41 Source: Ministry of Health/Directions, General Systems of Information. 1994.

42 Ibid.

43 From a letter of public appeal by Witness for Peace, Washington, D.C. 1994.

44 Quotes from Noam Chomsky, *What Uncle Sam Really Wants*, 1992. Odonian Press, Berkeley, CA. pp. 42, 44.

45 Ibid., p. 43.

46 Ibid., pp. 42, 44.

47 Ibid., p. 46.

48   David Korten, *When Corporations Rule the World,* (Kumarian Press and Berrett-Koehler, West Hartford, CT and San Francisco, CA), 1995.

49   David Sanders with Richard Carver, *The Struggle for Health: Medicine and the Politics of Underdevelopment* (London: Macmillan, 1985), p. 184.

50   Ibid., p. 207.

51   Medea Benjamin and Andrea Freedman, *Bridging the Global Gap,* Seven Locks Press, 1989, p. v.

52   James Hightower, "20 Questions," *Utne Reader,* January–February 1995, p. 79; Cited in David Korten, *When Corporations Rule the World,* (Kumarian Press, West Hartford, Connecticut) 1995, p. 293.

53   Worldwatch Institute, "Matters of Scale" *World Watch.* Vol. 7. No 5. Sept./Oct. 1994, p. 39, Washington D.C.

54   From *Justice Denied: Human Rights and the International Financial Institutions.* Published by Women's Institute for Human Rights; and International Institute for Human Rights, Environment and Development. 1994.

55   Najmi Kanji, Nazneen Kanji, Firoze Manji, "From development to sustained crisis: Structural adjustment, equity and health" *Soc. Sci. Med.* Vol. 33 No. 9. pp. 985–993. 1991.

56   "The Ukunda Declaration on Economic Policy and Health," *Health Policy and Planning,* 6(2), 1991, p. 173–175.

57   "Filthy Rich." *New Internationalist.* Sept. 1994. p. 17. Toronto, Canada.

1   Roger Sawyer, *Children Enslaved* (London: Routledge, 1988), p. 178. Cited in Kent, p. 184.

2   For example, in 1989 the Bush Administration threatened to cut off US funding of WHO if that agency accepted the recently pro-claimed Palestinian state as a member. "Baker Urges Cutting Off of Funds if UN Agencies Upgrade PLO," *New York Times,* May 2, 1989, p. A6.

3   For example, in 1984, the Reagan Administration halted US funding of the United Nations Educational, Scientific and Cultural Organization (UNESCO) because the agency had become too "political". Graham Hancock, *Lords of Poverty: The Power, Prestige, and Corruption of the International Aid Business,* p. 49; William Preston Jr., *Hope and Folly: The United States and UNESCO 1945–1985* (University of Minnesota Press) 1989, p. 10.

4   George Kent, *The Politics of Children's Survival* (London: Praeger, 1991), p. 185.

5   See, for example, UNICEF, *Within Human Reach: A Future for Africa's Children* (New York: UNICEF, 1985), p. 64; Giovanni Andrea Cornia, Richard Jolly, and Frances Stewart, eds., *Adjust-ment with a Human Face: Protecting the Vulnerable and Promot-ing Growth* (Oxford: Clarendon Press, 1987), Vol. I, p. 2.

6   UNICEF, *The State of the World's Children, 1989,* pp. 1–28.

7   UNICEF, *The State of the World's Children, 1989,* pp. 21, 23.

8   UNICEF, *The State of the World's Children, 1989,* p. 34.

9   UNICEF, *The State of the World's Children, 1995.*

10   From a statement issued by *50 Years is Enough* (a coalition opposing the policies of the World Bank and IMF) at the Global Summit in Copenhagen, March, 1995.

11   From a statement by Peggy Antrobus, General Coordinator of Development Alternatives for Women for a New Era (DAWN), circulated at the Social Summit in Copenhagen, March, 1995.

12   From the Copenhagen Alternative Declaration as drafted by the NGO Forum during the Social Summit of March, 1995.

13   UNICEF, *State of the World's Children Report, 1995,* p. 54.

About the Authors

David Werner

David Werner, a biologist by training, has spent the last 30 years working to help poor farming families in the mountains of western Mexico to protect their health and rights. Project Piaxtla, the villager-run program to which he has been a facilitator and advisor since 1965, has contributed to the early conceptualization and evolution of Primary Health Care. The three main books he has written and illustrated—*Where There Is No Doctor, Helping Health Workers Learn,* and *Disabled Village Children*—are among the most widely used in the field of community-based health care and community based rehabilitation. He has worked in more than 50 countries—mostly in the Third World—helping to facilitate workshops and training programs, and as a consultant.

In recent years, David Werner has become increasingly involved in social, political, and economic factors, local to global, that affect disadvantaged people's health and lives. David has received several awards for his ground-breaking work, including the World Health Organization's first International Award in Health Education in 1985, and the MacArthur "genius" fellowship in 1991. He is a founding member of the International People's Health Council and of HealthWrights (Workgroup for People's Health and Rights).

David Sanders

David Sanders was born in South Africa and grew up and was educated in Zimbabwe where he qualified as a medical doctor. During the 1970s he lived and worked in Britain where he specialised in Paediatrics and later in Tropical Public Health. While there he was actively involved in campaigns to defend the National Health Service and in solidarity work with the liberation struggles in the former Portuguese African Colonies, Zimbabwe and South Africa. He was also a founder member of ZIMA (Zimbabwe Medical Aid) and the "Politics of Health" Group.

In 1980 David Sander returned to newly-independent Zimbabwe as Coordinator of a rural health programme developed by OXFAM in association with the Zimbabwe Ministry of Health. He also initiated and helped develop a national children's supplementary feeding programme and actively contributed to the reconstruction and development of Zimbabwe's health system. He joined the Department of Paediatrics and Child Health of the Medical School in Harare and later transferred to the Department of Community Medicine in which he was latterly Associate Professor and Chairperson. During this period he was centrally involved in the restructuring of the Medical Undergraduate Curriculum.

In 1992 he became Director of Staff/Student Development at the Medical School of the University of Natal in South Africa where he became actively involved in health policy development with the African National Congress (ANC) and SAHSSO (South African Health and Social Services Organisation). In 1993 he was appointed as Professor and Director of a new Public Health Programme at the University of the Western Cape, Cape Town, South Africa which provides practice-oriented education and training in public health and primary health care to a wide range of health and development workers. He is the author of a book: *The Struggle for Health: Medicine and the Politics of Underdevelopment,* as well as several booklets and articles on the political economy of health, structural adjustment, child nutrition and health personnel education.